*GEORGE WASHINGTON
IN AMERICAN LITERATURE
1775-1865*

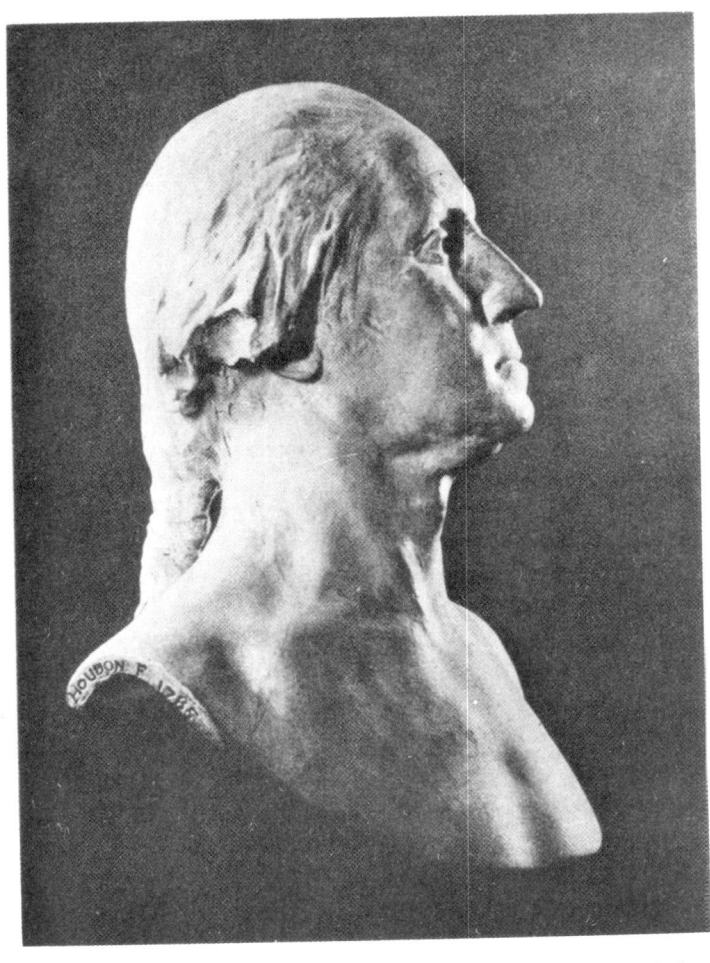

THE FAMOUS BUST OF GEORGE WASHINGTON MADE FROM LIFE AT MOUNT VERNON BY THE GREAT FRENCH SCULPTOR, JEAN ANTOINE HOUDON, IN 1785

Courtesy of the Mount Vernon Ladies' Association

GEORGE WASHINGTON IN AMERICAN LITERATURE
1775-1865

BY WILLIAM ALFRED BRYAN

GREENWOOD PRESS, PUBLISHERS
WESTPORT, CONNECTICUT

Copyright © 1952 by Columbia University Press, New York

Reprinted by permission
of Columbia University Press

First Greenwood Reprinting 1970

Library of Congress Catalogue Card Number 72-100146

SBN 8371-3258-4

PRINTED IN UNITED STATES OF AMERICA

FOREWORD

WILLIAM ALFRED BRYAN was born on October 21, 1907, in Sumter, South Carolina. He did his undergraduate work at the College of Charleston, where he received the Alumni Medal for highest scholastic average in 1927, and took his Master of Arts degree in English at Duke University in 1933. From 1929 until 1940 he taught in the public schools and did educational work in Civilian Conservation Corps units. In June, 1940, he began study at Duke toward a doctorate in the field of American literature. He held three graduate appointments and in 1944 and 1945 was an instructor in the Navy V-12 program.

From 1945 to 1948 Mr. Bryan was acting Assistant Professor of English at the University of Mississippi, and in 1948-1949 he was Associate Professor of English at East Carolina Teachers College.

He spent the last several months of his life writing the present work, which was intended to be his doctoral dissertation. He completed it and had fulfilled the other requirements for the degree, but illness prevented his taking the final examination. He died of a heart attack on December 17, 1950.

Mr. Bryan's research on the subject of Washington in literature was extensive, and he was the author of the following articles: "The Genesis of Weems' 'Life of Washington,'" *Americana*, XXXVI (April, 1942), 147-165; "Three Unpublished Letters of Parson Weems," *William and Mary College Quarterly*, XXIII (July, 1943), 272-277; "Minor Washingtoniana," *Tyler's Quarterly Historical and Genealogical Magazine*, XXV (January, 1944), 164-

170; "George Washington, Symbolic Guardian of the Republic," *William and Mary Quarterly*, Third Series, VII (January, 1950), 53–63.

ENID P. BRYAN

Rome, Georgia
January 21, 1952

PREFACE

UNTIL LINCOLN appeared as challenger for the title of foremost American hero, George Washington had no rival for that title. Washington's role in literature has been greater than that of any other American, with the possible exception of Lincoln, and also greater than that of any Englishman except Shakespeare, and possibly the legendary King Arthur. When I began work on this most attractive subject, I found myself confronted with five-volume biographies and short poems; newspaper editorials and novels; epics, dramas, ballads, orations—a little of everything, ranging in date from the seventeen-fifties to the present. I discovered that George Washington's role in American literature is a field that an editor with a board of several readers might not cover exhaustively for many years. Numerous periodicals contain significant material, especially in the February issues. Authors of books which do not deal with Washington directly often go out of their way to eulogize him. He has been a literary subject for nearly two centuries, and he was internationally famous nearly a century before Lincoln. I found it necessary to limit my subject, and one logical step was to consider only the material written between 1775 and 1865, when Lincoln's fame began to compete with that of Washington.

The materials, even so, are staggering. Every newspaper published in America has carried Washingtonian material occasionally, on February 22 as well as on other dates. Any issue of almost any magazine may contain a pertinent sketch or poem. These facts led me to accept the premise that a representative portion of the writing about Washington eventually found its way into books, and accordingly I have made them the largest body of material studied. In addition, I have gone through the files of three magazines representing different sections of the United States: the *Southern Literary Messenger*, the *North American Review*, and the *Knickerbocker;* and through the use of Poole's and other indexes I have examined numerous items in other magazines. On a few occasions I have looked into newspapers, but I have felt it practicable to depend for the most part upon compilations and secondary sources for an impression of material originally published in newspapers. Thus I have endeavored to determine the essential facts of Washingtonian literature by study of a very large sample. The materials which I have examined include, I feel sure, practically everything of literary importance.

Although the primary purpose of my research has been to discover and evaluate the treatment accorded Washington by poets, dramatists, and writers of fiction in the period 1775–1865, I have found that a consideration of biography and oratory dealing with Washington is essential to an understanding of the belles-lettres. It will be apparent that a great part of the material treated in every category is of little literary merit. Yet I have tried to maintain my sense of literary values, and I have made a special effort to find and study carefully what our major writers have had to say about Washington.

Although I have searched chiefly in American literature, I have in a few instances found Washington in the works of English authors, and I hope eventually to consider some English views of Washington in one or more magazine articles. The story of Washington in American literature reveals a phase of the interaction between it and English literature, and I have considered Thackeray in the text because his portrait of Washington provoked a strong critical reaction in America.

This study necessarily touches upon large allied fields, some of which offer alluring bypaths: Washington's own writings, moot points of his career and character, the lives of his contemporaries, the lives and works of various writers who have treated him, his role as a subject in sculpture and painting. Lord Mahon, writing history in the eighteen-fifties, said that Washington's refusal to allow André to be shot rather than hanged was a blot upon his character. What was Washington's attitude on the case, as revealed in his own letters written at the time? What have his biographers had to say on this question? John Adams is reputed to have objected in 1777 to the idolatrous veneration paid to Washington by all Americans. Was Adams quoted accurately? What were his feelings toward Washington at the time and what inspired them? John Neal in 1823 presented a fictitious character who criticizes a Stuart portrait of Washington as being too sublimated, idealized, and unrealistic. Where did Neal get his concept of Washington? What did he know about Stuart or about the art of portrait painting? When did Stuart paint his portraits, and when and by whom were they copied? What effect have they had upon the popular conception of Washington? Only momentary glances can be cast at such questions, because each is an *ignis fatuus*, to lead the student away from the study of Washington in literature into some other Washingtonian field equally vast and perhaps equally fascinating. I might add that in some instances I have gone further into such questions than may be apparent to the reader.

I am indebted to a long line of Washingtonian scholars who have preceded me: biographers, editors, and compilers. Among the biographers I may mention Washington Irving, Rupert Hughes, John C. Fitzpatrick, Nathaniel Wright Stephenson, Waldo Hilary Dunn, and Douglas Southall Freeman, two volumes of whose monumental work have now appeared. I am indebted also to the three great editors of Washington's writings: Jared Sparks, Worthington Chauncey Ford, and John C. Fitzpatrick. The compilations of such men as Winthrop Sargent, William Spohn Baker, Burton Egbert Stevenson, and Gilbert Chinard have supplied convenient collections of materials that are basic to my work. Miss Margaret B. Stillwell's bibliography of the funeral orations of 1800 has been very useful. I should mention also Roy P. Basler, whose study of Lincoln in literature set a kind of precedent for my study of Washington.

I have done most of my research in the Duke University Library, all departments of which have been helpful. The pleasant and efficient staff of the Library of Congress made my research there highly profitable. The interlibrary loan departments of the Duke University Library, the library of the University of Mississippi, and the library of East Carolina Teachers College patiently met large demands and made available material from the Boston Athenaeum, the Library of Congress, the New York State Library (Albany), and the libraries of the University of North Carolina, the American Antiquarian Society, Yale University, Harvard University, Brown University, Columbia University, the University of Pennsylvania, the University of Virginia, the University of Michigan, the University of Texas, the University of Chicago, Tulane University, and others.

Many friends in the graduate school and on the faculty of Duke University furnished useful leads and quotations. Foremost of these was Professor Lewis Leary, and second was Benjamin W. Early.

The direction of Professor Jay B. Hubbell has been at all times helpful and inspirational.

My indebtedness to my wife, who has been at various times listener, secretary, research assistant, and critic is beyond my power to express.

W.A.B.

Durham, North Carolina
October 27, 1950

ACKNOWLEDGMENTS

SPECIAL ACKNOWLEDGMENT is made to the following, who have granted permission for the reprinting of copyrighted material from the books and periodicals listed below:

THE AMERICAN PHILOSOPHICAL SOCIETY: The Autobiography of Benjamin Rush, ed. George W. Corner, 1948. (Originally issued as Vol. XXV of the Memoirs of the Society.)

APPLETON-CENTURY-CROFTS, INC.: Complete Works of Abraham Lincoln, ed. John G. Nicolay and John Hay, 2 vols., 1902.

BARNES & NOBLE, INC.: The Literary History of the American Revolution, 1763–1783, by Moses Coit Tyler, 2 vols., 1941.

THE BOBBS-MERRILL COMPANY, INC.: Correspondence of John Adams and Thomas Jefferson, 1812–1826, selected by Paul Wilstach, 1925.

MR. ALBERT BONI: The Journal of William Maclay, United States Senator from Pennsylvania, 1789–1791, with Introduction by Charles A. Beard, 1927.

DOUBLEDAY & COMPANY, INC.: Leaves of Grass, by Walt Whitman, 3 vols. in 1, 1920.

THE RALPH WALDO EMERSON MEMORIAL ASSOCIATION and COLUMBIA UNIVERSITY PRESS: The Letters of Ralph Waldo Emerson, ed. Ralph L. Rusk, 6 vols., 1939.

HOUGHTON MIFFLIN COMPANY: Reminiscences of an American Loyalist, 1738–1789, by Jonathan Boucher, ed. Jonathan Bouchier,

Acknowledgments

1925; Tendencies in Modern American Poetry, by Amy Lowell, 1926; The Complete Poetical Works of James Russell Lowell, 1897.

THE NEW ENGLAND QUARTERLY: "Contemporary Songs and Verses about Washington," by Mary W. Smyth, *New England Quarterly*, V (April, 1932), 281–292.

UNIVERSITY OF PENNSYLVANIA PRESS: Benjamin Rush, Physician and Citizen, 1746–1813, by Nathan Gerson Goodman, 1934.

PRINCETON UNIVERSITY PRESS: George Washington as the French Knew Him, ed. Gilbert Chinard, 1940.

LIBRARY OF PRINCETON UNIVERSITY: The Poems of Philip Freneau, Poet of the American Revolution, ed. Fred Lewis Pattee, 3 vols., 1902–1907.

G. P. PUTNAM'S SONS: The Writings of Thomas Jefferson, ed. Paul Leicester Ford, 10 vols., 1892–1899.

CHARLES SCRIBNER'S SONS: The Spy, a Tale of the Neutral Ground, by James Fenimore Cooper, 1931; George Washington, a Biography, by Douglas Southall Freeman, 4 vols. (of 6 projected), 1948–1951.

MRS. EMILY ELLSWORTH FORD SKEEL: Mason Locke Weems, His Works and Ways, ed. Mrs. Skeel, 3 vols., 1929.

MR. BURTON EGBERT STEVENSON: Poems of American History, ed. Mr. Stevenson, Houghton Mifflin, 1922.

WILLIAM AND MARY QUARTERLY: "A Visit to Mount Vernon—a Letter of Mrs. Edward Carrington to Her Sister, Mrs. George Fisher," *William and Mary College Quarterly*, Series 2, XVIII (April, 1938), 198.

WM. H. WISE & CO., INC.: The Life and Works of Thomas Paine, ed. William M. Van der Weyde, 10 vols., copyright 1925 by the Thomas Paine National Historical Association.

CONTENTS

I.	INTRODUCTION	3
II.	WASHINGTON AS SEEN BY HIS CONTEMPORARIES	23
III.	ORATORY	51
IV.	BIOGRAPHY	86
V.	VERSE	121
VI.	DRAMA	171
VII.	FICTION	190
VIII.	CONCLUSION	234
	APPENDIX	243
	SELECTIVE BIBLIOGRAPHY	247
	INDEX	271

GEORGE WASHINGTON
IN AMERICAN LITERATURE
1775-1865

CHAPTER I

INTRODUCTION

*T*O CONSIDER INTELLIGENTLY the voluminous literature written about Washington, one needs a certain basic knowledge of his character and personality, which often appear in distorted or idealized forms in the literature. Some such background can be acquired from a study of the writings of his contemporaries. There is also need of a knowledge of the chief periods and incidents of Washington's life. The casual reader does not always realize that he was not only a soldier and a statesman, but also a boy and a man, a planter and a private citizen, a husband and a foster father. The present chapter contains a brief sketch of his life and a survey of the course of his renown in the period under consideration.

I

George Washington's life may be divided into seven periods:

I.	1732–1752	Child and youth
II.	1752–1759	Colonial officer
III.	1759–1775	Virginia planter
IV.	1775–1783	Commander-in-Chief
V.	1784–1789	Retired General
VI.	1789–1797	President
VII.	1797–1799	Retired President[1]

[1]Similar outlines have been used in other studies of Washington, but the present one and the sketch which follows are based upon three recent authoritative biographies: Nathaniel Wright Stephenson and Waldo Hilary Dunn, *George Washington*, 2 vols. (New York and London, 1940); John C. Fitzpatrick, *George*

Introduction

Washington's childhood, like the early years of many other great men, is obscure, and this fact has made it easy for the legend-makers to fashion a picture of the youthful Washington which is not justified by historical research. There is little evidence to determine what manner of woman his mother was,[2] and his father died when George was only eleven. A number of school exercises in mathematics, geography, and other subjects, which the boy wrote apparently between his seventh and fifteenth years, are still extant, but who his teachers were and where he studied are unknown. Sixty-two "Rules of Civility," copybook maxims written when he was about thirteen, have been emphasized on the ground that he followed them all his life, but the life of any great man displays conscious or unconscious adherence to many copybook maxims.

The diary which he kept when a member of a party engaged in surveying the wild lands of Lord Fairfax reveals a youth of sixteen who was used to clean sheets and frequent changes of clothing but who could endure a verminous bed or a blanket on the cold ground with an admirable sense of humor. He wrote a few verses and corresponded with several young ladies. At nineteen he made a trip to Barbados with his half brother Lawrence, who was fourteen years his senior. The intrepid young man of twenty who was appointed District Adjutant of Virginia militia, with the title of Major, had already supported himself for several years. He was equally at home alone in the forests, with Indians and backwoodsmen, or in the best Virginia drawing rooms of his day.

At the age of twenty-one Washington inherited Mount Vernon, which was throughout his life a center for his thoughts and a haven of refuge. The journal of his mission to Fort Le Boeuf shows him cool in the face of danger, prodigiously hardy, daring, and tenacious of purpose. This journal was published in Virginia and in

---

Washington Himself ... (Indianapolis, [1933]); Douglas Southall Freeman, *George Washington, a Biography*, 6 vols. projected, 4 published (New York, 1948–1951).

[2] See Freeman, *op cit.*, I, Introduction, xix-xx; I, 45 ff; *et passim*. See also Bernhard Knollenberg's review of Freeman, *William and Mary Quarterly*, Series 3, VI (January, 1949), 111–121. Freeman presents Mary Ball Washington as a cantankerous, difficult person, and Knollenberg thinks he was unfair to her.

Introduction

England in 1754 along with one or two letters written after his surprise and destruction of Jumonville's party of Frenchmen. Records of several months between the time of his surrender at Fort Necessity in 1754 and Braddock's defeat in 1755 are imperfect; in fact, history does not reveal where Washington was or what he was doing for many days, weeks, and months of the seven years 1752–1759.

After the catastrophe of Braddock's defeat, Washington was known in Virginia as he later came to be known universally: a man capable of extraordinary expenditures of physical, mental, and moral energy. His years as Colonel of Virginia militia in charge of frontier defense gave him experience on a small scale with most of the problems which he was to encounter as General: troops ill-clothed, ill-lodged, ill-fed, and ill-trained, often the dregs of their communities; squabbles between officers over rank, pay, and authority; misunderstanding and poor cooperation from the Governor and the Burgesses; misunderstanding and poor cooperation from the citizenry; insufficient forces and supplies. He saw the burned cabins and the scalped bodies left by Indian raids. But there was also a lighter aspect of the young Colonel's experiences. When he was in the settlements he enjoyed cards, dancing, and the theater; his favorite play was Addison's *Cato*. He sometimes rode accompanied by servants in fine liveries, and with the Washington arms upon the trappings of his horses. The man who married Mrs. Custis in 1759 was mature, and he was far above average in everything he attempted except spelling and public speaking.[3]

After he took his wife to Mount Vernon, Washington found his chief interest in the management of the estates he had acquired. He became a scientific farmer, experimenting with various agricultural innovations. Eventually he abandoned tobacco and the one-crop system that was then commonly practiced in Virginia, in favor of wheat and wool. His agricultural pursuits led him into related activities: in order to grind his own wheat he purchased a mill. He

---

[3]Freeman, *op cit.*, gives excellent discussions of Washington's social life in this period.

was aware of the West, and he advocated the development of the Potomac as a means of transportation from the coast to the lands beyond the Alleghenies. He was also interested in a plan to drain the Dismal Swamp. Nevertheless, he was "land poor," for most of his income from the soil went back into it; he was often lacking in ready money. Occasionally he traded in slaves, buying or selling a few, although he grew dissatisfied with slavery much as he did with the one-crop system; he saw that it was inefficient and undesirable from an economic point of view. As a large planter and man of affairs, he occupied a seat in the House of Burgesses, where he was an influential committee member though not conspicuous on the floor; he became familiar with behind-the-scenes politics. He also took an active part in Masonry and in the activities of the Anglican Church. His manifold serious activities still left him time for fishing, shooting, fox hunting, entertaining, and reading in "agriculture and English history." His stepchildren were usually in the household, and Washington supervised their education.

General Washington led in the Revolutionary War the embattled third of the American people in revolt against the British crown. It must be remembered that another third favored the crown and that the remaining third were by comparison indifferent.[4] He was moving on a scene larger than any he had previously entered, and at first he placed his main reliance upon Congress. As the affairs of the Patriots grew desperate, Congress proved inadequate, and he had to rely on his own efforts to hold together some sort of opposition. He was a systematic military executive, handling over his desk enormous quantities of paper work and so directing events far removed from his immediate surroundings.[5] He inspired almost un-

[4] Sydney George Fisher, *The True History of the American Revolution* (Philadelphia and London, 1902), and *The Struggle for American Independence*, 2 vols. (Philadelphia and London, 1908), *passim.*

[5] A current interpretation of General Washington is that his temperament followed an up-and-down rhythm in which periods of berserk energy were followed by periods of comparative inactivity and recuperation. Stephenson and Dunn, *op. cit., passim;* Dixon Wecter, *The Hero in America, a Chronicle of Hero-Worship* (New York, 1941), p. 109; Kenneth Umbreit, *Founding Fathers; Men Who Shaped Our Tradition* (New York and London, 1941), pp. 239 ff; Freeman, *op. cit., passim.*

Introduction

limited loyalty in a small body of officers and men, with whom he seems to have been hard but just; his punishments, judged by modern standards, were harsh, but he was no sterner than other eighteenth-century commanders. The Commander-in-Chief sometimes played ball with his officers and occasionally enjoyed dancing. The quality of his military genius has been the subject of many volumes; perhaps the most valid reason advanced for not classing him with Alexander and Napoleon is the small size of the armies engaged in such actions as Trenton and Yorktown.

After the war Washington tried to take up again the life he had lived at Mount Vernon before 1775, but he never quite succeeded. He backed the Potomac Company, worked toward the development of his western lands, turned again to the scientific study of agriculture, and took a lively interest in education; but now he was an internationally known figure, continually visited and continually busy with an enormous correspondence. He saw the need for the Constitutional Convention and helped arrange for it. While presiding over it, he was very close to James Madison, whose share in writing the Constitution was as great as that of any other one man.

When he became President, Washington realized that his every move, public or private, might constitute a precedent. Like other military men who have held political offices, he was sometimes annoyed by the necessity of conciliating all manner of associates. He had little time for riding and other outdoor activities to which he was accustomed. Furthermore, he was not in good health; serious illnesses had attacked him at all periods of his life, and the strain of the Revolution told on him now. Displeased and alarmed by the rise of political parties, he tried in vain to remain neutral. History has justified his financial and foreign policies, but in 1800 the American people rejected the presidential formality and ceremony which seemed desirable to the elderly Virginian. During his second administration, party feeling grew so strong that for almost a century thereafter few American writers could present Washington, Jefferson, and Hamilton in a cool light.

Retiring again to Mount Vernon in 1797, Washington once more vainly tried to escape the public eye. Less than a year after his retirement he felt it his duty to accept responsibility for the organization of an army to afford protection against France. He directed this by correspondence, with his habitual efficiency, and he was Lieutenant-General and Commander-in-Chief of the armies of the United States when he died. In his will he provided that his slaves should be freed upon the death of his widow.[6]

2

In 1750 Washington was known to his circle of Virginia acquaintances merely as a young man of exceptional ability. The next few years were important ones. Through his mission to Fort Le Boeuf, his skirmish with Jumonville, and his surrender at Fort Necessity, Washington's reputation spread in the colonies, and upon the publication of his journal in 1754 he became known also to such observers as Horace Walpole in England.[7] His exploits in Braddock's campaign in 1755 increased his fame in Virginia and the near-by colonies, although it seems that general knowledge of these adventures did not reach England for several generations.[8] Through his activities as Colonel of Virginia militia and later as member of the Virginia House of Burgesses he became acquainted with a few leading men throughout the colonies and known to many others. In addition, he acquired the standing of a solid and substantial citizen in his native colony during the peaceful years at Mount Vernon before the Revolution. People knew him as a soldier, a squire, a planter, a legislator, and a man of affairs.

Then came Lexington and Concord, and Gage's army of redcoats

[6] A table of the more important dates and events of Washington's life is included as an appendix.

[7] Walpole to Horace Mann, October 6, 1754, in Walpole, *The Letters . . .* , ed. Mrs. Paget Toynbee, 16 vols. (New York, 1903-1905), III, 254.

[8] M. Darnell Davis, "British Newspaper Accounts of Braddock's Defeat," *Pennsylvania Magazine of History and Biography*, XXIII (January, 1899), 310-328; "Braddock's Defeat," *Niles' Weekly Register*, X (June 15, 1816), 249-251; Winthrop Sargent, ed., *The History of an Expedition against Fort Duquesne . . .* in *Memoirs of the Historical Society of Pennsylvania*, Vol. V, 1856.

Introduction

was besieged in Boston by a group of New England farmers. Washington was appointed leader of these poorly trained militiamen and so stepped abruptly into the glare of intense publicity. The process by which he became in a short while the hero of the American Patriots was an old and natural one. In time of war the military commander is the symbol of his people's cause, and all possible praise is heaped upon him in order to glorify that cause. In the eyes of the Patriots a remark disparaging of Washington was traitorous. William Goddard, a New Jersey printer, was mobbed because he published some of Charles Lee's attacks upon the Commander.[9] The name of Washington became the signal for unlimited eulogy in prose and verse; he was the pride and glory of America.

It should not be forgotten that to the Tories of the same day, in America as well as in England, the rebel General was an object of contempt and ridicule. Instead of dimming his light, scurrility seemed ultimately to make it shine brighter. Every attempt to "smear" Washington redounded to his credit; none of the mud which was hurled at him stuck. On the other hand, the excessive praise which the Patriots heaped upon him tended to obscure the outlines of his actual personality.

English Tories aided the American Tories by publishing preposterous biographical sketches, libelous pamphlets, and letters falsely attributed to Washington.[10] Yet even while the war was being

---

[9] Frank Luther Mott, *American Journalism* . . . (New York, 1941), p. 92.

[10] The propaganda of the American Revolution is a large and interesting subject. James Rivington's *Gazette* was a particularly effective organ of Tory propaganda in this country. British Tory writers were equally energetic, and their works were widely circulated. For example, a pamphlet published in London in 1776 had it that Washington kept a woman named Mary Gibbons at a boardinghouse and went to see her in disguise, late at night. See John C. Fitzpatrick, *The George Washington Scandals* (Alexandria, Va., 1929), p. 2.

Propaganda of both the Patriots and the Tories is preserved in verse and dramatic satires of the Revolutionary period, as well as in pamphlets, newspaper editorials, and magazine articles. Of American publications, more Whig than Tory propaganda is extant, so that the former seems to have predominated, whether it actually did so or not. Yet esteem and respect for Washington were by no means constant even among the Patriots during the war. History records many instances of faintheartedness and dissatisfaction as the weary months passed and Washington lost battle after battle. Dixon Wecter has handled this subject briefly but well: *op. cit.*, pp. 107-112. The fluctuation in the attitude of Americans is apparent in letters, diaries, and newspaper writing, but not to any marked extent in the litera-

fought, the American Commander was a hero to some of the British Whigs, who were politically opposed to the war with the American colonies.

The many French officers, observers, and soldiers of fortune who came to the aid of the American rebels were most favorably impressed by the leader of the cause they had adopted. For the edification of their countrymen back home they wrote of him in eloquent terms and so established a heroic French view of Washington which lasted, despite occasionally recurring charges that he had murdered Coulon de Jumonville in a border skirmish in 1754.[11]

By the end of the Revolutionary War, Washington had about halfway completed his progress toward Olympus. He had proved himself a great military leader, but he was yet to show himself a great statesman. During the few years between the war and the Constitutional Convention his reputation grew much less rapidly

---

ture of the period. See, however, *The Motley Assembly, infra,* Chapter VI, Section 1.

For larger aspects of the subject: Frank Moore, *Diary of the American Revolution, from Newspapers and Original Documents,* 2 vols. (New York, 1860); Philip Davidson, *Propaganda and the American Revolution, 1763-1783* (Chapel Hill, N.C., 1941); Mott, *op. cit.,* pp. 113-134.

[11] The nature and growth of Washington's reputation abroad are well outlined by Gilbert Chinard in "The American Dream," in *Literary History of the United States,* ed. Robert E. Spiller, Willard Thorp, Thomas H. Johnson, Henry Seidel Canby, 3 vols. (New York, 1948), I, 198-200.

French writers who championed Jumonville had the idea that he was carrying a flag of truce when shot by Washington. See St. John de Crèvecoeur, *Sketches of Eighteenth Century America* . . . , ed. Henri L. Bourdin, Ralph H. Gabriel, and Stanley T. Williams (New Haven, 1925), p. 176. Francis Parkman studied the Jumonville incident in detail: *Montcalm and Wolfe* . . . , 3 vols. (Boston, 1897-1898), I, 145-150; II, 421-422. A recent publication shows continued interest in the subject: Gilbert Francis Leduc, *Washington and the Murder of Jumonville* (Lowell, Mass., 1943), not seen by the present writer. The work of Leduc, a Catholic priest, is reviewed in the *Commonweal,* XL (September, 1944), 521.

The Jumonville incident was the basis of a French epic poem of 1759: *infra,* Chapter V, note 45. In the seventeen-fifties Washington was, of course, in the service of the British, and they found no fault with his action. But during the Revolution the Tory editor Rivington published in his New York *Royal Gazette* a long and detailed account of the cruel Mr. Washington's action as set forth in the French poem. Such excellent propaganda proved still serviceable in a later period, when Washington was again under attack, this time at the hands of the Republicans. The story was rehashed in Benjamin Franklin Bache's *Aurora* in 1795 and 1797, and other newspapers carried discussion and comment. See Stephenson and Dunn, *op. cit.,* II, 160; Bernard Faÿ, *The Two Franklins: Fathers of American Democracy* (Boston, 1933), pp. 273-274, 315.

than it had grown during the war, but it did not decrease. Numerous visitors who sought out the world-famous leader of the victorious American Patriots continued to spread abroad reports of his dignity and impressiveness. His part in the Constitutional Convention was of paramount importance because his prestige as well as his strength of character and good sense enabled the diverse elements to erect "a standard to which the wise and honest" could repair.

Washington's name was one of the strongest arguments of those who fought successfully for the adoption of the Constitution between 1787 and 1789. An attack on the Constitution seemed to be an attack on him. His election to the presidency was an integral part of the process of setting the new government firmly on its foundation. No other man had won the confidence and respect of all Americans as had Washington. Writers throughout the length and breadth of the land celebrated his glory in enthusiastic, though unskillful, verses. Indeed, from this time onward he was a fashionable subject for versifiers, one to be treated by many in the most ambitious encomium that they could produce.

No man holds an important post without exposing himself to adverse criticism, and during his presidency Washington's reputation was shaped by forces somewhat similar to those that had molded it in Revolutionary days. The Federalists praised him to the skies and assumed that he was infallible; the opposition, at first unorganized but later centered in the Republican Party, often sought to besmirch him along with their favorite target, Hamilton. Political feeling grew strong and bitter during his second administration, and the mudslinging of the Republicans of 1795 was much like that which has been a feature of American politics at frequent intervals ever since. The questions of Franco-American and Anglo-American relations became enormously important, and the Republican Party of Jefferson, favoring France, took definite shape in opposition to the Federalist Party of Hamilton, which favored England. The Federalists, who had the greater influence with Washington, had already prevailed in disagreements over national finance. The Republicans, as an opposition party, were the more vociferous of the two, and they accused the administration of drifting toward monarchy. The signing of the Jay Treaty in 1795 particularly enraged them. James Madison, Philip Freneau, Benjamin Franklin Bache, William Duane, James Thompson Callender, and others produced a continual barrage of pamphlets and articles attacking the administration.[12] For the Federalists, Hamilton, John Fenno, William Cobbett ("Peter Porcupine"), and others took up the cudgels. Thus twice during his lifetime Washington's name was the object of

---

[12]Because of his enormous prestige, Republicans were at first timid about attacking Washington, but before the end of his second term his name and actions were so roughly handled that a writer a century later could say that "with one exception—Johnson—no president ever went out of office so loaded with odium as Washington." Moncure Daniel Conway, *The Life of Thomas Paine* . . . , 2 vols. (New York, 1892), II, 176-177.

Benjamin Franklin Bache, a grandson of Benjamin Franklin, carried on a most prolonged and virulent campaign in his Philadelphia newspaper, the *Aurora*. Bache seems to have felt that since attempts to win the President over to the pro-French attitude had failed, the proper move was to force him out of office. In the summer of 1795, on through the remainder of Washington's administration, the *Aurora* published Bache's own invectives and similar articles sent in by readers, usually anonymous or pseudonymous. In 1796 Bache wrote: "If ever a nation was debauched by a man, the American nation has been debauched by Washington. If ever a nation has suffered from the improper influence of a man, the American nation has suffered from the influence of Washington. If ever a nation was deceived by a man, the American nation has been deceived by Washington. . . . Let the history of the federal government instruct mankind, that the masque of patriotism may be worn to conceal the foulest designs against the liberties of the people." *Aurora*, December 23, 1796.

Even on the last day of Washington's administration Bache issued a bitter attack, declaring that the day should be one of jubilee. Bache's part in the political propaganda of the nineties is treated by Faÿ, *op. cit.*; see especially pp. 264-274, "Benny Bache and George Washington."

Tom Paine's *Letter to George Washington* also appeared in 1796, as did William Duane's *A Letter to George Washington* . . . (Philadelphia, 1796, published anonymously), wherein the President was represented as the tool of Britain. William Cobbett, a Federalist hack, found a particularly effective way to answer Paine: in *A Letter to the Infamous Tom Paine, in Answer to His Letter to General Washington* (Philadelphia, 1796), he printed in parallel columns selections from the letter of 1796 which condemned Washington and selections from Paine's earlier writings which praised him.

In 1800, when the country was united in panegyrical funeral orations on the lamented hero, James Thompson Callender was publishing *The Prospect before Us* (Richmond, Va., 1800-1801), including a review of all the major political issues of the preceding decade, with emphasis upon the perfidy of Washington.

The pamphlet wars of the seventeen-nineties constitute a large subject, of more than passing interest. But the violence of feeling then aroused is reflected but dimly in the literature treating Washington, notably in a few verses and dramas.

bitter invective and at the same time the rallying cry of his supporters.

When he published his Farewell Address (1796) and of his own volition left the presidency in 1797, Washington completed the solid foundation of his permanent fame. The address, with its strong plea for cooperation between sections and its warning against political divisions based upon geographical considerations, was a bulwark of the Constitution and of the federal government until the permanence of the Union was tested during the administration of Lincoln. Its clear statement of the foreign policy of Washington's administration—a policy of friendship with all nations, yet avoidance of "the insidious wiles of foreign influence"—served as a guide for American foreign policy for generations thereafter. Upon his death in 1799 Americans were tireless in pouring encomiums upon their great leader; for the most part, political differences were temporarily forgotten, and Federalists and Republicans united in confirming Washington as America's hero.

In 1800 the nation was still in its formative stage, in danger of breaking up through the conflict of diverse factions. The infant republic needed some symbol to which all of its people could turn with pride, a unifying force. Only the hero Washington, general and statesman, filled that need. Divested of most of his personal traits, made into an abstract catalogue of virtues, he was straightway elevated to the Valhalla of national heroes, and there he has remained to this day. The process is clearly evident in the terms of the numerous orations which were delivered in the first few months of 1800 by political leaders, educators, and clergymen all over America. The abstract Washington that they held up to the admiration of their countrymen has persisted despite attempts to portray him more humanly in history, biography, fiction, sculpture, and painting.

The official biography that John Marshall produced between 1804 and 1807 did nothing to dispel the abstract conception of Washington. Judge Marshall was an old friend of Washington and was in many ways qualified for the task. But he seems to have had no sympathy with Dr. Johnson's theory that the biographer should show the foibles, even the weaknesses, of his subject in order to reveal him as a human being. The reader who has persistence enough to continue through Marshall's five volumes obtains a grasp of considerable background material and of the facts of Washington's public career and achievements, but of the man's personal traits he learns little. John Adams passed definitive judgment: "Marshall's [book] is a Mausoleum, 100 feet square at the base, and 200 feet high."[13]

Parson Weems's *Life* was written in protest against Marshall's impersonal portrayal and that of the funeral orations. Weems felt that he could satisfy the taste of his readers by emphasizing private life and personal characteristics, particularly those of Washington as boy and youth. A minister himself, Weems made his hero a saint from early childhood. Reaction against deism was in full swing in the first decade of the nineteenth century, and Weems's Washington fitted the teachings of the orthodox evangelicals. Since his work did more to form the popular conception of Washington than that of any other writer in the period under consideration, it is indeed unfortunate that Weems made a prig out of the robust leader who had held the loyalty of the ragged Patriot armies of 1778.

It has been noted that at Washington's death most of his political enemies joined in the lamentation and praise. The Republicans probably felt—rightly, as it proved—that the Federalist Party would soon lose its strength when it could no longer summon the authority and rely upon the popularity of the living hero. Yet the Federalist tone of a great part of the funeral oratory had its significance. The Federalists hoped still to use Washington's prestige to their advantage. Still more dangerous from the Republican point of view was the Federalist bias of Marshall's biography of Washington. Thomas Jefferson soon saw that it would be a mistake to let the Federalists pin a tag of permanent ownership on Washington. In 1814 he ad-

---

[13]John Adams to Thomas Jefferson, July, 1813, in Jefferson, *The Writings* . . . , ed. Albert Ellery Bergh, 20 vols. (Washington, D.C., 1904–1905), XIII, 301. This letter is not included in Adams, *Works* (1850–1856).

Introduction

vised a friend, then engaged in political activity, not to regard Washington's name and prestige as the property of the Federalists: "I am convinced that he is more deeply seated in the love and gratitude of the republicans, than in the Pharisaical homage of the federal monarchists."[14]

Jefferson's most important aid in preventing a Federalist monopoly of Washington's glory was none other than the lowly, almost ridiculous Parson Weems aforementioned, who was not unaware of this aspect of his masterpiece. Writing to Jefferson for an endorsement of his biography, Weems said that he presented Washington not as "an Aristocrat . . . to mislead and enslave the nation, but a pure Republican."[15] His biography was indeed an antidote to Marshall, for he made the first President less formidable and dignified, consequently more acceptable to the voters who had brought about the political revolution of 1800. The leaders of the Federalist Party, however, continued to claim Washington for their own as long as that party existed; the name of their auxiliary organization, the Washington Benevolent Society, is good evidence, if there were no other. A great part of the oratory and verse that celebrated Washington in the first quarter of the nineteenth century was frankly Federalist.

There were earlier attempts to portray Washington in fiction, as well as in drama, but the first important effort was that of James Fenimore Cooper in *The Spy*, published in 1821. Other romancers immediately followed Cooper's example, but none met with popular favor. To picture Washington in fiction seemed irreverent. Americans considered him a fit subject for eulogies, not for novels.

Despite the works of Marshall, Weems, Cooper, and many others, interest in Washington remained on a plateau, so to speak, for a generation after his death. This was the period of the Virginia dynasty, which was Republican. Yet Washington remained a na-

---

[14]To Dr. Walter Jones, January 2, 1814, in Jefferson, *The Writings* . . . , ed. Paul Leicester Ford, 10 vols. (New York, 1892-1899), IX, 447-449. The letter is quoted at length, *infra*, Chapter II, Section 4.

[15]February 1, 1809, in Emily Ellsworth Ford Skeel, ed., *Mason Locke Weems, His Works and Ways*, 3 vols. (Norwood, Mass., 1929), II, 389.

tional symbol. Speakers and writers whose ideas were formed by Weems, Marshall, or the funeral orators could easily produce something comparable to the Stuart portraits, and many did so. On the occasion of the centennial of his birth a member of Congress could declare, "The praise of Washington is an exhausted subject." Voicing his praise in sonorous phrases had become a national—and to some extent an international—habit.

The appearance of Jared Sparks's edition of Washington's own writings in 1834–1837 was followed by a renaissance of interest on all sides. Sparks's work included a biography, and several others were published shortly thereafter. In the eighteen-fifties Washington Irving's biography appeared, and in 1857–1859 Thackeray used the American hero as a character in *The Virginians*, though he found it difficult to get material on Washington's personality. At one point, upon hearing a typical American description of Washington, Thackeray exclaimed, "No, no, Kennedy, that's not what I want. Tell me, was he a fussy old gentleman in a wig? Did he take snuff and spill it down his shirt front?" Furthermore, American hero-worshippers were outraged by the liberties that Thackeray took in fitting Washington into his story.

Before 1865 most American writers agreed that Washington's character was perfect, but they were not completely unified with regard to what constituted perfection. For instance, the exact nature of his religious belief occasioned some disagreement. Many of the funeral orators were ministers, and they put a heavy emphasis upon the great man's piety. So too did Parson Weems. His anecdote of a Quaker named Potts, who found Washington praying in the woods near Valley Forge, became a favorite with writers and speakers, as did a tale that at one time during the Revolution, when far from a church of his own denomination, Washington attended a Presbyterian communion service. But there were a few doubts. Even nineteenth-century readers might notice that while Washington often referred to God or Providence in his speeches, he never mentioned Christ. When in 1836 the Reverend E. C. M'Guire published *The Religious Opinions and Character of Washington*, a re-

Introduction

viewer remarked that Washington was often considered an infidel.[16] Some twenty years later Theodore Parker wrote: "In his latter years he had no more belief in the popular theology than John Adams or Benjamin Franklin, though, unlike them, he was not a speculative man."[17]

But most Americans thought otherwise. Moreover, they often failed to take account of the difference between the Episcopal Church of eighteenth-century Virginia and the churches, in many cases evangelical, to which they themselves belonged. Perhaps the most extreme view of Washington's piety is that presented in William Meade's *Old Churches, Ministers, and Families of Virginia*,[18] an influential book which went through several editions. Bishop Meade, who led an evangelical movement in the Episcopal Church of Virginia, repeated Weems's story of the Quaker and pointed out that Washington always demanded a chaplain for his army. Continuing, he proved to his own satisfaction that Washington was opposed to intemperance, profanity, card playing, dancing, the theater, and hunting.[19] Meade's marshaling of evidence from Washington's own writings to show that he constantly relied on Providence is impressive and convincing, but he made him even more puritanical than did the New England funeral orators of 1800. On the other hand, there are chapters on "Washington as a Sportsman" and "Birth Night Balls and the Theatre" in *Recollections and Private Memoirs of Washington* (1860), by George Washington Parke Custis, Washington's adopted son.[20]

Some writers who accepted the conventional idea of Washington's religious zeal felt they must combat or ignore the notion that he was guilty of profane swearing upon certain occasions, notably

---

[16]"Review of M'Guire's *Religious Opinions of Washington*," *New York Review*, I (March, 1837), 225–237.

[17]"George Washington," in Theodore Parker, *Historic Americans*, ed. Samuel A. Eliot (Boston, [1908]), p. 88. Freeman (*op. cit.*, II, 388) is nearly in agreement with Parker.

[18]2 vols. (Philadelphia, 1857).

[19]*Ibid.*, II, 242–255.

[20]Custis's sketches had appeared in newspapers much earlier: *infra*, Chapter IV, Section 4.

when he met General Charles Lee at the Battle of Monmouth. Others emphasized it and maintained that the Commander-in-Chief's rage was an indication of the depth and richness of his nature.[21] One important characteristic, his tolerance in religious matters, was generally overlooked, unless the story of his attending a Presbyterian communion service may be considered in that category. John Bell at an early date wrote of his tolerance, his complete freedom from religious prejudices,[22] but subsequent writers ignored this trait.

For more than a decade before the Civil War, leaders of thought in both the North and the South called upon the name of Washington in their appeals for national unity. His "magic name" was also invoked in matters of controversy. He had been opposed to the extension of slavery, and his Farewell Address gave emphatic counsel against sectionalism and disunion. On the other hand, he was himself a Southerner and a slaveholder; the South had no intention of repudiating the greatest of all great Virginians.

A British observer wrote in 1860 that although names of parties in America were so numerous as to be "scarcely intelligible," the deep and lasting political division was between the disciples of Washington and the disciples of Jefferson. The Jeffersonians were handicapped by "the necessity of depreciating the policy, and, to a certain extent, unavoidably disparaging the character of Washington." The writer hastily added that love and veneration for Washington's name had remained and doubtless would remain deep-seated in the heart of every true American; yet it was evident that not all turned to the great man's Farewell Address with unqualified enthusiasm and conviction.[23]

[21]For example, Edwin P. Whipple, *infra*, Chapter III, Section 4; Henry A. Wise, *infra*, Chapter III, Section 4; and John Neal, *infra*, Chapter VII, Section 1. Perhaps the fullest study of the evidence on Washington's remarks to Lee at Monmouth is in Rupert Hughes, *George Washington* . . . , 3 vols. (New York, 1926–1930), III, 362–366. There is apparently no proof that Washington used profanity on this occasion.

[22]*Infra*, Chapter IV, Section 1. Washington's actions bear this out. See John C. Fitzpatrick, *Washington as a Religious Man* (Washington, D.C., 1931), a Bicentennial pamphlet.

[23]"Review of an Inquiry into the Formation of Washington's Farewell Address," *Quarterly Review*, CVII (April, 1860) 382–383.

Introduction

Several movements of national extent served to focus attention on Washington during the turbulent fifties. The cornerstone of the Washington Monument, long the subject of discussion and debate, had been laid in 1848, and the campaign for subscriptions in the ensuing years kept the hero's memory particularly green.[24] In 1850 the United States Senate discussed and passed a motion for the purchase of the manuscript of the Farewell Address. A Southern woman in 1853 began the agitation which resulted in the Mount Vernon Ladies' Association. Edward Everett, the Massachusetts scholar and statesman, toured the entire country in behalf of this organization and raised nearly seventy thousand dollars toward the purchase and restoration of Washington's home. His widely repeated Washington's Birthday oration ended with a plea that North and South cling together in memory of Washington and his principles.

From being the symbol of the nation itself, Washington became the symbol of national unity, and although both North and South used his name in eloquent appeals for harmony, their invocations had discordant overtones. Northerners presented a logical case,

---

[24]Political overtones were sometimes present in discussions of a suitable mausoleum or memorial for Washington. In 1811 a Federalist criticized the Republican administration for failure to provide an impressive tomb for the national hero. See Alexander Graydon, *Memoirs of a Life* . . . (Harrisburg, Pa., 1811), pp. 328–329.

But various practical and aesthetic considerations were involved in the matter of a mausoleum and, later, a monument. Not only Congress but the citizens at large took an interest and made suggestions. In 1816 a contributor to the *North American Review* considered the possibilities of the arch, the pyramid, and other architectural forms, but decided that a column was the proper memorial for Washington, because only in that form could America surpass the whole world. Eight years later a writer in the same magazine bitterly resented a statement of a British traveler who compared Washington's tomb to "a pig stye." See W. Tudor, "Monument to Washington," *North American Review*, II (March, 1816), 329–340; "Faux's *Memorable Days in America*," ibid., XIX (July, 1824), 120.

Nathaniel Beverley Tucker, in an unsigned review (*Southern Literary Messenger*, I [February, 1835], 308), took the position that no memorial could appropriately express the feeling of Americans for their hero, and that consequently no memorial was needed. A decade later Hiram Powers said that the monument to Washington should be so high and the figure on the top so large that the features would be recognizable fifty miles away. See [Lewis Gaylord Clark], "Gossip with Readers," *Knickerbocker*, XXVI (October, 1845), 364–366.

Robert Mills's design, adopted but later modified, called for a figure of Washington in a triumphal chariot atop the obelisk. The history of the monument itself is intensely interesting. See F. L. Harvey, *History of the Washington Monument and the National Monument Society* (Washington, D.C., 1903).

often quoting strongly Federalist portions of the Farewell Address and pointing to Washington's stand against the spread of slavery into the Northwest Territory.[25] Lincoln's Cooper Institute speech is the classic example. Southern pleas were more varied, and were often less logical and more sentimental than Northern ones. Some Southern writers hoped to avoid intersectional ill-will by reminding all Americans of their high regard for Washington, a Virginian who had been chief agent in founding the nation and who had expected and desired it to be one nation.

But Southern speakers and writers were likely to let their regional pride get the upper hand even when they called for national unity. Many emphasized heavily the fact that America's greatest hero was a Southerner; this theme was particularly attractive to Virginians. Another motif in Southern literature was the charge or implication that although sectionalism had arisen, contrary to Washington's wish and counsel, the North was to blame because it had encroached upon the rights of the South. Governor Henry A. Wise of Virginia well expressed this attitude in his speech upon the unveiling of a statue of Washington at the Virginia Military Institute in 1856. The next logical step for Southerners was a dangerous one which few were ready to take before 1861: to declare that freedom was at stake and that the South must rebel against Northern oppression even as Washington had done against the British. John C. Calhoun had brought this analogy to the attention of the United States Sen-

[25] Criticism of the institution of slavery began long before 1800, and to Washington himself was addressed a letter, published in Ireland, on the subject of his slaveholding. See Edward Rushton, *Expostulatory Letter to George Washington* ... (Liverpool, 1797).

Dr. Benjamin Rush, a signer of the Declaration of Independence, wrote against slavery before the Revolution. See Benjamin Rush, *Autobiography* ..., ed. George W. Corner ([Princeton, N.J.], 1948), pp. 82–83.

Benjamin Franklin in his last years joined antislavery movements, and in 1789 he wrote "An Address to the Public from the Pennsylvania Society for Promoting Abolition of Slavery." Bernard Faÿ (*op. cit.*, p. 166) thinks he may have had Washington in mind as he composed this denunciation of slavery and of those who maintained the institution.

Washington in his will directed that his slaves be freed upon his widow's death. At least one funeral orator (Timothy Bigelow) said that other Southerners should follow his example and free their slaves.

Theodore Parker's essay on Washington (*op. cit.*) is devoted partly to the matter of slavery; he regretted that Washington did not take a firm stand against it in the Constitutional Convention.

Introduction

ate in his famous speech of March 4, 1850. Thus Southern reasoning on the theme of Washington ran the gamut from the desirability of national union to the necessity for disunion.[26]

Reverence for the name and principles of America's first hero did not serve to avert conflict. After the war had actually begun, the Southern cause seemed to its supporters much like that of 1776, a struggle for freedom. The character of Robert E. Lee, the Southern Commander, resembled that of Washington and added force to the analogy.[27] Lee was steeped in the Washington tradition from childhood, and the great Virginian who had been his father's friend was his own model in a very real and personal sense.[28] Those who rallied to the Southern cause could unite in one clear conception of Washington: a son of the South who had led an earlier war for freedom.[29]

After the smoke of battle cleared, new heroes took their places in the American hall of fame. For a time Lee himself tended to

---

[26] An interesting Southern expression on Washington occurs in Mrs. Elizabeth Anne Poyas's *Our Forefathers* . . . (Charleston, S.C., 1860), pp. 10–33. Mrs. Poyas began with a long discussion of Washington's genealogy and family connections, continued with amusing anecdotes of his marriage and family life, and concluded with a stirring call to the defense of Southern rights. Cf. Beverley Tucker, "A Discourse on the Genius of the Federal System of the United States," *Southern Literary Messenger*, IV (December, 1838), 761–769; G. W. Bagby, "Editor's Table," *ibid.*, XXXI (December, 1860), 473; George Fitzhugh, "Bonaparte, Cromwell, and Washington," *De Bow's Review*, XXVIII (February, 1860), 139–154. The role of Washington in prewar controversy is treated more fully by the present writer in "George Washington: Symbolic Guardian of the Republic, 1850–1861," *William and Mary Quarterly*, Series 3, VII (January, 1950), 53–63.

[27] Douglas Southall Freeman, *R. E. Lee, a Biography*, 4 vols. (New York, 1934–1935), IV, 185, 248, *et passim*.

[28] Lee chanced to read Everett's biography of Washington in the early days of 1861, while he was stationed at Fort Mason, Texas. On January 23 of that year he wrote to his family: "How his [Washington's] spirit would be grieved could he see the wreck of his mighty labors! I will not, however, permit myself to believe, until all the ground for hope has gone, that the fruit of his noble deeds will be destroyed and that his precious advice and virtuous example will so soon be forgotten by his countrymen."
Lee thought that the South had just grievances, but although four states had already seceded at this time, he hoped that the Union might yet be saved. See A. L. Long, *Memoirs of Robert E. Lee* . . . (New York, 1886), p. 87.
After he accepted command of the Confederate forces, Lee may have reflected from time to time that Washington likewise led a rebel army. Cf. Freeman, *R. E. Lee*, I, 419–420, 440, 453, 465; IV, 202.

[29] Confederate poetry and songs carried this motif: *infra*, Chapter V, Section 7.

eclipse Washington in the affections of Southerners, and Lincoln, the martyr-President, held the spotlight in the North. Today the names of Washington and Lincoln are frequently coupled, and both have secure positions in the hearts of their countrymen. The primacy perhaps belongs to Lincoln, for Washington has usually been more admired than loved. Yet his sun has never been hidden, and it may in the end prove to be the brightest of all.

The process by which Washington became the Father of His Country while many facets of his personality were forgotten is neither unprecedented nor unnatural. "Time dissipates to shining ether the solid angularity of facts," says Emerson. Many of the details which the name of George Washington called to the minds of those who knew him personally were lost sight of when he came to be remembered as the leader of the Patriot forces of the Revolution and as the first President of the United States. With the passage of still more time the "ether" increased. Americans who had grown up under the Stars and Stripes did not realize that for forty-three years Washington had been a Colonial and a loyal subject of British kings. And men who more and more lived their lives in cities and towns failed to understand the psychology and way of life of a Virginia planter and slaveholder.

Some facts simply did not fit into the picture of the man who was to serve as the symbol of a nation. Puritanical persons even before Washington's death did not like to be reminded that he was at times furious in his rage and was said to swear occasionally. Historians may quarrel as to whether he smoked the pipes that he ordered from England or merely kept them for visiting friends, but there is abundant evidence that he liked his wine at dinner. He was fond of the theater, and on one social occasion during the Revolution he danced for three hours without once sitting down. He likewise enjoyed fox hunting and other outdoor sports. As a young man, he played cards for fairly high stakes. In short, George Washington was a real person in eighteenth-century Virginia. But, to quote Emerson again, "Who cares what the fact was, when we have made a constellation of it to hang in heaven an immortal sign?"

CHAPTER II

WASHINGTON AS SEEN BY HIS CONTEMPORARIES

THE READER who has encountered only modern presentations of George Washington is sometimes surprised when he examines what those who actually knew the man had to say about him. Some of the contemporary accounts reveal traits which in the nineteenth century were forgotten, and in them Washington often appears as a living man rather than an American symbol. One purpose of the present chapter is to suggest a rounded picture of the actual George Washington who moved among his contemporaries. They saw him as a soldier, as a statesman, and as a private citizen at Mount Vernon, and especially important are the comments of those who knew him best.

The second purpose of the chapter is to reveal the specious, ethereal, Jovian Washington of the nineteenth century in the formative stages. In Revolutionary days there were two main attitudes toward Washington, that of the Patriots and that of the Tories. After the Revolution, however, the Tories were gone or silenced. The contrasting views were in the last decade of his life those of the Federalists, who claimed him as one of them, and those of the Republicans, who opposed many of his policies and thought he favored their political rivals. Much of the panegyric voiced and written by Washington's friends has echoed and re-echoed through the years, but the remarks of his critics and enemies have been for the most part forgotten; yet some of these have value.

The first two sections of the present chapter present the opinions first of his friends and then of his critics or opponents in Revolutionary days. The third and fourth sections reveal a somewhat similar contrast during his presidency.

I

The best brief physical description of young Washington, the soldier who had distinguished himself at the Monongahela, is that given by George Mercer, who served with Washington in the colonial wars. In 1760 Mercer wrote to a friend in Europe:

Although distrusting my ability to give an adequate account of the personal appearance of Col. George Washington, late commander of the Virginia Provincial troops, I shall, as you request, attempt the portraiture. He may be described as being as straight as an Indian, measuring six feet two inches in his stockings, and weighing 175 pounds when he took his seat in the House of Burgesses in 1759. His frame is padded with well-developed muscles, indicating great strength. His bones and joints are large, as are his feet and hands. He is wide shouldered, but has not a deep or round chest; is neat waisted, but is broad across the hips, and has rather long legs and arms. His head is well shaped though not large, but is gracefully poised on a superb neck. A large and straight rather than a prominent nose; blue-gray penetrating eyes, which are widely separated and overhung by a heavy brow. His face is long rather than broad, with high round cheek bones. He has a clear though rather a colorless pale skin, which burns with the sun. A pleasing, benevolent, though a commanding countenance, dark brown hair, which he wears in a cue. His mouth is large and generally firmly closed, but which from time to time discloses some defective teeth. His features are regular and placid, with all the muscles of his face under perfect control, though flexible and expressive of deep feeling when moved by emotions. In conversation he looks you full in the face, is deliberate, deferential and engaging. His voice is agreeable rather than strong. His demeanor at all times composed and dignified. His movements and gestures are graceful, his walk is majestic, and he is a splendid horseman.[1]

[1] In W. S. Baker, ed., *Early Sketches of George Washington* . . . (Philadelphia, 1894), pp. 13-14. Baker (p. 9) compares the portrait painted by Charles Willson Peale in 1772.
  Shortly after Braddock's defeat Christopher Gist, a fellow soldier, wrote to

Washington as Seen by His Contemporaries

When Washington was appointed Commander-in-Chief of the Patriot army in 1775, a Northern member of Congress wrote home that

His election was unanimous, his acceptance of the high trust, modest and polite, his Character I need not enlarge on but will only say to his honor, that he is said to be as fixed and resolute in having his orders on all occasions executed, as he is cool and deliberate in giving them.[2]

Benjamin Rush, physician, representative of Pennsylvania in the Second Continental Congress, and signer of the Declaration of Independence, gives us a picture of a dinner at which Washington was present shortly after his acceptance of the appointment noted above. The first toast drunk was to "The Commander-in-chief of the American Armies," and Washington rose for a response. Rush describes the reaction of the group:

The whole company instantly rose, and drank the toast standing. This scene, so unexpected, was a solemn one. A silence followed it as if every heart was penetrated by the awful, but great events which were to follow the use of the sword of liberty which had just been put into General Washington's hands by the unanimous voice of his country.[3]

By 1778 Major Samuel Shaw was writing to a friend in the rhetorical fashion which soon became standard for Patriots speaking of Washington:

It would be paying very little attention to that warm attachment which you so justly have to our illustrious Commander-in-chief, were I to omit acquainting you, that he enjoys a perfect state of health and is the same steady, amiable character he has ever been. His fortitude, patience, and equanimity of soul, under the discouragement he has been obliged to encounter, ought to endear him to his country,—it has done it exceed-

---

Washington from Philadelphia: "Your name is more talked of than any other person of the army." Quoted in Nathaniel Wright Stephenson and Waldo Hilary Dunn, *George Washington*, 2 vols. (New York and London, 1940), I, 155.

[2] Silas Deane to Joseph Trumbull, n.p., n.d., in Edmund C. Burnett, ed., *Letters of Members of the Continental Congress*, 8 vols. (Washington, D.C., 1921–1936), I, 133. On this appointment cf. comments made by John Adams at this time and later: *The Works of John Adams* . . . , ed. Charles Francis Adams, 10 vols. (Boston, 1850–1856), I, 175–176; X, 36.

[3] Benjamin Rush, *Autobiography* . . . , ed. George W. Corner, ([Princeton, N.J.], 1948), pp. 112–113.

ingly to the army. When I contemplate the virtues of the man, uniting in the citizen and soldier, I cannot too heartily coincide with the orator for the Fifth of March last who so delicately describes him, as a person that appears to be raised by Heaven to show how high humanity can soar. It will afford you no small pleasure to be told, that the faction which was breeding last winter to traduce the first character on the Continent is at an end.[4]

> The Battle of Monmouth and Washington's difficulty with General Charles Lee, his second in command, caused Patriots to rally more fervently than ever in defense and eulogy of their leader. Governor William Livingston of New Jersey conveyed popular sentiment when he wrote in a letter addressed to Lee:

I should be extremely unhappy in having reasons to believe, what is most frequently & perhaps injuriously reported of you, that you endeavored to lessen the estimation in which General Washington is held by the most virtuous citizens of America; and which estimation, not Sir, from a blind attachment to men of high rank, nor from any self-interested motive whatsoever, but from a full conviction of his great personal merit & public importance, I deem it my duty to my country, to use my utmost influence to support.[5]

Elias Boudinot, of New Jersey, commissary-general of prisoners, wrote concerning the incident: "The General I always revered and loved ever since I knew him, but in this instance he rose superior to himself— Every lip dwells on his praise, for even his pretended friends (for none dare to acknowledge themselves his enemies) are obliged to croak it forth."[6]

Boudinot recorded an interview which he had with the General at a dark moment in 1778. The scene has a human warmth which is rare in firsthand characterizations of Washington:

When I found every application to obtain hard money from Congress for the Cloathing of our Prisoners in vain, I waited on Genl Washing-

[4]Samuel Shaw to the Reverend John Eliot, April 12, 1778, in *The Journals of Major Samuel Shaw* . . . , ed. Josiah Quincy (Boston, 1847), p. 45; cf. p. 104.
[5]To Charles Lee, January 16, 1779, in *The Lee Papers*, 4 vols., in *Collections of the New York Historical Society* (IV–VII) (New York, 1871–1874), III, 297.
[6]To Alexander Hamilton, July 8, 1778, *ibid.*, II, 474.

ton, and proposed my resignation, as my Character was at stake, having (on the promise of the Secret Committee to yield me every necessary aid) pledged myself to the officers in Confinement that they should be regularly supplied with every necessary, but they now suffered more than ever. In much distress with Tears in his Eyes, he assured me that if he was deserted by the Gentn of the Country, he should despair. He could not do everything— He was Genl. Quarter Master and Commissary. Every thing fell on him and he was unequal to the task. He gave me the most positive Engagement that if I would contrive any mode for their Support and Comfort he would confirm it as far as was in his Power— On this I told him, I knew of but one way and that was to borrow Money on my private Security. He assured me that in Case I did, and was not reimbursed by Congress, he would go an equal share with me in the loss.[7]

The *Memoirs* of Alexander Graydon are among the most readable of the reminiscences of old Revolutionary soldiers. The author came directly from harum-scarum adventures in school to join the army when the war began. Washington comes into the story frequently. Captain Graydon found him venerable but says that he made mistakes, for instance at Fort Washington.[8] The Commander is characterized as possessing the qualifications desirable for one in his position "in a degree not to be surpassed: a manner which at once inspired confidence and attachment; a figure preeminently gentlemanly, dignified, commanding, equally removed from heaviness and flippancy, and blending the gravity of the sage with the animation of the soldier."[9]

Alexander Garden, another old soldier, published his reminiscences in 1822 under the title *Anecdotes of the Revolutionary War*. Several of the anecdotes treat Washington, but much of the material was obtained by hearsay, and much was stilted, as, for instance a little story of the fall of Yorktown. The author said he heard this

[7]Elias Boudinot, "Reminiscences," July 31(?), 1778, in Burnett, *op. cit.*, III, 356.
[8]Alexander Graydon, *Memoirs of a Life* . . . (Harrisburg, Pa., 1811), p. 171; cf. pp. 275-276, 279.
[9]*Ibid.*, p. 276. Cf. William Heath, *Memoirs of Major-General Heath* . . . (Boston, 1798); James Thacher, *A Military Journal* . . . (Boston, 1823); James Wilkinson, *Memoirs of My Own Times* (Philadelphia, 1816); Elkanah Watson, *Men and Times of the Revolution* . . . (2d ed.; New York, 1857); Charles Fraser, *Reminiscences of Charleston* . . . (Charleston, S.C., 1854).

from a Dr. M'Caula, of Charleston, and the story was that as the British were to march out from the garrison and deliver up their arms, Washington urged the men near him to refrain from boisterous clamor: "My brave fellows, let no sensation of satisfaction for the triumph you have gained, induce you to insult your fallen enemy—let no shouting, no clamorous huzzaing increase their mortification. It is sufficient satisfaction to us that we witness their humiliation. Posterity will huzza for us."[10]

The works of Garden and Graydon, typifying, as they do, accounts of Washington by his men, have particular importance because Thackeray is known to have perused them in preparation for his treatment of Washington in *The Virginians*.[11] Since these soldiers did not publish their memoirs until twenty years after Washington's death, it is likely that their descriptions are less realistic than they would have been had they been written nearer the time of the Revolution.

Patriot ladies who were fortunate enough to see or meet the Commander-in-Chief were impressed by his "great personal merit & public importance" as were their menfolk, but they also afford us a few glimpses of Washington the gentleman, at his ease in polite society. The brilliant Abigail Adams found the gentleman and soldier agreeably blended in him; she quoted Dryden in describing her reaction to the hero when he arrived in Boston to take command of the army in 1775.[12] Four years later a young belle expressed a more frivolous point of view. She wrote to John Jay, her brother-in-law, that Washington entertained widely and with elegance and that he wore on occasion a suit of clothes made by the Countess du la Luzerne [*sic*].[13] Mrs. Richard Bache wrote to her father, Benjamin

[10]*Anecdotes of the Revolutionary War in America* . . . (Charleston, S.C., 1822), p. 394. A second series of the *Anecdotes* was published in 1828.
[11]Henry T. Tuckerman, *The Life of John Pendleton Kennedy* (New York, 1871), p. 364.
[12]Abigail Adams to John Adams, July 16, 1775, in *Letters of Mrs. Adams* . . . , ed. Charles Francis Adams, 2 vols. (Boston, 1840), I, 51–52.
[13]Kitty Livingston to John Jay, Philadelphia, December 26, 1779, in John Jay, *The Correspondence and Public Papers* . . . , ed. Henry P. Johnston, 4 vols. (New York and London, 1890–1893), I, 308.

Franklin, of informal conversation with the General at balls and other social gatherings:

> I have been several times invited abroad with the General and Mrs. Washington. He always inquires after you in the most affectionate manner, and speaks of you highly. We danced at Mrs. Powell's on your birth-day, or night, I should say, in company together, and he told me it was the anniversary of his marriage; it was just twenty years that night.[14]

In reply Franklin, writing from France, asked his daughter to tell Washington that the old French generals studied his operations with approval.[15] In 1780 Franklin invited the General to come to France, where he would be known at once as he would be a thousand years thereafter, free from petty enmities and inconveniences, because, as he said, a thousand leagues have the same effect upon a reputation as a thousand years.[16] On the fall of Yorktown he wrote Washington a letter of congratulation, saying, "It has made a great addition to the military reputation you had already acquired, and brightens the glory that surrounds your name, and that must accompany it to the latest posterity."[17]

A member of Congress who was present when Washington resigned his authority as Commander-in-Chief described the scene feelingly: "The spectators all wept, and there was hardly a member of Congress who did not drop tears. The General's hand which held the address shook as he read it. . . . all conspired to render it a spectacle inexpressibly solemn and affecting."[18]

Writing from France, John Adams expressed strong approval of Washington's method of handling the officers and men who at Newburgh demanded their back pay. Adams pronounced the character of Washington "above all praise, as every character is whose

---

[14]Sarah Franklin Bache to Benjamin Franklin, January 17, 1779, quoted in W. S. Baker, *Itinerary of General Washington* . . . (Philadelphia, 1892), p. 149.

[15]To Mrs. Sarah Bache, June 3, 1779, in *The Writings of Benjamin Franklin* . . . , ed. Albert H. Smyth, 10 vols. (New York and London, 1905-1907), VII, 349-350.

[16]Franklin to Washington, March 5, 1780, *ibid.*, VIII, 28-29.

[17]April 2, 1782, *ibid.*, VIII, 411.

[18]James McHenry to Miss Margaret Caldwell, December 23, 1783, in Burnett, *op. cit.*, VII, 394-395.

rule and object are duty, not interest, nor glory; which I think has been strictly true with the General from the beginning . . ."[19] But Adams was at times disturbed and annoyed by the people's adulation of Washington. Benjamin Rush quoted Adams as early as 1777 on the subject of the "superstitious veneration" paid to General Washington by certain members of Congress; according to Rush, Adams said they were idolizing an image wrought by their own hands.[20] In 1785, after the Commander's retirement, Adams returned to this theme:

Instead of adoring a Washington, mankind should applaud the nation which educated him. . . . I glory in the character of a Washington, because I know him to be only an exemplification of the American character. . . . Now, I ask, what occasioned this dangerous enthusiasm for him? I answer, that, great as his talents and virtues are, they did not altogether contribute so much to it as his serving without pay, which never fails to turn the heads of the multitude.[21]

French soldiers and diplomats who saw Washington during the Revolution wrote of him with remarkable uniformity. An especially vivid description was penned by François, later Marquis de Barbé-Marbois, who was attached to the French Legation in America from 1779 to 1785. He is felicitous in choosing concrete details of Washington's physical characteristics, and his mention of the ballplaying is unique. Of a visit to Washington's headquarters in 1779 Barbé-Marbois wrote:

He received us with a noble, modest, and gentle urbanity and with that graciousness which seems to be the basis of his character. He is fifty years old, well built, rather thin. He carries himself freely and with a sort of military grace. He is masculine looking, without his features being less gentle on that account. I have never seen anyone who was more naturally and spontaneously polite. His eyes are blue and rather large, his mouth and nose are regular, and his forehead open. His uniform is exactly like that of his soldiers. Formerly, on solemn occasions,

[19] John Adams to Secretary Livingston, June 16, 1783, in *Works*, VIII, 73.
[20] Rush, *op. cit.*, p. 141.
[21] Adams to John Jebb, London, September 10, 1785, in *Works*, IX, 540–542.

that is to say on days of battle, he wore a large blue sash, but he has given up that unrepublican distinction. I have been told that he preserves in battle the character of humanity which makes him so dear to his soldiers in camp. I have seen him for some time in the midst of his staff, and he has always appeared even-tempered, tranquil, and orderly in his occupations, and serious in his conversation. He asks few questions, listens attentively, and answers in a low tone and with few words. He is serious in business. Outside of that, he permits himself a restricted gaiety. His conversation is as simple as his habits and his appearance. He makes no pretensions, and does the honors of his house with dignity, but without pompousness or flattery. His aides-de-camp preside at his table and offer the toasts. Before being the head of the American army, he did not disdain the care of his farm. To-day, he sometimes throws and catches a ball for whole hours with his aides-de-camp. He is reverent without bigotry, and abhors swearing, which he punishes with the greatest severity. As to his public conduct, ask his compatriots, and the universe. If you like historical parallels, I might compare him to Timoleon who freed the Sicilians from the tyranny of the Carthaginians . . .[22]

Frenchmen who became interested in the American cause had an exalted preconception of the great leader of that cause and were not disappointed upon meeting him. Somewhat similar to the words of Barbé-Marbois are those written by Mathieu, Count Dumas, in 1781. The latter's account reveals traits of sympathy and kindness in Washington:

We had been impatient to see the hero of liberty. His dignified address, his simplicity of manners and mild gravity, surpassed our expectation, and won every heart. After having conferred with Count Rochambeau, as he was leaving us to return to his head-quarters near West Point, I received the welcome order to accompany him as far as Providence. We arrived there at night; the whole of the population had assembled from the suburbs, we were surrounded by a crowd of children carrying torches, reiterating the acclamations of the citizens; all were eager to approach the person of him whom they called their father, and pressed so closely around us that they hindered us from proceeding.

[22]François, Marquis de Barbé-Marbois, *Our Revolutionary Forefathers, the Letters of François, Marquis de Barbé-Marbois . . . 1779–1785*, ed. Eugene Parker Chase (New York, 1929), pp. 113–114.

General Washington was much affected, stopped a few moments, and pressing my hand, said, "We may be beaten by the English; it is the chance of war; but behold an army which they can never conquer."

. . . . .

The general gave me a most cordial reception. . . . Being invited to dinner, which was remarkably plain, I had leisure to admire the perfect harmony of his noble and fine countenance, with the simplicity of his language and the justice and depth of his observations. He generally sat long at table, and animated the conversation by unaffected cheerfulness. Much was said of the treachery of Arnold . . . I was particularly struck with the marks of affection which the general showed to his pupil, his adopted son the marquis de La Fayette. Seated opposite to him, he looked at him with pleasure, and listened to him with manifest interest.

. . . . .

After having visited the forts and reviewed the garrison, as the day was declining, and we were going to mount our horses, the general perceived that M. de la Fayette, in consequence of his old wound, was very much fatigued. "It will be better," said he, "to return by water; the tide will assist us in ascending the stream." A boat was soon manned with good rowers, and we embarked. The cold became excessive; we had to make our way between the large flakes of ice which the river brought down. A heavy snow and obscurity of the night soon rendered the danger more imminent; and the management of the boat, filled with water, became increasingly difficult. We coasted the rocks which lined the right bank of the Hudson, between West Point and New Windsor, at the foot of which it is impossible to land. General Washington perceiving that the master of the boat was very much alarmed, took the helm, saying, "Courage, my friends; I am going to conduct you, since it is my duty to hold the helm." After having with much difficulty made our way against the stream and the tide, we landed, and had to walk a league before we reached the head-quarters.[23]

[23]Mathieu Dumas, *Memoirs of His Own Time* . . . , 2 vols. (Philadelphia, 1839), as quoted in Gilbert Chinard, ed., *George Washington as the French Knew Him* . . . (Princeton, N.J., 1940), pp. 40–42. Lafayette's correspondence with Washington (*ibid.*, pp. 3–13) shows a warm attachment on both sides.

Chinard's collection of texts is an excellent foundation for a study of Washington in French literature. He includes the famous observations of Chastellux (pp. 43–61) and Chateaubriand (pp. 93–98).

Partly because they lacked complete information as well as perspective, Washington's contemporaries did not often analyze his military strategy and soldierly characteristics as such. Instead, they were impressed upon sight by his commanding mien and upon acquaintance by his noble character. Among the recurring words and phrases are "fortitude," "patience," "modesty," "politeness," "fixed resolution," and "devotion to duty." Yet in the descriptions and brief anecdotes given by some of those Patriots Washington is a very real personality, not a mere collection of abstractions.

2

When the Patriots, or Whigs, won the war and independence was assured, most of the leaders of the Loyalist or Tory third of the American population of 1775-1783 were harried out of the land, and they and their works were soon forgotten. But during the war the Tories were busily trying to undermine Washington's reputation. Of Tories whose writing has survived, few actually knew Washington personally; their defamation was largely a matter of malicious rumor and propaganda.[24]

The Reverend Jonathan Boucher, who had been a tutor of Washington's stepson, knew the General better than any other Tory whose writing is extant. In 1775 Boucher found himself forced out of his pulpit because of the Tory doctrines that he preached. Shortly before leaving for England, he wrote to Washington in bitter terms of reproach, concluding:

You cannot say that I deserved to be run down, vilified, and injured in the manner which you know has fallen to my lot, merely because I cannot bring myself to think on some political points just as you and your party would have me think. And yet you have borne to look on at least as an unconcerned spectator, if not an abetter, whilst like the poor frogs in the fable, I have in a manner been petted to death. I do not ask if such conduct in you was friendly: was it either just, manly, or generous? It was not; no, it was acting with all the base malignity of a virulent Whig. As such, Sir, I resent it: and oppressed and overborne as

[24]*Supra*, Chapter I, Section 2.

I may seem to be by popular obloquy, I will not be so wanting in justice to myself as not to tell you, as I now do with honest boldness, that I despise the man who, for any motives, could be induced to act so mean a part. You are no longer worthy of my friendship; a man of honour can no longer without dishonour be connected with you. With your Cause I renounce you; and now, for the last time, subscribe myself, Sir,
Your humble servant

J. B.[25]

Some ten years after his return to England Boucher wrote more dispassionately of Washington in his *Reminiscences*. After several pages on the young Washington's adventures in the colonial wars, Boucher gives his calm, considered judgment:

At Braddock's defeat, and every subsequent occasion throughout the war, he acquitted himself much in the same manner as in my judgment he has since done, i.e. decently, but never greatly. I know Mr. Washington well; and tho' occasions may call forth traits of character that never would have been discovered in the more sequestered scenes of life, I cannot conceive how he could, otherwise than through the interested representations of party, have ever been spoken of as a great man. He is shy, silent, stern, slow, and cautious, but has no quickness of parts, extraordinary penetration, nor an elevated style of thinking. In his moral character he is regular, temperate, strictly just and honest (excepting that as a Virginian he has lately found out that there is no moral turpitude in not paying what he confesses he owes to a British creditor) and, as I always thought, religious: having heretofore been pretty constant, and even exemplary, in his attendance on public worship in the Church of England. But he seems to have nothing generous or affectionate in his nature. Just before the close of the last war he married the widow Custis, and thus came into the possession of her large jointure. He never had any children; and lived very much like a gentleman at Mount-Vernon in Fairfax County, where the most distinguished part of his character was that he was an admirable farmer.[26]

In 1797, after Washington had retired from public life, Boucher dedicated to him a book entitled *A View of the Causes and Con-*

---

[25]To Washington, August 6, 1775, in Jonathan Boucher, *Reminiscences of an American Loyalist* . . . , ed. Jonathan Bouchier (Boston and New York, 1925), pp. 136-141.
[26]*Ibid.*, pp. 49-50.

sequences of the American Revolution, in Thirteen Discourses, Preached in North America between the Years 1763 and 1775. The inconsistency of dedicating to the former Commander-in-Chief a work hostile to the American cause is obvious. But Boucher approved of Washington's presidency, and as a Christian minister he was most favorably impressed by certain portions of the Farewell Address. At last he was willing to concede the American leader a certain amount of greatness: "That you possessed talents eminently well adapted for the high post you lately held, friends and foes have concurred in testifying . . ."[27]

The story of Washington's altercation with General Charles Lee, his second in command during the early years of the war, is a long and distressing one. Lee, an English-born Whig and professional soldier, was ambitious for personal glory and hoped eventually to gain the highest command himself. He began to cast mild aspersions upon Washington at least as early as July, 1776:

No man loves, respects, and reverences another more than I do General Washington. I esteem his virtues, private and public. I know him to be a man of sense, courage and firmness, but if a hero should start up . . . who would charge himself with the mighty task of political salvation, General Washington ought, and, I am convinced, would resign the truncheon . . .[28]

After the fall of Fort Washington in the same year, he was more explicit in a letter to a young officer who admired his military ability:

I received your most obliging, flattering letter—lament with you that fatal indecision of mind which in war is a much greater disqualification than stupidity, or even want of personal courage—accident may put a decisive blunder in the right—but eternal defeat and miscarriage must attend the man of the best parts if cursed with indecision. . . . I really think our Chief will do better with me than without me.[29]

[27] (London, 1797), Dedication.
[28] Charles Lee to Richard Henry Lee, July 19, 1776, in *Lee Papers*, II, 147-148.
[29] Charles Lee to Joseph Reed, November 24, 1776, *ibid.*, II, 305.

At the Battle of Monmouth, Lee was guilty of conduct which led to his trial and disgrace. For a time he defended his action in letters to the newspapers as well as to his friends. He bitterly denounced Washington. At one point he optimistically wrote to General Gates that

Our Great Gargantua, or Lama Babak (for I know not which Title is the properest) begins to be no longer considered as an infallible divinity— . . . no art no artifice shall . . . prevail upon me to draw my sword again at least while Gargantua or Lama Babak is at the head of our Armies. I am sorry for the poor American Soldiers, who have certainly merit, virtue and courage—but they must inevitably be beat or rather drown'd if they depend on such a bladder of emptiness and pride . . .[30]

Lee's attitude did not change. After Yorktown, when Washington was the toast of two continents, Lee wrote to his sister:

All I say is, that (the New England men excepted) the Americans (tho' they fancy and sometimes call themselves Romans) have not a single Republican qualification or Idea. They have always a God of the day, whose infallibility is not to be disputed; to him every man must bow down on pain of political damnation. Washington has long been in this state of divinity—but I think, of late the legality of his apotheosis begins to be called in question. You will naturally be curious to be acquainted with a character that has made so much noise; Shakespeare has drawn it in some measure in his Merchant of Venice, but it wants finishing. There are a sort of men, whose visages do cream & mantle like a standing pool; and do a wishful stilness entertain, with purpose to be dress'd in an opinion of wisdom, gravity & profound conceit &c &c—in fact the bearing of a mysterious carriage of the body, to hide the defects of the mind, is his great talent & his only talent. For tho' he is not without understanding, his understanding is of so slow a sort, as not to be of any use (at least) in that situation to which the infatuation of the people has rais'd him; but *en revanche*, as the French say, he has an ample share of cunning, which enables him, by direct or indirect means (but the latter is his favorite mode) to work the ruin of every Man who has excited his jealousy or offended his pride, and whoever sins in either of these two points has no chance of being forgiven by the most essential services. I do not wonder (such is the weakness of the multitude) that

[30] To Horatio Gates, March 29, 1779, *ibid.*, III, 319-321.

a man who has not really great parts or sterling Virtues, but who has something specious and shining about him, or that a General who is not really a great soldier, but who has blundered himself into success at different times, should impose for a while; but how a man without fashion, air, manners, or language enough to relieve a Corporals Guard, and who has blundered himself into innumerable defeats & disgraces, and only stumbled (and then notoriously not his own measure) into one successful surprise of a drunken Hessian, should ever become the object of popular adoration, I confess astonishes me. Indeed it is so astonishing, that if this letter was publish'd, I have no doubt, it would be considered as the mere effusion of personal pique and resentment; let them think so if they please; but should the Avenue of truth be once open'd, the World will be asham'd of the gross delusion they have been so long kept in, with respect to this puffed up Charlatan. I shall mention two others of his amiable qualities, and then have done with him, he is extremely prodigal of other men's blood and a great economist of his own.[31]

The few who have read this letter have usually considered it a "mere effusion of personal pique and resentment," as Lee said they would, but he was not without influential friends in his own day. Benjamin Rush wrote of him as "the soul of our army," and said he was "most unjustly condemned by a court martial for saving our army . . . General Washington was his accusor."[32] An interesting detail is the emphasis that Lee as well as Boucher (also, "no quickness of parts") puts upon Washington's slowness. The General's friends were wont to speak of his calm deliberation, prudence, and composure.

At the time of the Conway Cabal the enemies of Washington in his own ranks were emboldened to whisper that he was cruel to his slaves and guilty of "immorality of life."[33] General Conway himself wrote to the Commander with studied disrespect:

The general and universal merit, which you wish every promoted officer might be endowed with, is a rare gift. We see but few of merit so generally acknowledged. We know but the great Frederic in Europe,

[31] To Miss Sidney Lee, June, 1782, *ibid.*, IV, 9–10. Cf. *The Merchant of Venice*, I, 1, 88.
[32] Rush to John Adams, October 27, 1778, in Nathan G. Goodman, *Benjamin Rush, Physician and Citizen, 1746–1813* . . . (Philadelphia, 1934), p. 116.
[33] Joseph Reed to Nathanael Greene, November 5, 1778, in *Lee Papers*, III, 250.

and the Great Washington on this continent. I certainly never was so rash as to pretend to such a prodigious height.[34]

Occasionally, of course, those who were otherwise loyal supporters found themselves at variance with Washington on some specific matter. For example, General John Armstrong, unlike John Adams, did not approve of the Commander's treatment of the dissatisfied officers and men at Newburgh in 1783. He wrote to General Gates:

You will find something to admire from the Illustrissimo of the age. Of all his illustrious foibles, I think the affectation of Zeal in a cause he strove so anxiously to damn is the most ridiculous; and like the lies of Falstaff, or Falstaff himself, it is gross and palpable.[35]

In the following year Stephen Higginson, of Massachusetts, disapproved of Washington's favorable stand on a 5 per cent impost and was disposed to attach much significance to it. Higginson wrote that

He would in my Opinion have rendered his Character much more perfect had he have given us in his valedictory strong evidence that he still retained his republican Ideas and principles . . . and could never be induced by foreign or domestic Influence to aid those measures that have the most remote tendency to subvert the government which he once affected to revere and for the support of which he repeatedly declared he would hazard his All.[36]

3

By 1787 the American scene had changed radically. The need, which was great, was for statesmen rather than military leaders. But Washington commanded the confidence and respect of all Americans as did no other man. He consented to serve as a delegate from Virginia to the Constitutional Convention and was unani-

---
[34]Thomas Conway to Washington, December 31, 1778, in Burnett, *op. cit.*, III, 23.
[35]John Armstrong, Jr., to Horatio Gates, May 30, 1783, *ibid.*, VII, 175, note.
[36]To Arthur Lee, January 17, 1784, *ibid.*, VII, 423-424.

mously elected chairman. Shortly after the adjournment, Gouverneur Morris wrote to him:

> Should the idea prevail that you will not accept the Presidency, it would prove fatal in many parts. The truth is, that your great and decided superiority leads men willingly to put you in a place, which will not add to your personal dignity, nor raise you higher than you already stand. But they would not readily put any other person in the same situation, because they feel the elevation of others, as operating by comparison the degradation of themselves, and, however absurd this idea may be, yet you will agree with me, that men must be treated as men, and not as machines, much less as philosophers, and least of all things as reasonable creatures, seeing that in effect they reason not to direct, but to excuse their conduct.[37]

Morris's shrewd words are significant both of early American individualism and of the high regard evinced for Washington by all groups at this time. The gradual development of political parties was yet to come.

Washington's daily life at home was quite different from that into which he was plunged when he became President. His secretary, Tobias Lear, writing between the Constitutional Convention and Washington's first inauguration, has given an excellent brief description of his routine at Mount Vernon:

> I have lived with him near two years, have received as many marks of his affection and esteem as perhaps any young man ever did—and have occasions to be with him in every situation in which a man is placed in his family—have eaten and drank with him constantly, and almost every evening play at cards with him, and I declare I have never found a single thing that could lessen my respect for him—a complete knowledge of his honesty, uprightness and candour in all his private transactions has sometimes led me to think him more than a man.—His industry is unparalleled—he rises every day before the sun—writes till breakfast (which never exceeds ½ past 7) then mounts his horse, and rides around his farm till ½ past 2, sees that everything is in proper order—and if there is no company he writes till dark, and in the evening plays a game of whist—this is the general round which he pursues with little varia-

[37]October 30, 1787, in Jared Sparks, *The Life of Gouverneur Morris* . . . , 3 vols. (Boston, 1832), I, 290.

tion.—He raises no tobacco on his lands here, but is introducing the present mode of Husbandry practiced in England on his farms.[38]

About a year after the above passage was written, Washington was on his way to New York for his installation as President, and his progress from town to town was like a Roman triumph, for the populace thronged out everywhere to salute the hero with the grandest festivities that each place could afford. His arrival in New York was "a scene of triumphal rejoicings and acclamations," according to an eye witness who, in 1821, wrote of sitting up on a roof as a young girl to witness the inauguration:

> His entrance on the balcony was announced by universal shouts of joy and welcome. His appearance was most solemn and dignified. Advancing to the front of the balcony, he laid his hand on his heart, bowed several times, and then retired to an arm-chair near the table. The populace appeared to understand that the scene had overcome him, and were at once hushed in profound silence . . .[39]

As Washington kissed the Bible after taking the oath, cannon were fired, and bells rang out all over the city.

By 1792 a political alignment was well under way, and Alexander Hamilton, leader of the Federalists, enjoyed President Washington's friendship and confidence. As his first term drew to a close, Hamilton wrote him a cogent argument against retiring; the main point he presented was that the Constitution was still on trial and needed Washington's support.[40] When Hamilton resigned as a cabinet member in 1795, he wrote in appreciation of Washington's friendship:

> As often as I may recall the vexations I have endured, your approbations will be a great and precious consolation. . .
>
> Whatsoever may be my destination hereafter, I entreat you to be persuaded (not the less for my having been sparing in professions) that

[38]Tobias Lear to William Prescott, March 2, 1788, in George S. Hellman, "Irving's Washington; and an Episode in Courtesy," *Colophon*, Vol. I, Pt. 1 (March, 1930).

[39]Eliza Quincy, *Memoir of the Life of Eliza Susan Morton Quincy* (Boston, 1861), pp. 51-52. See also Hellman, *op. cit.*

[40]July 30, 1792, in Alexander Hamilton, *The Works* . . . , ed. Henry Cabot Lodge, 9 vols. (New York, 1886), VIII, 274.

I shall never cease to render a just tribute to those eminent and excellent qualities which have been already reproductive of so many blessings to your country, that you will always have my fervent wishes for your public and personal felicity, and that it will be my pride to cultivate a continuance of that esteem, regard, and friendship of which you do me the honor to assure me. With true respect and affectionate attachment, etc.[41]

Commenting on Washington's intention to retire in 1796, Hamilton wrote that knowledge of it should be withheld from the public until the last moment; he mentioned the draft of "a certain paper," Washington's Farewell Address, which was also to be kept private till the proper time.[42] Though no longer a cabinet member, Hamilton was still one of Washington's advisers.

Party candidates for the presidency appeared for the first time in 1796, when John Adams, a Federalist, was elected. Discussing the occasion of his own inauguration, Adams wrote to his wife that Washington seemed to be saying with an air of triumph: "Now I am fairly out and you are fairly in." Adams added that there were no dry eyes in the house, because one sun was setting and another, less splendid, was rising.[43] A witness of Adams's inauguration wrote to Rufus King, minister to England, that Washington, plainly dressed and unattended, was the sensation of the day, and that the good-humored faces in the crowd showed that the lies maliciously spread about had been unable to hurt his reputation.[44]

[41] February 3, 1795, *ibid.*, VIII, 334. Cf. Alexander Hamilton to General Pinckney, December, 1799, *ibid.*, VI, 276, and to Tobias Lear, January 2, 1800, *ibid.*, VIII, 538.

[42] Hamilton to Washington, July 5, 1796, *ibid.*, VIII, 421.
Later in the same year, when a French diplomat's conduct was such that it could be neither approved nor condemned conveniently, Hamilton conferred with John Jay and then wrote Washington their opinion: "That the true rule on this point would be to receive the minister at your levee with a *dignified reserve*, holding to an *exact medium* between an *offensive coldness* and *cordiality*. The point is a nice one to be hit, but no one will know better how to do it than the President." November 4, 1796, *ibid.*, VIII, 422.

[43] To Abigail Adams, March 5, 1797, in *Works*, I, 506.

[44] Theodore Sedgwick to Rufus King, March 14, 1799, in Rufus King, *The Life and Correspondence* . . . , ed. Charles R. King, 6 vols. (New York, 1894–1900), II, 158. King wrote to America at about the same time that all in England were calling Washington not only "the most illustrious but also the most meritorious character" of all time; he was second only to the King in the affections of the people. Rufus King to Alexander Hamilton, February 6, 1797, *ibid.*, II, 142.

To Washington in retirement, Adams wrote: "I must tax you sometimes for advice. We must have your name, if you will in any case permit us to use it. There will be more efficacy in it than in many an army."[45] In the same year, 1798, he publicly stated that the last act of Washington's political life, coming out of retirement at the call of his country, would be recorded as one of history's most brilliant examples of public virtue.[46]

Adams was a thoroughgoing patriot and a man of great ability, but he was somewhat vain, and especially in later life he was probably envious of Washington's extraordinary reputation. In private correspondence he at one point supported a proposition with the query: "Would Washington have ever been commander of the revolutionary army or president of the United States if he had not married the rich widow of Mr. Custis?"[47] In another private letter he stated that his own position in November, 1779, as "Minister Plenipotentiary" to make peace and to negotiate a commercial treaty with England far surpassed in danger, difficulty, and importance Washington's commission as Commander-in-Chief of the army.[48]

Yet Adams genuinely admired Washington, and there is no reason to doubt the sincerity of his eulogy in the address he delivered to the Senate when news of Washington's death arrived:

> The life of our Washington cannot suffer by a comparison with those of other countries who have been most celebrated and exalted by fame. The attributes and decorations of royalty could have only served to eclipse the majesty of those virtues which made him, from being a modest citizen, a more resplendent luminary. Misfortune, had he lived, could hereafter have sullied his glory only with those superficial minds, who believing that characters and actions are marked by success alone, rarely deserve to enjoy it. Malice could never blast his honor, and envy

---

[45]Philadelphia, June 22, 1798, in *Works*, VIII, 573.
[46]"To the Senate and Assembly of the State of New York, August 31, 1798," *ibid.*, IX, 220.
[47]To John Taylor, April, 1814, *ibid.*, VI, 462.
[48]To Mercy Warren, July 30, 1807, in *Correspondence between John Adams and Mercy Warren* . . . in *Collections of the Massachusetts Historical Society*, Fifth Series, IV (Boston, 1878), 377.

made him a singular exception to her universal rule. For himself, he had lived enough to life and to glory. For his fellow-citizens, if their prayers could have been answered, he would have been immortal. . . .

His example is now complete, and it will teach wisdom and virtue to magistrates, citizens, and men, not only in the present age, but in future generations, as long as our history shall be read. If a Trajan found a Pliny, a Marcus Aurelius can never want biographers, eulogists, or historians.[49]

Abigail Adams felt that a careful consideration of Washington's career could be of benefit to her husband. She wrote to him shortly before the end of Washington's second administration:

Take his character all together, and we shall not look upon his like again; notwithstanding which, he was reviled and abused, his administration perplexed, and his measures impeded. What is the expected lot of a successor? He must be armed as Washington was with integrity, with firmness, with intrepidity.[50]

In his last days Washington received many visitors at Mount Vernon, among them a Mrs. Edward Carrington, who commented very favorably upon the respect shown by Nellie Custis Lewis "to her aged Grandmother & the General, whom she always calls Grampa." Mrs. Carrington gives a delightful glimpse of the lighter side of Washington's personality. Writing to her sister, she opened her account of the visit as follows:

Yes we arrived at this venerable mansion in perfect safety, where we are experiencing every mark of hospitality & kindness that the good old General's continued friendship to Col. C. could lead us to expect; his reception of my husband was that of a Brother; he took us each by the hand & with a warmth of expression not to be described, pressed mine, & told me that I had conferred a favor, never to be forgotten, in bringing his old friend to see him; then bidding a servant to call the ladies entertained us most facetiously till they appeared.[51]

[49]"Reply to the Address of the Senate, on the Death of George Washington, December 23, 1799," in *Works*, IX, 142–143; cf. III, 92–93; VII, 282; IX, 45, 163.
[50]November 8, 1796, in *Letters of Mrs. Adams*, II, 233.
[51]"A Visit to Mount Vernon—a Letter of Mrs. Edward Carrington to Her Sister, Mrs. George Fisher," *William and Mary College Quarterly*, Series 2, XVIII (April, 1938), 198. The letter is dated "Mount Vernon, November 22nd, 1799."

4

Washington's relations with the Senate and with society are seen from a Republican standpoint in the *Journal* of William Maclay. Coming to the first Senate from a farm in Pennsylvania, with a bookish attitude toward practical politics and with high hopes for a Republic founded upon the principles of the best days of Rome, Maclay in the beginning felt that the President was "the first character in the world."[52] His book shows a steady decline from roseate illusions to something like cynicism in his attitude toward the new government and, to a lesser degree, toward its head.

Maclay gives realistic rather than flattering pictures of Washington addressing the Senate at various times, for he found the President an unconvincing speaker. After attending a production of *The School for Scandal* with the President's party, the unworldly Senator reported that the play and the company were frivolous. His accounts of the levees and dinners at Washington's home reveal his impatience with the grandeur, ceremony, and dullness of these occasions. Of one dinner he wrote:

I looked around the company to find the happiest faces. Wisdom, forgive me if I wrong thee, but I thought folly and happiness most nearly allied. The President seemed to bear in his countenance a settled aspect of melancholy. No cheering ray of convivial sunshine broke through the cloudy gloom of settled seriousness. At every interval of eating or drinking he played on the table with a knife and fork; like a drumstick. Next to him, on his right, sat Bonny Johnny Adams, ever and anon mantling his visage with the most unmeaning simper that ever dimpled the face of folly.[53]

[52]*The Journal of William Maclay, United States Senator from Pennsylvania, 1789-1791*, with Introduction by Charles A. Beard (New York, 1927), p. 4. A bowdlerized edition of the *Journal* was privately printed in 1880; the Maclay family considered it disrespectful to several of the Founding Fathers.
At the first levee Maclay attended, he and Washington had an interesting tête-à-tête on the subject of farming in Virginia and Pennsylvania: pp. 41-42.

[53]*Ibid.*, p. 201. Cf. pp. 13, 29, 40, 128, 135, *et passim.*

Maclay disapproved of most administration measures, and he came to feel that the President's name and popularity were being used by the Federalist Party to support unwise laws:

> Republicans are borne down by fashion and a fear of being charged with a want of respect to General Washington. If there is treason in the wish, I retract it, but would to God this same General Washington were in Heaven! We would not then have him brought forward as the constant cover to every unconstitutional and irrepublican act.[54]

A far more personal and bitter condemnation was written by Thomas Paine near the end of Washington's second administration. Paine had rendered the Patriot cause signal service during the Revolution. His writings of that period and of the years immediately following express unlimited admiration for Washington.[55] Later Paine was active in Revolutionary politics in France, where he was thrown into prison as a result of Robespierre's rise to power. He reversed his attitude toward Washington because the President did not take measures adequate to secure his release. Washington's policy was to remain on good terms with both France and England if possible, and the misfortunes of such a stormy petrel as Tom Paine were but a detail in his impersonal view of the welfare of the infant nation he had been chosen to guide. Paine's "Letter to George Washington," published in 1796, is largely an expression of personal resentment, but it is to some extent representative of Republican sentiment at that time.

The letter begins with the statement that the presidency caused grave deterioration in Washington's character. Dwelling upon the "disguised traitors" and the "corruption and perfidy" to be seen in the President's advisers, Paine says that Washington owed it to him as an old friend to get him out of prison. He maintains that others, too, had begun to lose faith in Washington: "From being the chief

---

[54]*Ibid.*, p. 341. One strong Federalist opined that although Washington's death aroused more regret and deeper sorrow than any such previous event, the leaders of the opposition were secretly pleased. Theodore Sedgwick to Rufus King, December 29, 1799, in King, *op. cit.*, III, 162.

[55]Thomas Paine, *The Life and Works* . . . , ed. William M. Van der Weyde, 10 vols. (New Rochelle, N.Y., 1925), I, 235; II, 269; III, 261; IV, 134 ff.; VI, 291; VII, 149–150; *et passim*.

of government, he . . . made himself the chief of a party; and his integrity was questioned, for his politics had a doubtful appearance."[56] After a tirade on the foreign relations of Washington's administration, the burden of which is that the President was ungrateful to France even as he was to Paine, the writer divagates into Washington's military career. Completely reversing many of his own *dicta* of past times, he exclaims: "No wonder we see so much pusillanimity in the President when we see so little enterprise in the General!" Paine concludes on a note of strong invective:

> And as to you, Sir, treacherous in private friendship (for so you have been to me, and that in the day of danger) and a hypocrite in public life, the world will be puzzled to decide whether you are an apostate or an impostor; whether you have abandoned good principles, or whether you ever had any.[57]

Ferdinand Bayard, a French Republican who traveled in America in 1791, wrote a description of Washington which makes an interesting contrast with those written by Barbé-Marbois and Count Dumas several years earlier. According to Bayard, Washington's movements were free but lacked grace and vigor; he spoke seldom and listened to others without interest and almost without attention. Bayard understood that even as a child he had been grave and stiff, "un de ces enfans machines sans vivacité . . . qui se meuvent, parlent, agissent avec la régularité d'un horloge." He attached much importance to Washington's childlessness: "La nature lui a refusé ce principe de vie qui perpétue les êtres, les rend passionés, généreux et aimans. On ne cite de lui aucun de ces traits qui parte de l'âme, que les historiens des hommes célèbres se gardent bien d'omettre."[58]

The party in America which for a time favored the French Revolutionists was, of course, led by Thomas Jefferson. Washing-

[56]*Ibid.*, V, 162. The letter occupies pp. 139–201.
[57]*Ibid.*, V, 201. Paine's letter "To the Citizens of the United States," published in 1803 (*ibid.*, X, 122–124) repeats many of the ideas he advanced in 1796.
[58]Ferdinand M. Bayard, *Voyage dans l'interieur des États-Unis . . .* (2d ed.; Paris, [1798]), p. 310. Bayard based some of his details and impressions upon spurious Washington letters printed in London during the American Revolution. Cf. pp. xii, 311 ff. Chinard gives unfavorable comments on Washington by Citizens Genêt and Adet, *op. cit.*, pp. 105–109.

ton and Jefferson were associated in varying capacities and relationships over a long period. In Jefferson's *Anas*, a notebook written in large part during Washington's first administration and the early months of his second, the first President appears frequently. On one occasion, during a cabinet meeting, Washington said that if Congress should fail to function effectively, the government would have to assume a different form; Jefferson waited patiently for details, but none was given.[59] Apropos of the articles in Freneau's paper and in others of Republican persuasion, Washington told Jefferson that he believed there might be *"desires"* to establish a monarchy but no *"designs"* for it.[60] Jefferson gleefully tells of Washington's indignation when David Humphreys announced his arrival at a levee in a loud voice, with the formality usually attached to royalty.[61] Similar is the tale of a plan to have the President and Mrs. Washington at a public ball sit on a sofa elevated on a dais and receive with monarchical ceremony, a plan which caused amusement when Mrs. Knox tried to join them on the sofa.[62]

One of the best known of the incidents in the *Anas* concerns a cabinet meeting in which Washington lost his temper:

Knox, in a foolish incoherent sort of a speech, introduced the Pasquinade lately printed, called the funeral of George W———n, and James W———n [Wilson], King and judge, &c. where the President was placed on a guillotine. The Presid't was much inflamed, got into one of those passions when he cannot command himself, ran on much on the personal abuse which had been bestowed on him, defied any man on earth to produce one single act of his since he had been in the govmt, which was not done on the purest motives, that he had never repented but once the having slipped the moment of resigning his office, and that was every moment since, that *by god* he had rather be in his grave than in his present situation. That he had rather be on his farm than to be made *emperor of the world* and yet they were charging him with wanting to

[59]Thomas Jefferson, *The Writings* . . . , ed. Paul Leicester Ford, 10 vols. (New York, 1892–1899), I, 191.
[60]*Ibid.*, I, 199.
[61]*Ibid.*, I, 216.
[62]*Ibid.*, I, 234. Jefferson got this story from hearsay. Ford points out that it cannot be accurate. Cf. Rufus W. Griswold, *The Republican Court* . . . (New York, 1854), p. 156.

be a king. That that *rascal Freneau* sent him 3 of his papers every day, as if he thought he would become the distributor of his papers, that he could see in this nothing but an impudent design to insult him. He ended in this high tone. There was a pause. Some difficulty in resumg [*sic*] our question . . .[63]

Jefferson later wrote an introduction for the published form of the *Anas* in which he indicated that during his second administration Washington was almost senile and that he became the tool of the Federalists.[64] In 1824 he wrote Martin Van Buren a letter stating that Washington, surrounded by his second cabinet, could not hear all sides of any question because he was presented with nothing but the biased opinions of the Federalists.[65]

Jefferson set down his considered estimate of the first President in a letter written fourteen years after Washington's death. Several circumstances make this sketch invaluable. As he says, Jefferson had known Washington long and intimately. His strong Republicanism, which caused him to oppose many of Washington's policies, protects him from the charge of bias to which Federalists are open. In addition, the caliber of the man himself lends authority to his words. It is indeed fortunate that we have his detailed opinion, written when he could forget partisan politics and see important matters in perspective.

Instead of praising Washington in vague, eulogistic terms, Jefferson analyzes his characteristics and his greatness with discernment and discrimination. For example, he qualifies his praise of the General's military ability; the reader recalls the slowness criticized by Jonathan Boucher and Charles Lee. Furthermore, Jefferson did not think Washington warmhearted; he pronounces him "naturally distrustful of men." (Romancers were to take a different view.) Federalists might, of course, have argued with Jefferson about what seemed to him a distrust of democratic government on Washington's part.

[63]Jefferson, *op. cit.*, I, 254.
[64]Introduction to the *Anas, ibid.*, I, 168.
[65]*Ibid.*, X, 314.

All things considered, this letter is probably the best word portrait of Washington that we have from one who knew him. It may serve as a touchstone against which to try other portraits:

I think I knew General Washington intimately and thoroughly; and were I called on to delineate his character, it should be in terms like these.

His mind was great and powerful, without being of the very first order; his penetration strong, though not so acute as that of a Newton, Bacon, or Locke; and as far as he saw, no judgment was ever sounder. It was slow in operation, being little aided by invention or imagination, but sure in conclusion. Hence the common remark of his officers, of the advantage he derived from councils of war, where hearing all suggestions, he selected whatever was best; and certainly no General ever planned his battles more judiciously. But if deranged during the course of the action, if any member of his plan was dislocated by sudden circumstances, he was slow in re-adjustment. The consequence was, that he often failed in the field, and rarely against an enemy in station, as at Boston and York. He was incapable of fear, meeting personal dangers with the calmest unconcern. Perhaps the strongest feature in his character was prudence, never acting until every circumstance, every consideration, was maturely weighed; refraining if he saw a doubt, but when once decided, going through with his purpose, whatever obstacles opposed. His integrity was most pure, his justice the most inflexible I have ever known, no motives of interest or consanguinity, of friendship or hatred, being able to bias his decision. He was, indeed, in every sense of the words, a wise, a good, and a great man. His temper was naturally high toned; but reflection and resolution had obtained a firm and habitual ascendancy over it. If ever, however, it broke its bonds, he was most tremendous in his wrath. In his expenses he was honorable, but exact; liberal in contributions to whatever promised utility; but frowning and unyielding on all visionary projects and all unworthy calls on his charity. His heart was not warm in its affections; but he exactly calculated every man's value, and gave him a solid esteem proportioned to it. His person, you know, was fine, his stature exactly what one would wish, his deportment easy, erect, and noble; the best horseman of his age, and the most graceful figure that could be seen on horseback. Although in the circle of his friends, where he might be unreserved with safety, he took a free share in conversation, his colloquial talents were not above mediocrity, possessing neither copiousness of ideas, nor fluency of words. In public, when called on for a sudden opinion, he was unready, short and embarrassed. Yet he wrote readily, rather diffusely, in an easy and correct style. This he had acquired by conversation with the world, for his education was merely reading, writing and common arithmetic, to which he added surveying at a later day. His time was employed in action chiefly, reading little, and that only in agriculture and English history. His correspondence became necessarily extensive, and, with journalizing his agricultural proceedings, occupied most of his leisure hours within doors. On the whole, his character was, in its mass, perfect, in nothing bad, in few points indifferent; and it may truly be said, that never did nature and fortune combine more perfectly to make a man great, and to place him in the same constellation with whatever worthies have merited from man an everlasting remembrance. For his was the singular destiny and merit, of leading the armies of his country successfully through an arduous war, for the establishment of its independence; of conducting its councils through the birth of a government, new in its forms and principles until it had settled down into a quiet and orderly train; and of scrupulously obeying the laws through the whole of his career, civil and military, of which the history of the world furnishes no other example. . . .

He has often declared to me that he considered our new constitution as an experiment on the practicability of republican government, and with what dose of liberty man could be trusted for his own good; that he was determined the experiment should have a fair trial, and would lose the last drop of his blood in support of it. . . . I do believe that General Washington had not a firm confidence in the durability of our government. He was naturally distrustful of men, and inclined to gloomy apprehensions; and I was ever persuaded that a belief that we must at length end in something like a British constitution, had some weight in his adoption of the ceremonies of levees, birth-days, pompous meetings with Congress, and other forms of the same character, calculated to prepare us gradually for a change which he believed possible, and to let it come on with as little shock as might be to the public mind.

These are my opinions of General Washington, which I would vouch at the judgment seat of God, having been formed on an acquaintance of thirty years. . . . I felt on his death, with my countrymen, that "verily a great man hath fallen this day in Israel."[66]

[66]To Dr. Walter Jones, January 2, 1814, *ibid.*, IX, 448-451.

CHAPTER III

ORATORY

AT THE PRESENT TIME, with daily newspapers accessible to all, and an infinite number of books and magazines almost as easy to obtain, it is hard to comprehend a period when public opinion was determined and expressed largely by pulpit and courthouse speakers. The advent of radio has tended to revive interest in public address and so in a way to bring us closer to our forefathers. Early America was oratory-conscious, and one can hardly overemphasize the importance of speechmaking in American life before the Civil War and long afterward. The founders established a government dependent for its very operation upon free public discussion; they and their immediate descendants were keenly aware of the power of the spoken word. Indeed, it has been said that no people since the ancient Athenians spoke so often, so copiously, or even so well as did these Americans.[1]

Ever-growing audiences of plain folk eager to hear discussion and debate upon all manner of subjects soon brought about a change to a more emotional rhetorical style than that which had been brought over from eighteenth-century England. Of such eloquence Daniel Webster, Henry Clay, and John C. Calhoun were masters, and their heyday may be called the golden age of oratory in the United States.[2]

[1] Bower Aly and Grafton P. Tanquary, "The Early National Period: 1788–1860," in William Norwood Brigance, ed., *A History and Criticism of American Public Address*, 2 vols. (New York, 1943), I, 109. Cf. Ota Thomas, "The Teaching of Rhetoric in the United States during the Classical Period of Education," *ibid.*, I, 193–213.

[2] Harold F. Harding, Everett L. Hunt, and Willard Thorp, "The Orators," in *Lit-*

The oratory which was spoken in 1799 and 1800 at the time of Washington's death is highly significant for the investigator of his reputation. Many of the orations were printed, as were many others before and afterward. In fact, Puritan New England had by this time a long tradition of elegiac oratory. Even before his death Washington was occasionally a subject for American orators, and a brief discussion of pre-1800 oratory is included here not because the orations have great literary value, but because they reveal the elements of which the funeral orations were composed. The funeral orations had no great literary value either, but he who would understand the Washington legend must ponder them. Oratory from 1800 until about 1840 is the subject of a third section; it frequently shows some political intent on the part of the speaker, even though he spoke upon or about Washington. As the sections of the nation began to grow apart, the exponents of conflicting viewpoints used Washington to fortify their own logical positions; their speeches are the subject of the fourth and final section of the present chapter. Throughout the period from 1800 to 1865, orators often considered their productions works of great literary value. Much more frequently than similar works are today, they were printed to be handed down to posterity.

I

The Reverend Samuel Davies made in 1755 a famous mention of Washington which was often quoted in the period under consideration. It has been said that in prophecy "men mark when they hit, and never mark when they miss." Two months after Braddock's last fight, in which two horses were shot under Washington and four bullets tore his clothes, Davies ventured to prophesy. Addressing a company of Virginia soldiers, he declared that God raised Alexander, Caesar, William III, and Marlborough for warlike purposes, just as He created Homer, Milton, Newton, and Tubal-cain for other purposes. Then the preacher added: "As a

erary History of the United States, ed. Robert E. Spiller, Willard Thorp, Thomas H. Johnson, Henry Seidel Canby, 3 vols. (New York, 1948), I, 543–553.

Oratory

remarkable instance of this, I may point out to the public that heroic youth, Colonel Washington, whom I cannot but hope Providence has hitherto preserved in so signal a manner, for some important service to his country."[3]

When that service became a reality, ministers were still more impressed. Two months after Yorktown a Massachusetts pastor presented in his Thanksgiving Day message an elaborate parallel between Washington and Gideon. He outlined Jewish history in Gideon's day and compared it with American Revolutionary history; Gideon was called the Jewish Cincinnatus and Washington the American Cincinnatus.[4] Much of the oratory to be considered here shows the influence of Plutarch.

As in other forms of oratory involving Washington, 1800 was the year of great beginnings, but the Independence Day oration was an established institution long before that date. Joel Barlow, author of *The Vision of Columbus*, made one at Hartford in 1787. After tracing the history of the Revolution without reference to particular individuals, he paid tribute to various heroes, including Lafayette, Greene, and others. Washington was first and foremost though the reference to him was not lengthy.[5] At Marietta, Ohio, a year later one of the judges of the territory commented upon the high state of commerce, law, justice, and other phases of culture among his hearers. He also alluded to Washington incidentally and rhetorically.[6]

---

[3]Samuel Davies, *Sermons on Important Subjects* . . . , 3 vols. (New York, 1842), III, 45. Davies later became president of Princeton. Cf. Irving Allen, "Providential Events in the Life of Washington," in Robert H. Schauffler, ed., *Washington's Birthday* (New York, 1932), pp. 227–238.

[4]John Murray, *Jerubbaal; or, Tyranny's Grove Destroyed, and the Altar of Liberty Finished* . . . (Newburyport, Mass., 1784). Cf. Ezra Stiles, *The United States Elevated to Glory and Honor. A Sermon* . . . (New Haven, Conn., 1783). Byron's comparison of Washington with Cincinnatus is very famous.

[5]"An Oration, Delivered at the North Church in Hartford . . . July the Fourth, 1787 . . . ," *American Museum*, II (August, 1787), 135–142.

[6]James M. Varnum, "An Oration Delivered July 4, 1788, at Marietta . . . ," *American Museum*, V (May, 1789), 452–456.

Edmund Pearson, in *Queer Books* (Garden City, N.Y., 1928), p. 20, says that at least five orations were delivered in the states and territories on July 4, 1787. For the celebration of July 4, 1788, see Aly and Tanquary, *op. cit.*, I, 70.

February 22 was often celebrated as a holiday while Washington was still alive. As early as 1793 the day was one of festivity in Salem, Massachusetts, where salutes were fired by the town's artillery, bells rang, musicians played, and flags were displayed from the courthouse cupola. The speaker of the day, a local minister, declared that the most important period in the history of the world began with Washington: "His happy Revolution has robbed Tyranny of its spell, and taught mankind that, could they find an hero like him, as great in virtue as in arms, they might by one generous effort, ensure the highest ends of Government, and trample oppression in the dust." The preacher thought that in time America would civilize the Indians and free the Negroes, and he found opportunity to praise free schools. He likewise praised Salem and its ships, as they had been in Revolutionary days and as they were in 1793.[7]

An oration delivered by the youthful William Munford, first American translator of Homer, on Independence Day in the same year was somewhat similar. Some of Munford's remarks reveal a Plutarchian turn of mind which is the most obvious characteristic of the funeral oratory:

Immortal Washington! thou shield of the wide-spread states of America! revered by thy enemies—beloved as a father by those who followed thy steps to glory—where shall we find thy parallel?—Shall the annals of Greece and Rome be ransacked for this purpose? But who of all those heroes, whose names are handed down to us with undiminished lustre has achieved such glorious and important exploits with equal advantages? Let Trenton—let Princeton—let our native York bear witness to thy matchless vigilance and glory . . .[8]

Near the beginning of an oration delivered on July 4, 1795, Jonathan Maxcy praised Washington; then he prophesied the future greatness of America, and the spread of independence, as in France,

---

[7] [William Bentley], "Washington's Birth-Day Oration at Salem, Mass., February 22, 1793," *Historical Magazine*, Series 2, VII (January, 1870), 3–8; quotation, p. 3.

[8] "An Oration on the Subject of American Independence Spoken at Williamsburg on the Fourth of July, 1793," in William Munford, *Poems and Compositions in Prose on Several Occasions* (Richmond, Va., 1798), p. 157.

Oratory

which he saw with a most friendly eye.[9] Four years later, on the same day, the same speaker grew enthusiastic upon the subject of "the brave youth, the flower and strength of our country," rushing into the field to oppose the French butchers, while "the eye of immortal WASHINGTON lightens along their embattled ranks."[10]

2

The funeral eulogies delivered in the last days of 1799 and well into 1800 comprise a large block of material highly important in crystallizing and to a limited degree in forming popular conceptions of Washington. The critic was now silent, and, as a contemporary British traveler put it, orators all over the country "called all their tropes and metaphors together; collected all the soldiers and statesmen of history, and made them cast garlands at the feet of his statue."[11] Some 350 of these productions were printed.[12]

On December 19, 1799, four days after Washington's death, John Marshall presented to the House of Representatives a set of resolutions prepared by Henry Lee. Marshall began his speech with the idea that Americans should deliver and hear funeral orations, continued with a short biographical sketch of Washington, and concluded with the three resolutions, the last of which contained Lee's famous words, "first in war, first in peace, and first in the hearts of

---

[9] Jonathan Maxcy, "An Oration Delivered in the Baptist Meeting House in Providence . . . ," in *The Literary Remains* . . . (New York, 1844), pp. 362–377. Cf. Abiel Holmes, *A Sermon on the Freedom and Happiness of America* . . . (Boston, 1795).

[10] "An Oration Delivered in the First Congregational Meeting House, in Providence, on the Fourth of July, 1799," in Maxcy, *op. cit.*, p. 394.

[11] John Davis, *Travels of Four Years and a Half in the United States of America; during 1798, 1799, 1800, 1801, and 1802*, ed. A. J. Morrison (New York, 1909), p. 145. Davis's *Travels* was first published in 1803.

[12] Margaret Bingham Stillwell, *Washington Eulogies; a Checklist of Eulogies and Funeral Orations on the Death of George Washington* . . . (New York, 1916). Miss Stillwell speaks of 346 eulogies known to have been printed, of which the texts of thirty-eight are not known to be extant.
Cf. Franklin B. Hough, *Bibliographical List of . . . Eulogies . . . Relating to the Death of General Washington* . . . (Albany, N.Y., 1865); Appleton P. C. Griffin, *A Catalogue of the Washington Collection in the Boston Athenaeum* . . . (Cambridge, Mass., 1897).

his countrymen."[13] On December 24 motions were passed authorizing a period of mourning throughout the nation and the erection of an appropriate monument, under which the body of the hero might be deposited.[14]

A prominent Federalist who remembered the funeral eulogies from his youth wrote a thoughtful though somewhat inaccurate comment upon them in 1834:

> It is worth remarking, that the general sentiment of respect and affection for this eminent man was so exalted, that few of the orators did, or could, come up to the demand. The feeling of these public speakers was, and must have been that of deep veneration, a feeling not adapted to bring forth the touching expressions which would be grateful to a numerous audience. Washington's character was rather to be contemplated than talked of. He was to be estimated by comparison with other men and an eulogy does not permit of this. His eminent worth was to be found in no one brilliant act, nor in any remarkable achievements, but in a whole life of useful, dignified and honorable service. Most of the eulogists were compelled to resort to biographical sketches, which do not admit of much eloquence.[15]

These old orations are dull reading now, and at least one critic found them so in 1800. Charles Brockden Brown or one of his assistants reviewed dozens of them within a few months of their appearance. Although the reviewer apparently made a serious effort to evaluate the crowning American literary output of the year, he did not like the task. After reading several of the eulogies, Brown published "Hints for a Funeral Oration." Here he specified ironically that the eulogist must reveal elaborate grief on the part of himself and his audience; then he must cover Washington's career in detail, skipping from Braddock's defeat to 1775, when the hero accepted command of the Revolutionary armies on June 16 in Independence Hall in Philadelphia, after being suggested for the post by John Adams on June 15 and being approved by unanimous vote

[13]*Annals of Congress*, X (December 19, 1799), 203–204.
[14]*Ibid.*, X (December 23–24, 1799), 208–210.
[15]William Sullivan, *The Public Men of the Revolution* . . . (Philadelphia, 1847), p. 168. The work was first published in Boston in 1834 as *Familiar Letters on Public Characters, and Public Events, from the Peace of 1783, to the Peace of 1815.*

of the Congress—and so on through a prolonged series of bromidic details.[16]

The first dozen of Brown's reviews often ran three or four pages each, but as the months passed and the speeches kept pouring in, the reviewer was by November ready to dismiss two in a paragraph:

So many performances, on this melancholy occasion, have passed in review before us that we have to be excused from bestowing any particular attention on those which remain, unless they possess either novelty of matter or manner, or some distinguished attributes of eloquence that may claim the attention of our readers. The two here offered to our notice contain the same succession of incidents in the life of the American patriot which have been so often repeated and possess no qualities of style that distinguish them above others of the same class, or to entitle them to a more critical examination.[17]

A likely source for biographical material in the funeral orations was Thomas Condie's "Memoirs of George Washington . . . ," the only approach to a full-length biography of Washington to appear before his death. Condie published the "Memoirs" in five installments in his *Philadelphia Monthly Magazine*, a journal that existed only in the year 1798. The work consists largely of Washington's account of his mission to Fort Le Boeuf and similar documents dating from all periods of his life. It ends with a character sketch that brings in Moses, Camillus, Leonidas, Gustavus, Sydney, and several other notables.[18] Also available to the eulogist was an excellent sketch of Washington in Jedidiah Morse's *The American Geography*, first published in 1789. Unlike Condie, Morse includes many details of Washington's daily routine at Mount Vernon.[19]

Although the funeral orators frequently elaborated on the fact that Washington retired to private life after the Revolution and

[16]*Monthly Magazine and American Review*, II (February, 1800), 102–105.

[17]*Ibid.*, III (November, 1800), 377; cf. *ibid.*, III (October, 1800), 272.

[18]*Philadelphia Monthly Magazine; or, Universal Repository of Knowledge and Entertainment*, I (January, February, March, May, June, 1798), 15–20, 65–71, 121–127, 241–249, 297–308.

[19]Jedidiah Morse, *The American Geography* . . . (Elizabeth Town, N.J., 1789), pp. 127–132. W. S. Baker (*Early Sketches of George Washington* . . . [Philadelphia, 1894], pp. 7–8) points out that Condie used Morse's sketch and also one written by John Bell; all are considered again in Chapter IV.

again after his presidency, none of them said much about that private life. As is natural in speeches delivered to public gatherings, the military and political achievements of the hero were emphasized. Most of the speakers said that he was apparently chosen by Divine Providence for a special purpose, as Samuel Davies had observed in 1755; sometimes Davies was quoted in this connection, sometimes the idea was stated directly, and sometimes it was implied. One of the most striking aspects of these orations is their mention of other great names of almost all periods. Washington was compared to, or contrasted with, a wide variety of classical, Biblical, and contemporary worthies, practically always to their disadvantage. His early training was mentioned occasionally, as were his skill in writing and his fine physique. Nearly all the eulogists stressed his piety; they varied in their lists of virtues, but few omitted piety. Nearly all made the point that he was a proper model, upon which young and old should pattern themselves. Usually the speaker included somewhere in his remarks an apology for the inadequacy of his own literary and oratorical ability when confronted with such a subject.

Many of the funeral eulogies must have consumed hours in delivery. One given by the Reverend Phillips Payson at Chelsea, Massachusetts, on January 14, 1800, had a plainer style than most of them and had in addition the merit of brevity. Payson's first two paragraphs were mournful, ending thus:

The solemnities of the day, with the gloomy tokens of death in our view keep fresh in all our minds, a painful sense of that sorrowful event, that excites the public grief; and mentioning of it, will but increase the sorrow. It is the death of General WASHINGTON, that has raised the loud voice of weeping through the United States. And the death of such an illustrious personage, the first and most accomplished general and statesman of his country, and the age; such a disinterested patriot, such a defender, deliverer and father of his country, must needs be deeply lamented in every heart, that is not totally void of all sensibility, gratitude and piety.[20]

[20]Phillips Payson, *A Sermon, Delivered at Chelsea, January 14, 1800* . . . (Charlestown, Mass., 1800), p. 6.

Oratory

Payson observed that "as the free and federal citizens" of America, his hearers should be filled with piety and should offer prayers of gratitude to God. Proceeding to Washington's part in the Revolution, Payson said that he was raised up by God even as were Moses and Cyrus, and that all should be grateful for his achievements. The dire results that would have ensued had Washington failed in the Revolution were considered briefly.[21]

After speaking of Washington's disbanding the army which wished to make him king, Payson stressed the prosperity of the nation under the first President. His transitional sentence at this point is fairly typical:

Let us now, under the impression both of grief and gratitude, follow our great leader, from the scene of war, the field of victory, to the chair of state as the first supreme magistrate and President of the Union, to which he was called by the united voice of his country.[22]

The speaker made a comparatively mild apology for his own shortcomings and then came to Washington's second retirement and his Farewell Address:

These imperfect hints (for I possess neither materials nor abilities to do justice to the subject) I say, what has been but very imperfectly mentioned, must impress our minds with profound respect and reverence to the memory of the deceased . . . I do not recollect ever hearing of a single instance of mistake, error, or blame, that was ever justly charged upon him nor did I ever read of a person in any age of the world, to whom, such real greatness and purity of character, would more justly apply; or that ever merited more highly of this country.

After a series of the most eminent services for his country, for the space of five and forty years, enough to bear down the firmest constitution, he declined being considered as a candidate for the office of President, and thought proper to retire to the private walks of life. But still retaining his disinterested affection for his country, left it a legacy fraught with the most tender, parental advice, counsels, warnings, and cautions, that human wisdom could devise, which ought to be engraven on the heart of every American citizen.[23]

[21]*Ibid.*, pp. 6–9.
[22]*Ibid.*, pp. 10–11.
[23]*Ibid.*, pp. 11–13.

The next paragraph was devoted to Washington's calm in the face of death, and another compared the mourning of America for him to that of Israel for Moses, Samuel, or Josiah. In the following section pious prayer for improvement along the lines suggested by Washington's example and counsel was urged upon all; his successor and other public officials were adjured to follow in his footsteps. In the peroration Payson mentioned the funeral ceremonies held all over the country.[24]

Payson's speech was unlike many in that it contained no attack on the Republican Party. The funeral orations were delivered in an election year, and many Federalists could not resist the opportunity to attack the Jeffersonians. Republicans left politics out of their eulogies, and when the votes were counted, the Federalists appeared to have done themselves no good by endeavoring to use Washington's prestige. John Adams, writing to Jefferson sixteen years later, recalled this deluge of funeral eulogy, in disillusioned, almost cynical phrases:

> The death of Washington diffused a general grief. The old Tories, the hyper-federalists, the speculators, set up a general howl. Orations, prayers, sermons, mock funerals were all employed, not that they loved Washington, but to keep in continuance the funding and banking system; and to cast into the background and the shade, all others who had been concerned in the service of their country in the revolution.[25]

Few of the orators—especially in New England—could have known Washington well. Although the orations were not confined to any section of what was then the United States, about two thirds of the 346 known to have been printed were delivered in New England. It must be remembered that New England was more advanced in printing than the other sections. Furthermore, New England was strongly Federalistic at the time, and it seems likely that Washington was somewhat less a hero to the Republicans than to

[24] *Ibid.*, pp. 13–15.
[25] September 3, 1816, in Adams, *Correspondence of John Adams and Thomas Jefferson (1812–1826)*, ed. Paul Wilstach (Indianapolis, 1925), p. 140.

the Federalists of 1800. In any case, the New England stamp is noticeable, for the funeral orations as a whole make Washington seem something of a Puritan. Many of the speakers, incidentally, were clergymen.

Numerous eulogies were delivered in Boston. There Fisher Ames, addressing the legislature, briefly compared Washington with Fabius but spent most of his time attacking Revolutionary France and the Republican Party,[26] so that Brockden Brown's reviewer was moved to remark: "Mr. Ames takes a wider range, and deviates more into the tract of political discussion, than at first sight may be thought suitable to the chief purpose of his oration."[27] The Reverend Caleb Alexander, beginning with the omnipotence of death, gave a short biographical sketch and so arrived back at the inescapability of death.[28] George Richards Minot touched upon the sadness of the occasion and then traced Washington's career, stressed his retirements, sketched his character, praised the Constitution and some local heroes, and in conclusion noted the universal acclaim of Washington and the cessation of envy at his death.[29] Timothy Bigelow, who addressed a Masonic gathering, mentioned Socrates, Belisarius, Columbus, Alexander, Solon, Lycurgus, Chatham, Sully, and Fabius.[30] John Davis spoke to the American Academy of Arts and Sciences in Boston on February 19 and talked much of public credit and stability in government. He followed a biographical outline and sought in vain for a parallel to Washington in Gustavus, Alexander, Pompey, Marc Antony, Peter the Great, and many others, but found something like one at last in Timoleon,

[26] *Eulogies and Orations on the Life and Death of General George Washington* . . . (Boston, 1800), pp. 108–130.
[27] *Monthly Magazine and American Review*, II (May, 1800), 355–361.
[28] Caleb Alexander, *A Sermon; Occasioned by the Death of His Excellency George Washington* . . . (Boston, 1800).
[29] George Richards Minot, *An Eulogy on George Washington, Late Commander in Chief of the Armies of the United States* . . . (2d ed.; Boston, 1800).
[30] In *Eulogies and Orations*, pp. 130-141. Cf. George Blake, *A Masonic Eulogy, on the Life of the Illustrious Brother George Washington, Pronounced before the Brethren of St. John's Lodge, on the Evening of the 4th Feb. 5800* . . . (Boston, 5800 [1800]). Later Masonic addresses were distinctive only in their emphasis on the Masonic details of Washington's life. See Benjamin B. French, *An Address on the Masonic Character and Standing of Washington* . . . (Washington, 1851).

and ended by striking at "the leprosy of false knowledge," or, in other words, the deism of Jefferson.[31]

President Joseph Willard opened the exercises at Harvard College with a brief but enthusiastic Latin speech, which Brockden Brown took to pieces sentence by sentence in a review longer than the speech itself. Dr. David Tappan, Professor of Divinity, followed with a sketch of Washington in which he presented the idea that men are made in the image of God, and that Washington was the most nearly perfect man and consequently the most godlike: "Well may he be ranked among Earthly Gods, who, to other great accomplishments united a 'humble,' yet near resemblance of HIM, who is the standard of human perfection, and the EXPRESS IMAGE of divine glory."[32]

The Reverend Abiel Holmes, father of Oliver Wendell Holmes, speaking at Cambridge on the day after the exercises of Harvard, said that he did not intend to give a character sketch because his audience had heard one the day before, but that he would instead give some of the ideas to be drawn from Washington's counsels. He quoted the Farewell Address at length, with elucidative comments, gave the character sketch he had said he was not going to give, and repeated briefly in his own words ideas quoted from Washington, all in a diffuse style.[33] By comparison, the oration which Aaron Bancroft delivered at Worcester was simple and unadorned. Bancroft referred to Washington at one point as the American Joshua, and at another point he stated: "In other countries, individuals have been illustrious as Heroes and Statesmen. The talents which immortalized their respective names were united in our American Alfred; and he was free from the vices and weak-

[31] In *Eulogies and Orations*, pp. 152–158. Also included in this volume are the speeches of Henry Lee, Gouverneur Morris, Robert Treat Paine, and several others. The John Davis quoted here should not be confused with the English traveler of the same name quoted *supra*.

[32] *An Address in Latin, by Joseph Willard . . . and a Discourse in English, by David Tappan* . . . ([Charlestown, Mass.], 1800). Brown's review: *Monthly Magazine and American Review*, III (July, 1800), 47.

[33] Abiel Holmes, *The Counsel of Washington, Recommended in a Discourse Delivered at Cambridge, February 22, 1800* (Boston, 1800).

nesses, which were the shades of their characters."³⁴ Jedidiah Morse, at Charlestown, gave the life of Moses, then the life of Washington, and proceeded to show that Washington was appointed to lead America to liberty even as Moses had been appointed to lead Israel to the promised land; the details of the comparison were minute.³⁵

Original observations in the funeral orations were few. But sometimes a minister was alarmed by the extravagance of national mourning and by the idolatry implicit in some of the orations. In western New York Seth Williston preached a sermon which was later published as *The Agency of God, in Raising up Important Characters, and Rendering Them Useful*.³⁶ He feared that men were worshiping Washington instead of the God who sent him to deliver his people from bondage. "Nothing is too hard for the LORD," declared Williston. "HE that has raised up one WASHINGTON, can, with infinite ease, raise up another. It is impious, therefore, to say 'Our loss is irreparable.' Let us respect the memory of this great man, but let us not limit the Omnipotent." In similar vein Peter Whitney, of Northborough, Massachusetts, emphasized the fact that men, including Washington, are but instruments in effecting the will of God. Whitney also pointed out that Washington himself was always careful to acknowledge that others as well as he had a share in securing American freedom and happiness.³⁷

Despite the great volubility and skill of New England orators, it was Henry Lee, of Virginia, who wrote the words that were destined to outlive all others spoken on the occasion of Washington's death. "Light Horse Harry," who was a personal friend of Washington, drew up the resolutions offered in Congress on De-

---

³⁴Aaron Bancroft, *An Eulogy on the Character of the Late Gen. George Washington* . . . (Worcester, Mass., 1800).

³⁵Jedidiah Morse, *A Prayer and Sermon* . . . (Charlestown, Mass., 1800). Cf. Pliny Merrick, *An Eulogy on the Character of the Late Gen. George Washington* . . . (Brookfield, Mass., 1800); Daniel Dana, *A Discourse on the Character and Virtues of General George Washington* . . . (Newburyport, Mass., 1800); and Josiah Dunham, *A Funeral Oration on George Washington* . . . (Boston, 1800).

³⁶Geneva, N.Y. [1800].

³⁷Peter Whitney, *Weeping and Mourning at the Death of Eminent Persons a National Duty. A Sermon* . . . (Brookfield, Mass., 1800).

cember 19, 1799, by John Marshall.³⁸ Lee's tribute as a whole is no better than many others, but a few phrases won popular favor. On December 26, Lee spoke his complete oration before the House of Representatives, who requested a copy. The most famous of his sentences is certainly the best known to be found in the funeral oratory:

First in war, first in peace, and first in the hearts of his countrymen, he was second to none in the humble and endearing scenes of private life; pious, just, humane, temperate, and sincere; uniform, dignified, and commanding; his example was as edifying to all around him as were the effects of that example lasting.³⁹

3

Thomas Jefferson regretted, toward the end of his first Inaugural Address, that he did not possess the enormous prestige Washington had when beginning his first administration, and he applied a few glowing terms to his illustrious predecessor.⁴⁰ But during Jefferson's administration Washington's fame tended to be slightly overcast. In fact, one Fourth of July oration delivered in 1802 attributed American success in the Revolution to Providence, and paid no attention whatsoever to Washington personally.⁴¹ Probably more typical was a speech made at Savannah a few years later, when a forgotten colonel listed American heroes and made the name of Washington the climax. The colonel praised him as a model for youth, mentioned his judicious appointments while President, and urged the audience to heed his counsels, especially those regarding political parties. This was mild electioneering for the campaign of 1808.⁴²

³⁸*Annals of Congress*, X (December 19, 1799), 204.
³⁹*Ibid.* (Sixth Congress, December 2, 1799–March 3, 1801), Appendix, pp. 1310–1311. See also pp. 203–211, 222–223 (December, 1799). Lee's speech was delivered at Philadelphia and was printed several times in 1800.
⁴⁰Jefferson, *The Writings* . . . , ed. Paul Leicester Ford, 10 vols. (New York, 1892–1899), VIII, 5.
⁴¹John Leland, *An Oration . . . Cheshire, Massachusetts, July 5, 1802.* (2d ed.; Hudson, Mass., 1802).
⁴²Colonel John Macpherson Berrien, *An Oration, Commemorative of the Anniversary of American Independence . . .* (Savannah, Ga., 1808).

A speech made by a Philadelphia physician two years later is an example of Washington's Birthday oratory with a strong political bias. After apologizing for his inability as a speaker, the doctor launched into a biographical sketch adorned by many tributes to Washington's character and military skill. He took occasion to contrast the roseate days of the first presidential administration with the "cowardly proclamations, sullen nonintercourse laws and ruinous embargoes" of Jefferson and Madison.[43] Before closing he lamented the nation's failure to provide an appropriate tomb for its hero.

In 1812 the Federalists, who were opposed to war, were very voluble, and Washington was their guiding light. Of these Daniel Webster was destined to be one of the most influential. A speech he delivered before the Washington Benevolent Society of Portsmouth, New Hampshire, on July 4, 1812, was definitely political and was quite typical. At this time, Webster spoke as a New Englander; twenty years later he was an energetic nationalist and opponent of sectionalism. Webster criticized the current war on the grounds that it interfered with commerce, and he argued that Washington's administration would have avoided it. He stated that the Revolution had left precedents for future ages, and he noted the "well considered and settled principles" of Washington. Passing over analysis of Washington's character, Webster concentrated instead on his principles of civil administration, which he found "on the subject of commerce and foreign relations . . . plain and consistent." In connection with foreign relations Webster pointed out that Washington had planned to have an adequate navy, but that his plans had not been put into execution:

This, gentlemen, is an imperfect view of the principal maxims of Washington's administration. Universal protection; honest, impartial negotiation; spirited preparations for defence; utter aversion to all foreign

---

[43]Charles Caldwell, *An Oration Commemorative of the Character and Administration of Washington, Delivered before the American Republican Society of Philadelphia* (Philadelphia, 1810), p. 34. Cf. Charles W. Hanson, *Oration Delivered before the Washington Benevolent Society of Maryland, February 22, 1811* (Baltimore, 1811).

connections; the love of peace; the observance of justice; these are the pillars on which he sought to establish national prosperity. Would to God, that the spirit of his administration might actuate the government to its latest moment . . ."[44]

The Washington Benevolent Society of Rutland County, Vermont, heard on February 22, 1814, a typical sermon against the Republican Party: "What imbecility in counsel! What bombastic proclamations and insignificant exploits! What bravado and cowardice! . . . Happy was thy situation, Oh America, my native, my beloved country, when Washington ruled thy destinies!"[45]

[44]"Daniel Webster, *The Writings and Speeches* . . . , 18 vols. (Boston, 1903), XV, 583–598; quotation, p. 593.
Cf. Samuel Austin, *Apology of Patriots; or, the Heresy of the Friends of Washington and Peace Policies Defended* . . . . (Worcester, Mass., 1812); Edward D. Bangs, *An Oration . . . Sutton, Mass., July 5, 1815* . . . (Boston, 1813); Isaac C. Bates, *An Oration Pronounced before the Washington Benevolent Society of the County of Hampshire on Their First Anniversary, 1812* . . . (Northampton, Mass., 1812); Francis Blake, *An Oration Pronounced . . . on the Thirty-sixth Anniversary of American Independence* (Worcester, 1812); Samuel M. Burnside, *Oration at Worcester, April 30, 1813, before the Washington Benevolent Society, in Commemoration of the First Inauguration of General Washington* (Worcester, Mass., 1813); William Crafts, Jun., *An Oration . . . on the Fourth of July* . . . (Charleston, S.C., 1812); George Washington Parke Custis, *An Address Occasioned by the Death of General Lingan, Who Was Murdered by the Mob at Baltimore* . . . (Boston, 1812); Josiah Dunham, *An Oration in Commemoration of the Birth of Our Illustrious Washington* . . . (Windsor, Vt., 1812); Hosea Hildreth, *Discourse before the Washington Benevolent Society in Exeter, May 4, 1813* (Exeter, Mass., 1813); Abiel Holmes, *An Address Delivered before the Washington Benevolent Society at Cambridge . . . July 5, 1813* (Cambridge, Mass., 1813); Samuel L. Knapp, *Address before "The Associated Disciples of Washington," February 22, 1812* (Newburyport, Mass., 1812); Elijah H. Mills, *Oration at Northampton at the Request of the Washington Benevolent Society . . . on the Thirty-seventh Anniversary of American Independence* (Northampton, Mass., 1813); David Raymond, *An Oration Delivered on the 22d of February, 1813, at Washington Hall in the City of New York* (New York, 1813); William Sullivan, *An Oration Delivered before the Washington Benevolent Society of Massachusetts . . . on the Thirtieth Day of April, 1812* . . . (Boston, 1812).

[45]Henry Bigelow, *A Sermon Delivered . . . in Commemoration of the Birth of Washington* (Middlebury, Vt., 1814), pp. 11–12.
Cf. Timothy Bigelow, *Address on the 3d Anniversary of the Washington Benevolent Society, April 30, 1814* (Boston, 1814); Richard H. Dana, *Oration before the Washington Benevolent Society of Cambridge, July 4, 1814* (Cambridge, Mass., 1814); Josiah Dunham, *An Oration in Commemoration of Our Illustrious Washington . . . February 22, 1814* (Windsor, Vt., 1814); Abraham Haskell, *Oration Pronounced . . . before the Washington Benevolent Society of Leominster and Fitchburg, July 4, 1814* (Worcester, Mass., 1814); Francis Scott Key, *An Oration, Delivered . . . before the Washington Society of Alexandria* (Alexandria, Va., 1814); George Washington Warner, *Oration Delivered before the Washington*

Oratory   67

In 1816, because Virginians had begun a movement to transfer the remains of Washington from Mount Vernon to Richmond, a committee was appointed by Congress to take steps to put into effect its resolution of 1799 to have a suitable mausoleum erected.[46] James Ervin four years later made a motion providing that some action be taken to carry out that same resolution. He spoke in conventional manner:

> Greece may tell of her legislators; Rome may tell of her heroes, but what age or country can boast a Washington—a man so renowned both in peace and war? Leonidas was patriotic; Aristides just; Hannibal was patient; Fabius prudent; Scipio was continent; Caesar merciful; Marcellus courageous, and Cato of inflexible integrity; yet, those virtues which separately distinguished those mighty men of antiquity, were all united in the character of this singular great man, and raised him above the level of mankind; he was so preeminent that envy never dared to raise its malignant glance to the elevation of his virtues. Other heroes are renowned for subjugating—he for liberating his country.[47]

This sort of thing typifies remarks likely to be heard in Congress whenever the name of Washington was mentioned, 1800–1865, and Congressional oratory is typical American oratory of its day.

A Washington's Birthday speech which is interesting because of its peroration upon the glory of America in war, manufacturing, internal improvements, the conquest of the wilderness, architecture, literature, oratory, and government, as contrasted with the unhappy lot of freedom in South America, Spain, Greece, and other nations was delivered at Albany, New York, in 1824. This oration very nearly typified the Washington's Birthday oratory of the period under consideration. The opening was, as usual, a biographical sketch of the subject, and certain incidental remarks favoring the

---

Benevolent Society of the County of Columbia . . . (Hudson, N.Y., 1814); *An Oration, Delivered . . . on Board the Nassau Prison Ship, at Chatham, England, July 4, 1814. By an American Seaman, Prisoner of War* (Boston, 1815).

[46]*Annals of Congress*, XXIX (February 16, 1816), 1007–1010.

[47]*Ibid.*, XXXVI (April 6, 1820), 1792–1799; quotation p. 1798.

The oratory of Congress upon the subject of Washington has been made easily available. See U. S. Library of Congress, Legislative Reference Service, *The United States Congress on George Washington* . . . , compiled by Myrtis Jarrell . . . (Washington, D.C., 1932).

internal improvements made by the Whigs gave a slightly political cast to this production.⁴⁸

The centennial of Washington's birth in 1832 was of course marked by numerous orations. At a public dinner in New York, Senator Daniel Webster spoke of the new age that began with America's freedom:

> Washington stands at the commencement of a new era, as well as at the head of the New World. A century from the birth of Washington has changed the world. The country of Washington has been the theatre on which a great part of the change has been wrought; and Washington himself a principal agent by which it has been accomplished. His age and his country are equally full of wonders; and of both he is the chief.⁴⁹

Webster talked of the growth and spread of liberty throughout the world and then proceeded to Washington's principles as seen in the Farewell Address; about half of the speech was concerned with that document. Webster's strong nationalism in 1832 is almost a reversal of his sectional criticism of the War of 1812.

The nullification movement in South Carolina reached its crisis in 1832, and speakers of lesser note than Webster recalled Washingtonian principles as an anchor in a time of turbulent ideas. An oration delivered before the Massachusetts legislature consisted of a lengthy biographical sketch and much praise of representative government.⁵⁰ The president of the University of Nashville told his audience of the Washington eulogies he had heard in 1800, when "the whole land wore the garb of bereavement," and, after biographizing Washington briefly, contrasted the history of Europe for

---

⁴⁸Salem Dutcher, Jr., *An Oration Commemorative of the Birth of Washington; Delivered at the Baptist Church* . . . (Albany, N.Y., 1824).

Cf. Timothy Flint, *An Oration, Delivered* . . . *July 4, 1815, before the Washington Benevolent Societies of Lancaster and Sterling, and of Leominster and Fitchburg* (Worcester, Mass., 1815); Edward Wigglesworth Andrews, *An Address before the Washington Benevolent Society* . . . *February 22, 1816* (Newburyport, Mass., 1816); Solomon Drowne, *An Oration Delivered in the First Baptist Meeting-House, in Providence, at the Celebration, February 23, A.D. 1824* . . . (Providence, R.I., 1824); Webster, *op. cit.*, I, 231–255; II, 1–11, 69–82; V, 213; VI, 43, 118–119.

⁴⁹"The Character of Washington," in Webster, *op. cit.*, II, 69–82; quotation p. 71.

⁵⁰Francis C. Gray, *Oration* . . . *on the Hundredth Anniversary of the Birth of George Washington* (Boston, 1832).

Oratory 69

a generation with that of America. He too extolled the principles of the Farewell Address.[51]

Congress debated in 1832 the project of removing Washington's remains to the city of Washington and interring them with appropriate ceremonies on the hundredth anniversary of his birth. The debate included such points as Virginia's prior claim, Washington's provision in his will for interment at Mount Vernon, the possibility of removal of the capital to the West, and of disunion. When Congress finally attempted to take action, it was blocked by Washington's relatives.[52] In the course of the discussion, Representative Augustin Clayton, of Georgia, voiced one memorable idea: "The praise of Washington is an exhausted subject . . ."[53]

Learned societies have ever been patrons of oratory, and Washington was the subject of an address made before the Virginia Historical and Philosophical Society in 1837. The speaker said that though American history lacked antiquity, it compensated by the splendor of character of such persons as John Smith, Pocahontas, and especially Washington; he regretted that there was no fitting monument to the greatest of these and went on to say that his hearers should strive to make the government as pure as it was in Washington's day.[54]

Partly because of his strong Federalism, Daniel Webster's speeches on all manner of occasions were sprinkled with allusions to Washington. Often he cited the hero's example in connection with current measures that he advocated or opposed. For instance, he

[51]Philip Lindsley, *An Address* . . . (Nashville, Tenn., 1832).
Cf. Charles Burroughs, *Oration on the Moral Grandeur of George Washington, February 22, 1832* . . . (Portsmouth, N.H., 1832); Charles Caldwell, *A Discourse . . . Delivered by Request to the Citizens of Lexington, Ky.* . . . (Lexington, Ky., 1832); Robert R. Collier, *An Oration* . . . *Petersburg, Virginia, February 22, 1832* (Petersburg, 1832); Solomon Lincoln, *An Oration Pronounced at Plymouth, on the Centennial Anniversary of the Birth of George Washington* (Plymouth, Mass., 1832); John Pitman, *Oration* . . . *February 22, 1832* (Providence, R.I., 1832).
[52]*Register of Debates in Congress*, VIII, pt. 2 (February 13–16, 1832), 1782–1820.
[53]*Ibid.*, VIII, pt. 2 (February 13, 1832), 1798.
[54]Thomas W. Gilmer, "An Address . . . ," *Southern Literary Messenger*, III (February, 1837), 97–102.
Cf. John Quincy Adams, *An Oration* . . . *July 4, 1837* (Newburyport, Mass., n.d.).

cited the first President's stand on monetary matters, particularly a national bank, in at least four speeches, the first made in 1837 at Wheeling, Virginia.[55]

Memorial and anniversary exercises at various points of historic interest were frequently occasions for oratory touching Washington. One example was an address which John Tyler, later President, delivered at Yorktown in 1837. Tyler observed that although Leonidas and his men were killed and Moses could not enter the promised land, Washington overcame all his difficulties and entered into peace with his countrymen. The speaker's strain was exalted: "Ye ambitious ones of the earth, how vile and contemptible do you appear when compared with *Washington.*"[56]

Abraham Lincoln's words about Washington have a unique interest because he was himself destined to take a place beside the first President in the hearts of his countrymen. Like thousands of Americans, Lincoln read Weems's *Life of Washington* in his youth.[57] Frequently he expressed his high regard for Washington's authority and example. Lincoln's early oratorical style was ornate, as may be seen from his remarks on Washington made in an address before the Young Men's Lyceum of Springfield in 1837. His words were directed against violence, for the country was then stirred by the recent burning of a mulatto in St. Louis. He concluded his speech:

Passion has helped us, but can do so no more. It will in the future be our enemy. Reason—cold, calculating, unimpassioned reason—must furnish all the materials for our future support and defense. Let those materials be molded into general intelligence, sound morality, and, in particular, a reverence for the Constitution and laws; and that we improved to the last, that we remained free to the last, that we revered his name to the last, that during his long sleep we permitted no hostile foot to pass over

---

[55]Webster, *op. cit.,* II, 241; III, 9–10, 163; VII, 97.

[56]John Tyler, "An Oration . . . ," *Southern Literary Messenger,* III (December, 1837), 747–752.
Cf. James Ewell Heath, "A Lecture . . . ," *Southern Literary Messenger,* IV (November, 1838), 705–707.

[57]"Address to the Senate of New Jersey, February 21, 1861," in Lincoln, *Complete Works . . . ,* ed. John G. Nicolay and John Hay, 2 vols. (New York, 1902), I, 688.

or desecrate his resting-place, shall be that which to learn the last trump shall awaken our Washington.⁵⁸

The Catholic bishop of Charleston, South Carolina, speaking there on February 22, 1838, based his address in large part upon Jared Sparks's biography of Washington, to which he made several references. Declaring that Providence had chosen Washington for the role he played, the Bishop urged all Americans to make him their model. The speaker found the work of a surveyor and the early expedition to Fort Le Boeuf good training to prepare the youth "for a period of equal difficulties upon a more extended scale, for a nobler purpose." The Bishop spoke of Washington as a "Southron," and he called on his audience to be loyal Southerners and Carolinians.⁵⁹

A year later John Quincy Adams addressed the New York Historical Society on the semicentennial of Washington's first inauguration, which was called the Jubilee of the Constitution. He said that Washington's part in establishing the Constitution was ordained by Providence. Elaborating on Washington's character, Adams found blended in him "the spirit of command and the spirit of meekness" more than in Aeneas or King David.⁶⁰ His address is a little like a rebuttal to certain expressions of the Southern bishop.

Expressing a typical American viewpoint, Ralph Waldo Emerson said in 1838 that when he saw a great figure like Washington or Epaminondas, he was filled with admiration of a beauty to be desired.⁶¹ Apparently Emerson felt some such respect or admiration for Washington most of the time, for he mentioned the hero occasionally in his essays—usually they grew out of lectures—but, like most of the other great writers of his day, he never treated him at any length. Probably most of the New England Brahmins sympa-

⁵⁸*Ibid.*, I, 15.
⁵⁹John England, "Oration Delivered before the Washington Light Infantry," in *The Works* . . . , ed. Ignatius Aloysius Reynolds, 5 vols. (Baltimore and New York, 1849), IV, 485–503.
⁶⁰John Quincy Adams, *The Jubilee of the Constitution* . . . (New York, 1839).
⁶¹"Divinity School Address," in *The Complete Works* . . . , ed. Edward Waldo Emerson, 12 vols. (Boston and New York, 1903), I, 133.

thized with the belief of Representative Clayton that "The praise of Washington is an exhausted subject." Emerson on at least one occasion seconded this in fairly definite language: "Every hero becomes a bore at last. . . . They cry up the virtues of George Washington,—'Damn George Washington!' is the poor Jacobin's whole speech and confutation."[62] Emerson's attitude toward Washington must be gleaned from pithy sentences in essays, journals, and letters, and probably more typical than the impatient remark quoted above is a paragraph on the Stuart portrait of Washington in his dining room: Emerson says this portrait reveals a calm like that of the Alleghenies, which contrasts vividly with the hysteria of contemporary politicians.[63]

4

At Lafayette College on July 4, 1840, Willis Gaylord Clark, popular Philadelphia littérateur, spoke with understanding on the subject of Lafayette and Washington. He considered Lafayette's career and then that of Washington, his theme being that they were kindred spirits, both inspired with zeal for noble action. Concluding, Clark quoted verses comparing Washington with several Roman heroes and other verses describing General Washington's entry into heaven.[64]

Two years later, on February 22, Abraham Lincoln addressed the Springfield Washingtonian Temperance Society, of which he was a member. He attacked slavery as well as drunkenness, and he again mentioned Washington only at the end of his remarks. Then he said the name of Washington was the "mightiest name of earth—

[62]"Uses of Great Men," *ibid.*, IV, 27.

[63]Ralph Waldo Emerson, *Journals* . . . , ed. Edward Waldo Emerson and Waldo Emerson Forbes, 10 vols. (Boston and New York, 1909–1914), VIII, 300; cf. X, 350. Cf. Emerson, *The Complete Works*, II, 83, 258, 263; III, 89; V, 7; VIII, 102; XI, 78; *The Letters* . . . , ed. Ralph L. Rusk, 6 vols. (New York, 1939), I, 188, 330, 345, 349, 382; II, 426; IV, 408; V, 481.

[64]Willis Gaylord Clark, "Lafayette and Washington, an Address Pronounced before the Washington Society . . . ," in Clark, *The Literary Remains* . . . , ed. Lewis Gaylord Clark (New York, 1844); reviewed by L. G. Clark in *Knickerbocker*, XVI (November, 1840), 446–447.

Oratory

long since mightiest in the cause of civil liberty, still mightiest in moral reformation." Lincoln added: "On that name no eulogy is expected. It cannot be. To add brightness to the sun or glory to the name of Washington is alike impossible. Let none attempt it. In solemn awe pronounce the name, and in its naked deathless splendor leave it shining on."[65]

Upon the completion of the Bunker Hill monument in 1843, Daniel Webster pronounced one of his most memorable passages on Washington, beginning: "America has furnished to the world the character of Washington! And if American institutions had done nothing else, that alone would have entitled them to the respect of mankind." Declaring that Washington was purely American, although all of Europe recognized his preeminence, Webster said the monument was an appropriate, though inadequate, symbol of the greatest American, because it too was entirely American. He went on to justify the American effort to reconcile freedom with security.[66] Much of the oratory about Washington is, of course, somewhat chauvinistic.

Washington's reputation was approaching its peak in 1847, when a Virginia minister, after comparing him with Moses and Joshua, found his greatest service to be that of a leader toward religious liberty. The speaker mentioned Demosthenes and Alfred the Great, praised motherhood, and so arrived at an implied Washington-Jesus parallel: "And to 'Mary the Mother of Washington,' whose incomplete monument at Fredericksburg lies shamefully neglected, we owe all the mighty debt due from mankind to her immortal son."[67]

At the laying of the cornerstone of the Washington Monument

---

[65] Lincoln, *op. cit.*, I, 63–64.

[66] Webster, *op. cit.*, I, 281–282. Cf. Charles Fraser, *Address on the Birth Day of General Washington* ... (Charleston, S.C., 1845); W. S. Norman, *An Oration, Containing a Biographical Sketch of George Washington* ... (Savannah, Ga., 1847); William Buell Sprague, *An Address Delivered the Evening of the 22d of February, 1847* ... (Albany, N.Y., 1847).

[67] J. N. Danforth, "Thoughts on the Fourth of July, 1847," *Southern Literary Messenger*, XIII (August, 1847), 502–505. For a stronger and more sentimental comparison of Washington with Jesus, see Beverley R. Wellford, Jr., "Address Delivered before the Ladies' Mount Vernon Association ... ," *Southern Literary Messenger*, XXI (September, 1855), 562–566.

on July 4, 1848, Robert C. Winthrop, who also made the speech at its dedication nearly thirty-seven years later, discussed the appropriateness of such a memorial and of the occasion. He touched upon the European view of Washington, gave a conventional biographical sketch, and then attempted to analyze the power that enabled the man to keep a nation behind him. Unable to attribute Washington's strength of character to scholarship, wit and eloquence, personal magnetism, a reckless spirit of adventure, or even "solid information and judgment," he finally concluded that it lay in his valor and modesty and particularly in his incorruptible honesty. Winthrop pointed out that Washington disliked being a politician and that though circumstances forced that role upon him, he remained free of any tendency toward demagoguery.[68]

The very sentimental or ambitious panegyric of Washington occasionally—as we have seen in the words of Representative Clayton and of Ralph Waldo Emerson—aroused protests. Lecturing at Boston in 1850, a literary critic of the day voiced one which is unusually thoughtful and incisive:

Mediocrity has a bad trick of idealizing itself in eulogizing him, and drags him down to its own level while assuming to lift him to the skies. . . . Accordingly, in the panegyric of cold spirits, Washington disappears in a cloud of commonplaces; in the rodomontade of boiling patriots, he expires in the agonies of rant. Now, the sooner this bundle of mediocre talents and moral qualities, which its contrivers have the audacity to call George Washington, is hissed out of existence, the better it will be. . . . Again, some eulogists have caricatured him as a passionless, imperturbable, "proper" man; but at the battle of Monmouth, General Lee was privileged to discover, that from those firm, cold lips could leap words hotter and more smiting than the hot June sun that smote down upon their heads.[69]

The rift between North and South brought new overtones into every mention of Washington. In the year of the Great Compro-

[68]Robert C. Winthrop, "An Oration . . . ," in Winthrop, *Addresses and Speeches on Various Occasions*, 4 vols. (Boston, 1852–1886), IV, 70–89.
[69]Edwin P. Whipple, "Washington and the Principles of the Revolution," in Whipple, *Character and Characteristic men* (Boston, 1866), pp. 305-306.

mise, 1850, the Senate passed a motion for the purchase of the manuscript of the Farewell Address. Henry Clay, who introduced the motion, said that all would find it refreshing to reread Washington's words at that critical time, "amid the discordance and ungrateful sounds of disunion and discord which assail our ears in every part of this country and in both halls of Congress." He also mentioned Washington's paternal warning "to beware of sectional division, to beware of demagogues, to beware of the consequences of indulging a spirit of disunion," as Clay put it.[70]

Six weeks after Clay spoke these words, another Senator brought Washington to the attention of his colleagues, but the reasoning and conclusion he advanced were startlingly original. John C. Calhoun, with less than a month of life before him, was too weak to address the Senate, but he was present on March 4 when James Mason, of Virginia, read for him his last speech on the slavery controversy. His words on Washington were not a mere mention:

> Nor can the Union be saved by invoking the name of that illustrious Southerner whose mortal remains repose on the western bank of the Potomac. He was one of us—a slaveholder and a planter. We have studied his history, and find nothing in it to justify submission to wrong. On the contrary, his great fame rests on the solid foundation, that, while he was careful to avoid doing wrong to others, he was prompt and decided in repelling wrong. I trust that in this respect, we profited by his example.
>
> Nor can we find any thing in his history to deter us from seceding from the Union, should it fail to fulfil the objects for which it was instituted, by being permanently and hopelessly converted into the means of oppressing instead of protecting us. On the contrary, we find much in his example to encourage us, should we be forced to the extremity of deciding between submission and disunion.

In a further paragraph Calhoun pointed out that the young Washington was a soldier of the crown and a defender of the union

---

[70]"Speech in the Senate, January 24, 1850," in Calvin Colton, ed., *The Life, Correspondence, and Speeches of Henry Clay*, 6 vols. (New York, 1857), III, 110. It has been said that, because of his part in incurring war with Britain in 1812, Clay "was as quick to defy Washington as to deify him." Harding, Hunt, and Thorp, *op. cit.*, I, 546.

between the crown and the colonies, but that when such union became oppressive and unprofitable to his own country, he did not hesitate to draw his sword to destroy it.[71]

Daniel Webster a year before his death expressed his genuine veneration for Washington in a nonpolitical speech made at the invitation of the young men of Albany, New York, on May 24, 1851. Webster was not debating, but the trend of his remarks is clearly opposed to that of Calhoun's:

> If I were now to describe a patriot President, I would draw his [Washington's] master-strokes and copy his design; I would present his picture before me as a constant study; I would display his policy, alike liberal and just, narrowed down to no sectional interests, bound to no personal objects, held to no locality, but broad and generous and open, as expansive as the air which is wafted by the winds of heaven from one part of the country to another.[72]

A Washington's Birthday speech delivered at Baltimore in 1852 put particular emphasis upon Washington's views on national union and foreign relations, as set forth in the Farewell Address. The orator expressed comparisons: "Others have those traits which awaken feelings akin to the terrible—such are Genghis Khan, Tamerlane, and Bonaparte. But in Washington we have an approximation to the highest order of the moral sublime. What virtue was wanting in him, or what vice was ever laid to his charge?"[73]

[71] John C. Calhoun, "Speech on the Slavery Question, Delivered in the Senate, March 4th 1850," in Calhoun, *The Works* . . . , ed. Richard K. Crallé, 6 vols. (New York, 1854–1860), IV, 561.

[72] Webster, *op. cit.*, IV, 281. Cf. *ibid.*, III, 228–230; IV, 314; VII, 115; XIII, 423–428; XIV, 343–344.

[73] Alexander H. Stephens, *Address . . . before the Maryland Institute . . .* (Washington, D.C., 1852).

A little pamphlet containing a dozen or so speeches made at a banquet given on February 22, 1852, is a storehouse of mid-nineteenth-century American rhetoric: William Hincks and F. H. Smyth, *Washington's Birthday; Congressional Banquet in Honor of George Washington, and the Principles of Washington* (Washington, 1852).

Cf. Alfred B. Ely, *American Liberty . . . an Oration . . . before the Order of United Americans . . .* (New York, 1850); Henry H. Tator, *An Oration Commemorative of the Birthday of Washington . . .* (Albany, N.Y., 1851); Clement Butler, *Our Country and Our Washington . . .* (Washington, 1852); "Address before the Mount Vernon Association, July 4th, 1855," *Southern Literary Messenger*,

At the unveiling of the statue of Washington in Union Square, New York, on July 4, 1856, the orator discussed the inadequacy of historical portraiture of Washington and debated whether crises make great men or great men make crises; he seemed vaguely aware of the approach of civil war, and he found in classic times—in Fabius, Cato, Scipio Africanus, Cincinnatus—no such harmonious union of virtues as in Washington.[74]

Also on July 4, 1856, Governor H. A. Wise, of Virginia, delivered a memorable oration at Lexington. The occasion was the unveiling of a replica of Houdon's statue by the Virginia Military Institute.[75] Wise's speech was long and for the most part conventional. He sketched Washington's career and analyzed his greatness, declaring that his hearers could and should make him their model. He mentioned the hero's temper and pronounced him "no Northern iceberg which repelled by coldness."[76] But when he spoke of the framing of the Constitution and the establishment of the Union, Wise found reason to fear that in his own day certain persons in Massachusetts might "trample . . . upon the oaths of organic law, and madly rushing over the grave at Mount Vernon, make a wreck of this master work of wisdom and virtue . . ." In such case, he continued, Virginia would "remain loyal like her leader" and would "defend the holy places of the mighty dead and the glorious work of their master minds!!" Concluding this portion of his address, he cried: "The Constitution and the Union shall be preserved!!"[77] The meaning and the political implication here become somewhat clearer when it is recalled that in the Virginia convention of 1861 Wise advocated a fight-within-the-Union policy rather than secession.

XXI (August, 1855), 514–518; John Minor Botts, *Speech . . . Delivered before the Order of United Americans . . .* (New York, 1859); Thomas S. Bocock, *Oration Delivered February 22, 1860 . . .* (n.p., n.d.).

[74] George Washington Bethune, "Address Delivered . . . at the Unveiling of the Equestrian Statue of Washington . . . ," in W. S. Baker, ed., *Character Portraits of Washington . . .* (Philadelphia, 1889), pp. 274–276.

[75] "Gov. Wise's Oration . . . ," *Southern Literary Messenger*, XXIII (July, 1856), 1–19.

[76] *Ibid.*, p. 15.   [77] *Ibid.*, p. 13.

The most famous of February 22 orations is the one that Edward Everett repeated 129 times in the period 1856–1860, when he toured the entire country in behalf of the Mount Vernon Ladies' Association of the Union.[78] Everett was a student of Washington long before 1856, and many of the ideas of his Birthday oration, entitled "The Character of Washington," may be seen taking shape in earlier speeches delivered on all manner of occasions.[79]

Everett discussed Washington's career in some detail and then sketched the background against which the man and his achievements must be considered. The founders appear all the more remarkable to one who has studied European society and political history. In Everett's words: "Washington and the men of his age, like the great Columbus, were compelled, against adverse tempests, to sound their way along the unvisited coasts of republican government and constitutional liberty."[80]

The question at hand was to determine wherein the greatness of Washington consisted. As for certain supposed shortcomings, such as his apparent lack of cleverness in speech and of some other qualities that impress the unthinking, most of these would have been out of place in him, for popular judgment is often attracted by superficialities or actual defects.[81] Washington had what Everett termed the unpopular qualities: prudence, justice, modesty, and common sense, all in one harmonious whole: "To complain of the character of Washington that it is destitute of brilliant qualities, is to complain of a circle that it has no salient points and no sharp angles in its circumference . . ."[82] His greatness was the result of his character: "He was great as he was good . . . he was great because he was good . . ."[83] Believing that Washington's virtue in maturity was the natural result of the fact that the hero was a good boy, the

[78]Edward Everett, *Orations and Speeches on Various Occasions*, 4 vols. (2d ed.; Boston, 1850–1868), IV, 3–51.
[79]*Ibid.*, I, 378, 461, 564; II, 268; III, 11, 58, 357, 615, 636–637.
[80]*Ibid.*, IV, 31–34.
[81]*Ibid.*, IV, 34–37.
[82]*Ibid.*, IV, 37–40. Cf. James Russell Lowell's lines on Washington in "Under the Old Elm," *infra*, Chapter V, Section 7.
[83]*Ibid.*, IV, 40–41.

Oratory

which he saw with a most friendly eye.[9] Four years later, on the same day, the same speaker grew enthusiastic upon the subject of "the brave youth, the flower and strength of our country," rushing into the field to oppose the French butchers, while "the eye of immortal WASHINGTON lightens along their embattled ranks."[10]

2

The funeral eulogies delivered in the last days of 1799 and well into 1800 comprise a large block of material highly important in crystallizing and to a limited degree in forming popular conceptions of Washington. The critic was now silent, and, as a contemporary British traveler put it, orators all over the country "called all their tropes and metaphors together; collected all the soldiers and statesmen of history, and made them cast garlands at the feet of his statue."[11] Some 350 of these productions were printed.[12]

On December 19, 1799, four days after Washington's death, John Marshall presented to the House of Representatives a set of resolutions prepared by Henry Lee. Marshall began his speech with the idea that Americans should deliver and hear funeral orations, continued with a short biographical sketch of Washington, and concluded with the three resolutions, the last of which contained Lee's famous words, "first in war, first in peace, and first in the hearts of

---

[9] Jonathan Maxcy, "An Oration Delivered in the Baptist Meeting House in Providence . . . ," in *The Literary Remains* . . . (New York, 1844), pp. 362-377. Cf. Abiel Holmes, *A Sermon on the Freedom and Happiness of America* . . . (Boston, 1795).

[10] "An Oration Delivered in the First Congregational Meeting House, in Providence, on the Fourth of July, 1799," in Maxcy, *op. cit.*, p. 394.

[11] John Davis, *Travels of Four Years and a Half in the United States of America; during 1798, 1799, 1800, 1801, and 1802*, ed. A. J. Morrison (New York, 1909), p. 145. Davis's *Travels* was first published in 1803.

[12] Margaret Bingham Stillwell, *Washington Eulogies; a Checklist of Eulogies and Funeral Orations on the Death of George Washington* . . . (New York, 1916). Miss Stillwell speaks of 346 eulogies known to have been printed, of which the texts of thirty-eight are not known to be extant.
Cf. Franklin B. Hough, *Bibliographical List of . . . Eulogies . . . Relating to the Death of General Washington* . . . (Albany, N.Y., 1865); Appleton P. C. Griffin, *A Catalogue of the Washington Collection in the Boston Athenaeum* . . . (Cambridge, Mass., 1897).

his countrymen."[13] On December 24 motions were passed authorizing a period of mourning throughout the nation and the erection of an appropriate monument, under which the body of the hero might be deposited.[14]

A prominent Federalist who remembered the funeral eulogies from his youth wrote a thoughtful though somewhat inaccurate comment upon them in 1834:

> It is worth remarking, that the general sentiment of respect and affection for this eminent man was so exalted, that few of the orators did, or could, come up to the demand. The feeling of these public speakers was, and must have been that of deep veneration, a feeling not adapted to bring forth the touching expressions which would be grateful to a numerous audience. Washington's character was rather to be contemplated than talked of. He was to be estimated by comparison with other men and an eulogy does not permit of this. His eminent worth was to be found in no one brilliant act, nor in any remarkable achievements, but in a whole life of useful, dignified and honorable service. Most of the eulogists were compelled to resort to biographical sketches, which do not admit of much eloquence.[15]

These old orations are dull reading now, and at least one critic found them so in 1800. Charles Brockden Brown or one of his assistants reviewed dozens of them within a few months of their appearance. Although the reviewer apparently made a serious effort to evaluate the crowning American literary output of the year, he did not like the task. After reading several of the eulogies, Brown published "Hints for a Funeral Oration." Here he specified ironically that the eulogist must reveal elaborate grief on the part of himself and his audience; then he must cover Washington's career in detail, skipping from Braddock's defeat to 1775, when the hero accepted command of the Revolutionary armies on June 16 in Independence Hall in Philadelphia, after being suggested for the post by John Adams on June 15 and being approved by unanimous vote

[13] *Annals of Congress*, X (December 19, 1799), 203–204.
[14] *Ibid.*, X (December 23–24, 1799), 208–210.
[15] William Sullivan, *The Public Men of the Revolution* . . . (Philadelphia, 1847), p. 168. The work was first published in Boston in 1834 as *Familiar Letters on Public Characters, and Public Events, from the Peace of 1783, to the Peace of 1815.*

of the Congress—and so on through a prolonged series of bromidic details.[16]

The first dozen of Brown's reviews often ran three or four pages each, but as the months passed and the speeches kept pouring in, the reviewer was by November ready to dismiss two in a paragraph:

So many performances, on this melancholy occasion, have passed in review before us that we have to be excused from bestowing any particular attention on those which remain, unless they possess either novelty of matter or manner, or some distinguished attributes of eloquence that may claim the attention of our readers. The two here offered to our notice contain the same succession of incidents in the life of the American patriot which have been so often repeated and possess no qualities of style that distinguish them above others of the same class, or to entitle them to a more critical examination.[17]

A likely source for biographical material in the funeral orations was Thomas Condie's "Memoirs of George Washington . . . ," the only approach to a full-length biography of Washington to appear before his death. Condie published the "Memoirs" in five installments in his *Philadelphia Monthly Magazine*, a journal that existed only in the year 1798. The work consists largely of Washington's account of his mission to Fort Le Boeuf and similar documents dating from all periods of his life. It ends with a character sketch that brings in Moses, Camillus, Leonidas, Gustavus, Sydney, and several other notables.[18] Also available to the eulogist was an excellent sketch of Washington in Jedidiah Morse's *The American Geography*, first published in 1789. Unlike Condie, Morse includes many details of Washington's daily routine at Mount Vernon.[19]

Although the funeral orators frequently elaborated on the fact that Washington retired to private life after the Revolution and

[16]*Monthly Magazine and American Review*, II (February, 1800), 102–105.
[17]*Ibid.*, III (November, 1800), 377; cf. *ibid.*, III (October, 1800), 272.
[18]*Philadelphia Monthly Magazine; or, Universal Repository of Knowledge and Entertainment*, I (January, February, March, May, June, 1798), 15–20, 65–71, 121–127, 241–249, 297–308.
[19]Jedidiah Morse, *The American Geography* . . . (Elizabeth Town, N.J., 1789), pp. 127–132. W. S. Baker (*Early Sketches of George Washington* . . . [Philadelphia, 1894], pp. 7–8) points out that Condie used Morse's sketch and also one written by John Bell; all are considered again in Chapter IV.

again after his presidency, none of them said much about that private life. As is natural in speeches delivered to public gatherings, the military and political achievements of the hero were emphasized. Most of the speakers said that he was apparently chosen by Divine Providence for a special purpose, as Samuel Davies had observed in 1755; sometimes Davies was quoted in this connection, sometimes the idea was stated directly, and sometimes it was implied. One of the most striking aspects of these orations is their mention of other great names of almost all periods. Washington was compared to, or contrasted with, a wide variety of classical, Biblical, and contemporary worthies, practically always to their disadvantage. His early training was mentioned occasionally, as were his skill in writing and his fine physique. Nearly all the eulogists stressed his piety; they varied in their lists of virtues, but few omitted piety. Nearly all made the point that he was a proper model, upon which young and old should pattern themselves. Usually the speaker included somewhere in his remarks an apology for the inadequacy of his own literary and oratorical ability when confronted with such a subject.

Many of the funeral eulogies must have consumed hours in delivery. One given by the Reverend Phillips Payson at Chelsea, Massachusetts, on January 14, 1800, had a plainer style than most of them and had in addition the merit of brevity. Payson's first two paragraphs were mournful, ending thus:

The solemnities of the day, with the gloomy tokens of death in our view keep fresh in all our minds, a painful sense of that sorrowful event, that excites the public grief; and mentioning of it, will but increase the sorrow. It is the death of General WASHINGTON, that has raised the loud voice of weeping through the United States. And the death of such an illustrious personage, the first and most accomplished general and statesman of his country, and the age; such a disinterested patriot, such a defender, deliverer and father of his country, must needs be deeply lamented in every heart, that is not totally void of all sensibility, gratitude and piety.[20]

[20]Phillips Payson, *A Sermon, Delivered at Chelsea, January 14, 1800* . . . (Charlestown, Mass., 1800), p. 6.

Oratory

Payson observed that "as the free and federal citizens" of America, his hearers should be filled with piety and should offer prayers of gratitude to God. Proceeding to Washington's part in the Revolution, Payson said that he was raised up by God even as were Moses and Cyrus, and that all should be grateful for his achievements. The dire results that would have ensued had Washington failed in the Revolution were considered briefly.[21]

After speaking of Washington's disbanding the army which wished to make him king, Payson stressed the prosperity of the nation under the first President. His transitional sentence at this point is fairly typical:

Let us now, under the impression both of grief and gratitude, follow our great leader, from the scene of war, the field of victory, to the chair of state as the first supreme magistrate and President of the Union, to which he was called by the united voice of his country.[22]

The speaker made a comparatively mild apology for his own shortcomings and then came to Washington's second retirement and his Farewell Address:

These imperfect hints (for I possess neither materials nor abilities to do justice to the subject) I say, what has been but very imperfectly mentioned, must impress our minds with profound respect and reverence to the memory of the deceased . . . I do not recollect ever hearing of a single instance of mistake, error, or blame, that was ever justly charged upon him nor did I ever read of a person in any age of the world, to whom, such real greatness and purity of character, would more justly apply; or that ever merited more highly of this country.

After a series of the most eminent services for his country, for the space of five and forty years, enough to bear down the firmest constitution, he declined being considered as a candidate for the office of President, and thought proper to retire to the private walks of life. But still retaining his disinterested affection for his country, left it a legacy fraught with the most tender, parental advice, counsels, warnings, and cautions, that human wisdom could devise, which ought to be engraven on the heart of every American citizen.[23]

[21]*Ibid.*, pp. 6–9.
[22]*Ibid.*, pp. 10–11.
[23]*Ibid.*, pp. 11–13.

The next paragraph was devoted to Washington's calm in the face of death, and another compared the mourning of America for him to that of Israel for Moses, Samuel, or Josiah. In the following section pious prayer for improvement along the lines suggested by Washington's example and counsel was urged upon all; his successor and other public officials were adjured to follow in his footsteps. In the peroration Payson mentioned the funeral ceremonies held all over the country.[24]

Payson's speech was unlike many in that it contained no attack on the Republican Party. The funeral orations were delivered in an election year, and many Federalists could not resist the opportunity to attack the Jeffersonians. Republicans left politics out of their eulogies, and when the votes were counted, the Federalists appeared to have done themselves no good by endeavoring to use Washington's prestige. John Adams, writing to Jefferson sixteen years later, recalled this deluge of funeral eulogy, in disillusioned, almost cynical phrases:

The death of Washington diffused a general grief. The old Tories, the hyper-federalists, the speculators, set up a general howl. Orations, prayers, sermons, mock funerals were all employed, not that they loved Washington, but to keep in continuance the funding and banking system; and to cast into the background and the shade, all others who had been concerned in the service of their country in the revolution.[25]

Few of the orators—especially in New England—could have known Washington well. Although the orations were not confined to any section of what was then the United States, about two thirds of the 346 known to have been printed were delivered in New England. It must be remembered that New England was more advanced in printing than the other sections. Furthermore, New England was strongly Federalistic at the time, and it seems likely that Washington was somewhat less a hero to the Republicans than to

[24]*Ibid.*, pp. 13-15.
[25]September 3, 1816, in Adams, *Correspondence of John Adams and Thomas Jefferson (1812-1826)*, ed. Paul Wilstach (Indianapolis, 1925), p. 140.

Oratory

the Federalists of 1800. In any case, the New England stamp is noticeable, for the funeral orations as a whole make Washington seem something of a Puritan. Many of the speakers, incidentally, were clergymen.

Numerous eulogies were delivered in Boston. There Fisher Ames, addressing the legislature, briefly compared Washington with Fabius but spent most of his time attacking Revolutionary France and the Republican Party,[26] so that Brockden Brown's reviewer was moved to remark: "Mr. Ames takes a wider range, and deviates more into the tract of political discussion, than at first sight may be thought suitable to the chief purpose of his oration."[27] The Reverend Caleb Alexander, beginning with the omnipotence of death, gave a short biographical sketch and so arrived back at the inescapability of death.[28] George Richards Minot touched upon the sadness of the occasion and then traced Washington's career, stressed his retirements, sketched his character, praised the Constitution and some local heroes, and in conclusion noted the universal acclaim of Washington and the cessation of envy at his death.[29] Timothy Bigelow, who addressed a Masonic gathering, mentioned Socrates, Belisarius, Columbus, Alexander, Solon, Lycurgus, Chatham, Sully, and Fabius.[30] John Davis spoke to the American Academy of Arts and Sciences in Boston on February 19 and talked much of public credit and stability in government. He followed a biographical outline and sought in vain for a parallel to Washington in Gustavus, Alexander, Pompey, Marc Antony, Peter the Great, and many others, but found something like one at last in Timoleon,

[26] *Eulogies and Orations on the Life and Death of General George Washington* . . . (Boston, 1800), pp. 108-130.
[27] *Monthly Magazine and American Review*, II (May, 1800), 355-361.
[28] Caleb Alexander, *A Sermon; Occasioned by the Death of His Excellency George Washington* . . . (Boston, 1800).
[29] George Richards Minot, *An Eulogy on George Washington, Late Commander in Chief of the Armies of the United States* . . . (2d ed.; Boston, 1800).
[30] In *Eulogies and Orations*, pp. 130-141. Cf. George Blake, *A Masonic Eulogy, on the Life of the Illustrious Brother George Washington, Pronounced before the Brethren of St. John's Lodge, on the Evening of the 4th Feb. 5800* . . . (Boston, 5800 [1800]). Later Masonic addresses were distinctive only in their emphasis on the Masonic details of Washington's life. See Benjamin B. French, *An Address on the Masonic Character and Standing of Washington* . . . (Washington, 1851).

and ended by striking at "the leprosy of false knowledge," or, in other words, the deism of Jefferson.[31]

President Joseph Willard opened the exercises at Harvard College with a brief but enthusiastic Latin speech, which Brockden Brown took to pieces sentence by sentence in a review longer than the speech itself. Dr. David Tappan, Professor of Divinity, followed with a sketch of Washington in which he presented the idea that men are made in the image of God, and that Washington was the most nearly perfect man and consequently the most godlike: "Well may he be ranked among Earthly Gods, who, to other great accomplishments united a 'humble,' yet near resemblance of HIM, who is the standard of human perfection, and the EXPRESS IMAGE of divine glory.[32]

The Reverend Abiel Holmes, father of Oliver Wendell Holmes, speaking at Cambridge on the day after the exercises of Harvard, said that he did not intend to give a character sketch because his audience had heard one the day before, but that he would instead give some of the ideas to be drawn from Washington's counsels. He quoted the Farewell Address at length, with elucidative comments, gave the character sketch he had said he was not going to give, and repeated briefly in his own words ideas quoted from Washington, all in a diffuse style.[33] By comparison, the oration which Aaron Bancroft delivered at Worcester was simple and unadorned. Bancroft referred to Washington at one point as the American Joshua, and at another point he stated: "In other countries, individuals have been illustrious as Heroes and Statesmen. The talents which immortalized their respective names were united in our American Alfred; and he was free from the vices and weak-

[31] In *Eulogies and Orations*, pp. 152–158. Also included in this volume are the speeches of Henry Lee, Gouverneur Morris, Robert Treat Paine, and several others. The John Davis quoted here should not be confused with the English traveler of the same name quoted *supra*.

[32] *An Address in Latin, by Joseph Willard . . . and a Discourse in English, by David Tappan . . .* ([Charlestown, Mass.], 1800). Brown's review: *Monthly Magazine and American Review*, III (July, 1800), 47.

[33] Abiel Holmes, *The Counsel of Washington, Recommended in a Discourse Delivered at Cambridge, February 22, 1800* (Boston, 1800).

Oratory

nesses, which were the shades of their characters."[34] Jedidiah Morse, at Charlestown, gave the life of Moses, then the life of Washington, and proceeded to show that Washington was appointed to lead America to liberty even as Moses had been appointed to lead Israel to the promised land; the details of the comparison were minute.[35]

Original observations in the funeral orations were few. But sometimes a minister was alarmed by the extravagance of national mourning and by the idolatry implicit in some of the orations. In western New York Seth Williston preached a sermon which was later published as *The Agency of God, in Raising up Important Characters, and Rendering Them Useful*.[36] He feared that men were worshiping Washington instead of the God who sent him to deliver his people from bondage. "Nothing is too hard for the LORD," declared Williston. "HE that has raised up one WASHINGTON, can, with infinite ease, raise up another. It is impious, therefore, to say 'Our loss is irreparable.' Let us respect the memory of this great man, but let us not limit the Omnipotent." In similar vein Peter Whitney, of Northborough, Massachusetts, emphasized the fact that men, including Washington, are but instruments in effecting the will of God. Whitney also pointed out that Washington himself was always careful to acknowledge that others as well as he had a share in securing American freedom and happiness.[37]

Despite the great volubility and skill of New England orators, it was Henry Lee, of Virginia, who wrote the words that were destined to outlive all others spoken on the occasion of Washington's death. "Light Horse Harry," who was a personal friend of Washington, drew up the resolutions offered in Congress on De-

---

[34]Aaron Bancroft, *An Eulogy on the Character of the Late Gen. George Washington* . . . (Worcester, Mass., 1800).

[35]Jedidiah Morse, *A Prayer and Sermon* . . . (Charlestown, Mass., 1800). Cf. Pliny Merrick, *An Eulogy on the Character of the Late Gen. George Washington* . . . (Brookfield, Mass., 1800); Daniel Dana, *A Discourse on the Character and Virtues of General George Washington* . . . (Newburyport, Mass., 1800); and Josiah Dunham, *A Funeral Oration on George Washington* . . . (Boston, 1800).

[36]Geneva, N.Y. [1800].

[37]Peter Whitney, *Weeping and Mourning at the Death of Eminent Persons a National Duty. A Sermon* . . . (Brookfield, Mass., 1800).

cember 19, 1799, by John Marshall.[38] Lee's tribute as a whole is no better than many others, but a few phrases won popular favor. On December 26, Lee spoke his complete oration before the House of Representatives, who requested a copy. The most famous of his sentences is certainly the best known to be found in the funeral oratory:

First in war, first in peace, and first in the hearts of his countrymen, he was second to none in the humble and endearing scenes of private life; pious, just, humane, temperate, and sincere; uniform, dignified, and commanding; his example was as edifying to all around him as were the effects of that example lasting.[39]

3

Thomas Jefferson regretted, toward the end of his first Inaugural Address, that he did not possess the enormous prestige Washington had when beginning his first administration, and he applied a few glowing terms to his illustrious predecessor.[40] But during Jefferson's administration Washington's fame tended to be slightly overcast. In fact, one Fourth of July oration delivered in 1802 attributed American success in the Revolution to Providence, and paid no attention whatsoever to Washington personally.[41] Probably more typical was a speech made at Savannah a few years later, when a forgotten colonel listed American heroes and made the name of Washington the climax. The colonel praised him as a model for youth, mentioned his judicious appointments while President, and urged the audience to heed his counsels, especially those regarding political parties. This was mild electioneering for the campaign of 1808.[42]

[38] *Annals of Congress*, X (December 19, 1799), 204.

[39] *Ibid.* (Sixth Congress, December 2, 1799–March 3, 1801), Appendix, pp. 1310–1311. See also pp. 203–211, 222–223 (December, 1799). Lee's speech was delivered at Philadelphia and was printed several times in 1800.

[40] Jefferson, *The Writings* . . . , ed. Paul Leicester Ford, 10 vols. (New York, 1892–1899), VIII, 5.

[41] John Leland, *An Oration . . . Cheshire, Massachusetts, July 5, 1802*. (2d ed.; Hudson, Mass., 1802).

[42] Colonel John Macpherson Berrien, *An Oration, Commemorative of the Anniversary of American Independence* . . . (Savannah, Ga., 1808).

A speech made by a Philadelphia physician two years later is an example of Washington's Birthday oratory with a strong political bias. After apologizing for his inability as a speaker, the doctor launched into a biographical sketch adorned by many tributes to Washington's character and military skill. He took occasion to contrast the roseate days of the first presidential administration with the "cowardly proclamations, sullen nonintercourse laws and ruinous embargoes" of Jefferson and Madison.[43] Before closing he lamented the nation's failure to provide an appropriate tomb for its hero.

In 1812 the Federalists, who were opposed to war, were very voluble, and Washington was their guiding light. Of these Daniel Webster was destined to be one of the most influential. A speech he delivered before the Washington Benevolent Society of Portsmouth, New Hampshire, on July 4, 1812, was definitely political and was quite typical. At this time, Webster spoke as a New Englander; twenty years later he was an energetic nationalist and opponent of sectionalism. Webster criticized the current war on the grounds that it interfered with commerce, and he argued that Washington's administration would have avoided it. He stated that the Revolution had left precedents for future ages, and he noted the "well considered and settled principles" of Washington. Passing over analysis of Washington's character, Webster concentrated instead on his principles of civil administration, which he found "on the subject of commerce and foreign relations . . . plain and consistent." In connection with foreign relations Webster pointed out that Washington had planned to have an adequate navy, but that his plans had not been put into execution:

This, gentlemen, is an imperfect view of the principal maxims of Washington's administration. Universal protection; honest, impartial negotiation; spirited preparations for defence; utter aversion to all foreign

---

[43]Charles Caldwell, *An Oration Commemorative of the Character and Administration of Washington, Delivered before the American Republican Society of Philadelphia* (Philadelphia, 1810), p. 34. Cf. Charles W. Hanson, *Oration Delivered before the Washington Benevolent Society of Maryland, February 22, 1811* (Baltimore, 1811).

66   Oratory

connections; the love of peace; the observance of justice; these are the pillars on which he sought to establish national prosperity. Would to God, that the spirit of his administration might actuate the government to its latest moment . . ."[44]

The Washington Benevolent Society of Rutland County, Vermont, heard on February 22, 1814, a typical sermon against the Republican Party: "What imbecility in counsel! What bombastic proclamations and insignificant exploits! What bravado and cowardice! . . . Happy was thy situation, Oh America, my native, my beloved country, when Washington ruled thy destinies!"[45]

[44]"Daniel Webster, *The Writings and Speeches* . . . , 18 vols. (Boston, 1903), XV, 583–598; quotation, p. 593.
Cf. Samuel Austin, *Apology of Patriots; or, the Heresy of the Friends of Washington and Peace Policies Defended* . . . . (Worcester, Mass., 1812); Edward D. Bangs, *An Oration . . . Sutton, Mass., July 5, 1815* . . . (Boston, 1813); Isaac C. Bates, *An Oration Pronounced before the Washington Benevolent Society of the County of Hampshire on Their First Anniversary, 1812* . . . (Northampton, Mass., 1812); Francis Blake, *An Oration Pronounced . . . on the Thirty-sixth Anniversary of American Independence* (Worcester, 1812); Samuel M. Burnside, *Oration at Worcester, April 30, 1813, before the Washington Benevolent Society, in Commemoration of the First Inauguration of General Washington* (Worcester, Mass., 1813); William Crafts, Jun., *An Oration . . . on the Fourth of July* . . . (Charleston, S.C., 1812); George Washington Parke Custis, *An Address Occasioned by the Death of General Lingan, Who Was Murdered by the Mob at Baltimore* . . . (Boston, 1812); Josiah Dunham, *An Oration in Commemoration of the Birth of Our Illustrious Washington* . . . (Windsor, Vt., 1812); Hosea Hildreth, *Discourse before the Washington Benevolent Society in Exeter, May 4, 1813* (Exeter, Mass., 1813); Abiel Holmes, *An Address Delivered before the Washington Benevolent Society at Cambridge . . . July 5, 1813* (Cambridge, Mass., 1813); Samuel L. Knapp, *Address before "The Associated Disciples of Washington," February 22, 1812* (Newburyport, Mass., 1812); Elijah H. Mills, *Oration at Northampton at the Request of the Washington Benevolent Society . . . on the Thirty-seventh Anniversary of American Independence* (Northampton, Mass., 1813); David Raymond, *An Oration Delivered on the 22d of February, 1813, at Washington Hall in the City of New York* (New York, 1813); William Sullivan, *An Oration Delivered before the Washington Benevolent Society of Massachusetts . . . on the Thirtieth Day of April, 1812* . . . (Boston, 1812).

[45]Henry Bigelow, *A Sermon Delivered . . . in Commemoration of the Birth of Washington* (Middlebury, Vt., 1814), pp. 11–12.
Cf. Timothy Bigelow, *Address on the 3d Anniversary of the Washington Benevolent Society, April 30, 1814* (Boston, 1814); Richard H. Dana, *Oration before the Washington Benevolent Society of Cambridge, July 4, 1814* (Cambridge, Mass., 1814); Josiah Dunham, *An Oration in Commemoration of Our Illustrious Washington . . . February 22, 1814* (Windsor, Vt., 1814); Abraham Haskell, *Oration Pronounced . . . before the Washington Benevolent Society of Leominster and Fitchburg, July 4, 1814* (Worcester, Mass., 1814); Francis Scott Key, *An Oration, Delivered . . . before the Washington Society of Alexandria* (Alexandria, Va., 1814); George Washington Warner, *Oration Delivered before the Washington

Oratory

In 1816, because Virginians had begun a movement to transfer the remains of Washington from Mount Vernon to Richmond, a committee was appointed by Congress to take steps to put into effect its resolution of 1799 to have a suitable mausoleum erected.[46] James Ervin four years later made a motion providing that some action be taken to carry out that same resolution. He spoke in conventional manner:

> Greece may tell of her legislators; Rome may tell of her heroes, but what age or country can boast a Washington—a man so renowned both in peace and war? Leonidas was patriotic; Aristides just; Hannibal was patient; Fabius prudent; Scipio was continent; Caesar merciful; Marcellus courageous, and Cato of inflexible integrity; yet, those virtues which separately distinguished those mighty men of antiquity, were all united in the character of this singular great man, and raised him above the level of mankind; he was so preeminent that envy never dared to raise its malignant glance to the elevation of his virtues. Other heroes are renowned for subjugating—he for liberating his country.[47]

This sort of thing typifies remarks likely to be heard in Congress whenever the name of Washington was mentioned, 1800–1865, and Congressional oratory is typical American oratory of its day.

A Washington's Birthday speech which is interesting because of its peroration upon the glory of America in war, manufacturing, internal improvements, the conquest of the wilderness, architecture, literature, oratory, and government, as contrasted with the unhappy lot of freedom in South America, Spain, Greece, and other nations was delivered at Albany, New York, in 1824. This oration very nearly typified the Washington's Birthday oratory of the period under consideration. The opening was, as usual, a biographical sketch of the subject, and certain incidental remarks favoring the

---

Benevolent Society of the County of Columbia . . . (Hudson, N.Y., 1814); *An Oration, Delivered . . . on Board the Nassau Prison Ship, at Chatham, England, July 4, 1814. By an American Seaman, Prisoner of War* (Boston, 1815).

[46] *Annals of Congress*, XXIX (February 16, 1816), 1007–1010.

[47] *Ibid.*, XXXVI (April 6, 1820), 1792–1799; quotation p. 1798.

The oratory of Congress upon the subject of Washington has been made easily available. See U. S. Library of Congress, Legislative Reference Service, *The United States Congress on George Washington* . . . , compiled by Myrtis Jarrell . . . (Washington, D.C., 1932).

internal improvements made by the Whigs gave a slightly political cast to this production.⁴⁸

The centennial of Washington's birth in 1832 was of course marked by numerous orations. At a public dinner in New York, Senator Daniel Webster spoke of the new age that began with America's freedom:

> Washington stands at the commencement of a new era, as well as at the head of the New World. A century from the birth of Washington has changed the world. The country of Washington has been the theatre on which a great part of the change has been wrought; and Washington himself a principal agent by which it has been accomplished. His age and his country are equally full of wonders; and of both he is the chief.⁴⁹

Webster talked of the growth and spread of liberty throughout the world and then proceeded to Washington's principles as seen in the Farewell Address; about half of the speech was concerned with that document. Webster's strong nationalism in 1832 is almost a reversal of his sectional criticism of the War of 1812.

The nullification movement in South Carolina reached its crisis in 1832, and speakers of lesser note than Webster recalled Washingtonian principles as an anchor in a time of turbulent ideas. An oration delivered before the Massachusetts legislature consisted of a lengthy biographical sketch and much praise of representative government.⁵⁰ The president of the University of Nashville told his audience of the Washington eulogies he had heard in 1800, when "the whole land wore the garb of bereavement," and, after biographizing Washington briefly, contrasted the history of Europe for

⁴⁸Salem Dutcher, Jr., *An Oration Commemorative of the Birth of Washington; Delivered at the Baptist Church* . . . (Albany, N.Y., 1824).

Cf. Timothy Flint, *An Oration, Delivered . . . July 4, 1815, before the Washington Benevolent Societies of Lancaster and Sterling, and of Leominster and Fitchburg* (Worcester, Mass., 1815); Edward Wigglesworth Andrews, *An Address before the Washington Benevolent Society* . . . *February 22, 1816* (Newburyport, Mass., 1816); Solomon Drowne, *An Oration Delivered in the First Baptist Meeting-House, in Providence, at the Celebration, February 23, A.D. 1824* . . . (Providence, R.I., 1824); Webster, *op. cit.*, I, 231–255; II, 1–11, 69–82; V, 213; VI, 43, 118–119.

⁴⁹"The Character of Washington," in Webster, *op. cit.*, II, 69–82; quotation p. 71.

⁵⁰Francis C. Gray, *Oration . . . on the Hundredth Anniversary of the Birth of George Washington* (Boston, 1832).

Oratory 69

a generation with that of America. He too extolled the principles of the Farewell Address.[51]

Congress debated in 1832 the project of removing Washington's remains to the city of Washington and interring them with appropriate ceremonies on the hundredth anniversary of his birth. The debate included such points as Virginia's prior claim, Washington's provision in his will for interment at Mount Vernon, the possibility of removal of the capital to the West, and of disunion. When Congress finally attempted to take action, it was blocked by Washington's relatives.[52] In the course of the discussion, Representative Augustin Clayton, of Georgia, voiced one memorable idea: "The praise of Washington is an exhausted subject . . ."[53]

Learned societies have ever been patrons of oratory, and Washington was the subject of an address made before the Virginia Historical and Philosophical Society in 1837. The speaker said that though American history lacked antiquity, it compensated by the splendor of character of such persons as John Smith, Pocahontas, and especially Washington; he regretted that there was no fitting monument to the greatest of these and went on to say that his hearers should strive to make the government as pure as it was in Washington's day.[54]

Partly because of his strong Federalism, Daniel Webster's speeches on all manner of occasions were sprinkled with allusions to Washington. Often he cited the hero's example in connection with current measures that he advocated or opposed. For instance, he

[51] Philip Lindsley, *An Address* . . . (Nashville, Tenn., 1832).
Cf. Charles Burroughs, *Oration on the Moral Grandeur of George Washington, February 22, 1832* . . . (Portsmouth, N.H., 1832); Charles Caldwell, *A Discourse . . . Delivered by Request to the Citizens of Lexington, Ky.* . . . (Lexington, Ky., 1832); Robert R. Collier, *An Oration* . . . *Petersburg, Virginia, February 22, 1832* (Petersburg, 1832); Solomon Lincoln, *An Oration Pronounced at Plymouth, on the Centennial Anniversary of the Birth of George Washington* (Plymouth, Mass., 1832); John Pitman, *Oration* . . . *February 22, 1832* (Providence, R.I., 1832).
[52] *Register of Debates in Congress*, VIII, pt. 2 (February 13–16, 1832), 1782–1820.
[53] *Ibid.*, VIII, pt. 2 (February 13, 1832), 1798.
[54] Thomas W. Gilmer, "An Address . . . ," *Southern Literary Messenger*, III (February, 1837), 97–102.
Cf. John Quincy Adams, *An Oration* . . . *July 4, 1837* (Newburyport, Mass., n.d.).

cited the first President's stand on monetary matters, particularly a national bank, in at least four speeches, the first made in 1837 at Wheeling, Virginia.[55]

Memorial and anniversary exercises at various points of historic interest were frequently occasions for oratory touching Washington. One example was an address which John Tyler, later President, delivered at Yorktown in 1837. Tyler observed that although Leonidas and his men were killed and Moses could not enter the promised land, Washington overcame all his difficulties and entered into peace with his countrymen. The speaker's strain was exalted: "Ye ambitious ones of the earth, how vile and contemptible do you appear when compared with *Washington.*"[56]

Abraham Lincoln's words about Washington have a unique interest because he was himself destined to take a place beside the first President in the hearts of his countrymen. Like thousands of Americans, Lincoln read Weems's *Life of Washington* in his youth.[57] Frequently he expressed his high regard for Washington's authority and example. Lincoln's early oratorical style was ornate, as may be seen from his remarks on Washington made in an address before the Young Men's Lyceum of Springfield in 1837. His words were directed against violence, for the country was then stirred by the recent burning of a mulatto in St. Louis. He concluded his speech:

Passion has helped us, but can do so no more. It will in the future be our enemy. Reason—cold, calculating, unimpassioned reason—must furnish all the materials for our future support and defense. Let those materials be molded into general intelligence, sound morality, and, in particular, a reverence for the Constitution and laws; and that we improved to the last, that we remained free to the last, that we revered his name to the last, that during his long sleep we permitted no hostile foot to pass over

---

[55] Webster, *op. cit.*, II, 241; III, 9–10, 163; VII, 97.

[56] John Tyler, "An Oration . . . ," *Southern Literary Messenger*, III (December, 1837), 747–752.
Cf. James Ewell Heath, "A Lecture . . . ," *Southern Literary Messenger*, IV (November, 1838), 705–707.

[57] "Address to the Senate of New Jersey, February 21, 1861," in Lincoln, *Complete Works . . .* , ed. John G. Nicolay and John Hay, 2 vols. (New York, 1902), I, 688.

or desecrate his resting-place, shall be that which to learn the last trump shall awaken our Washington.[58]

The Catholic bishop of Charleston, South Carolina, speaking there on February 22, 1838, based his address in large part upon Jared Sparks's biography of Washington, to which he made several references. Declaring that Providence had chosen Washington for the role he played, the Bishop urged all Americans to make him their model. The speaker found the work of a surveyor and the early expedition to Fort Le Boeuf good training to prepare the youth "for a period of equal difficulties upon a more extended scale, for a nobler purpose." The Bishop spoke of Washington as a "Southron," and he called on his audience to be loyal Southerners and Carolinians.[59]

A year later John Quincy Adams addressed the New York Historical Society on the semicentennial of Washington's first inauguration, which was called the Jubilee of the Constitution. He said that Washington's part in establishing the Constitution was ordained by Providence. Elaborating on Washington's character, Adams found blended in him "the spirit of command and the spirit of meekness" more than in Aeneas or King David.[60] His address is a little like a rebuttal to certain expressions of the Southern bishop.

Expressing a typical American viewpoint, Ralph Waldo Emerson said in 1838 that when he saw a great figure like Washington or Epaminondas, he was filled with admiration of a beauty to be desired.[61] Apparently Emerson felt some such respect or admiration for Washington most of the time, for he mentioned the hero occasionally in his essays—usually they grew out of lectures—but, like most of the other great writers of his day, he never treated him at any length. Probably most of the New England Brahmins sympa-

[58]*Ibid.*, I, 15.
[59]John England, "Oration Delivered before the Washington Light Infantry," in *The Works* . . . , ed. Ignatius Aloysius Reynolds, 5 vols. (Baltimore and New York, 1849), IV, 485-503.
[60]John Quincy Adams, *The Jubilee of the Constitution* . . . (New York, 1839).
[61]"Divinity School Address," in *The Complete Works* . . . , ed. Edward Waldo Emerson, 12 vols. (Boston and New York, 1903), I, 133.

thized with the belief of Representative Clayton that "The praise of Washington is an exhausted subject." Emerson on at least one occasion seconded this in fairly definite language: "Every hero becomes a bore at last. . . . They cry up the virtues of George Washington,—'Damn George Washington!' is the poor Jacobin's whole speech and confutation."[62] Emerson's attitude toward Washington must be gleaned from pithy sentences in essays, journals, and letters, and probably more typical than the impatient remark quoted above is a paragraph on the Stuart portrait of Washington in his dining room: Emerson says this portrait reveals a calm like that of the Alleghenies, which contrasts vividly with the hysteria of contemporary politicians.[63]

4

At Lafayette College on July 4, 1840, Willis Gaylord Clark, popular Philadelphia littérateur, spoke with understanding on the subject of Lafayette and Washington. He considered Lafayette's career and then that of Washington, his theme being that they were kindred spirits, both inspired with zeal for noble action. Concluding, Clark quoted verses comparing Washington with several Roman heroes and other verses describing General Washington's entry into heaven.[64]

Two years later, on February 22, Abraham Lincoln addressed the Springfield Washingtonian Temperance Society, of which he was a member. He attacked slavery as well as drunkenness, and he again mentioned Washington only at the end of his remarks. Then he said the name of Washington was the "mightiest name of earth—

[62]"Uses of Great Men," *ibid.*, IV, 27.

[63]Ralph Waldo Emerson, *Journals* . . . , ed. Edward Waldo Emerson and Waldo Emerson Forbes, 10 vols. (Boston and New York, 1909-1914), VIII, 300; cf. X, 350. Cf. Emerson, *The Complete Works*, II, 83, 258, 263; III, 89; V, 7; VIII, 102; XI, 78; *The Letters* . . . , ed. Ralph L. Rusk, 6 vols. (New York, 1939), I, 188, 330, 345, 349, 382; II, 426; IV, 408; V, 481.

[64]Willis Gaylord Clark, "Lafayette and Washington, an Address Pronounced before the Washington Society . . . ," in Clark, *The Literary Remains* . . . , ed. Lewis Gaylord Clark (New York, 1844); reviewed by L. G. Clark in *Knickerbocker*, XVI (November, 1840), 446-447.

long since mightiest in the cause of civil liberty, still mightiest in moral reformation." Lincoln added: "On that name no eulogy is expected. It cannot be. To add brightness to the sun or glory to the name of Washington is alike impossible. Let none attempt it. In solemn awe pronounce the name, and in its naked deathless splendor leave it shining on."[65]

Upon the completion of the Bunker Hill monument in 1843, Daniel Webster pronounced one of his most memorable passages on Washington, beginning: "America has furnished to the world the character of Washington! And if American institutions had done nothing else, that alone would have entitled them to the respect of mankind." Declaring that Washington was purely American, although all of Europe recognized his preeminence, Webster said the monument was an appropriate, though inadequate, symbol of the greatest American, because it too was entirely American. He went on to justify the American effort to reconcile freedom with security.[66] Much of the oratory about Washington is, of course, somewhat chauvinistic.

Washington's reputation was approaching its peak in 1847, when a Virginia minister, after comparing him with Moses and Joshua, found his greatest service to be that of a leader toward religious liberty. The speaker mentioned Demosthenes and Alfred the Great, praised motherhood, and so arrived at an implied Washington-Jesus parallel: "And to 'Mary the Mother of Washington,' whose incomplete monument at Fredericksburg lies shamefully neglected, we owe all the mighty debt due from mankind to her immortal son."[67]

At the laying of the cornerstone of the Washington Monument

---

[65] Lincoln, *op. cit.*, I, 63–64.

[66] Webster, *op. cit.*, I, 281–282. Cf. Charles Fraser, *Address on the Birth Day of General Washington* . . . (Charleston, S.C., 1845); W. S. Norman, *An Oration, Containing a Biographical Sketch of George Washington* . . . (Savannah, Ga., 1847); William Buell Sprague, *An Address Delivered the Evening of the 22d of February, 1847* . . . (Albany, N.Y., 1847).

[67] J. N. Danforth, "Thoughts on the Fourth of July, 1847," *Southern Literary Messenger*, XIII (August, 1847), 502–505. For a stronger and more sentimental comparison of Washington with Jesus, see Beverley R. Wellford, Jr., "Address Delivered before the Ladies' Mount Vernon Association . . . ," *Southern Literary Messenger*, XXI (September, 1855), 562–566.

on July 4, 1848, Robert C. Winthrop, who also made the speech at its dedication nearly thirty-seven years later, discussed the appropriateness of such a memorial and of the occasion. He touched upon the European view of Washington, gave a conventional biographical sketch, and then attempted to analyze the power that enabled the man to keep a nation behind him. Unable to attribute Washington's strength of character to scholarship, wit and eloquence, personal magnetism, a reckless spirit of adventure, or even "solid information and judgment," he finally concluded that it lay in his valor and modesty and particularly in his incorruptible honesty. Winthrop pointed out that Washington disliked being a politician and that though circumstances forced that role upon him, he remained free of any tendency toward demagoguery.[68]

The very sentimental or ambitious panegyric of Washington occasionally—as we have seen in the words of Representative Clayton and of Ralph Waldo Emerson—aroused protests. Lecturing at Boston in 1850, a literary critic of the day voiced one which is unusually thoughtful and incisive:

Mediocrity has a bad trick of idealizing itself in eulogizing him, and drags him down to its own level while assuming to lift him to the skies. . . . Accordingly, in the panegyric of cold spirits, Washington disappears in a cloud of commonplaces; in the rodomontade of boiling patriots, he expires in the agonies of rant. Now, the sooner this bundle of mediocre talents and moral qualities, which its contrivers have the audacity to call George Washington, is hissed out of existence, the better it will be. . . . Again, some eulogists have caricatured him as a passionless, imperturbable, "proper" man; but at the battle of Monmouth, General Lee was privileged to discover, that from those firm, cold lips could leap words hotter and more smiting than the hot June sun that smote down upon their heads.[69]

The rift between North and South brought new overtones into every mention of Washington. In the year of the Great Compro-

[68]Robert C. Winthrop, "An Oration . . . ," in Winthrop, *Addresses and Speeches on Various Occasions*, 4 vols. (Boston, 1852–1886), IV, 70–89.
[69]Edwin P. Whipple, "Washington and the Principles of the Revolution," in Whipple, *Character and Characteristic men* (Boston, 1866), pp. 305-306.

mise, 1850, the Senate passed a motion for the purchase of the manuscript of the Farewell Address. Henry Clay, who introduced the motion, said that all would find it refreshing to reread Washington's words at that critical time, "amid the discordance and ungrateful sounds of disunion and discord which assail our ears in every part of this country and in both halls of Congress." He also mentioned Washington's paternal warning "to beware of sectional division, to beware of demagogues, to beware of the consequences of indulging a spirit of disunion," as Clay put it.[70]

Six weeks after Clay spoke these words, another Senator brought Washington to the attention of his colleagues, but the reasoning and conclusion he advanced were startlingly original. John C. Calhoun, with less than a month of life before him, was too weak to address the Senate, but he was present on March 4 when James Mason, of Virginia, read for him his last speech on the slavery controversy. His words on Washington were not a mere mention:

Nor can the Union be saved by invoking the name of that illustrious Southerner whose mortal remains repose on the western bank of the Potomac. He was one of us—a slaveholder and a planter. We have studied his history, and find nothing in it to justify submission to wrong. On the contrary, his great fame rests on the solid foundation, that, while he was careful to avoid doing wrong to others, he was prompt and decided in repelling wrong. I trust that in this respect, we profited by his example.

Nor can we find any thing in his history to deter us from seceding from the Union, should it fail to fulfil the objects for which it was instituted, by being permanently and hopelessly converted into the means of oppressing instead of protecting us. On the contrary, we find much in his example to encourage us, should we be forced to the extremity of deciding between submission and disunion.

In a further paragraph Calhoun pointed out that the young Washington was a soldier of the crown and a defender of the union

---

[70]"Speech in the Senate, January 24, 1850," in Calvin Colton, ed., *The Life, Correspondence, and Speeches of Henry Clay*, 6 vols. (New York, 1857), III, 110. It has been said that, because of his part in incurring war with Britain in 1812, Clay "was as quick to defy Washington as to deify him." Harding, Hunt, and Thorp, *op. cit.*, I, 546.

between the crown and the colonies, but that when such union became oppressive and unprofitable to his own country, he did not hesitate to draw his sword to destroy it.[71]

Daniel Webster a year before his death expressed his genuine veneration for Washington in a nonpolitical speech made at the invitation of the young men of Albany, New York, on May 24, 1851. Webster was not debating, but the trend of his remarks is clearly opposed to that of Calhoun's:

> If I were now to describe a patriot President, I would draw his [Washington's] master-strokes and copy his design; I would present his picture before me as a constant study; I would display his policy, alike liberal and just, narrowed down to no sectional interests, bound to no personal objects, held to no locality, but broad and generous and open, as expansive as the air which is wafted by the winds of heaven from one part of the country to another.[72]

A Washington's Birthday speech delivered at Baltimore in 1852 put particular emphasis upon Washington's views on national union and foreign relations, as set forth in the Farewell Address. The orator expressed comparisons: "Others have those traits which awaken feelings akin to the terrible—such are Genghis Khan, Tamerlane, and Bonaparte. But in Washington we have an approximation to the highest order of the moral sublime. What virtue was wanting in him, or what vice was ever laid to his charge?"[73]

[71] John C. Calhoun, "Speech on the Slavery Question, Delivered in the Senate, March 4th 1850," in Calhoun, *The Works* . . . , ed. Richard K. Crallé, 6 vols. (New York, 1854–1860), IV, 561.

[72] Webster, *op. cit.*, IV, 281. Cf. *ibid.*, III, 228–230; IV, 314; VII, 115; XIII, 423–428; XIV, 343–344.

[73] Alexander H. Stephens, *Address . . . before the Maryland Institute . . .* (Washington, D.C., 1852).

A little pamphlet containing a dozen or so speeches made at a banquet given on February 22, 1852, is a storehouse of mid-nineteenth-century American rhetoric: William Hincks and F. H. Smyth, *Washington's Birthday; Congressional Banquet in Honor of George Washington, and the Principles of Washington* (Washington, 1852).

Cf. Alfred B. Ely, *American Liberty . . . an Oration . . . before the Order of United Americans . . .* (New York, 1850); Henry H. Tator, *An Oration Commemorative of the Birthday of Washington . . .* (Albany, N.Y., 1851); Clement Butler, *Our Country and Our Washington . . .* (Washington, 1852); "Address before the Mount Vernon Association, July 4th, 1855," *Southern Literary Messenger,*

At the unveiling of the statue of Washington in Union Square, New York, on July 4, 1856, the orator discussed the inadequacy of historical portraiture of Washington and debated whether crises make great men or great men make crises; he seemed vaguely aware of the approach of civil war, and he found in classic times—in Fabius, Cato, Scipio Africanus, Cincinnatus—no such harmonious union of virtues as in Washington.[74]

Also on July 4, 1856, Governor H. A. Wise, of Virginia, delivered a memorable oration at Lexington. The occasion was the unveiling of a replica of Houdon's statue by the Virginia Military Institute.[75] Wise's speech was long and for the most part conventional. He sketched Washington's career and analyzed his greatness, declaring that his hearers could and should make him their model. He mentioned the hero's temper and pronounced him "no Northern iceberg which repelled by coldness."[76] But when he spoke of the framing of the Constitution and the establishment of the Union, Wise found reason to fear that in his own day certain persons in Massachusetts might "trample . . . upon the oaths of organic law, and madly rushing over the grave at Mount Vernon, make a wreck of this master work of wisdom and virtue . . ." In such case, he continued, Virginia would "remain loyal like her leader" and would "defend the holy places of the mighty dead and the glorious work of their master minds!!" Concluding this portion of his address, he cried: "The Constitution and the Union shall be preserved!!"[77] The meaning and the political implication here become somewhat clearer when it is recalled that in the Virginia convention of 1861 Wise advocated a fight-within-the-Union policy rather than secession.

XXI (August, 1855), 514-518; John Minor Botts, *Speech . . . Delivered before the Order of United Americans . . .* (New York, 1859); Thomas S. Bocock, *Oration Delivered February 22, 1860 . . .* (n.p., n.d.).

[74]George Washington Bethune, "Address Delivered . . . at the Unveiling of the Equestrian Statue of Washington . . . ," in W. S. Baker, ed., *Character Portraits of Washington . . .* (Philadelphia, 1889), pp. 274-276.

[75]"Gov. Wise's Oration . . . ," *Southern Literary Messenger*, XXIII (July, 1856), 1-19.

[76]*Ibid.*, p. 15. [77]*Ibid.*, p. 13.

The most famous of February 22 orations is the one that Edward Everett repeated 129 times in the period 1856–1860, when he toured the entire country in behalf of the Mount Vernon Ladies' Association of the Union.[78] Everett was a student of Washington long before 1856, and many of the ideas of his Birthday oration, entitled "The Character of Washington," may be seen taking shape in earlier speeches delivered on all manner of occasions.[79]

Everett discussed Washington's career in some detail and then sketched the background against which the man and his achievements must be considered. The founders appear all the more remarkable to one who has studied European society and political history. In Everett's words: "Washington and the men of his age, like the great Columbus, were compelled, against adverse tempests, to sound their way along the unvisited coasts of republican government and constitutional liberty."[80]

The question at hand was to determine wherein the greatness of Washington consisted. As for certain supposed shortcomings, such as his apparent lack of cleverness in speech and of some other qualities that impress the unthinking, most of these would have been out of place in him, for popular judgment is often attracted by superficialities or actual defects.[81] Washington had what Everett termed the unpopular qualities: prudence, justice, modesty, and common sense, all in one harmonious whole: "To complain of the character of Washington that it is destitute of brilliant qualities, is to complain of a circle that it has no salient points and no sharp angles in its circumference . . ."[82] His greatness was the result of his character: "He was great as he was good . . . he was great because he was good . . ."[83] Believing that Washington's virtue in maturity was the natural result of the fact that the hero was a good boy, the

[78] Edward Everett, *Orations and Speeches on Various Occasions*, 4 vols. (2d ed.; Boston, 1850–1868), IV, 3–51.
[79] *Ibid.*, I, 378, 461, 564; II, 268; III, 11, 58, 357, 615, 636–637.
[80] *Ibid.*, IV, 31–34.
[81] *Ibid.*, IV, 34–37.
[82] *Ibid.*, IV, 37–40. Cf. James Russell Lowell's lines on Washington in "Under the Old Elm," *infra*, Chapter V, Section 7.
[83] *Ibid.*, IV, 40–41.

orator contrasted the profligacy of Alexander. Further contrasts involved the hardness of Caesar in his dealings with the Germans, and the graft of the Duke of Marlborough, who kept on his rolls the names of men killed in his campaigns, in order to collect their pay for himself. Marlborough's palatial residence and grounds, a show place in England, seemed to Everett to cry out, "Avarice, Plunder, Eternal Shame!" Mount Vernon, a simple but dignified home, probably cost less than the dog kennels of the shrine of Marlborough.[84]

Having made his appeal for Mount Vernon, Everett alluded to the belief that Washington could never have led Napoleon's armies into Russia and commented that Napoleon was unable to lead them out. After some further consideration of Washington as a military figure and a few words in praise of the Farewell Address, the speaker closed with a tactfully worded plea:

It was well said by Mr. Jefferson in 1792, writing to Washington to dissuade him from declining a renomination: "North and South will hang together while they have you to hang to." Washington in the flesh is taken from us; we shall never behold him as our fathers did; but his memory remains, and I say, let us hang to his memory.[85]

Pleas for national unity in the name of Washington were numerous, and Governor Wise, of Virginia, made a notable one at the unveiling of Thomas Crawford's equestrian statue in Richmond on February 22, 1858. The occasion was a great and festive one; high national officials and the governors of all the states were invited, and many dignitaries were among the thousands who poured into Richmond from all directions. Governor Wise's speech of welcome was brief but gracious and eloquent. Speaking the name of Washington, he exclaimed:

Magic name! If none other under Heaven can draw us to each other, that talisman can touch the chords of unison, and clasp us hand to hand, and bind us heart to heart, in the kindred heirship of one Patriot Father! —Before that august name Feud and Faction stand abashed:—Civil Discord hushes into awed silence:—schisms and sections are subdued and

[84]*Ibid.*, IV, 41-45.
[85]*Ibid.*, IV, 49-51.

vanish; for, in the very naming of that name, there is . . . the strength and beauty of *National Union*.[86]

Edward Everett was among the out-of-state visitors present for the ceremonies at Richmond, and on February 23 he was called upon to deliver his famous oration to a large audience there. Making his introductory remarks, he touched upon no controversial topic, but at one point he said that he would be happy if through his activity for the Mount Vernon cause he softened "the asperity of sectional feeling" by reminding Americans of their common respect and love for Washington.[87]

At Richmond Everett was presented by the Mount Vernon Ladies' Association with a Washington relic in appreciation of his services, as was William Lowndes Yancey, one-time Congressman from Alabama. Yancey, a popular exponent of Calhoun's doctrine of states' rights, did not forget the burning issue of the day. He declared it the duty of all Americans to preserve and perpetuate the teachings of Washington's life, but, he continued, "Of these teachings the least, and that in which the subjects of the crowned despotisms of the old world are alike with him, a teacher, is the one which most eulogists dwell upon as the main lesson he taught—mere fealty to government." Washington lived in vain if he impressed no higher ideal upon mankind. Instead, his life was dedicated to "that other immortal, new-born, American principle," that governments are made for the benefit of the governed, and that it is not merely the people's right but even their duty to overthrow a government which fails to fulfill its purpose. Yancey exclaimed that it would indeed be a sad day if the South should ever have to justify itself by proclaiming "these mighty, yet blood-stained truths," and he added that such a day would never come if all Americans would follow

[86][Henry A. Wise], "The Celebration of the Twenty-second . . . ," *Southern Literary Messenger*, XXVI (April, 1858), 241-244; quotation, p. 243.
    The principal address at the ceremony was that of Senator Robert M. T. Hunter, who presented Washington as the prime agent in organizing and directing a great new movement in human society: American popular government. See "Inauguration of the Equestrian Statue of Washington," *Southern Literary Messenger*, XXVI (March, 1858), 167-184.
[87]Everett, *op. cit.*, III, 620-623.

Washington's lead in a course of justice and respect for the rights of others.[88]

The arguments of Yancey and other secessionists, which may have originated with Calhoun, eventually drew from Abraham Lincoln rebuttals equally logical. Lincoln's more important references to Washington were made in political speeches, including his first debate against Douglas, on August 21, 1858. On this occasion he stated that when the nation was established the leaders expected the ultimate eradication of slavery, and that his party was therefore following the principles of Washington, Jefferson, and Madison in trying to check its spread.[89] In the Cooper Institute speech, of February 27, 1860, Lincoln noted that secessionists as well as their opponents were quoting Washington's warning against sectional parties. But, Lincoln reminded his hearers, President Washington had approved and signed a Congressional act prohibiting slavery in the Northwest Territory. He continued:

Bearing this in mind, and seeing that sectionalism has since arisen upon this same subject, is that warning a weapon in your hands against us, or in our hands against you? Could Washington himself speak, would he cast the blame of that sectionalism upon us, who sustain his policy, or upon you, who repudiate it? We respect that warning of Washington, and we commend it to you, together with his example pointing to the right application of it.

A few minutes later Lincoln again referred to Washington:

Let us be diverted by none of those sophistical contrivances wherewith we are so industriously plied and belabored—contrivances such as groping for some middle ground between the right and the wrong; vain as the search for a man who should be neither a living man nor a dead man; . . . such as invocations to Washington, imploring men to unsay what Washington said and undo what Washington did.[90]

---

[88]"Washington's True Legacies," in *Library of Southern Literature*, ed. Edwin Anderson Alderman, Joel Chandler Harris, and Charles William Kent, 16 vols. (New Orleans, 1908-1913), XIII, 6027-6033.

[89]Lincoln, *op. cit.*, I, 291. Cf. I, 30, 32, 74, 136, 569, 693.

[90]*Ibid.*, I, 606, 612. Later campaign speeches also presented this argument (I, 615, 623, 629).

After his election and before his inauguration Lincoln several times alluded to Washington in a humble tone. Just before leaving Springfield, he said: "I now leave, not knowing when or whether I may return, with a task before me greater than that which rested upon Washington. Without the assistance of that Divine Being who ever attended him, I cannot succeed. With that assistance, I cannot fail."[91]

Before a deputation of Negro citizens in 1862 Lincoln discussed the proposal of a colony for Negroes in Central America; he said that it might not be easy for those who emigrated but that it might be beneficial to their race, and he cited the example of Washington: "General Washington himself endured greater physical hardships than if he had remained a British subject, yet he was a happy man because he was engaged in benefiting his race, in doing something for the children of his neighbors, having none of his own."[92]

Without disrespect to Lincoln, we can probably best illustrate the tone of many Washingtonian orations by presenting a burlesque of one. Charles Farrar Browne, who is often confused with his principal character, the traveling showman Artemus Ward, made a number of references to Washington in *Artemus Ward: His Book* (1862). Most of them are trifling compared to Ward's "Fourth of July Oration," which, as he said of his show, has seldom been equaled and never surpassed. After some criticism of the American colonists, Ward contrasted them with the heroes of the Revolution:

There was no discount, however, on them brave men who fit, bled and died in the American Revolushun. We needn't be afraid of setting 'em up two steep. Like my show, they will stand any amount of prase. G. Washington was abowt the best man this world ever sot eyes on. He was a clear-heded, warm-harted, and stiddy goin man. He never slopt over! The prevailin weakness of most public men is to SLOP OVER!

[91]*Ibid.*, I, 672. Cf. I, 675, 677; II, 64–65, 126.
[92]*Ibid.*, II, 224. In the same year Lincoln mentioned Washington in an order of Sabbath observance for the army and navy, reverentially quoting from "the first general order issued by the Father of his Country after the Declaration of Independence." *Ibid.*, II, 254. Cf. "A speech at the Celebration of the Birthday of Washington by the Boston Light Infantry Association, February 22, 1863," in Winthrop, *op. cit.*, II, 553–557.

Oratory 83

[Put them words in large letters.—A. W.] They git filled up and slop. They Rush things. They travel too much on the high presher principle. They git on to the fust poplar hobby-hoss whitch trots along, not carin a sent whether the beest is even goin, clear sited and sound or spavined, blind and bawky. Of course, they git throwed eventooually, if not sooner. When they see the multitood goin it blind they go Pel Mel with it, instid of exertin theirselves to set it right. They can't see that the crowd which is now bearin them triumfuntly on its shoulders will soon diskiver its error and cast them into the hoss pond of Oblivyun, without the slitest hesitashun. Washington never slopt over. That wasn't George's stile. He luved his country dearly. He wasn't after the spiles. He was a human angil in a 3 kornerd hat and knee britches, and we shan't see his like right away. My friends, we can't all be Washington's, but we kin all be patrits and behave ourselves in a human and a Christian manner.[93]

This is not the place for discussion of the status of the orator as a literary man; of the speakers here cited, only Lincoln, Webster, Calhoun, and possibly Everett, are generally conceded real literary merit. The importance of Washingtonian oratory lies in its impact upon the American people, including those who wrote and read biographies of Washington and stories and poems concerning him. The amount of this oratory is staggering. It seems unlikely that any other man in history, with the possible exception of Napoleon, was so widely "orated" upon in his latter years and for more than a half

[93]Charles Farrar Browne, *The Complete Works of Artemus Ward* . . . (London, 1899), p. 125.

For earlier burlesques of Washington oratory, not so clever as Browne's, see: "The Village on Fourth of July 183–," by "T. P., Alexandria," *Southern Literary Messenger*, I (December, 1834), 158–159; "John Phoenix's Fourth of July Oration in Oregon," *Knickerbocker*, XLVIII (December, 1856), 639–641; note on a rejected burlesque of similar nature, *Knickerbocker*, LVI (October, 1860), 444; Walter Blair, "Burlesques in Nineteenth Century American Humor," *American Literature*, II (November, 1930), 236–247.

There were occasionally speeches characterized by unintentional humor. See the Reverend C. W. Howard's speech before the Mnemosynean Literary Society on Commencement Day, 1858, "Editor's Table," *Southern Literary Messenger*, XXVII (September, 1858), 231–232; also a speech made by Dr. Hooper Cumming in New York (1824) and a most bombastic one made by Edwin H. Tenney, of Rome, Tennessee (1859), in Pearson, *op. cit.*, pp. 27–28 and 29–38. Pearson's amusing discussion of the humorous aspects of July 4 oratory is entitled "Making the Eagle Scream."

century after his death as George Washington. February 22 and the Fourth of July were annual occasions upon which he was sure to be eulogized in towns and hamlets all over the country, and public speakers found many other opportunities to focus attention upon him. Ministers, lawyers, educators, members of Congress, state governors and other public officials, scholarly lecturers, even humorists —anyone called upon to make a speech on any occasion of national importance—found in the Father of His Country an excellent subject.

The men who eulogized Washington from pulpit, lecture platform, and courthouse steps were fired with patriotic zeal; they pointed to the first President as the type of leader their country could and did produce, greater than any that Europe or Asia had ever nurtured. Many of the speakers had in addition special political programs or ideals to put across; these felt that their opinions and plans were those of Washington, and so they dwelt upon his greatness with the same enthusiasm as the more disinterested.

Naturally enough, the orators were concerned almost entirely with Washington's public career. They sketched his early life and mentioned his retirement, but the man they constantly recreated was the President and the Commander-in-Chief. Nathaniel Hawthorne facetiously expressed the feeling of Americans in general when he once mused, toying with the idea of a nude statue of Washington: "Did anybody ever see Washington nude? It is inconceivable. He had no nakedness, but I imagine he was born with his clothes on, and his hair powdered, and made a stately bow on his first appearance in the world."[94] The Fourth of July orator had no small part in fostering this impression.

In the orations Washington was essentially the same man of integrity and moral stamina that we see in his writings (as well as in his deeds) and those of his contemporaries. He was, to be sure,

[94]*Notes of Travel*, vols. XIX–XXII, in *Complete Writings*, Old Manse ed., 22 vols. (Boston and New York, 1903), XXII, 43. Cf. XXII, 86–87. Hawthorne wrote a couple of pages on Washington to accompany a portrait in *The American Magazine of Useful and Entertaining Knowledge* for March, 1836. See Arlin Turner, *Hawthorne as Editor* (University, La., 1941), pp. 17–20.

somewhat more formally and strictly pious; the funeral orators, especially the large number of New England ministers among them, share with Parson Weems the credit for this stamp. Later speakers and writers were slow to investigate its authenticity. But the major fault to be found with the orators is that they made Washington a catalogue of abstract virtues rather than a being of flesh and blood. In consonance with their motives and purposes as public speakers, they dealt largely in eulogistic generalizations; many used Biblical terms and comparisons. In short, the orators played a major role in the canonization of Washington, and they lent it their continual support through the years. As a result, the public long resented any attempt to humanize its demigod—as, for instance, to depict him as a young lover who wrote verses, or to describe his high temper that occasionally broke its bounds, or to picture his as being the life of an eighteenth-century Virginia planter, fond of dancing and fox hunting. Americans before 1865 learned how Washington looked from the Stuart portraits; they learned what he was like from the orators and from Parson Weems. Artemus Ward put it succinctly: "He was a human angil in a 3 kornerd hat and knee britches."

CHAPTER IV

BIOGRAPHY

BIOGRAPHY had not emerged from ministerial panegyric in America at the time of Washington's death, and its development for many years thereafter was slow and halting. In the early part of the nineteenth century there were in the struggling new country very few men with the scholarly equipment and the leisure to produce good biography.[1] In Britain the situation was far different; Boswell produced his masterpiece in 1791. But Washington had no Boswell. Indeed, the work of his early biographers left so much to be desired that, since 1850, a host of writers have busied themselves in uncovering the "true" or "real" George Washington.

Formal biographies of Washington were written during the period under discussion by John Marshall, Jared Sparks, and Washington Irving. Contemporaneous with the work of each of these three were lighter and more popular biographies, including those by Mason Locke Weems, James K. Paulding, and Caroline Matilda Kirkland. In addition, a number of short sketches and character studies preceded the appearance of Marshall's work, and many others were written later. For the sake of convenience, biography of Washington is here considered in the following order: first, early sketches; second, Marshall, Weems, and their contemporaries; third, Sparks and his contemporaries; fourth, Irving and his contemporaries; and fifth, short sketches and biographical studies. A final section deals with the role of Washington in the biographies of some of his associates.

[1] See Edward H. O'Neill, *A History of American Biography, 1800–1935* (Philadelphia, 1935), pp. 18–20.

Biography

I

Sketches of Washington written before his death are notable for their rarity and, with a few exceptions, their inconsequentiality. In 1789 John Bell, Revolutionary soldier and statesman, wrote a letter to a friend in Europe in which he included a detailed biographical sketch of Washington that soon found its way into print.[2] Beginning with a paragraph on the General's family and childhood, Bell treats his adventures in the colonial wars and his life at Mount Vernon before 1775. Then he considers the question of Washington's military skill: "I think I may venture to pronounce that General Washington will be regarded by mankind as one of the greatest military ornaments of the present age, and that his name will command the veneration of the latest posterity." The penultimate paragraph is a thoughtful characterization which contains the following: "He has an excellent understanding without much quickness; is strictly just, vigilant, and generous . . . a total stranger to religious prejudices, which have so often excited Christians of one denomination to cut the throats of those of another . . ." In his conclusion Bell contrasts Washington with Moses, Camillus, Gustavus Adolphus, and several other great men, and he declares that the American hero, chosen by the Almighty, performed a greater work than any of them.

The Reverend Jedidiah Morse included in *The American Geog-*

[2]Reprinted in W. S. Baker, ed., *Early Sketches of George Washington* . . . (Philadelphia, 1894), pp. 65-80. Various printings and editions are listed in W. S. Baker, *Bibliotheca Washingtoniana; a Descriptive List of the Biographies and Biographical Sketches of George Washington* (Philadelphia, 1889).
Early Sketches is a useful compilation of fifteen essays, in full or extracted, written by American and British writers before 1800. Included (pp. 149-150) is a very brief item from a Philadelphia magazine of 1795 containing the epithet "father of his country." The term is at least as old as Rome; it (*pater patriae*) was applied to Cicero, and he applied it to Marius (Cicero, *In L. Calpurnium Pisonem Oratio*, 3, 6). A biography of Peter the Great of Russia was published in England in 1758 under the title *The Father of His Country;* see Donald A. Stauffer, *The Art of Biography in Eighteenth Century England* (Princeton, N.J., 1941), I, 328. Baker (*Bibliotheca Washingtoniana*, p. 6, note) says that the earliest known application of the phrase to Washington occurred in a Pennsylvania German almanac of 1779, in which he was hailed as *Des Landes Vater.*

88   *Biography*

raphy (1789) a footnote sketch of Washington which contains some particularly interesting and apparently authentic material on his daily life at Mount Vernon. Specific details of his planting activities are given, e.g.: "He has, this year, raised two hundred lambs, sowed twenty-seven bushels of flax seed, and planted more than seven hundred bushels of potatoes."[3] Morse's original sketch was expanded and went through many reprintings and revisions, but he continued to give due attention to Washington's private life and to stress the importance of the years before 1775. Many full-length biographies and innumerable essays and partial treatments which have since appeared are not so graphic and readable as Morse's original sketch, but his style in the later expansions is somewhat overburdened by the mass of facts included.

Thomas Condie made use of the sketches of Bell and Morse when he published "Memoirs of George Washington . . ." in five installments in a short-lived Philadelphia magazine which he edited in 1798.[4] This, the longest biographical treatment of Washington to appear before his death, is for the most part a compilation of certain of his own writings, including his journal of 1753–1754 and several of his addresses and letters. The "Memoirs" was published in book form with slight changes and additions in 1800.[5]

At least a score of biographical sketches of Washington appeared in the months following his death. Some of these were reprinted several times, many with additions and expansions.[6] The usual sketch published in 1800 is a chronological outline of outstanding events in Washington's life, followed by an undiscriminating eulogy. The preponderance of abstract terms and generalities reminds the reader of the funeral orations. Typical is the "Biographical Outline of

[3]Jedidiah Morse, *The American Geography* . . . (Elizabeth Town, N.J., 1789), pp. 127–132. For reprintings see Baker, *Bibliotheca Washingtoniana*.

[4]*Philadelphia Monthly Magazine; or, Universal Repository of Knowledge and Entertainment*, I (January, February, March, May, June, 1798), 15–20, 65–71, 121–127, 241–249, 297–308.

[5]Thomas Condie, *Biographical Memoirs of the Illustrious Gen. Geo. Washington* . . . (Philadelphia, 1800).

[6]See Baker, *Bibliotheca Washingtoniana*.

General George Washington" written by one J. M. Williams; here the departed hero is praised as a model for future generations of Americans on various grounds, including his physique, reserve, dignity, grace, personal attractiveness, urbanity, integrity, and inflexibility in administration.[7]

The productions mentioned and all other early biographical sketches of Washington are unimportant in comparison with a pamphlet by Mason Locke Weems, four editions of which appeared in 1800. The work of Weems is considered in the following section.

2

Judge Bushrod Washington, George Washington's literary executor, labored for a time in the year 1800 over his uncle's voluminous manuscripts in an effort to write a biography. How far Judge Washington proceeded before calling in assistance and why he chose Judge John Marshall to take over the work are matters for conjecture. Albert J. Beveridge has in his biography of Marshall a lively chapter on the woes of the Judge when confronted with the problem of turning out a life of Washington from a mass of manuscripts that now comprise a large portion of thirty-nine printed volumes. There is, therefore, no need for more than the outline of the story here. Marshall had never written a scholarly work—his formal education was slight—and he had little time for it, but he had been George Washington's friend, he was a friend and associate of Bushrod Washington, he was a Federalist, and he was in debt. He expected to turn off four or five quartos, four or five hundred pages each, in a year, and he estimated the reward of his labors at fifty thousand dollars. Although Judge Washington had found it advisable to relinquish the task himself, he seems to have shared Marshall's optimism. C. P. Wayne, a Philadelphia publisher, assured the men that their estimate of the number of subscribers was beyond reason, but he was sanguine to the point of making a contract, and

[7] In *Washington's Political Legacies* . . . (Boston, 1800).

in 1802 he began taking subscriptions. The tale thenceforward is one of mishaps and disappointments.[8]

Confused by the unwieldy mass of material, Marshall committed himself wholeheartedly to the theory that a great man must be shown against the background of his times. Accordingly, the first volume, which came out in 1804, is a detailed history of America from the days of John Cabot to about 1760; Washington comes on the scene only for a half dozen pages in connection with the fight at Little Meadows and Braddock's disaster. The second volume, published at the same time, begins with one page on Washington's life before 1755, retells the story of Braddock's fight, and covers the years before the Revolution in less than three chapters. Most of the volume treats the opening years of the Revolution. Volume III, which appeared some months later, is, like the first two, largely a rewriting of readily available secondary sources, but the style and treatment are better. Marshall had been careless in the preparation of his manuscript for the earlier volumes, and the result, in print, was a disappointment to him and brought much criticism upon him. It is evident that he took more pains with the remainder of his work. Volume III continues the story of the Revolution to 1779, and in describing Revolutionary problems and hardships and the battles in which he had himself taken part Marshall is at times graphic and interesting. The fourth volume, published about a year later still, is better proportioned than the first three, although it is a history of the Revolution rather than a life of Washington. It brings the story only to the close of the war.

Marshall had consumed more time and enormously more space than any of the three men involved in the work had bargained for, and he had now to cover the years from 1783 to 1799 in the one remaining volume. There were no handy secondary sources that he could use for these years, which he remembered clearly himself. Of necessity he used his own knowledge and grappled to some ex-

---

[8]Albert J. Beveridge, "Biographer," in Beveridge, *The Life of John Marshall*, 4 vols. (Boston, 1916-1919), III, 223-274. Marshall became Chief Justice of the Supreme Court in 1801.

tent—it would appear for the first time—with the Washington manuscripts. In 1807 he produced his final volume, over seven hundred pages in length. It is far better than the others, even though the author frequently leaves Washington completely in order to discourse on matters of law and politics and on the rise of political parties in the United States.[9]

Marshall's style is heavy and somewhat diffuse, but the proportions of his work are worse than the style. More space is devoted to the Revolutionary years than to the remaining sixty years of Washington's life, and there are extensive digressions throughout. Marshall originally intended to show his subject against his historical background, but in reality Washington is lost in that background for very long intervals. In fact, he never emerges as a distinct personality.[10]

Marshall's *Life* was disappointing to his immediate readers for the reasons mentioned and others as well. Federalists were disgruntled because the first three volumes contained nothing against the Republicans, and Republicans were angered because the last part of Volume IV and much of Volume V were indirect attacks upon them. The Chief Justice realized some of the shortcomings of his work and labored at the task of revision off and on for many years. Later editions, the first of which was published in 1832, were improved in style and slightly abridged, but the proportions remained the same.[11] Yet Marshall seems to have felt no particular dissatisfaction with his treatment of Washington himself. Apparently he did not consult with others who had known the man, and his use of the manuscripts was slight. On the whole, his biographical effort was not a success even by early American standards for life-writing.[12]

---

[9]John Marshall, *The Life of George Washington . . . Compiled under the Inspection of the Honourable Bushrod Washington, from Original Papers . . . to Which Is Prefixed, an Introduction Containing a Compendious View of the Colonies Planted by the English on the Continent of North America . . .* , 5 vols. (Philadelphia, 1804–1807).

[10]Cf. O'Neill, *op cit.*, pp. 158–162. For John Adams's comment: *supra*, Chapter I, Section 2.

[11]Beveridge, *op. cit.*, III, 272. Cf. O'Neill, *op. cit.*, p. 162.

[12]Michael Kraus says that despite all its faults Marshall's work, particularly the

Biography

No one was more displeased with the work of Marshall, Judge Washington, and Wayne than was Mason Locke Weems, the most successful of Wayne's agents in the sale of what he called "the Washingtoniad." In 1805 Weems wrote to Wayne protesting a change in format:

> I am sorry you are under such a mistake. I told W. [Judge Washington] & Genl. M. [Marshall] that you had printed a 2d Edit. on a paper so thin as to make the vol. look but half as thick as the former, and this is to be given to *new* sub^s. I said *then*, and I shall *forever say* that this is utterly wrong. Sub^s. will all think themselves entitled to books of the same excellent quality, and will as Genl. M. well observed, think themselves *cheated* if worse books be put upon them. . . .
> But vain it is for me to counsel; my counsel has ever been contemned. For six long months before the work was printed I begg'd and pray'd as if for *salvation*, that you w^d have but one style of ornamenting the books. You have 2, 3, or 4 . . .[13]

Weems found Marshall's ponderous and expensive work hard to sell in any of its styles of ornamentation, and his dissatisfaction with it was probably the most powerful inducement that led him gradually to expand a sketch which he himself had first put out in 1800. He had done some of his writing before Washington's death, as may be seen in a letter written to Mathew Carey, the Philadelphia publisher, in the summer of 1799:

> I have nearly ready for the press a piece christen^d, or to be christen^d, "The Beauties of Washington." Tis artfully drawn up, enliven^d with

---

first volume, filled a need—as history, rather than biography—of the day. See Kraus, *A History of American History* (New York, [1937]), p. 159.

TREATMENT OF THE PERIODS OF WASHINGTON'S LIFE IN MARSHALL'S
The Life of George Washington

Years	References (Volume, Chapter, and Page)	Number of Pages
1732–1752	II, (1)	1
1753–1759	I, 10 (356–358), 12 (368–371); II, 1, (4–71)	75
1760–1774	II, 2 and 3 (71–190)	120
1775–1783	II, 3 to 9 (191–560); III (568 pp.); IV (626 pp.)	1576
1784–1788	V, 1 and 2	152
1789–1796	V, 3 to 9 (153–725)	573
1797–1799	V, 9 (726–779)	54

[13]Norfolk, January 25, 1805, in Emily Ellsworth Ford Skeel, ed., *Mason Locke Weems, His Works and Ways*, 3 vols. (Norwood, Mass., 1929), II, 311.

anecdotes, and in my humble opinion, marvellously fitted, "*ad captandum—gustum populi Americani*!!!! ["] What say you to printing it for me and ordering a copper plate Frontispiece of that Heroe, something in this way. George Washington Esqr. The Guardian Angel of his Country "Go thy way old George. Die when thou wilt we shall never look upon thy like again" M. Carey inver. &^c

NB. The whole will make but four sheets and will sell like flax seed at quarter of a dollar. I cou'd make you a world of pence and popularity by it.[14]

Some biographers of Weems have assumed that his biography of Washington grew out of a funeral sermon, but the letter quoted and one or two others written a short while after Washington's death make the assumption highly improbable.[15] Weems was a clergyman before he was a bookseller, and it is not unlikely that he delivered one or more funeral orations on Washington, but it is clear that he had had a pamphlet in mind for some time. He was motivated in his writing both by a desire for profit and by a desire to promote good works. As he wrote to Carey: "It is in our power to make this thing profitable and beneficial— Everybody will read about Washington—and let us hold up his Virtues— Some, may go and do likewise."[16] In another letter to Carey he explained his plan: to give Washington's history "sufficiently minute," then to show that his rise was due to "his Great Virtues. 1 His Veneration for the Diety [sic], or Religious Principles. 2 His Patriotism. 3^d his Magninmity [sic]. 4 his Industry. 5 his Temperance and Sobriety. 6 his Justice, &^c &^c."[17]

Weems's original pamphlet, about eighty pages in length, went through nine printings in the course of six years, during which time its text was in a state of flux. The first extensive expansion resulted in the book of 1806, twice as large as any previous edition: *The*

---

[14] June 24, 1799, *ibid.*, II, 120; cf. II, 122, 127.

[15] W. A. Bryan, "The Genesis of Weems' 'Life of Washington,'" *Americana*, XXXVI, (April, 1942), 147–165. Cf. Lawrence C. Wroth, *Parson Weems; a Biographical and Critical Study* (Baltimore, 1911), p. 64; Harold Kellock, *Parson Weems of the Cherry Tree* . . . (New York and London, [1928]), p. 80.

[16] February 2, 1800, in Skeel, *op. cit.*, II, 126.

[17] "Jan. 12 or 13," 1800, *ibid.*, II, 176.

Life of George Washington, with Curious Anecdotes Equally Honourable to Himself and Exemplary to His Young Countrymen . . . This edition, called the fifth, is the first to contain the cherry-tree story. Weems made further additions and changes for new editions in the next two years. An edition of 1808 contains the final form of the Preface and the story that a Quaker named Potts found Washington praying aloud in the woods at Valley Forge. About that year, 1808, the text seems to have become static.[18]

Parson Weems had traveled extensively through what was then the United States, and he knew the temper and the reading taste of the public far better than Judge Marshall did. His work is short and readable. Moreover, he was politically in tune with his time. Instead of the aristocrat of Federalist sympathies to be seen in Marshall's tomes, Weems presents a Washington pleasing to the most Republican taste. That this was intentional is clear from a letter in which Weems announced his decision to dissociate himself from the sale of Marshall's book: "It is not half so moralizing & Republican as my own of which by the way I publish^d here this winter and have nearly sold off the whole impression 1500 copies (of a 5th edition improv^d. without frontispiece) at half a do^{llr}."[19] Another happy idea—from the standpoint of salability—was to present Washington's "private deeds" rather than to deal only with the public achievements that the orators, as well as Marshall, were currently extolling.[20] In this effort to show Washington's personal and private side Weems included the anecdotes of dubious origin which have brought such an avalanche of criticism upon him through the years that no further comment is necessary here. Lastly, Weems's por-

[18] For further details of editions and publications see Skeel, *op. cit.*, and Bryan, *op. cit.*
[19] To Mathew Carey, Savannah, May 24, 1807, in Skeel, *op. cit.*, II, 362.
[20] By the biographical theory expressed in his Preface, Weems shows himself to be, consciously or unconsciously, a follower of Dr. Johnson and his circle. He says: "In most of the elegant orations pronounced to his praise, you see nothing of Washington below *the clouds*—nothing of Washington the *dutiful son*—the affectionate brother—the cheerful schoolboy—the diligent surveyor—the neat draftsman—the laborious farmer—the widow's husband—the orphan's father—the poor man's friend. No! this is not the Washington you see; 'tis only Washington, the HERO, and the demigod."

trayal was in line with the religious and ethical code of the ordinary public that he wished to reach. He therefore produced what might be called the poor man's Washington, not the aristocrat's and definitely not the scholar's or the critic's.[21]

The proportions of Weems's *Life* are somewhat better than those of Marshall's, although it is difficult to compare the two on this basis. Marshall found nothing about the young Washington in his secondary sources and so said nothing of him. Weems "enlivened" his story with several anecdotes of his hero's boyhood. Some, like the cherry-tree story, are dramatic scenes in which two characters converse. The boy George, according to Weems, was indeed a model useful to educators and preachers, as is evidenced by the following passage, among others:

About five years after the death of his father, he quitted school for ever, leaving the boys in tears for his departure; for he had ever lived among them, in the spirit of a brother. He was never guilty of so brutish a practice as that of fighting himself; nor would he, when able to prevent it, allow them to fight one another. If he could not disarm their savage passions by his arguments, he would instantly go to the master and inform him of their barbarous intentions.[22]

Like much American prose of the day, Weems's narrative frequently sounds like a burlesque of the elevated style of Homer or Milton. A short selection from his account of the battles of Concord and Lexington may serve to illustrate:

The enemy fell back, appalled! The shouting farmers, swift closing on their rear, followed their steps with death, while the British, as fast as they could load, wheeling on their pursuers, returned the deadly platoons [*sic*]. Like some tremendous whirlwind, whose soaring sweep all at once darkens the day, riding the air in tempests; so, sudden and terrible, amidst clouds of dust, and smoke, and flames, the flight of Britain's warriors thundered along the road. But their flight was not in safety.

[21] Even in 1800 Weems's pamphlet was damned by critics as a "harmless oddity" and a "literary antick" unworthy to be connected with the name of a great man. See *Monthly Magazine and American Review*, III (September, 1800), 210.
[22] Mason Locke Weems, *A History of the Life and Death, Virtues & Exploits of General George Washington* (New York, 1927), p. 36. The story of the cherry tree is on pp. 23-25 of this edition.

Every step of their retreat was stained with the trickling crimson. Every hedge or fence by which they passed, took large toll of hostile carcasses.[23]

Despite all shortcomings now apparent, nineteenth-century readers liked Weems's book. While Marshall was laboriously correcting and revising his biography, Weems was disposing of his at a rapid rate. It has been by far the most popular book on Washington ever written, running to forty editions by the time of Weems's death in 1825 and to eighty by 1932. As has been pointed out, the Parson knew what people would wish to read and believe about their great national hero, and he gave them just that. In addition, the style of much of his writing is above the average of his day; he has verve and enthusiasm, and his genuine patriotism is in evidence throughout the book. The most serious charge against him, of course, concerns his prudish portrayal of Washington as a boy and youth. The boy of the cherry-tree story, the boy who ran to the teacher to prevent the other boys from fighting, may be somewhat like young Weems, who early felt he was called to the ministry; certainly he is not young Washington.

The Reverend Aaron Bancroft, father of the better-known historian, saw that Marshall's *Life* would be more appealing to the public if the strictly biographical portions were separated from the history and other extraneous matter. He set about to abridge the work according to this sound biographical principle; in his Preface he makes no claim to originality.[24] His book, a single volume, appeared in the same year as Marshall's final volume, 1807, and was reasonably popular for some twenty-five years. Bancroft's tone and style are as formal as Marshall's.

Another to produce a Washington biography in 1807 was Dr. David Ramsay, a physician and historian of South Carolina. Dr. Ramsay had included a character sketch of Washington in his *History of the American Revolution*, which was first published in

---

[23]*Ibid.*, p. 117.
[24]Aaron Bancroft, *The Life of George Washington* . . . , 2 vols. in one (Philadelphia, 1808). The first edition appeared in 1807 under the title *An Essay on the Life of George Washington* . . .

1789. Furthermore, in 1800 he had delivered a funeral eulogy that contained more biographical detail than most such orations.[25] His *Life,* which went through several editions, is based on the material in Marshall and in histories of the Revolution, including his own. It is, therefore, primarily a military and political account and offers nothing new in the treatment of Washington. Ramsay sticks close to his subject, and his style is easier and less formal than Marshall's and Bancroft's.[26]

A biography of Washington written for the American Sunday School Union by Anna C. Reed came out first in 1829 and went through several editions, including a few in French and German. Though obviously moral in purpose, the book is not unctuous in tone. Miss Reed drew her material from both Marshall and Weems. Her first chapter treats the years 1732–1762, the second through the eighth treat the years 1763–1781, and the last four chapters deal with the remaining eighteen years of Washington's life.[27]

Samuel G. Goodrich, who under the name of Peter Parley produced a famous series of school textbooks, held the copyright on a biography of Washington designed for school use and first published in the centennial year, 1832. Clear, informative, and moralistic, this little book contains at the bottom of the pages questions which the children reading it are supposed to be able to answer. The chapters are divided into numbered paragraphs. Though the tone is very serious, a number of anecdotes, mostly from Weems, are included. Twenty pages treat Washington before the Revolution, about a hundred and twenty are devoted to the war period, and thirty-two to the remainder of his life.[28] Better-proportioned biog-

---

[25]Baker, *Early Sketches,* pp. 129–133; *Character Portraits,* pp. 155 ff.
[26]David Ramsay, *The Life of George Washington* . . . (New York, 1807).
[27][Anna C. Reed], *The Life of George Washington* . . . (Philadelphia, [1832]).
[28][Samuel G. Goodrich], *The Life of George Washington, Illustrated by Tales, Sketches and Anecdotes* . . . (New York, [1832]). Goodrich at times denied authorship of this book, which went through several editions. See Baker, *Bibliotheca Washingtoniana,* p. 175.

An interesting literary curiosity of the period is *A Life of George Washington in Latin Prose* (New York, 1835) written for the use of students by an Ohio pedagogue named Francis Glass. Writing in the *Southern Literary Messenger,* Edgar Allan Poe at first considered this work a hoax, but he later defended its Latin

raphies were to appear only after Sparks's edition of some of Washington's own writings made more material available to writers.

3

The first scholar to undertake a biography of Washington was Jared Sparks, a trained historian who in 1823, at the age of thirty-four, had left the ministry to become editor of the *North American Review*. At about the same period he conceived the idea of an extensive history of the American Revolution along biographical lines. He planned to begin it with the life of Washington and an edition of his writings. Accordingly, Sparks spent five years visiting historical places and collecting material both in the United States and abroad. He likewise visited Judge Marshall and entered into correspondence with Judge Washington. In 1827 he secured an arrangement whereby, for half the eventual profits of his work, the judges gave him a free hand with the largest collection of the Washington manuscripts.[29] The first volume published was Volume II of *The Writings of George Washington . . . with a Life of the Author*. The *Life*, Volume I of the set, did not appear until 1837.[30]

Sparks, a New Englander, deserves much credit for his patient study of original sources; he was the first American biographer to use them extensively. Although the proportions of his one-volume biography of Washington are not so bad as those of the five-volume

---

against the attacks of other critics. For reviews see: *Southern Literary Messenger*, II, (December, 1835), 52–54; *North American Review*, XLIII (July, 1836), 28–52; XLIV (January, 1837), 270; *Knickerbocker*, VI (October, 1835), 366–367; VIII (October, 1836), 473–480. Baker (*Bibliotheca Washingtoniana*, pp. 215, 402) finds that there were at least two other biographies of Washington written in Latin.

[29] John Spencer Bassett, *The Middle Group of American Historians* (New York, 1917), pp. 73–80.

Sparks's edition and Worthington Chauncey Ford's edition (New York, 1889–1893) of Washington's writings together contain only about half of the material included in the thirty-nine volumes of the bicentennial edition (1931–1944); see John C. Fitzpatrick, *George Washington Himself . . .* (Indianapolis, [1933]), Introduction.

[30] George Washington, *The Writings . . .* , ed. Jared Sparks, 12 vols. (Boston, 1834–1837).

Sparks produced several other biographies in the meantime. See O'Neill, *op. cit.*, pp. 38–40.

work by Marshall, he devotes about half of the book to the war years and about a fourth each to the years preceding and the years following. Approximately 10 per cent of his book consists of quotations from Washington's letters and other writings. Such use of quotations is an aid to a sound biographical method, but Sparks's judgment in the selection of material seems to have been influenced by his preconception of Washington. His characterization combines the augustness of Marshall's portrait with a good measure of the priggishness of Weems's. The style is restrained, dignified, and clear, but seldom lively.[31]

Some fourteen years after Sparks had completed his edition of Washington's writings, a serious charge was brought against him. It was discovered that he and his assistant, Samuel Atkins Eliot, had altered the papers considerably. Several Americans criticized him, but the strongest attack was made by Lord Mahon, the English historian, in 1851. Sparks, then professor of history at Harvard, defended his editorial policies vigorously, but he admitted that he had corrected errors in diction and grammar, changed sentences, and omitted some passages in Washington's letters. His defense was that Washington himself had corrected and rewritten some of the letters before his death and that he, Sparks, had merely continued his work. In the fifties, the Sparks-Mahon controversy over proper editorial methods raged through books, periodicals, and pamphlets.[32] Some critics who approved the general editorial principles of Sparks found fault with his judgment in such matters as changing Washington's "but a flea-bite at present" to "totally inadequate to our demands at this time" and "Old Put" to "General Putnam." The controversy was to some extent an Anglo-American affair, but before it ended the issues were so confused and the lines so vaguely drawn that nearly every writer of the time had expressed an indi-

---

[31]Sparks published a separate book, *The Life of George Washington*, in 1839. It is substantially the same work as the first volume of *The Writings*.

[32]Bassett, *op. cit.*, pp. 100–110; O'Neill, *op. cit.*, pp. 39–40. A contemporary summary of the affair appears in Evert A. and George L. Duyckinck, *Cyclopaedia of American Literature* . . . , 2 vols. (New York, 1856), I, 180. See also J. G. Palfrey, "The History of England . . . by Lord Mahon . . . ," *North American Review*, LXXV (July, 1852), 125–208.

vidual opinion. The final result was an advance of scholarly opinion toward the theory that an editor should make no changes in works issued after the author's death.

In editing his writings as well as in writing his biography, Sparks was eager to show Washington as a perfect being in every way. His alterations were not confined to matters of diction. He changed phrases that seemed to him vulgar and he toned down or omitted uncomplimentary comments on the New England militia, as well as other passages exhibiting anger, impatience, or disgust. In short, Sparks wished to perpetuate the traditional Washington, symbol of the American nation.[33]

The availability of the *Writings* gave a new impetus to the study of Washington's career. James Kirke Paulding, the novelist, published a two-volume life of Washington in 1835.[34] Designed for the use of schools and dedicated to the "pious, retired, domestic Mothers" of America, the book has a pleasing style and is interesting reading, although at times Paulding points his moral too obviously for present-day taste. For instance, after telling the familiar story that as a boy Washington rode to death his mother's favorite colt, Paulding takes care to say that when they have done something injudicious, young people should be perfectly frank in admitting it, as Washington was, instead of increasing their difficulties by attempts at deception. On the other hand, the descriptions of such dramatic events as the Commander's rage at the retreat of General Charles Lee at Monmouth do justice to the material at Paulding's disposal. Slightly more than a fifth of the work deals with the prewar period, about three fifths treat the Revolution, and less than a fifth covers the subsequent years. Paulding's work was reprinted several times, although it never became so popular as Weems's. Reviewing it for the *Southern Literary Messenger*, Edgar Allan Poe

---

[33]Before the charge of bowdlerizing was raised, reviewers praised Sparks's work highly. The reviews often assumed the form of essays on the greatness of Washington. See Nathaniel Beverley Tucker, "Literary Notices," *Southern Literary Messenger*, I (June, 1835), 591–594; cf. *ibid.*, I, 533.

[34]James K. Paulding, *A Life of Washington* . . . , 2 vols. (New York, 1835).

wrote that nothing further on "the great theme of Washington" seemed necessary: "Mr. Paulding has completely and most beautifully filled the vacuum which the works of Marshall and Sparks have left open."[35]

The demand for popular treatments of Washington was sufficient to attract several less talented writers during this period, among them Horatio Hastings Weld, the Reverend E. C. M'Guire, and Charles W. Upham. In 1836 M'Guire brought out *The Religious Opinions and Character of Washington*, of which the Introduction and the first chapter are biography, bristling with dates. In his Preface M'Guire wrote that Washington had been treated as Commander-in-Chief and as President but that he wished to show him in another light. Material from Weems is included as well as Washington quotations from the Sparks edition; M'Guire's gloss upon them drips with moral sentiment.[36] Upham, a strong Whig, remembered today chiefly for his part in having Nathaniel Hawthorne removed from his post in the Salem Customs House. His contribution to Washingtonian literature is a two-volume biography consisting of selections from Washington's letters and Upham's comments upon them. The comments become briefer after the first ten chapters, so that the work is chiefly a collection of didactic quotations, many Federalist in sentiment, from Washington.[37] The tone of Horatio Hastings Weld's *Pictorial Life of George Washington* (Philadelphia, 1845) may be gauged from a sentence in the Preface: "The first word of infancy should be mother, the second father, the third WASHINGTON." The book seems to be a rapidly written amalgamation of Paulding, Weems, and other secondary sources, but it includes many quotations from Washington's letters. Weld concludes with a contrast between Washington and Bonaparte, which

---

[35]*Southern Literary Messenger*, II (May, 1836), 396–399. Cf. *Knickerbocker*, VI (October, 1835), 370; VII (April, 1836), 429–431.
[36]New York, 1836. Reviewed in the *Knickerbocker*, IX (January, 1837), 87–88.
[37]Charles W. Upham, *The Life of Washington in the Form of an Autobiography . . .*, 2 vols. (Boston, 1840). This edition was suppressed as an infringement on Sparks's copyright, but another was published in London in 1851.

he borrowed from Paulding, and with a description of Washington's tomb.

A former minister and semiprofessional writer named J. T. Headley published in 1847 a work entitled *Washington and His Generals*. Headley, whom Edgar Allan Poe called "the Autocrat of all the Quacks," had written a similar book about Napoleon and so had discovered that there was a good market for books featuring the romantic aspects of warfare. His *Washington* was a best-seller for about two decades.[38] An account of the life of the central figure is followed by sketches of the chief military men with whom he was associated, and the protagonist is necessarily considered again and again throughout the book. Headley's organization within the chapters is somewhat haphazard, but his style is lively and nervous at times, as in his account of Washington's bad night on the island with Christopher Gist in 1753. The sketch of Washington with which the book opens is extravagantly eulogistic. *The Illustrated Life of Washington*, by the same author, was published in serial form in *Graham's Magazine* a few years later. The *Life*, which also appeared in book form in several editions, contains long passages from the author's earlier work; about two thirds of it treats the Revolutionary period. Here too, anecdotes are intermingled with sweeping generalizations in a rambling manner.[39]

Rufus W. Griswold, assisted by E. D. Ingraham, William Gilmore Simms, and possibly others, wrote *Washington and the Generals of the American Revolution*, which was in outline much like Headley's work of similar title. A competent literary anthologist, Griswold was not here in his proper sphere; yet the work proved popular.[40] Some years later Griswold published a more important work, entitled *The Republican Court; or, American Society in the*

[38] J. T. Headley, *Washington and His Generals* . . . , 2 vols. (New York, 1847).
[39] J. T. Headley, *The Illustrated Life of Washington* . . . (Social Circle, Ga., 1859); first published in *Graham's Magazine*, Vols. XLIV–XLVI (February, 1854 through March, 1855).
[40] [Griswold], *Washington and the Generals of the American Revolution* . . . , 2 vols. (Philadelphia, 1847).
George Lippard's fictional work entitled *Washington and His Generals* also appeared in 1847.

Days of Washington.⁴¹ The outline of the book is based upon the activities of Washington during his presidency, but Griswold follows for a time any important figure who comes into the story, discussing his family, his wife, her family, and the social status and activities of each and all. Social life is the prime interest: balls, levees, celebrations, and weddings; but the author includes also much information on politics, presented from an anti-Republican standpoint. The whole is interspersed with many anecdotes and bits of conversation in which Washington frequently has a part. For the most part, fact cannot here be distinguished from tradition.

4

Washington Irving for many years planned to write a biography, which he hoped would be his masterpiece, of the great man for whom he was named. There is a story, authenticated by Irving himself, that his nurse accosted Washington on the street and obtained his blessing for the boy, then six years old.⁴² The pressure of other duties, as well as what he termed his awe of the project, caused him to turn down two publishers' offers made to him for a life of Washington in the eighteen-twenties, but he collected material and by 1829 had definite plans for that work. Yet the first volume appeared only in 1855, and the fifth and last in 1859, a few months before his death. Most of the actual composition was done during his last eleven years, when he was far from well.

The long interval between the conception and the execution of his biography enabled Irving to gather and evaluate a great many materials. In 1841 he wrote to his bookseller asking for

two or three works that have been published on the subject, such as Paulding's Life of Washington. Weems D°. Custis Memoir of Mrs Washington, published in the 1st vol of American Portrait Gallery—

---

⁴¹New York, 1854. The edition of 1864 contains the author's final additions and corrections.

Griswold began a biography of Washington but wrote only about two hundred pages before the illness which led to his death. See *infra*, Section 4.

⁴²Stanley T. Williams, *The Life of Washington Irving*, 2 vols. (New York and London, 1935), I, 10.

These and any other works relative to the matter (excepting Sparks & Marshall which I have) I would thank you to procure for me.[43]

In addition to these secondary sources Irving made excellent use of the Washington correspondence in the files of the State Department and other manuscript material that he found in sundry out-of-the-way places in the course of his travels. He also corresponded and talked with surviving contemporaries of Washington and so gleaned many interesting anecdotes not previously published. But his greatest indebtedness was to Sparks's edition of Washington's writings, an indebtedness which Sparks thought was inadequately acknowledged in Irving's Preface.[44]

The first edition of Irving's biography is in five volumes, each about five hundred pages in length. Like Marshall, he includes a great deal of historical background, but, unlike his predecessor, he manages to keep Washington in the foreground most of the time. His outline is also superior to Marshall's. The first volume ends with Washington's appointment as Commander-in-Chief; the second, third, and part of the fourth treat the war years; and the last volume deals with Washington's presidency and last years.[45] A notable feature of the first volume is the inclusion of a chapter on the Washington family in England; previous biographers have very little information on this subject.

His biography of Washington is not today considered Irving's masterpiece, but he was reasonably successful at the time in accomplishing the purpose he had in mind. He himself had the highest admiration for Washington, but he felt that the portrayals by Marshall, Weems, and Sparks were too pompous and grandiose. Irving set out to present a living man rather than a marble statue, and, as he wrote to Henry T. Tuckerman, he purposed to use simple language as one means to this end. He further wrote to Tuckerman that he was trying to arrange his facts "in the most lucid order and place

[43]To Messr's. Langleys, December 13, 1841, as quoted *ibid.*, II, 227.
[44]*Ibid.*, II, 227-229, 397.
[45]Washington Irving, *Life of George Washington*, 5 vols. (New York, 1855-1859).

them in the most favourable light; without exaggeration or embellishment; trusting to their own characteristic value for effect."[46] Irving's language does not seem especially simple to the present-day reader, but it is simple when compared with that of most previous biographers of Washington. The *Life* does not, however, have the charm that characterizes many of Irving's writings. In judging it, the reader must consider the wide difference between this subject and the romantic themes with which the author was most at his ease.

Irving's last work met with a most favorable reception at the time of its publication, although a few critics found small errors of fact and others noted that in the attempt to point up warm, human traits Irving is at times sentimental. Jared Sparks thought that his rival had used too much background material in the work and so had written a chronicle of events, ornamented with anecdotes, rather than a biography.[47] The validity of this criticism is still a matter of opinion; one present-day authority on biography says there is nothing in Irving's book that does not have sufficient connection with Washington's career to justify its inclusion.[48] In his effort to present a less austere version of the first President than had been given by predecessors, Irving was probably as successful as a man of his generation in America could be. Certainly his is the best biography of Washington written in the period under consideration. It was generally recognized as such for a generation; only after the publication of much new source material, especially Worthington Chauncey Ford's edition of Washington's writings (1889-1893), was it superseded.

Various phases of Washington's career attracted writers of lesser stature than Irving during the fifties. In 1856 Richard Rush, diplo-

---

[46] January 8, [1855?], as quoted in Williams, *op. cit.*, II, 230.

[47] *Ibid.*, II, 230. Williams (*ibid.*, II, 230-231, 397-398) gives a good account of the reception of Irving's biography, including newspaper and periodical reviews. Reviews not mentioned by Williams occur in: *Southern Literary Messenger*, XXIII (August, 1856), 160; XXX (January, 1860), 73-75; *Knickerbocker*, XLVI (July, 1855), 74; XLVII (March, 1856), 34; XLVIII (August, 1856), 189-191; LI (June, 1858), 633; *Littell's Living Age*, LIV (July 25, 1857), 250; LV (October 17, 1857), 177.

[48] O'Neill, *op. cit.*, pp. 164-166; cf. pp. 7-8. O'Neill finds this one of the best examples of historical biography done by an American.

mat and a son of the eminent Dr. Benjamin Rush of Revolutionary days, wrote and published synopses of a number of letters written by Washington while President. Rush called his book *Washington in Domestic Life*. The letters are concerned mainly with arrangements at Mount Vernon, matters involving Washington's slaves, and other details of private business, and there is little mention of national affairs. Sparks did not include these letters in his edition, and consequently Rush's synopses were a contribution to Washingtoniana at the time of their appearance.[49]

One of the most interesting of the biographical works on Washington to appear before the Civil War is Caroline Matilda Kirkland's *Memoirs of Washington*.[50] By 1857, women readers were a sizable and important group in America, and there had emerged a number of women authors. Mrs. Kirkland, novelist and one-time editor of a popular magazine, was regarded by Edgar Allan Poe as a talented writer and a woman of unusual wit and penetration.[51] In the Foreword of her Washington *Memoirs* she states a purpose much like that of Parson Weems, whom she praises and whose anecdotes she uses: she aims to portray Washington in private life and to reach younger readers particularly. She also acknowledges indebtedness to the work of Jared Sparks and to the reminiscences of George Washington Parke Custis, presently to be considered. Mrs. Kirkland devotes fifteen chapters to the Revolution and twenty-five to Washington's life before and after the war; of these twenty-five, twenty deal with the period before 1775. Her style and tone are informal.

[49]Richard Rush, *Washington in Domestic Life* . . . (Philadelphia, 1857). The letters were in the possession of Tobias Lear, Washington's secretary.
    John Pickell's *A New Chapter in the Early Life of Washington, in Connection with the Narrative History of the Potomac Company* (New York, 1856) is a collection of hackneyed incidents, but it has significance in being an early monograph stressing one phase of Washington's career.
[50]New York, 1857. Before publishing her work complete, Mrs. Kirkland used some of her material in magazine articles entitled "Early Days of Washington," *Putnam's Monthly Magazine*, III (January and February, 1854), 1, 121.
[51]"The Literati," in Poe, *Complete Works* . . . , ed. James A. Harrison, 17 vols. in 11 (New York, 1902), XV, 84–88. Mrs. Kirkland's *A New Home—Who'll Follow?* (1839) is one of the best early accounts of the Midwest.

Mrs. Kirkland's biographical method is somewhat like that of André Maurois in *Ariel* and *Disraeli*, although she is less skillful. Emphasizing Washington's youth, as the letters included in Sparks's edition enabled her to do, she makes good use of his early love affairs. A chapter on eighteenth-century literature, featuring Swift, Pope, Lady Mary Wortley Montagu, and others, she justifies by the fact that these were the popular authors in his formative years. She takes care to quote several of Washington's more playful letters written at various times of his life, as well as the now-famous contract made with a gardener, stipulating that in return for certain services Washington would supply him with necessaries, including daily grog, and in addition money at certain times, with which he was to get drunk on certain stipulated days.[52]

As her fiction shows, Mrs. Kirkland was less the sentimentalist and less the prude than most women writers of her time. Her chapters on the Washingtons' married life at Mount Vernon are extraordinarily realistic, and she includes a few anecdotes which do not appear in earlier biographies. For instance, a visitor said that he once overheard Mrs. Washington lecturing her husband after the household had retired, and that in a slight pause the General hastily replied, "Now, good sleep to you, my dear."[53] Mrs. Kirkland quotes from the family's orders for supplies from England and gives an amusing scene, suggested by the orders but with details from the writer's imagination, in which Washington misspells the names of various articles as Mrs. Washington dictates to him a list of things needed by the ladies and children of the household. In the author's words, "the impression left on the reader's mind is that of a rather gay and dressy family, visiting and seeing company in the best style of the day . . ."[54] The last chapter reflects the burning issue of the time when it was written; Mrs. Kirkland sets forth Washington's views on slavery and shows that he considered it an evil temporarily necessary but to be eradicated in time.

[52]Kirkland, *Memoirs of Washington*, pp. 206–207.
[53]*Ibid.*, p. 225.
[54]*Ibid.*, pp. 181–182.

An attempt at another informal presentation of America's first hero was made by the Reverend John N. Norton, of Kentucky, who dedicated his biographical study[55] to the proposition "that Washington as a man and a Christian should not be overshadowed by the military man." In the Preface he goes on to say that he has worked entirely with secondary sources; he mentions Marshall, Irving, Mrs. Kirkland, and Bishop William Meade, author of *Old Churches, Ministers, and Families of Virginia*. Norton does not seem entirely successful in breaking through the military tradition, for nearly as much of his text is devoted to the war years as to the remainder of Washington's life. His chapters on Washington's youth are not so good as Mrs. Kirkland's, partly because the preacher is very zealous in his attacks on the use of profanity. Norton gives several anecdotes of Washington's relations with churches and ministers, and a reader of his book would conclude that the hero was a conventional, faithful, and reverent, though not strait-laced, Episcopalian.

An important epitome of Washingtonian lore is *Recollections and Private Memoirs of Washington*, written by George Washington Parke Custis, Mrs. Washington's grandson and Washington's adopted son.[56] Published posthumously in 1860, the book is a collection of reminiscences and anecdotes which Custis had written for the *United States Gazette* and the *National Intelligencer* from time to time during the period 1826–1830. Many of the more important and interesting portions had already been incorporated in other books, such as Mrs. Kirkland's, before the *Recollections* appeared, but it made readily available a vast store of material relating to Washington, much of it not connected with the Revolution. Occasionally the author or Benson J. Lossing, who wrote the

[55]John N. Norton, *Life of General Washington* . . . (New York, 1860), published by the General Protestant Episcopal Sunday School Union and Church Book Society.

[56]George Washington Parke Custis, *Recollections and Private Memoirs of Washington* . . . with . . . *Illustrative and Explanatory Notes by Benson J. Lossing* . . . (New York, 1860). A less inclusive edition appeared in 1859. For reviews see *North American Review*, CI (July, 1860), 265; *Littell's Living Age*, LXV (June 30, 1860), 771; *London Athenaeum*, May 5, 1860; *Southern Literary Messenger*, XXX (March, 1860), 239.

footnotes, makes some definite claim to historicity. More often the tone is simply conversational, and the book is a pleasing confusion of what Custis saw, heard, remembered, and read.

Sundry works of Benson J. Lossing, popular illustrator and writer, treat Washington directly or indirectly. In addition to a three-volume biography and several short sketches[57] of Washington himself, Lossing wrote a sketch of Martha Washington, edited a portion of Washington's diary, and produced an illustrated book on Mount Vernon.[58] His *Life of Washington* was projected and begun by Rufus W. Griswold, who selected the designs and illustrations but had written only about two hundred pages before succumbing to an illness which proved fatal. Solicited by the publisher, who had already issued Griswold's chapters, Lossing continued the work somewhat reluctantly;[59] Irving's biography was also in process at the time. Lossing's book has been generally overlooked for this very reason. It is similar to Irving's in length and proportion, but in style and interpretation Irving's is of course markedly superior. A more important contribution to knowledge at the time of its appearance was *The Pictorial Field-Book of the Revolution*,[60] which contains over a thousand wood engravings. Lossing spent five years traveling to all scenes of any importance in Revolutionary history, collecting facts and legends and making sketches. His book in outline follows the course of his travels, and in text and footnotes it contains scores of items about Washington, for anything concerning him was considered pertinent. Lossing wrote for the magazines and did much to stimulate interest in American history. Especially, he made considerable progress in identifying sites which figured in Washington's early life.[61]

---

[57]*Infra*, note 67.

[58]Benson J. Lossing, *Martha Washington* (New York, 1861); *The Diary of George Washington, from 1789 to 1791* . . . , ed. Benson J. Lossing (New York, 1860); *Mount Vernon and Its Associations* . . . (New York, 1859).

[59]Benson J. Lossing, *Life of Washington; a Biography, Personal, Military, and Political*, 3 vols. (New York, [1860]), Preface.

[60]2 vols. (New York, 1851–1852). Numerous later editions appeared.

[61]Cf. Albert Bushnell Hart, "A Study of Washington Biography," *Publishers' Weekly*, CXIX (February 19, 1931), 820–822.

Biography

In 1860 Edward Everett, who had so many times addressed large audiences on the subject of Washington, prepared an article on him for the *Encyclopaedia Britannica*. In the Preface which he added when his work was published separately, Everett mentions indebtedness to Sparks and Irving, but the influence of the latter seems very slight in this biography.[62] The style is rhetorical and the tone somewhat pompous. But contemporary readers probably felt that the style was suited to the subject. One reviewer wrote:

> He [Everett] looks upon the being he endeavors to portray with a reverence which no ordinary man, however conspicuous in the records of fame, could inspire, and which no other mortal ever deserved . . . but which Washington ought to inspire in right-minded and intelligent men, and which he, and he alone, most assuredly deserves.[63]

At the opposite pole from Everett's dignified style is the work of Morrison Heady, a writer of verse and prose who was sometimes called "the blind bard of Kentucky." His juvenile life of Washington, entitled *The Farmer Boy, and How He Became Commander-in-Chief*, was first published in 1863 and was subsequently issued also in embossed print for the blind. The story is told with much circumstance and embroidery in the words of "Uncle Juvinell," and the comments and reactions of several children to whom he is supposedly talking are given. Heady retells Weems's stories and even improves upon them with details of his own invention; for example, a pickaninny is at first blamed for the cherry-tree tragedy, but little George by his manly confession saves him from a flogging.[64] Material from Irving is also included, and the book gives a fair picture of social life at Mount Vernon. In the course of some three hundred pages the author takes his hero only to the assumption of supreme command in the Revolution. Uncle Juvinell misses no opportunity to point a moral.

A book with a special appeal for a limited circle of readers,

---

[62]Edward Everett, *The Life of George Washington* (New York, 1860).

[63]Cornelius C. Felton, "The Life of George Washington . . . ," *North American Review*, XCI (October, 1860), 580–582.

[64][Morrison Heady], *The Farmer Boy and How He Became Commander-in-Chief*, by Uncle Juvinell . . . (Boston, 1864), pp. 42–45.

Biography

Washington and His Masonic Compeers, appeared in 1866. The plan is the same as that of Headley's *Washington and His Generals.* The sketch of Washington, comprising about half the book, is unusual in that over a hundred pages are devoted to the postwar period of his life, while the Revolution is treated in sixty pages and the prewar period in less than forty.[65] In attempting to bring out the first President's Masonic character, the author produced a grandiloquently phrased mixture of well-known information about Washington and data regarding Masonic lodges, celebrations, and ceremonies.

5

Editors of biographical dictionaries and similar compilations usually base their work on secondary sources, and sketches appearing in them are of interest here only for the emphasis given to different phases and periods of Washington's life. Sketches written within a decade after his death are notable for a preponderance of material on the Revolutionary years.[66] Later compilers of biography made some use of the writings edited by Sparks, but the tendency to pass lightly over Washington's career before the age of forty-three remained constant.[67] In the case of biographical dictionaries and cyclopedias intended for ready reference this emphasis is, of course, in accord with the nature of the works and the limited space available.

It must not be thought that short sketches of the period are devoid of rhetorical ornament. One in a volume entitled *The Sages*

[65]Sidney Hayden, *Washington and His Masonic Compeers* (New York, 1866).
[66]See William Allen, *An American Biographical and Historical Dictionary* . . . (Cambridge, Mass., 1809); James Jones Wilmer, *The American Nepos* . . . (2d Baltimore ed.; Baltimore, 1811); John Lempriere, *Universal Biography* (New York, 1810).
[67]See John Frost, *Lives of the Heroes of the American Revolution* . . . (Boston, 1848); Frost, *The Presidents of the United States from Washington to Pierce* . . . (Boston, 1855); Benson J. Lossing, *Our Countrymen* . . . (New York, 1855); Lossing, *The Lives of the Presidents* . . . (New York, 1847); Francis L. Hawks, ed., *Appleton's Cyclopedia of Biography* (New York, 1856); Evert A. Duyckinck, *National Portrait Gallery of Eminent Americans* . . . , 2 vols. (New York, [1862]); John S. C. Abbott, *Lives of the Presidents* . . . (Boston, 1867).

and Heroes of the American Revolution begins with a parallel between Moses and Washington and includes near the end mention of a Philadelphia mechanic's gift of a marble sarcophagus for the tomb of Washington. In a description of the Battle of Trenton the author says:

> Justice looked at the purple current as it flowed and sighed. Mercy carried the tragic news to the ethereal skies—and the eagle of LIBERTY heard the mournful story—descended in a stream of liquid fire—planted the torch of freedom in the serum of the murdered patriots and bid eternal defiance to the British Lion.[68]

The style of most sketches is more restrained than that of the selection quoted, but many include eulogies of Washington which rival the eloquence of the funeral orations.

Popular magazines published in America before 1865 (as well as subsequently) contain many articles that feature Washington and are more or less biographical in nature, e.g., "George Washington's First Interview with Mrs. Custis," "The Battle of Princeton and the Death of General Mercer," and H. F. Harrington's "Anecdotes of George Washington," all in *Godey's Lady's Book*.[69] The last named is the most readable of these three. It includes a playfully worded dinner invitation written by Washington in 1779, in which

---

[68] L. Carroll Judson, *The Sages and Heroes of the American Revolution* (Philadelphia, 1852), p. 371.

[69] XXXII (April, 1846), 145; XXXVI (May, 1848), 283; XXXVIII (December, 1849), 427.

Among similar articles are the following: "Washington's Agricultural Notes," *American Almanac*, 1830, p. 99; "Letter to General Washington," *Southern Literary Messenger*, III (May, 1837), 304–306; "Historic Landmarks in Lower Virginia," *ibid.*, XXXVIII (August, 1861), 115–126; "Letters from George Washington," *Knickerbocker*, X (October, 1837), 356–358; "Everett at Dorchester," *ibid.*, XLVI (August, 1855), 213; D.P.T., "Original Anecdotes of George Washington," *Democratic Review*, XIII (December, 1843), 624–626; "George Washington as a Merchant," *Merchant's Magazine*, XVI (March, 1847), 298; "George Washington," *Harper's New Monthly Magazine*, XII (February, 1856), 290–314; "Washington at Morristown, 1779–1780," *ibid.*, XVIII (February, 1859), 289; "Sixty-six Years Ago—Washington at Boston," *Putnam's Monthly*, VII (February, 1856), 113–114; "The Boston Ladies' Reception of George Washington," *ibid.*, IX (February, 1857), 154–168; "George Washington and His Family . . . ," *Eclectic Magazine*, LIX (June, 1863), 261; "Letters from Mount Vernon," *Land We Love* (Charlotte, N.C.), VI (December, 1868), 122–125.

he apologizes for the shortcomings of his camp cook,[70] and also a tale of Washington's having, because of the exigencies of war, slept under the same cover with a colored body servant named Primus.

Studies and scholarly investigations connected with Washington found their way into periodicals, especially in the eighteen-fifties and -sixties. The *Historical Magazine*, of Boston and New York, 1857–1875, was one of the leading vehicles for studies which were in many instances first read before learned societies. The articles in its pages discuss such matters as Washington's ancestry (documented from the thirteenth century), his legendary appointment as the Marshal of France, various details in his private life, the incidents involving Jumonville and André, Washington's interest in the West, and many military affairs.

Short biographical studies of Washington often take the form of character studies. That by Henry T. Tuckerman, essayist and literary critic, is in parts very penetrating. Tuckerman says that Washington's lack of brilliance was more than compensated for by the orderliness, system, and practicality which may be seen in his letters: "His mental features beam through his correspondence. . . . In Washington's letters . . . perspicuity and propriety, wisdom and kindliness, self-respect and remembrance of every personal obligation, are obvious."[71]

6

An indirect approach to Washington's reputation might be made through a study of works about his prominent associates. Such an investigation could be carried to great length, but even a sampling

---

[70] To Dr. John Cochran, August 16, 1779, in Washington, *Writings* . . . , ed. John C. Fitzpatrick, 39 vols. (Bicentennial edition; Washington, D.C., [1931–1944]), XVI, 116–117.

[71] Henry T. Tuckerman, *Biographical Essays* . . . (Boston, 1857). The essay on Washington appeared first as a review of Irving's biography: *North American Review*, LXXXIII (July, 1856), 1–29; later it formed a part of Tuckerman's *The Character and Portraits of Washington* (New York, 1859). A review of Tuckerman's study is in the *Southern Literary Messenger*, XXIII (December, 1856), 472–476. His method of portraying character in a short study is somewhat like that used more recently by Gamaliel Bradford in *Damaged Souls* (1923).

is enlightening. Biographers of other early American statesmen, when favorable to their subjects, frequently show that their protagonists thought well of Washington and were liked by him; and dissensions between Jefferson and Washington or Hamilton and Washington, for instance, are minimized in biographies favorable to their subjects. Writers treating Revolutionary officers likewise point out that their subjects and Washington stood always high in mutual esteem; any question of supposed or real shortcomings on the part of one of these men often resolves itself into the question whether or not Washington approved of him. On the other hand, writers unfavorable to some associate of Washington are careful to emphasize any disagreement between the two.

A volume published anonymously in 1809 under the title *Memoirs of the Honorable Thomas Jefferson* was intended as Federalist campaign propaganda; here Washington is a hero and Jefferson a hypocritical rascal.[72] This work continued the pamphlet wars of the seventeen-nineties;[73] Jefferson's letter to Mazzei, the attacks in Bache's *Aurora*, and other items critical of Washington are presented as evidence against Jefferson. B. L. Rayner's biography of Jefferson, written twenty-three years later, gives an entirely different view of the relationship of the two. Rayner has in a conspicuous place Jefferson's letter to Dr. Walter Jones on the subject of Washington's character, and he criticizes only lesser Federalists, such as David Humphreys.[74] The letter to Dr. Jones is also quoted in George Tucker's life of Jefferson (first edition, 1837) and in Henry Stephens Randall's classic biography. Tucker gives a short eulogy of Washington in mentioning his death, and Randall says that in the last years of his administration Washington was misled by bad counselors.[75] Samuel Mosheim Schmucker's *The Life and Times of*

---

[72][Stephen Cullen Carpenter], *Memoirs of the Honorable Thomas Jefferson* . . . ([New York], 1809).

[73]*Supra*, Chapter I, Section 2.

[74]B. L. Rayner, *Life of Thomas Jefferson* . . . (Boston, 1834), pp. 307, 388.

[75]George Tucker, *The Life of Thomas Jefferson* . . . , 2 vols. (London, 1839), II, 65, 364, 384; Randall, *The Life of Thomas Jefferson*, 3 vols. (New York, 1858), II, 374; III, 642.

Thomas Jefferson is unfavorable to the subject; included are appendices entitled "Jefferson's Strictures on Washington's Administration" and "Jefferson's Celebrated Letter to Mazzei."[76] From Schmucker one again learns that Jefferson was a subtle rascal, and the fact that he criticized Washington is part of the proof.

Alexander Hamilton's reputation was low in the time of the Virginia dynasty but began to rise again with the increase of sectionalism.[77] Earlier study of him was most actively carried on by his sons. Their writings encountered opposition because the public, at that time unfamiliar with the employment of ghost writers by public officials, was loath to believe that Hamilton had a large share in composing Washington's cherished Farewell Address.[78] Political descendants of the Republicans of 1795 naturally wanted to hear as little as possible of Hamilton, and political descendants of his own Federalist Party found it embarrassing to give him credit for writing a document made sacred by Washington's signature. But those who wrote favorably of him laid stress upon the close friendship that existed between him and Washington.[79]

David Humphreys produced in 1790 a Weemsian biography of General Israel Putnam, "Old Put," full of hairbreadth escapes and

[76] Philadelphia, 1857.

[77] Douglass Adair, "The Authorship of the Disputed Federalist Papers" (Part I), *William and Mary College Quarterly*, Series 3, I (April, 1944), 97–122.

[78] In the eighteen-twenties Madison, Jefferson, Jared Sparks, John Jay, James A. Hamilton, and others were corresponding about the matter behind the scenes. See James A. Hamilton, *Reminiscences* . . . (New York, 1869), pp. 44 ff. One of Jay's letters, published in 1833 (to Richard Peters, March 29, 1811, in William Jay, *The Life of John Jay* . . . , 2 vols. [New York, 1833], II, 336), presented a misleading account which practically omitted the work of Hamilton and Madison in drafting the message. In 1837 Sparks rather apologetically published the facts of the matter in an appendix to his biography of Washington. The public was slow to accept the truth, and as late as 1859 Horace Binney, a Philadelphia writer, published *An Inquiry into the Formation of Washington's Farewell Address*, running to over two hundred pages.

[79] John C. Hamilton, *The Life of Alexander Hamilton* . . . (New York, 1834); "The Life of Alexander Hamilton by His Son," *American Quarterly Review*, XV (June, 1834), 311–351; William Coleman, *A Collection of the Facts and Documents, relative to the Death of Major-General Alexander Hamilton* . . .([1804]; reprinted, Boston and New York, 1904); James A. Hamilton, *Reminiscences* . . . (New York, 1869); [Henry B. and James Renwick], *Lives of John Jay and Alexander Hamilton* (New York, 1845); "Alexander Hamilton, the Master of Political Sagacity," *Knickerbocker*, XXXII (July, 1848), 1–15.

marvelous adventures. The work ends with a letter to Putnam from Washington, warmly eulogistic in tone.[80] Occasional attempts to "debunk" Putnam all ran afoul of this letter. The question whether he did what he should not have done or did not do what he should have done often resolved itself in the question whether Washington thought well of him. Controversy over Putnam came into magazines from time to time over a long period.[81]

Jared Sparks eloquently expressed the general belief that Washington's opinion of a man was infallible, when he reviewed a book defending General Pulaski from the charge that he was asleep in a barn when he should have been in combat in the Battle of Germantown:

> It needs not to be inquired whether Pulaski was found in a farm house, or what he did, or whether he did anything, at the Battle of Germantown; it is enough to know, that Washington was acquainted with all his conduct there much better than any other person, and that he never lisped a whisper of censure for neglect of duty, but on the contrary aided his future promotion.[82]

Just as Washington's glory was shared by his political and military associates, a portion of it also shone on his wife and mother. Martha Dandridge Custis Washington does not figure largely in

---

[80]David Humphreys, "An Essay on the Life ... of Major-General Israel Putnam," in *The Miscellaneous Works* ... (New York, 1790), pp. 185-330. Humphreys later expanded this biography, and it went through several editions. He examined military records at Mount Vernon, but if he found any evidence that Washington was at times impatient or dissatisfied with Putnam, he ignored it. Cf. Leon Howard, *The Connecticut Wits* (Chicago, [1943]), pp. 244-245.

[81]"*An Account of the Battle of Bunker Hill. By H. Dearborn ... A Letter to Major General Dearborn ...* by Daniel Putnam, Esq.," *North American Review*, VII (July, 1818), 225-258; further discussion in *Knickerbocker*, XVIII (August, 1841), 91-106, 176-177; (October, 1841), 356-357; XIX (January, 1842), 92-93.

[82]Jared Sparks, "Pulaski Vindicated from an Unsupported Charge ...," *North American Review*, XX (April, 1825), 357-392; quotation, p. 392.

Among other biographies which bring out and emphasize the relationship that existed between their subjects and Washington are the following: W. A. Duer, *Life of Lord Stirling* (New York, 1847), pp. 166-167; Isaac Q. Leake, *Memoir of the Life and Times of General John Lamb* ... (Albany, N.Y., 1850), pp. 260 ff.; Friedrich Kapp, *Life of Frederick William von Steuben* (New York, 1859), pp. 110-113. Kapp's eulogy of Washington contains some unusual features, as he makes him a direct product of a movement that began with Martin Luther and finds him an outstanding example of the triumphant "Teutonic" type.

published writing before 1830. By that date women readers in America were numerous enough to make writers consider their special interests. Possibly the popular view of Martha Washington was derived largely from the reminiscences which her grandson, George Washington Parke Custis, published as newspaper articles between 1825 and 1830. Sparks, who used Custis's description, sums up his account of her in these words: "Affable and courteous, exemplary in her deportment, remarkable for her deeds of charity and piety, unostentatious and without vanity, she adorned by her domestic virtues the sphere of private life, and filled with dignity every situation in which she was placed."[83] Mrs. Washington's virtues, like those of her husband, are frequently extolled in abstract terms, and she too is presented as a model for the young. The tale of Washington's first meeting with his wife-to-be is repeated by several writers, but more emphasis is placed upon their reverent observance of the Sabbath.[84]

Vague descriptive eulogy and a few anecdotes of George Washington's mother, Mary Ball Washington, were probably based also on the work of G. W. P. Custis. His great-grandmother seems rather formidable in a passage which Custis quotes from a letter of an acquaintance: "Whoever has seen that awe-inspiring air and manner so characteristic in the Father of his Country, will remember the matron as she appeared when the presiding genius of her well-ordered household, commanding and being obeyed."[85] The letter continues with the much-repeated tale of Washington's riding to death his mother's favorite unbroken colt. Perhaps more popular with nineteenth-century readers was the story of her interview with Lafayette after Yorktown, when the whole world was resounding with her son's praises. Mrs. Washington was plainly

---

[83] Jared Sparks, *The Life of George Washington* . . . (Boston, 1839), p. 99. Cf. Custis, *op. cit.*, p. 119.

[84] Custis, *op. cit.*, pp. 499 ff., 508. Cf. Mrs. E. F. Ellet, *The Women of the American Revolution*, 2 vols. (5th ed.; New York, 1851), II, 9–29; Mrs. L. H. Sigourney, "The Lady of Mount Vernon," in *Myrtis, with Other Etchings and Sketchings* (New York, 1846), pp. 193–206; Irving, *op. cit.*, I, 275 ff.; Norton, *op. cit.*, pp. 103–104; Griswold, *The Republican Court, passim.*

[85] Custis, *op. cit.*, p. 131.

dressed, for working in the garden, and when Lafayette spoke enthusiastically of Washington's achievements, she merely said, "I am not surprised at what George has done, for he was always a very good boy." Her last meeting with her illustrious son, when he was on his way to be inaugurated as President, was another favorite scene.[86] Sometimes referred to as "Mary, the mother of Washington," she reached a pinnacle in an apotheosis penned by Rufus W. Griswold, who compares her and her son with the Virgin Mary and Jesus.[87]

Of the many biographers who undertook to write of Washington in the period 1800–1865, only a few names stand out. Two somewhat different conceptions stem from Marshall and Weems, but in the works of later writers the two are blended in varying proportions. Marshall, like the funeral orators, made Washington august and awesome; Weems made him a prig. If one were to read only the biographies written before 1855, he would think Washington a demigod who descended to earth (his character already fully developed and flawless even in childhood), freed his people from oppression, steered their government for a few years, and then returned to heaven.

The publication of Jared Sparks's edition of Washington's writings was a milestone in that it made much primary source material available to the public for the first time. With the use of this material Washington Irving produced the one outstanding biography of Washington written before 1889, when Henry Cabot Lodge's *George Washington* appeared. Irving intended to present a less

---

[86] *Ibid.*, p. 145.
[87] Griswold, *The Republican Court*, pp. 124–125. Cf. Ellet, *op. cit.*, I, 24–36; Sparks, *The Life of George Washington*, pp. 4 ff.; "Monument to the Mother of Washington," *Knickerbocker*, II (July, 1833), 72–73; "Washington's Text Book," *Historical Magazine*, X (February, 1866), 47; Mrs. Sigourney, "The Mother of Washington," *Southern Literary Messenger*, I (August, 1834), 6; other brief items in the *Southern Literary Messenger*, XIII (August, 1847), 506; XXI (September, 1855), 562–566; XXIII (July, 1856), 8; XXXIII (April, 1861), 321.

austere and less pompous version of Washington than had yet appeared in a scholarly biography, and he was in a measure successful. His work was acclaimed and its merit recognized by the well educated, but it failed to attain real popularity. Its great length was partly to blame. Then too, the general public of mid-nineteenth-century America was not interested in the truth concerning Washington, or even in that portion of the truth revealed by Irving. Washington was a cherished American tradition, and the people were much more interested in that tradition than in the man himself.[88]

Among the less pretentious efforts, that of Caroline Matilda Kirkland, although not free of the Weems influence, gives a remarkably informal, human conception of both George and Martha Washington. This short, unscholarly book, replete with anecdotes, might have been expected to have a large sale, but such was not the case. The inescapable fact is that the nineteenth-century public liked the Washington presented by Parson Weems better than any other. The average American read few books, and, as he found life a serious matter, he welcomed books that were morally instructive. Perhaps the secret of the Parson's success lay chiefly in his knowledge that his readers really liked to be preached to.

Beginning with Judge Marshall, most biographers of Washington concentrated heavily on his public life, i.e., his military and civil career. Much more material was available for the Revolution and the years of Washington's presidency than for the fifty years when he was neither Commander-in-Chief nor President. Still more important, Americans liked to read of Washington's life as it related to the founding of their country. The nation was still young, and patriotism, or national pride, was an important motif in its literature. Furthermore, warfare had a great romantic appeal. General Washington on his horse was an enormously popular figure, as is

---

[88]Cf. O'Neill, *op. cit.,* p. 166. O'Neill finds that later biographers made little use of Irving: "In spite of Irving's investigations and judgments, the genteel tradition persisted for at least forty years after Irving. I have found more than a dozen lives of Washington written between 1855 and 1895, and hardly one of them made any use of Irving's book."

attested by the reception of Headley's *Washington and His Generals* and Lossing's *Pictorial Field-Book*. Private-life anecdotes which showed how great and good he was were highly acceptable, as were biographical treatments emphasizing his religion, but the public was not curious about Washington's social milieu, pastimes, farming methods, and private business dealings.

On the whole, early biography does not present a much clearer picture of the actual man George Washington than does the oratory of the same period. Yet the works of Sparks and Irving are important beginnings of the scholarly investigation and critical interpretation which were to continue for at least a century.

CHAPTER V

VERSE

Much verse has been written about Washington, but very little poetry. Lincoln, whose elegist was Whitman, has fared somewhat better.[1] During the Revolutionary War many versifiers celebrated the Commander's deeds as they were being accomplished. His retirement to Mount Vernon at the conclusion of the war inspired still more verse, and his inauguration and triumphal tour through the country were highly stimulating subjects. A few writers treated Washington in metrical measures during his presidency and his last years, and many turned off odes and elegies on the occasion of his death and funeral. Versifiers neglected him somewhat while the Republicans were in the ascendancy, but the issues of 1812 called forth some poetical efforts, and others appeared in the succeeding decades.

Washingtonian verse presents the appearance of an unbroken flow, at times stronger than at others, but a few units may be singled out for separate consideration. Philip Freneau's contribution to metrical treatment of the hero is the most considerable made by any one writer, and a poor second is that of David Humphreys. The ballads of the war years, together with literary ballads written later, constitute a reasonably clear line of development, and the epic is another distinct type in which Washington figures to some extent. But the great bulk of verse treating or calling upon him is heterogeneous and can best be considered in the order of its appearance.

[1] Roy P. Basler, *The Lincoln Legend* (Boston and New York, 1935), pp. 267-272, *et passim*.

I

Philip Freneau was the object of Washington's anger in the seventeen-nineties; however, he aroused the President's ire not by his verse but by articles published in the *National Gazette*, which Freneau at that time edited. Sometimes called the poet of the American Revolution, Freneau was the most gifted of those who enthusiastically sang of the glorious struggle for freedom. Shortly after Washington took command at Boston in 1775, Freneau began to sound the strain which was to be recurrent in his verse for some forty-seven years. Seven couplets from "American Liberty, a Poem" are ornately eulogistic:

> See Washington New Albion's freedom owns,
> And moves to war with half Virginia's sons,
> Bold in the fight, whose actions might have aw'd
> A Roman Hero, or a Grecian God.
> He, he, as first his gallant troops shall lead,
> Undaunted man, a second Diomede;
> As when he fought at wild Ohio's flood,
> When savage thousands issu'd from the wood,
> When Braddock's fall disgrac'd the mighty day,
> And Death himself stood weeping o'er his prey,
> When doubting vict'ry chang'd from side to side,
> And Indian sod with Indian blood was dy'd,
> When the last charge repuls'd th'invenom'd foe,
> And lightnings lit them to the shades below.[2]

Several others of Freneau's poems written during the war years include praise of Washington. One of the longer passages occurs in "An Address to the Commander-in-Chief, Officers, and Soldiers of

[2] In Philip Freneau, *The Poems* . . . , ed. Fred Lewis Pattee, 3 vols. (Princeton, N.J., 1902–1907), I, 149.
The texts of Freneau's poems went through many changes, some noted by Pattee, some not. See Lewis Leary, *That Rascal Freneau, a Study in Literary Failure* ([New Brunswick, N.J., 1941]), *passim*. The form given in Pattee's edition is used in the present chapter when possible; he did not include all the poems extant. A good selection of Freneau's poems is *Poems of Freneau*, ed. Harry Hayden Clark (New York, [1929]). See also *The Last Poems of Philip Freneau*, ed. Lewis Leary (New Brunswick, N.J., 1945).

the American Army." After lauding the officers and soldiers, Freneau addresses their Commander:

> O Washington, who leadst this glorious train,
> Still may the fates thy valued life maintain.—
> Rome's boasted chiefs, who to their own disgrace,
> Proved the worst scourges of the human race,
>
> . . . . . .
>
> Return to nothing when compared to you;
> Throughout the world your growing fame has spread.
> In every country are your virtues read.

The succeeding lines contain details of Washington's virtues and a prophecy of his peaceful death and his reception into heaven.[3]

In 1783 Freneau celebrated the return of peace, the hero's valiant deeds in war, his greatness in retiring, and the eternal glory of his name, as did many other versifiers of the day. "Verses Occasioned by General Washington's Arrival in Philadelphia, on His Way to His Seat in Virginia" consists of seventeen stanzas, of which the thirteenth, containing an allusion to Cincinnatus, is representative of the effusions of the years 1783–1788:

> Now hurrying from the busy scene,
>   Where thy Potomack's water flow,
> May'st thou enjoy thy rural reign,
>   And every earthly blessing know;
>   Thus he who Rome's proud legions sway'd,
>   Return'd and sought his sylvan shade.[4]

Freneau treated Washington in two other pieces written during the period of retirement. Of these his "Lines Intended for Mr. Peale's

---

[3] In Pattee, *op. cit.*, II, 82. Other wartime poems mentioning Washington are also in Pattee: "To Lord Cornwallis," II, 86; "On the Fall of General Earl Cornwallis," II, 98; "Dialogue at Hyde Park Corner," II, 141; "General Gage's Soliloquy," I, 156; "Hugh Gaine's Life," II, 207.

[4] *Ibid.*, II, 228. Pattee prints the fifth line of the stanza quoted with a typographical error—*whom* for *who*—which Freneau tried hard to correct. See C. T. Hallenbeck, "A Note for Future Editors of Freneau's Poems," *American Literature*, IV (January, 1933), 391-393.

Exhibition," an irregular ode, is the more notable; one section describes a portrait of the hero.[5]

In lines "To the President of the United States" (1789), Freneau once more seized an occasion which appealed to a great many writers and allowed his spirits to soar. He found Washington's fame above all praise, at that time and forever, and concluded with the following stanza, the seventh:

> For in the annals of mankind,
> Who ever saw a compact bind,
> An Empire's utmost bound;
> Who ever saw ambition stand,
> Without the power to raise her hand,
> While *one* the people crown'd?[6]

During Washington's first administration, when the Federalist Party was being severely criticized in Freneau's *National Gazette*, the editor wrote of Washington in several of his verse compositions, and the sentiments expressed are little different from those in his earlier verse. In "The Rising Empire" (1790), "On the Demolition of Fort George" (1790), "Occasioned by the Debate of This Day" (March 29, 1792), and especially the ode entitled "God Save the Rights of Man" (1793), Freneau continued to eulogize Washington.[7] The last-named poem was unusual in that it called for cooperation with France and at the same time sang of Washington as the protector of freedom.

The possibility of war with France toward the end of the century evoked among others Freneau's pieces entitled "On the War Projected with the Republic of France" and "On a Proposed Negotiation with the French Republic . . . 1799." In both Washington

---

[5] Pattee, *op. cit.*, II, 248-249. See also "Rivington's Confession," *ibid.*, II, 232-233.

[6] I am indebted to Professor Lewis Leary for a transcript of this, from the *Daily Advertiser*, V, No. 1315, 2. There is no positive proof that it is Freneau's.

[7] The first two titles are in Pattee, *op. cit.*, III, 5-18 and 24-26; the other two are from the *National Gazette*, I, No. 44, 3 (March 29, 1792), and II, No. 63, p. 4 (June 5, 1793). I am indebted to Professor Lewis Leary for transcripts of the two uncollected poems. "God Save the Rights of Man," which was published in the *National Gazette* as "New Ode. To a popular tune," is quoted in part in Leary's *That Rascal Freneau*, p. 234; the poem is quite different in later forms and does not include mention of Washington.

is mentioned incidentally. The first contains a prediction of evil for Americans if they should fight France:

> Fortune no more your toils would crown;
> Your flag would fall before her frown;
> No gallant men the foe would dare,
> No Greene's, no Washington's appear . . .[8]

Washington's funeral and the ensuing period of mourning called forth a flood of verse as well as of oratory. In his "Stanzas to the Memory of General Washington . . ." Freneau envisioned the hero departing for a just reward after acting the part for which heaven had designed him; art and the gratitude of the people would show that in virtue he was far superior to the classical heroes:

> Those monarchs, proud of pillaged spoils,
>   With nations shackled in their train,
> Returning from their desperate toils
>   With trophies,—and their thousands slain;
>   In all they did no traits are known
>   Like those that honor'd Washington.[9]

The poet concluded with the idea that no one could supply the place left vacant. In "Stanzas upon the Same Subject," he considered how difficult would be the task of sculptors and painters who would try to portray Washington:

> Vain is the attempt by force of art
> To impress his image on the heart;
> It lives, it glows, in every breast,
> And tears of millions paint it best.[10]

Freneau justly and vigorously criticized the many stilted panegyrics and hackneyed appreciations of Washington which appeared in January, 1800:

> No tongue can tell, no pen describe
> The phrensy of a numerous-tribe,

[8] In Pattee, *op. cit.*, III, 141; see also *ibid.*, III, 227.
[9] *Ibid.*, III, 223
[10] *Ibid.*, III, 234.

> Who, by distemper'd fancy led,
> Insult the memory of the dead.
>
> . . . . . .
>
> Was, Washington, your conquering sword
> Condemn'd to such a base reward?
> Was trash, like that we now review,
> The tribute to your valor due?[11]

References to Washington occur in five of Freneau's poems written during the War of 1812: "The Volunteer's March," "On the British Invasion," "To America: on the English Depredations on the American Coast," "A Dialogue at Washington's Tomb," and "The Parade and Sham Fight."[12] The first two are spirited war songs. In the third and the fourth, which is somewhat longer, Freneau lamented the approach of British troops near the sacred ashes of the hero. "The Volunteer's March," which echoes Burns's "Scots Wha Hae," opens with the stirring lines:

> Ye, whom Washington has led,
> Ye, who in his footsteps tread,
> Ye, who death nor danger dread,
>   Haste to glorious victory.

Among poems of Freneau's last years are "Epitaph upon a Spanish Horse Called Royal Gift, Sent Over and Presented to General Washington by the King of Spain . . ." (1816) and "Stanzas Written on a Visit to a Field Called 'The Military Ground,' near Newburgh, in the State of New-York, Where the American Army Was Disbanded by General Washington, Almost Forty Years Ago."[13] The latter piece, written in the poet's seventy-first year, lacks the fire of some of his earlier compositions but contains the same motifs:

> Here walked the man, to live to distant times,
> Born, to a world its freedom to restore,

---

[11]"Stanzas Occasioned by Certain Absurd, Extravagant, and Even Blasphemous Panegyrics and Encomiums . . . ," *ibid.*, III, 235, 236.
[12]*Ibid.*, III, 337, 342, 302, 352–353, 371.
[13]*The Last Poems of Philip Freneau*, ed. Leary, pp. 15, 57.

> While 'midst a war of rancour and of crimes,
> Fell at his feet the shafts of foreign power;
> And *they*, who trod this verge of Hudson's stream
> Won all he wished, with duty, love, esteem.

Freneau is known today as a precursor of American romanticism rather than as the poet of the American Revolution, for patriotic poetry is now somewhat out of fashion. Yet from the aesthetic standpoint the verses quoted above are better than those of his numerous contemporaries who used the same themes. Freneau's sincerity and spirit are unquestionable despite his frequent use of eighteenth-century mannerisms. From first to last he sang of Washington as the heaven-sent leader of the great struggle for freedom. It must be remembered that he was himself a Revolutionary soldier. Recurrent motifs in his verse are the Commander's military greatness and his virtues, particularly his lack of personal ambition. The last-mentioned quality was extremely important to Freneau, an ardent Republican who feared monarchical tendencies in America and worked against them. By 1791 he felt that there was grave danger in the influence that Alexander Hamilton wielded over Washington during his presidency.[14] But in Freneau's verse Washington is ever the Commander-in-Chief who led his countrymen to freedom and sought no reward. In other words, he is a symbol of the American cause of 1776.

2

On leaving Yale to join the army, David Humphreys enthusiastically wrote in a poem addressed to a lady friend: "I go to WASHINGTON and glory."[15] Rising rapidly in the service, he became a lieu-

---

[14] See Leary, *That Rascal Freneau*, particularly Chapter VIII, "The National Gazette," pp. 193-246.
[15] "A Letter to a Young Lady in Boston . . . ," in David Humphreys, *The Miscellaneous Works* . . . (New York, 1804), p. 201.
There is evidence that Humphreys wrote a poem on the deeds of Washington and sent it to Colonel Samuel B. Webb, an aide, on July 8, 1776, but this piece

tenant colonel and one of the Commander's aides before the war was over, and he remained thereafter one of Washington's close friends. If Humphreys' talents had been greater, he might have written a great poem about his General, for he knew him more intimately than did any other versifier, and certainly his admiration was unbounded.

After Yorktown, Humphreys narrated the events of the war in an "Address to the Armies of America." Somewhat less prosaic than most of his couplets are five that include an allusion to the prophecy made by Samuel Davies many years earlier:

> Nor less our woes. Now darkness gather'd round;
> The thunder rumbled, and the tempest frown'd;
> When lo! to guide us thro' the storm of war,
> Beam'd the bright splendor of Virginia's star.
> O first of heroes, fav'rite of the skies,
> To what dread toils thy country bade thee rise!
> "Oh rais'd by heav'n to save th'invaded state!"
> (So spake the sage long since thy future fate)
> 'Twas thine to change the sweetest scenes of life
> For public cares—to guide th'embattled strife—[16]

In the conclusion of this long poem Humphreys dilated upon the happy days to come in America, the new Golden Age, a favorite topic with poets of the day.

In "A Poem on the Happiness of America . . ." (1786) Humphreys again envisioned a rosy future for his country. In this instance he was striving to increase her prestige with European nations, particularly Britain. The poem begins with didactic couplets paraphrasing Washington's farewell speech to the army:

> "Beware the feuds whence Civil war proceeds:
> Fly mean suspicions; spurn inglorious deeds . . ."

---

has not been preserved. See Leon Howard, *The Connecticut Wits* (Chicago, [1943]), pp. 114–115.

[16] In Humphreys, *op. cit.*, pp. 16–29. Lines 65–74 are quoted. Howard (*op. cit.*, pp. 120 ff.) discusses several revisions of this poem. For Davies's prophecy, see *supra*, Chapter III, Section 1.

Verse

Humphreys describes sentimentally the Commander's resignation and his triumphant homeward journey:

> Each eye was red, each face with tears bedew'd;
>
> . . . . . .
>
> The towns in raptures and the roads in flowers
> Wher'er he pass'd! What monarch ever knew
> Such acclamations, bursts of joy so true?[17]

But the treatment of Washington includes a new note; in addition to his heroism he was to be praised for his part in opening waterways toward the West.

"Mt. Vernon, an Ode," also written in 1786, was probably composed while Humphreys was a house guest at the site described.[18] *A Poem on Industry*, written after Washington became President, presents in several hundred lines a rose-tinged preview of the Industrial Revolution.[19] In both poems only incidental mentions of Washington occur.

In 1800 Humphreys wrote a sonnet, "On Receiving the News of the Death of General Washington . . . ," and a long composition entitled "A Poem on the Death of General Washington . . ."[20] In an introductory note on the latter, the writer propounded the theory that contemporary epic poets devoted too little space to the details of battles, and he thereby justified his allocation of about one

---

[17] In Humphreys, *The Miscellaneous Works* . . . (New York, 1790), pp. 32–36. Lines 33–34, 76, and 98–100 are quoted. Howard (*op. cit.*, pp. 125–131) gives a full discussion.

[18] Humphreys, *Miscellaneous Works* (1790), pp. 116–118.

[19] *A Poem on Industry* . . . (Philadelphia, 1794). There are also two couplets in praise of Washington in "A Poem on the Love of Country" (in Humphreys, *Miscellaneous Works*, 1804, p. 142) written for the Fourth of July, 1799.

[20] In *Miscellaneous Works* (1804), pp. 238 and 149–187.

At least two other sonnets on Washington were written before 1865. A "Sonnet to Washington," by an Englishman named Dr. Aikin, appeared in the *Gazette of the United States* for November 12, 1791, and was reprinted in the *Massachusetts Magazine*, IV (June, 1792), 393 and also in the *Historical Magazine*, III (September, 1859), 277. A sonnet entitled "General Washington's Wine Glass" was published in the *Knickerbocker*, XXVI (September, 1845), 231, over the signature "J. H. H., Bayou Goula, La."

fourth of his composition to the Battle of Monmouth. Despite the battle description of over two hundred lines, the poem is biographical in outline and is essentially a funeral sermon in couplets, a type of which several others were produced at the same time.[21] Humphreys, then minister to Spain, recited this ambitious work at the American Legation in Madrid on July 4, 1800. The following lines occur in connection with Washington's policy of neutrality during his presidency:

> The tricks of state his soul indignant scorn'd,
> Thence candid policy his sway adorn'd:
> Faith, honour, justice, honesty his aim,
> And truth and Washington were but one name.[22]

From his lines on Washington as well as from his other verse it is evident that Humphreys regarded poetry as a highly formal exercise. One who read only his verse would not suspect that he was better acquainted with the great man than were others who sang of his glory in 1800 and earlier.

3

Revolutionary War ballads are more interesting than the effusions of Humphreys. One of the best known is "The Yankee's Return from Camp," or "Yankee Doodle." The tune to which this was—and is—sung seems to have originated with the Cavaliers of seventeenth-century England,[23] and there were almost infinite variations in wording both before and after 1775. But several stanzas about "Yankee Doodle" were popular in the American colonies by that date.[24] Among the stanzas written in 1775 or 1776 by Edward

---

[21] *Infra*, Section 6.
[22] Lines 597–600.
[23] "Yankee Doodle" is discussed in several short articles in the *Historical Magazine*, I (January, 1857), 22; I (March, 1857), 86, 93, *et passim*.
[24] Percy H. Boynton, "Patriotic Songs and Hymns," in *The Cambridge History of American Literature*, 4 vols. (New York, 1917–1921), IV, 493.

Bangs, a Harvard student, are two which treat Washington with delightful informality:

> And there was Captain Washington
> And gentlefolks about him,
> They say he's grown so tarnal proud
> He will not ride without 'em.
>
> He got him on his meeting clothes,
> Upon a strapping stallion,
> He set the world along in rows,
> In hundreds and in millions.[25]

Similar in rhythm is a Tory ballad which was composed somewhat later and entitled "The Trip to Cambridge":

> When Congress sent great Washington
> All clothed in power and breeches,
> To meet old Britain's warlike sons,
> And make some rebel speeches;
>
> 'Twas then he took his gloomy way
> Astride his dapple donkeys,
> And travelled well, both night and day
> Until he reach'd the Yankees.

Seven further quatrains include such details as Washington's having a sergeant brush his wig about three miles from camp and old Mother Hancock's running out with a pan of butter and expatiating upon the calving of her brindled cow.[26]

In the second year of the war a New England ballad, entitled "A Poem Containing Some Remarks on the Present War," cele-

---

[25] In Burton Egbert Stevenson, ed., *Poems of American History* (Boston and New York, [1922]), pp. 159–160. A variant wording is given by Evert A. and George L. Duyckinck, *Cyclopaedia of American Literature* . . . , 2 vols. (New York, 1856), I, 464.

[26] In Stevenson, *op. cit.*, p. 169. Authors of the ballads treated in the present section are given if they are known.

brated the British evacuation of Boston. Washington is treated with charming simplicity, especially in the stanza:

> Brave Washington did come
> To our relief:
> He left his native home,
> Filled with grief.
> He did not covet gain,
> The cause he would maintain
> And die among the slain
> Rather than flee.[27]

A more famous Revolutionary ballad is "War and Washington," by Jonathan Mitchell Sewall; each of the twelve stanzas ends with the name of Washington. The ballad opens:

> Vain Britons, boast no longer, with proud indignity
> By land your conquering legions, your matchless strength at sea,
> Since we, your braver sons incensed, our swords have girded on,
> Huzza, huzza, huzza, huzza, for War and Washington.[28]

Tories expressed their sentiments at this time in "The Congress. A Song. Wrote in the Spring of the Year 1776," which rambles through twenty-two stanzas, all ending with the word "Congress." The tenth stanza runs:

> There's Washington and all his men—
> Where Howe had one, the goose had ten—
> March'd up the hill, and down again;
> And sent returns to Congress.[29]

[27]In Duyckinck, *op. cit.*, I, 443–445; Stevenson, *op. cit.*, pp. 173–174. Washington's name occurs in "A Song," published in the *Connecticut Gazette* in 1776, and also in "A Ballad" sung "To the tune of 'Smile Britannia'" and published in the *Freeman's Journal or New Hampshire Gazette*, October 22, 1776. For the former see Stevenson, *op. cit.*, p. 172; the latter is given in Frank Moore, ed., *Songs and Ballads of the American Revolution* (New York, 1856), p. 147, and in part by Duyckinck, *op. cit.*, I, 447.

[28]In Stevenson, *op. cit.*, p. 170; George Cary Eggleston, ed., *American War Ballads and Lyrics* . . . , 2 vols. in one (New York and London, [1889]), I, 53–56.

[29]In Winthrop Sargent, ed., *The Loyalist Poetry of the Revolution* (Philadelphia, 1857), pp. 70–75.

In 1777 "General Howe's Letter," a feeble satire on the British, appeared,[30] as did a stronger piece in the same vein by Francis Hopkinson, entitled "Political Ballad, Written in the Year 1777." Hopkinson characterized Washington as a "god-like hero" on the border line between the human and the divine.[31]

The news of Burgoyne's fate inspired "Saratoga Song," "The Gamester," and Wheeler Case's "The Fall of Burgoyne," all of which bring in Washington incidentally.[32] In "The Gamester," which is somewhat labored, the story of Burgoyne is told after the analogy of a card game. The composer of "Saratoga Song" put Benedict Arnold in a company from which he was later estranged:

> Now here's a health to Arnold,
> And our commander Gates,
> To Lincoln and to Washington,
> Whom every Tory hates.

Between the fall of Saratoga and the surrender of Yorktown, Samuel St. John's "American Taxation," or "Taxation of America," reached its final form.[33] The last words of each of some forty stanzas

---

[30] In Stevenson, *op. cit.*, pp. 205-206.

[31] Pp. 164-168 of "Poems on Several Subjects," included with separate paging in the back of the third volume of Francis Hopkinson, *The Miscellaneous Essays* . . . , 3 vols. (Philadelphia, 1792).
"The Battle of Trenton," which was characterized by General Winfield Scott as "a noble ballad," treats the entire army from the point of view of a soldier; Washington is mentioned only incidentally. See Stevenson, *op. cit.*, p. 188; Eggleston, *op. cit.*, I, 46; Rufus W. Griswold, *Curiosities of American Literature* (Philadelphia, 1843; bound with Isaac Disraeli's *Curiosities of Literature*), p. 31. General Scott quoted this ballad in a speech; see William Hincks and F. H. Smyth, *Washington's Birthday; Congressional Banquet* . . . (Washington, D.C., 1852), p. 14.
"Trenton and Princeton" (1777) consists of a dozen ballad stanzas and ends with a toast to Washington, Gates, and Putnam. See Stevenson, *op. cit.*, pp. 188-189.

[32] "Saratoga Song" is in Stevenson, *op. cit.*, pp. 202-204, and, under the title "The North Campaign," in Griswold, *op. cit.*, p. 32. "The Fall of Burgoyne" is in Wheeler Case, *Revolutionary Memorials* . . . , ed. Stephen Dodd (New York, 1852), p. 33. "The Gamester" is in Moore, *op. cit.*, pp. 191-195.

[33] In Moore, *op. cit.*, p. 1, and, with slightly different wording, in Duyckinck, *op. cit.*, I, 461-463.
Among other ballads which appeared in this interval are "A Poem on Washington Dated in 1779," "The Old Man's Song," and Major André's "The Cow-Chace." The first, which is more literary than most ballads of the time, is quoted in Duyckinck, *op. cit.*, I, 457, from the *New Hampshire Gazette*, October 12, 1779; the second, a tribute to the patriotic women of 1778, is in Moore, *op. cit.*, pp. 205-206; and André's famous mock-heroic is in Stevenson, *op. cit.*, pp. 233-236.

are "North America." The action herein contained begins a decade or so before the outbreak of hostilities and continues through Saratoga; from internal evidence the ballad seems to have grown as the years passed. The name of Washington is mentioned several times, usually with praise, as in the twenty-seventh stanza:

> We have a bold commander,
>   Who fears not sword or gun,
> The second Alexander,
>   His name is Washington.
> His men are all collected,
>   And eager for the fray,
> To fight they are directed
>   For North America.

The surrender of Cornwallis was celebrated in numerous ballads. One, in which the names of Burgoyne and the Compte de Grasse are simplified to "Bugwine" and "Countergrass," contains a striking narration of Cornwallis's movements when surrounded at Yorktown:

> He looked to the East, he saw Washington advance,
> He looked to the West, he espied the flag of France;
> Beside he saw bold Countergrass come floating down the bay,
> The fellow he arose trembling but could not get away.[34]

Washington has a more prominent role in a ballad called "Cornwallis's Surrender," or "Cornwallis Burgoyned," which includes the triumphant decree:

> Be peace, the glorious end of war,
>   By this event effected;
> And be the name of Washington
>   To latest times respected . . .[35]

One of the cleverest of the Revolutionary ballads is "The Dance," in which the movements of Greene and Cornwallis before York-

---

[34]Published for the first time by Mary W. Smyth, "Contemporary Songs and Verses about Washington," *New England Quarterly*, V (April, 1932), 281–292.

[35]In Stevenson, *op. cit.*, pp. 256–257; Moore, *op. cit.*, p. 367. The stanzas are of eight lines, *abcbdede*.

town are described as if they were parts of a country dance. The only passage on Washington is brief but unusual and effective:

> And Washington, Columbia's son,
>   Whom easy nature taught, sir
> That grace which can't by pains be won,
>   Or Plutus's gold be bought, sir.[36]

In ballads of later years Washington's name sometimes appears with a word or two of praise, as in "The 'Constellation' and the 'Insurgente' " (1813), which concerns the capture of a French vessel by an American vessel on February 9, 1799. The ballad concludes with the lines:

> Then to St. Kitt's we steered, we bro't her safe in port,
> The grand salute was fired and answered from the fort,
>   John Adams in full bumpers toast,
>   George Washington, Columbia's boast,
>   And now "The girl we love the most!"
>   My brave Yankee boys.[37]

"Passaic: a Group of Poems Touching That River" (1826) includes a narrative called "The Retreat of Seventy-six," wherein Washington is seen addressing his troops before the attack on Trenton.[38] The treatment lacks spontaneity, as does that in eight quatrains, untitled and anonymous, devoted to Washington's mission to Fort Le Boeuf at the age of twenty-one.[39]

Literary ballads in patriotic strain appeared in increasing numbers in the fifties. "Washington's First Battle; or, Braddock's Defeat"

---

[36] In Stevenson, *op. cit.*, p. 256. See also "The Surrender of Cornwallis," *ibid.*, p. 257, and "A Song, the Soldier at Home," in Moore, *op. cit.*, p. 347.

[37] In Eggleston, *op. cit.*, I, 110–112.

Possibly composed in the early years of the nineteenth century was a "Revolutionary War Song," containing praise of Washington, which appears in *Folk Songs of Florida*, ed. Alton C. Morris (Gainesville, Fla., 1950), pp. 22–23. The song was recorded from the singing of Miss Elsie Surber, of Panama City.

Washington is mentioned in "Noble Lads of Canada" (1812 ?), a ballad reprinted in George Stuyvesant Jackson, ed., *Early Songs of Uncle Sam* . . . (Boston, 1933), p. 92.

[38] *Knickerbocker*, XVI (October, 1840), 335–338.

[39] In John F. Watson, *Annals of Philadelphia and Pennsylvania, in the Olden Time* . . . , 2 vols. (Philadelphia, 1855; first published in 1843), II, 129.

(1851), by William Starbuck Mayo, consists of sixty eight-line stanzas. The narrative is told in the words of an aged survivor of the disaster, and much prominence is given to Washington's miraculous escape and the belief of the Indians that he bore a charmed life thereafter:

> Six times a chief his rifle points
> Against his manly breast,
> With careful and delib'rate sight
> And firm and steady rest.
> Six times at that same noble mark
> His braves aim fair and nigh—
> Six times the hissing volleys pass
> The hero harmless by.[40]

"The Lament of Washington" portrays the hero as a venerable sire shedding a tear over the fate of Lafayette, then in prison.[41] George Henry Calvert's "Washington" (1858) describes Mount Vernon and the surrounding region and tells of a British sea captain who refused to destroy that shrine in 1812.[42] "Fort Duquesne" (1858), by Florus B. Plimpton, an Ohio journalist, has more verve than most of the literary ballads. A couplet may serve to illustrate:

> And calm and tall above them all, i' the red November sun,
> Like Saul above his brethren, rode Colonel Washington.[43]

4

For several decades after the Revolution a few young men of literary aspirations felt that the events they had witnessed, or of which they had heard firsthand accounts, could be suitably treated in epic

[40] In William Starbuck Mayo, *Romance Dust from the Historic Placer* (New York, 1851), p. 72. The work was republished in 1855 as *Flood and Field*.

[41] In Rufus W. Griswold, *The Republican Court* . . . (New York, 1854), p. 395. The poem is attributed to a Mr. Bradford, who is said to have witnessed the scene described.

[42] In George Henry Calvert, *A Nation's Birth and Other National Poems* (Boston, 1876).

[43] In Stevenson, *op. cit.*, p. 119.
A rambling piece called "Patriotic Hymn" (*Knickerbocker*, XLV [February, 1855], 148–149) treats various scenes and events in the course of eighteen stanzas, the tenth of which is a tribute to Washington.

verse. Their college training was in the classical tradition, and their material—a great war and the founding of a new nation—was somewhat similar to that of Homer and Virgil. There was no dampening suspicion that the epic was already an obsolete literary genre. In 1785 John Adams wrote to congratulate his young friend Trumbull upon the merit of the mock-heroic *M'Fingal*. Adams believed Trumbull capable of weightier literary composition, and he remarked that it was his hope "to live to see our young America in possession of an Heroick Poem, equal to those the most esteemed in any country."[44]

When Timothy Dwight published *The Conquest of Canaan* in 1785,[45] an English critic reviewed it unfavorably and stated that its only interest would be for Americans who saw in it an allegory of the Revolutionary War, with Joshua representing Washington.[46] In a letter to Noah Webster, Dwight denied that he had intended any such allegory; he declared that the epic was practically complete before the Revolution and that any resemblances between Joshua and Washington were such as might exist between any two great men.[47] As recently as 1926 a historian of American literature spoke of the analogy of the American Revolution in *The Conquest of Canaan* as "sufficiently obvious."[48] He was in turn contradicted by a biographer of Dwight, who maintains that the poem was complete by 1775 except for slight revisions.[49] The case for the allegory

[44]Adams to John Trumbull, Antenil, April 28, 1785, "Stray Leaves from an Autograph Collection," *Historical Magazine*, IV (July, 1860), 193–203; quotation, p. 195.
[45]Timothy Dwight, *The Conquest of Canaan, a Poem in Eleven Books* . . . (Hartford, Conn., 1785; reprinted, London, 1788).
Washington is by implication the villain of a French epic in four books, *Jumonville* (1759), by a Monsieur Thomas, member of the French Academy. Washington's name is not mentioned, perhaps because it does not fit easily into the French meter. See "The 'Jumonville' of Thomas and Washington," *Historical Magazine*, VI (July, 1862), 201–203. Here the poem, not seen by the present writer, is paraphrased and quoted at length.
[46]*European Magazine and London Review*, XIII (February, 1788), 81–84; XIII (March, 1788), 175–178; XIII (April, 1788), 266–271.
[47]June 6, 1788. See Theodore A. Zunder, "Noah Webster and *The Conquest of Canaan*," *American Literature*, I (May, 1929), 200–202.
[48]Vernon L. Parrington, ed., *The Connecticut Wits* (New York, [1926]), p. 154.
[49]Charles E. Cuningham, *Timothy Dwight* . . . (New York, 1942), pp. 74, 130, 397–398, *et passim*.

may be weakened by too short an excerpt, but some of Dwight's lines on Joshua strikingly resemble many of those written about Washington:

> By nature fashion'd millions to controul
> In peace, in war, the great all-moving soul,
>
> . . . . . .
>
> Patient, serene, as ills and injuries tried,
> Meek without meanness, noble without pride,
> Frank yet impovious [sic], manly yet refined,
> As the sun watchful, and as angels kind.[50]

By 1785 Americans felt that such phrases exactly suited Washington,[51] for he was foremost of "wisest heads and noblest hearts" to inspire "epic rage."

The American hero comes in for bits of eulogy in several mock-heroic or Hudibrastic epics, beginning with John Trumbull's *M'Fingal*,[52] but Joel Barlow's *The Vision of Columbus* (1787) contains the first clear-cut treatment of Washington in heroic verse.[53] Singing enthusiastically of America's past and future, young Barlow introduced Washington in Book V, in connection with Braddock's fight:

> Brave Washington, in that young martial frame,
> From yon lost field begins a life of fame,

[50]Dwight, *op. cit.*, Book VI, lines 19-20, 25-28. Dwight dedicated his epic to Washington.

[51]Cf. Howard, *op. cit.*, p. 90; Nathaniel Wright Stephenson and Waldo Hilary Dunn, *George Washington*, 2 vols. (New York and London, 1940), II, 61-62.

[52]In John Trumbull, *The Poetical Works* . . . , 2 vols. (Hartford, Conn., 1820), II, 162. See also Joel Barlow and David Humphreys, *The Anarchiad*, ed. Luther G. Riggs (New Haven, Conn., 1861), p. 23 *et passim;* "The Cornwalliad," *United States Magazine*, I (February through October, 1779), 63, 133, 181, etc.; Samuel Knox, "A Dream," *Maryland Gazette*, October 10, 1786; Hugh Henry Brackenridge, untitled verses, *Pittsburgh Gazette*, November 3 and 10, 1787; "Satannical Instructions," *Massachusetts Centinel*, October 22, 1788. The newspaper pieces, not seen by the present writer, are discussed by Louie M. Miner, *Our Rude Forefathers; American Political Verse, 1783-1788* (Cedar Rapids, Iowa, 1937), pp. 120, 206, 225.

[53]Joel Barlow, *The Vision of Columbus: a Poem, in Nine Books, with Explanatory Notes (from a Revised Edition of the Author)* . . . (Hagerstown, Md., 1820). The poem was expanded when republished as *The Columbiad* in 1807; the characterization of Washington was not essentially changed.

> 'Tis he, in future strife and darker days,
> Desponding states to sovereign rule to raise,
> When the weak empire in his arm shall find
> The sword, the shield, the bulwark of mankind.

Washington is on the scene frequently in Books VI, VII, and VIII, which deal with the Revolution. The portions which treat the Commander have little of the divine fire in them, as may be seen from a part of the account of the Battle of Yorktown:

> O'er all great Washington his arm extends,
> Points every movement, every toil defends,
> Bids closer strife and bloodier strokes proceed,
> New batteries blaze and heavier squadrons bleed . . .

The Vision of Columbus is restrained in comparison with some of the other heroic verse of the day. The *Massachusetts Magazine* used as filler in issues from June, 1789, to December, 1792, a poem dealing with the Revolution and entitled "Zenith of Glory," by George Richards. Although it runs to over twelve hundred lines of bathos, the editors described it as "An Unpublished Ode." A stanza on the Battle of Germantown is enough to illustrate this work:

> Great Washington, athwart the gloom,
> Saw warring chieftains ope one tomb
>   And mingle yellow dust.
> Fir'd at the view—borne rapid on
> Bright as the ray of glory's morn
>   His form refulgent burst.[54]

Washington is the central figure of Richard Snowden's *The Columbiad*, which begins:

> That chief I sing: Columbia's fav'rite son,
> His acts record, and glorious conquests won.

---

[54]*Massachusetts Magazine*, IV (December, 1792), 747. The author's name, with some discussion, is given by William Bradley Otis, *American Verse, 1625–1807; a History* (New York, 1909), p. 290.

After treating Braddock's defeat, Snowden turned his attention to various scenes of the Revolution, choosing many in which Washington appeared. Here is the hero at Trenton:

> Again the chief prepares to save the land,
> His well-known voice is heard along the strand;
> The valiant remnant muster'd at the call;
> Resolv'd with him to conquer or to fall:
> Above all pain, all passion and all pride
> His courage rises as the flowing tide.
> Stung by reproach, by love of country fir'd,
> His brave example other chiefs inspired;
> The sacred unction spread throughout the host;
> To arms they fly, then seize th'envied post.
> The Hessians droop and give the town for lost.[55]

In a different tradition is *The Death of Washington*, written in the manner of Ossian by John Blair Linn in 1800. Calling his hero "Fingal," Linn reviewed several scenes from Washington's life. The description of the crossing of the Delaware is among the best passages in this work:

The darkened Delaware rolled beneath the winds. The spirit of destruction guarded his shores, and shrieked amid the angry deep. Fingal approached. The light glimmered on the distant way. His joy arose amid the storm, like the lightning's path through the sky of darkness. He pointed with his spear the course to his friends. He dashed the waters beneath him—and leapt on the ground of his foe. The foe awoke amid the arms of Fingal— Strike the harp, sons of Columbia!—let the voice of the song arise—such as the hero might hear, while he leaned upon his shield and his warriors slumbered around.[56]

From time to time, later versifiers aspired to epic heights when handling patriotic themes.[57] Hiram Haines, a friend of Edgar Allan

---

[55] Richard Snowden, *The Columbiad; or, A Poem on the American War, in Thirteen Cantoes* . . . (Baltimore, n.d.). Evans dates this 1796. No personal data are now available for Snowden, who also wrote histories.

[56] John Blair Linn, *The Death of Washington, a Poem, in Imitation of the Manner of Ossian* . . . (Philadelphia, 1800). Brockden Brown, brother-in-law of Linn, reviewed this in the *Monthly Magazine and American Review*, II (April, 1800), 307.

[57] In his Preface to "The Henriade" (1846), James McConochie stated that he would have written of Washington if he had not felt that the subject was too

Poe, included several stanzas on Washington in "The Virginiad," published in 1825. Haines wrote of a poet's reaction to the greatest American hero:

> His name still awes the soul while it inspires
> The Bard, to raise his first and purest fires;
> And with just praise, deep adoration blend,
> For him, our country's saviour—mankind's friend.[58]

"The Washingtonian, an Epic Poem" (1835), by Robert Francis Astrop, consists of two hundred ballad stanzas, including one on the incident of 1753 in which Washington and Christopher Gist arrested but soon released an Indian who had fired at them:

> And mark his [Washington's] nobleness of soul,
>   In one so young and warm,
> Although the savage he did take,
>   He done to him no harm [sic].[59]

On the same plane is *The Western World*, written in 1837 by Walter Marshall McGill, of Tennessee.[60] Extending to some eight thousand lines of blank verse interspersed with couplets, tetrameters, and prose, McGill's poem brings in ghosts, angels, elephants, cannibals, and the voice of the Lord.

A relatively brief poem in epic style is William Ross Wallace's

---

ambitious. He declared Washington the proper model for youth and called for future Washingtons and Patrick Henrys in America's times of need. See McConochie, *Leisure Hours* (Louisville, Ky., 1846), pp. 35 ff.

[58] In Hiram Haines, *Mountain Buds and Blossoms* . . . (Petersburg, Va., 1825), p. 36.

Washington's ghost is introduced at least once, and he is mentioned several times in Richard Emmons's epic of the War of 1812, *The Fredoniad* . . . , 4 vols. (Boston, 1827), I, iv, 146, 151, 155; IV, 141 ff.

[59] In Robert Francis Astrop, *Original Poems* . . . (Philadelphia, 1835), p. 69. The volume contains four shorter pieces that treat Washington.

[60] Walter Marshall McGill, *The Western World; a Poem, Founded on the Facts Recorded of the Revolutionary War* . . . (Maryville, Tenn., 1837).

William Emmons's epic on the Battle of Bunker Hill, copyrighted in 1839, contains incidental allusions to Washington. See Emmons, *The Battle of Bunker Hill* . . . (10th ed.; Boston, 1859), pp. 20, 63–64.

"Last Words of Washington" (1851), which in its opening seems to show the influence of Tennyson's "The Passing of Arthur":

> . . . So had the Hero lain all night,
> With folded arms, and large white brow serene,
> Like the calm statue of a deity,
> Reposing after some benignant work,
> That Grecian genius wrought adoringly . . .

Washington eventually speaks and, after reviewing his youth, the Revolution, and his presidency, prophesies a united and peaceful world.[61] Somewhat more realistic is Alfred Mitchell's *The Coloniad*, which was written in a month, according to the Preface, for the inauguration of Crawford's statue of Washington in Richmond on February 22, 1858. In couplets, it runs to fifteen hundred lines, concluding:

> Princeton was thy jewel—Monmouth was thy crown;
> But what completes thy glory, is thy battle at Yorktown![62]

Likewise biographical in outline is *The Washingtoniad* of Henry Richard Gibson, one-time Congressman from Tennessee. Gibson's poem, in meters reminiscent of Scott's metrical romances, was read to his fellow students at Hobart College on February 22, 1861.[63]

5

The stirring events of the Revolution inspired a great variety of verse in which Washington figures prominently.[64] In general, that

[61] In William Ross Wallace, *Meditations in America* . . . (New York, 1851). John Olin Eidson, in his *Tennyson in America* . . . (Athens, Ga., 1943), p. 114, to which I am indebted for a reference to this item, has it listed as illustrating the influence of Tennyson's "Ulysses." Wallace was a friend of Edgar Allan Poe. See Hervey Allen, *Israfel* . . . , 2 vols. (New York, 1929), II, 613.

[62] Alfred Mitchell, *The Coloniad, a Narrative in Verse on Washington's War* . . . (Richmond, Va., 1858).

[63] Henry Richard Gibson, *The Washingtoniad* . . . (Geneva, N.Y., 1861). Washington is mentioned several times in Burkitt J. Newman's *The Eagle of Washington: a Story of the American Revolution* (Louisville, Ky., 1859), which concerns young ladies and gentlemen moving against a Revolutionary War background. Almost every page contains one or two grammatical or metrical atrocities.

[64] A number of metrical curiosities date from the Revolutionary period. "A Revolutionary Puzzle" appears in Sophie Lee Foster, ed., *Revolutionary Reader* . . . (Atlanta, Ga., 1913) and in William F. Stone, ed., *Ballads and Poems Relating to*

Verse

which remains to be considered lacks the spontaneity of the ballads and is inferior in quality to the work of Freneau. An above-average example is John Trumbull's "The Genius of America, an Ode" (1777–1778), one stanza of which reads:

> And lo, where Victory spreads her eagle wings,
> O'er Trenton's stream and Princeton's classic plain;
> With warlike shouts th'aerial concave rings,
> O'er legions captived and the piles of slain!
> Through varying dangers, with unequal force,
> The godlike hero guides the dubious day,
> Foils the proud Howe, and checks his haughty course,
> With Fabian art, victorious by delay.
> O'er loss, o'er fortune and th'insulting foes,
> His innate virtue shines, his conqu'ring courage glows.[65]

The dramatic attack on Trenton furnished a particularly good theme for poetry. Among those who rose to the challenge was the Reverend Wheeler Case, who wished to show that Jehovah took especial interest in the Patriot cause. Case's management of the eighteenth-century couplet was naïve, but his enthusiasm in a degree compensated for his lack of metrical skill:

> Let's eye that Providence, adore the hand,
> That raised for us a *Joshua* in our land.

. . . . .

---

the *Burgoyne Campaign* (Albany, N.Y., 1893). See also "Rebus 8, on a Distinguished Personage," in John Parke, *Translations from the Greek and Latin, with Original Poems* (Philadelphia, 1786), p. 312.

Acrostics are in the following: *Massachusetts Magazine*, II (November, 1790), 700; *Historical Magazine*, VIII (June, 1864), 208, a reprint from the *Massachusetts Magazine* of September, 1789; *Boston Gazette and Country Journal*, No. 1823, September 14, 1789. Miss Louie M. Miner very kindly furnished a transcript of the last-mentioned item.

A Latin ode, "*In Geo. Washington, ducis supremi . . .* ," from the *Pennsylvania Magazine* of October, 1775, is reprinted in the *Historical Magazine*, VIII (April, 1864), 154, with an English translation in the Latin meter, *ibid.*, VIII (June, 1864), 209.

Probably the earliest mention of Washington in verse occurs in a metrical summary of contemporary history entitled "A Brief Chronology of Remarkable Events, Relating Chiefly to the Present War," and published in 1763. See Sam Briggs, ed., *The Essays, Humor and Poems of Nathaniel Ames . . . of Dedham* (Cleveland, Ohio, 1891), p. 270; also Rupert Hughes, *George Washington . . .* 3 vols. (New York, 1926–1930), II, 3-4.

[65] In Trumbull, *op. cit.*, II, 99.

> O what a blessing to the States! it is our bliss,
> Great Washington was rais'd for such a day as this.
>
> . . . . . .
>
> When these affairs are view'd and duly scann'd,
> He's blind that does not see Jehovah's hand.
>
> . . . . . .
>
> A gloom is spread around, alas! what grief,
> We know not where to go to find relief.
> A storm of snow and hail the Lord sent down,
> A blessed season this for *Washington:*
> He now return'd, and thro' the storm he press'd,
> And caught twelve hundred Hessians in their nest.[66]

"His Excellency General Washington," written in the early part of the war by Phillis Wheatley, the Negro poetess, is almost as rough as Case's lines and much less lively.[67]

Patriot soldiers were cheered and inspired by the lyrics of Jonathan Mitchell Sewall, whose ballad "War and Washington" has already been mentioned. Sewall repeatedly expressed in verse his passion for the American cause and his unbounded confidence in the Commander-in-Chief. Especially eloquent are some lines from the Epilogue which he wrote for a production of Addison's *Cato* in Portsmouth, New Hampshire, in 1778.[68] The poet here likened Washington to the old Roman hero of the play:

> A chief in all the ways of battle skill'd,
> Great in the council, glorious in the field!
> Thy scourge, O Britain! and Columbia's boast,
> The dread, and admiration of each host!

---

[66]Wheeler Case, "An Answer to the Messengers of the Nation" (1778), in *Case, Revolutionary Memorials* . . . , ed. Stephen Dodd (New York, 1852), pp. 40-47.

[67]In Phillis Wheatley, *Poems and Letters* . . . , ed. Charles Fred. Heartman (New York, [1915]). This poem was first published in the *Pennsylvania Magazine or American Monthly Museum*, II (April, 1776), 193, with a letter addressed to Washington and sent with the poem. Washington's reply was very gracious. See Washington, *The Writings* . . . , ed. John C. Fitzpatrick, IV, 360-361. Miss Wheatley's "On Major General Lee" (1776) contains a tribute to "Godlike Washington."

[68]In Jonathan Mitchell Sewall, *Miscellaneous Poems* . . . (Portsmouth, N.H., 1801), pp. 104-110.

Verse 145

> Whose martial arm, and steady soul, alone
> Have made thy legions quake, thy empire groan,
> And thy proud monarch tremble on his throne.

Sewall sometimes became more rhetorical, as in a later poem wherein John Adams is likened to Pallas in wisdom and Washington is proclaimed the equal of Jove.[69]

Another who gave the Patriots the moral support of his lyric ability was the versatile Francis Hopkinson, who early in 1777 wrote:

> On Heaven and Washington placing reliance,
> We'll meet the bold Briton, and bid him defiance;
> Our cause we'll support, for 'tis just and 'tis glorious—
> When men fight for freedom, they must be victorious.[70]

Hopkinson was especially successful with his satiric works, in both prose and verse.[71] His "A Political Catechism," a prose work of 1777, concludes with a glowing tribute to Washington; here it is stated that "Had he lived in the days of idolatry he had been worshipped as a God."[72]

One of the most impressive tributes to the Washington of Revolutionary days is Charles Henry Wharton's "A Poetical Epistle to George Washington, Esquire, Commander-in-Chief of the Armies

---

[69] "Festival Song," *ibid.*, pp. 169–171. Others of Sewall's poems which treat Washington are "On Congress Investing General Washington for a Season with the Supreme Military Power" (1776), "Song" (1777), "Song for Washington's Birth Day" (1799), "An Ancient Fable Modernized," and "Song for President Adams's Birthday," all included in the same volume.

Among poems which connect the name of Washington with the Olympian pantheon are "The Jerseys" (1777), in Moore, *op. cit.*, p. 156; "Song in Praise of Washington," *American Museum*, IV (August, 1788), 196; "Ode, Humbly Inscribed to the Illustrious PRESIDENT of the UNITED STATES OF AMERICA," by "J. L.," *Massachusetts Magazine*, I (May, 1789), 584; "To Washington" or "On General Washington," *Massachusetts Magazine*, II (September, 1790), 571–572 and *American Museum*, VII (January–June, 1790), Appendix i, 4.

[70] Final stanza of "Camp Ballad," pp. 174–175 of "Poems on Several Subjects," included with separate paging in the back of the third volume of Hopkinson, *op. cit.* Stevenson (*op. cit.*, p. 178) publishes this poem in slightly different form as "American Independence." It is not a ballad.

[71] The humorous "Battle of the Kegs" was very popular. Cf. his "Political Ballad," *supra*, Section 3.

[72] In Hopkinson, *op. cit.*, I, 120.

of the United States of America." Wharton, a Roman Catholic priest, was an American but was living in England when the war began. His sympathies were with his native land, and the "Epistle" expressed his comment on the entire situation. He satirized the conduct of the British Tory government, lauded Washington, and urged his fellow Americans to keep their sights high. After original publication in this country, probably in 1779, the poem was republished in London, where fifteen thousand copies were sold with the understanding that proceeds would be used for the relief of American prisoners of war. Such occurrences throw interesting side lights on the attitude of the British toward the war with the American colonies. Wharton's words on Washington are the stronger for their restraint:

> Great without pomp, without ambition brave,
> Proud not to conquer fellow-men, but save;
> Friend to the wretched, foe to none but those
> Who plan their greatness on their brethren's woes;
> Awed by no titles, faithless to no trust,
> Free without faction, obstinately just . . .[73]

It must not be forgotten that Tories were abroad in the land and that they too produced a quantity of verse. Their lines on the rebel army and its Commander vary from the inoffensively humorous to the scurrilous. One of their more effective attacks is entitled "American Times, a Satire in Three Parts," which includes a passage on the ragged condition of the Patriot troops:

> Strike up, Hell's music! roar, infernal drums!
> Discharge the cannon— Lo! the warrior comes!
> He comes, not tame as on Ohio's banks,
> But rampant at the head of ragged ranks.
> Hunger and itch are with him—Gates and Wayne—
> And all the lice of Egypt in his train.

[73] As quoted by Moses Coit Tyler, *The Literary History of the American Revolution, 1763-1783*, 2 vols. (New York, [1941]), II, 168-169. Tyler gives a full discussion. He believes the poem was first published at Annapolis in 1779. A part of it appears anonymously under the title "On General Washington," *American Museum*, VII (January-June, 1790), Appendix i, 43.

Verse

Sure these are Falstaff's soldiers, poor and bare;
Or else the rotten regiments of Rag-fair . . .[74]

Prominent among Loyalist versifiers were Joseph Stansbury and the Reverend Jonathan Odell. In a "Song for a Venison Dinner at Mr. Bunyan's, New York, 1781," evidently written before Yorktown, Stansbury bragged about the plentiful food possessed by the British army and speculated upon the ache in Washington's jaws at the time.[75] Odell tossed off spirited couplets such as:

Back to his mountains Washington may trot:
He take this city—yes, when ice is hot.[76]

But he also wrote and published in Rivington's *Royal Gazette* libelous doggerel on Washington and other Patriot leaders.[77]

After Yorktown the taunts of the Tories, never very effective in their ridicule of Washington, were forgotten. The return of peace was celebrated in verse, as was the General's retirement to Mount Vernon. The many poets who, like David Humphreys, heralded the dawning of a new age in America were almost sure to speak of Washington's part in bringing it to pass.[78] As early as 1785 an

---

[74]"By Camillo Querno, Chaplain to the Congress," in Sargent, pp. 9–10. Cf. the anonymous "To Washington from the British Light Infantry," in Moore, *op. cit.*, p. 224.

[75]In Joseph Stansbury and Jonathan Odell, *The Loyal Verses of Joseph Stansbury and Doctor Jonathan Odell* . . . , ed. Winthrop Sargent (Albany, N.Y., 1860), p. 79.

[76]"The Congratulation," *ibid.*, p. 46. Cf. "The Epilogue," published in Rivington's *Royal Gazette*, October 24, 1779, and republished in Moore, *op. cit.*, pp. 220–223.

[77]In particular, "The Word of Congress," Rivington's *Royal Gazette*, September 18, 1779; reprinted in Sargent, *Loyalist Poetry*, p. 46.

[78]See "The Genius of America—an Ode: Inscribed to His Excellency George Washington, Esq., on His Return to Mount Vernon, December, 1783," *American Museum*, V (January, 1789), 102–103; "Virginia's Invitation. Imitated from . . . Horace . . . ," *Gentleman and Lady's Town and Country Magazine*, I (June, 1784), 73–74; "Five Stanzas for February 22, 1784," by "Civis," *New York Gazetteer*, February 11, 1784, reprinted in *Historical Magazine*, V, Series 2 (February, 1869), 135; Samuel Low, "Peace," in Low, *Poems*, 2 vols. (New York, 1800), I, 125; Timothy Dwight, "Letter to Colonel Humphreys," in Elihu H. Smith, ed., *American Poems* . . . (Litchfield, Conn., 1793), p. 82; Joseph Brown Ladd, "The Prospect of America, Inscribed to His Excellency General Washington," in Ladd, *Poems of Arouet* (Charleston, S.C., 1786), pp. 14–15; Peter Markoe, "Ode on the Birth-Day of General Washington," *American Museum*, I (February, 1787), 161–162; "Toast for General Washington's Birthday" (1784), in Robert H. Schauffler, ed., *Wash-*

obscure verse writer foresaw that the hero would not long be suffered to enjoy his retirement:

> The virtues which his bosom warm,
> Shall force him to supreme command;
> And make him quit his much lov'd farm,
> To save his dearer native land.
> Americans unite! to Washington be true!
> And all the world can't conquer you.[79]

The Constitutional Convention inspired a fresh flow of verse. Samuel Low wrote lines expressing confidence in the group of patriots, "Their country's guardian guides," over whom Washington presided.[80] More spirited stanzas were written by William Milns, who concluded with the lines:

> Fame's trumpet shall swell in Washington's praise,
> And time grant a furlough to lengthen his days;
>   May health weave the thread
>   Of delight round his head.
>   No nation can boast
>   Such a name, such a toast,
> The Federal Constitution, boys, and Washington forever.[81]

At the time of Washington's inauguration as President, his visits to various towns were important occasions for local poets laureate. Wherever he went, his arrival was celebrated in ode or lyric. Some of these productions were sweet and simple, like the unusually short ode sung by the ladies at Trenton, where a boy in the guise of

---

ington's Birthday (New York, 1932), p. xvi; "Thanksgiving Hymn" (1784) in Stevenson, op. cit., pp. 264–265; "Address to His Excellency George Washington . . . ," American Museum, V (April, 1789), 409–410.

[79] An imitation of "Rule Britannia" from the Virginia Gazette and Independent Chronicle, March 26, 1785; Miss Louie M. Miner very kindly gave me a transcript of this; the stanza quoted is the last of seven.

[80] "The Constitution" (1789), in Low, op. cit., I, 97; cf. his "Ode Occasioned by the Adoption of the Present Constitution . . . ," op. cit., I, 102.

[81] "The Federal Constitution," in Stevenson, op. cit., pp. 272–273. See also Noah Webster, "The News-Boy's Address to His Customers," in Poems . . . , ed. Ruth Farquhar Warfel and Harry Redclay Warfel (College Park, Md., 1936); "American Independence," American Museum, I (February, 1787), 167. Several poems on the Constitution which treat Washington are discussed by Miss Louie M. Miner, op. cit., pp. 195 ff., 249.

Cupid crowned Washington with laurel as he passed beneath a bower:

> Welcome, mighty chief, once more!
> Welcome to this grateful shore!
> Now no mercenary foe
> Aims again the fatal blow,
> Aims at thee the fatal blow.
>
> Virgins fair and matrons grave,
> Those thy conquering arm did save,
> Build for thee triumphal bowers.
> Strew, ye fair, his way with flowers.
> Strew your hero's way with flowers.[82]

Other writers to welcome the first President soared aloft in ambitious Pindarics or regular odes of some length and formality, as may be seen from a short section of "An Ode upon the Arrival of THE PRESIDENT OF THE UNITED STATES," composed in Boston:

> 2 RECITATIVE
>
> He comes! the Chieftain comes! All hail!
> 'Twas his on *Trenton's* crimson'd vale—
> And *Princeton's* lawn—and *Brandywine,*
> To whelm in dust *Britannia's* line;
> 'Twas his, to lead *Columbia's* train
> To deathless deeds, on Monmouth plain;
> Or bid the storm of battle cease,
> When proud *Cornwallis* su'd for peace.
>
> AIR
>
> Swell the paean divine;
> Earth repeat it again!
> Ocean echo the strain!
> Heaven thunder amen!
> Columbia! George Washington's thine.[83]

---

[82]"Ode," in C. W. Bowen, "The Inauguration of Washington," *Century Magazine*, XXXVII (April, 1889), 817; also in Schauffler, *op. cit.*, p. 60. Similar poems of 1789 are "Ode to Columbia's Favorite Son," *Massachusetts Magazine*, I (October, 1789), 659; "Valedictory Ode," *ibid.*, I (November, 1789), 723; James Allen, "On Washington's Visit to Boston, 1789," in Samuel Kettell, ed., *Specimens of American Poetry* . . . , 3 vols. (Boston, 1829), I, 171.

[83]*Massachusetts Magazine*, I (October, 1789), 653. Similar pieces include the following: "Address to His Excellency General Washington, by His Excellency Gov-

150   Verse

One of the features of Washington's regime which eventually incurred Republican criticism was the ceremoniousness attached to celebration of the President's birthday.[84] The tendering and recital of odes was an important part of this ceremony. Certainly many of the Birthday odes and similar compositions dating from the period of Washington's presidency are highly obsequious as well as artificial. Invocations to the muse are followed by elaborate comparisons and contrasts between America's hero and those of all previous ages. Personifications abound. One versifier of 1792, who styled himself "The Volunteer Laureate," thus described the coming of the Revolutionary War:

> See, Demon Danger's horrid form,
> With dire Oppression strong allied,
> Hangs o'er the land—and wakes the storm:
> And swells, of deep calamity, the tide.

The same writer concluded his ode with a tribute only slightly more abstract and fulsome than the average of its kind:

> Favor'd of Heaven! the Muse in rapture faints,
> Thy grateful country strives, in vain to sing!
>
> . . . . . .
>
> "Long may'st thou live"—the Soul of Nature cries,
> "Greatest of Mortals—Favourite of the Skies."[85]

ernor Livingston, of New Jersey," *American Museum*, V (March, 1789), 300–301; "Address to His Excellency George Washington, Esq. . . . ," *ibid.*, V (April, 1789), 409–410; Samuel Knox, "An Ode . . . ," *ibid.*, VI (July, 1789), 85–86; [Sarah Wentworth Morton], "Ode to the President of the United States . . . ," *Massachusetts Magazine*, I (October, 1789), 660–661, also published in revised form as: Sarah Wentworth Morton, "Ode for Music, Inscribed to George Washington, upon His Public Entrance in the Town of Boston . . . ," in *My Mind and Its Thoughts* . . . (Boston, 1823); "Ode Sung in Boston, June 1, 1789," *American Museum*, VII (January–June, 1790), Appendix i, 10–11; Samuel Low, "Ode on the Arrival of the President . . . in the City of New York," in Low, *op. cit.*, I, 104–105.

[84]See Jefferson's letter to Dr. Jones, *supra*, Chapter II, Section 4.

[85]"An Ode; for the Birth Day of the President of the United States," *Massachusetts Magazine*, IV (February, 1792), 118. Cf. a piece spoken by Master Edmund Bacon, "When the President of the United States of America Honoured, with His Presence the Examination of the Students of the Richmond Academy in Georgia," *American Museum*, X (July–December, 1791), Appendix i, 2–3; "On the Death of

Verse

Poetasters of a more practical turn of mind continued to associate Washington's name with the dawning period of prosperity in America. An anonymous writer of magazine verse contrasted the happy lot of free American farmers with that of European serfs and peasants. Details include the fertility of the land, the healthfulness of the climate, and other advantages to be found in the new country. The poem ends with a dedication to Washington, to whom "the farmer's warmest thanks" were due.[86]

Verse which treats Washington during the period of his presidency is for the most part free of political overtones. But during his second administration his policies were attacked in Republican newspapers, and a small part of the criticism took the form of verse. In 1793 a series of "Probationary Odes" appeared in Philip Freneau's *National Gazette* under the pseudonym "Jonathan Pindar, a cousin of Peter's; and a candidate for the post of Poet-Laureate." Although Freneau was at first believed to be the author, the odes were actually the work of one of his friends, St. George Tucker, a jurist of Virginia. Tucker attacked Hamilton and Adams savagely, but his references to Washington were few and carefully phrased.[87] A direct address was "Ode V, to a Truly Great Man." Here Tucker gave Washington credit for saving the nation but declared him a man, after all, and therefore subject to error. Coming to his point, the writer inveighed against the establishment of a national

---

Dr. Franklin, a Fragment," *Massachusetts Magazine*, II (May, 1790), 309; "ODE, on the PRESIDENT's Birth Day, February 11, 1791," *ibid.*, III (February, 1791), 111; "Independence: an Ode," *ibid.*, VI (July, 1794), 440; "To the Hero, Deliverer, and Protector of America, on His Arrival in the Affectionate and Patriotic City of Charleston, on Monday the 2d of May, 1791," *Daily Advertiser*, June 8, 1791, p. 2; Margaretta V. Faugeres, "Verses Addressed to the Members of the Cincinnati of the State of New York, on the 4th of July" (1795?) in Rufus W. Griswold, *The Female Poets of America* (2d ed.; Philadelphia, 1859), p. 37; "Stanzas on the President's Birth Day," signed "A South Carolinian, Aged 17," in *The Columbian Muse* . . . (New York, 1794).

[86]"The American Farmer," *American Museum*, VII (January, 1790), 38–39. Cf. "On the American and French Revolutions," *ibid.*, VII (January–June, 1790), Appendix i, 44.

[87]See "A Dedicatory Ode, to a Would-Be Great Man [John Adams]," "Ode VI, Cousin Jonathan to Cousin Peter," and "Ode XIII, to the Democratic Societies," in [Tucker], *The Probationary Odes* . . . (Philadelphia, 1796), pp. 9–11, 70–73, 92–93. The first poem is in Part 1; the latter two are in Part 2 of the book.

bank, which he compared to a crocodile, ready to feast on the bowels of the nation unless the President withdrew his approval and killed it.[88] An interesting item is an untitled poem in which Tucker "*apostrophizes* a Great Man without stain," advising Washington not to resign his office:

> Still, as a Father to *thy country* dear,
> Regard not those who seek to wound thy peace,
> Nor to their impious falsehoods lend an ear,
> Who would persuade Thee *her* regards can cease.
> Still at the helm go on our Bark to steer,
> Nor quit it, *till thou leave thine Equal There.*[89]

The author or the publisher (Benjamin Franklin Bache) here added a footnote, evidently written when the poems were collected for book publication, saying that perhaps it would have been better, after all, had Washington left his office while his glory was "*unobscured.*"

On the other side of the ledger, Jonathan Mitchell Sewall expressed in verse his approval of Washington's refusal to allow Congress to examine the diplomatic correspondence relative to the Jay Treaty,[90] and St. John Honeywood came out with immediate endorsement of the sentiments of the Farewell Address and of the President's decision to retire at the end of his second term.[91]

The verse of Robert Treat Paine was greatly admired by his contemporaries. One of his youthful effusions, "The Invention of Letters" (1795), was dedicated to Washington.[92] With evident reference to the vicious attacks of the Republicans, Paine wrote:

> Can'st thou, great Chief, her thankless sons forgive,
> Who owe to thee the soil on which they live?
> These senseless reptiles, who, with Slander's bane,
> The bright medallion of thy life would stain,

[88] *Ibid.* (Part I), pp. 23–24.
[89] "Ode XII," *ibid.* (Part I), pp. 39–41.
[90] "The Inflexible Patriot . . . ," in Sewall, *op. cit.*, pp. 150–154.
[91] "On General Washington's Declining a Re-Election to the Presidency of the United States," in St. John Honeywood, *Poems* . . . (New York, 1801).
[92] In Robert Treat Paine, *The Works* . . . (Boston, 1812), pp. 171–172.

> Yield to the glories of thy deathless name,
> The strictest tribute ever paid by fame.
>
> . . . . . .
>
> Oh, WASHINGTON! thou hero, patriot, sage!
> Friend of all climates; pride of every age!
> Were thine the laurels, every soil could raise,
> The mighty harvest were penurious praise.

During Washington's final retirement versifiers were comparatively quiet, but the Franco-American situation of 1798 aroused a martial spirit and directed fresh attention to his military prowess. He is the subject of a stanza of Paine's "Adams and Liberty,"[93] and of two stanzas of Joseph Hopkinson's "Hail Columbia." Both songs were immediately popular. And so in 1798 and for many years thereafter Americans were singing:

> Sound, sound the trump of fame,
>   Let Washington's great name
> Ring through the world with loud applause . . .[94]

One of the last bards to celebrate the living Washington was Royall Tyler, better known as a playwright. For a Fourth of July celebration in 1799 Tyler wrote a "Convivial Song" containing the enthusiastic lines:

> Here's Washington, the brave, boys,
>   Source of all Columbia's joys,
> Here's Washington, the brave, boys,
>   Come rise and toast him standing:

---

[93] *Ibid.*, pp. 245–247. Griswold relates that Paine was constrained to compose this stanza because his friends would not let him have any wine until he introduced Washington's name into the song. See Rufus W. Griswold, *The Poets and Poetry of America* . . . (Philadelphia, 1842), p. 38. Paine treated Washington also in "The Green Mountain Farmer," *op. cit.*, pp. 267–269, and "The Ruling Passion," *op. cit.*, p. 175.

A few reverent and rhetorical lines on Washington's leaving retirement to answer his country's call occur in [Richard Alsop, Lemuel Hopkins, and Theodore Dwight], *The Political Green-house for the Year 1798* . . . (Hartford, Conn., [1799]).

[94] In Kettell, *op. cit.*, I, 350. The opening of the third stanza of "Hail Columbia" is quoted. See also "Poem on the Acceptance of the Appointment of Lieutenant General of the Armies of the United States by George Washington," *The Desert to the True American*, I (July 14, 1798), i.

> For he's the hero firm and brave,
> Who all our country's glory gave,
> And once again he shall us save,
> Our armies bold commanding.[95]

6

The vocabulary of poetic eulogy was exhausted long before the news of Washington's death spread over the country at the close of 1799. The verse of 1800 abounds in hackneyed phrases; the only new note is that of grief. The anonymous "Washington, My Son, a Lamentation," runs in part:

> Thence by thy country call'd to toils of state,
> He then was first chosen the chief in command,
> He beat the brave warriors all by his great skill,—
> Now where is the man that his station can fill?
> Oh, I fear, greatly fear, he lives not on this hemisphere.[96]

Among the better poems to mark the occasion were those of Freneau, who was annoyed by the enormous output of inferior verse on Washington.[97] In addition to short elegies and odes, there appeared a number of lengthy pieces which touch the high spots of Washington's career, usually in didactic couplets, and have many characteristics of the funeral sermons that were pronounced all over America at the time. "A Poem on the Death of General Washington," by David Humphreys, is an example of this biographical-elegiac type of composition.[98] A very long one which was widely read is Richard Alsop's *A Poem: Sacred to the Memory of George Washington . . . Adapted to the 22nd of February, 1800*.[99] After

---

[95] In Duyckinck, *op. cit.*, I, 416.
[96] In Smyth, *op. cit.*
[97] *Supra*, Section 1.
[98] *Supra*, Section 2.
[99] Hartford, Conn., 1800. Alsop's *The Charms of Fancy*, published posthumously, contains a few lines on the "patriot chief" in the same strain. See the portion quoted in Duyckinck, *op. cit.*, I, 496.

expressions of grief and a profession of dismay at the difficulty of the subject, Alsop began with Braddock's fight and then traced Washington's career in considerable detail. His style can be judged from a few lines at the point where Washington leaves Mount Vernon to become President:

> When Britain, proud Britain, invaded our land,
> Of public cares to assume the important weight,
> She saw thy fame with added splendors glow,
> New beams of glory radiate round thy brow.
> —But from the arduous toil, the task severe,
> The Muse despairing shrinks in conscious fear;
> To trace that brilliant course the hope were vain
> Though eagle's pinions should her flight sustain . . .[100]

A contemporary reviewer, probably Brockden Brown, pronounced the work correct but uninspired.[101]

At Lenox, Massachusetts, Eldad Lewis wrote and delivered a funeral oration in couplets.[102] Copies of another long poem were printed on satin and presented to subscribers by a Philadelphia newspaper publisher.[103] A few similar pieces were written in later years.[104]

Shorter poems were still more numerous. Samuel Low's "Ode on the Death of General George Washington" was recited by John Hodgkinson, a popular actor, at the New-York Theatre on January 8, 1800. Low, whose patriotism far surpassed his poetic gifts, reveled

---

[100] Richard Alsop, *A Poem* . . . , p. 13.

[101] *Monthly Magazine and American Review*, II (April, 1800), 309–312. The same critic remarked that few poets, compared to the number of orators, grasped the opportunity presented by Washington's death. To a present-day student the versifiers seem numerous.

[102] Eldad Lewis, *An Eulogy, on the Life and Character of His Excellency George Washington . . . Published at the Request of the Audience* (Pittsfield, Mass., 1800). Cf. Samuel Ellis, "Eulogy of George Washington," published in part (for the first time) by Smyth, *op. cit.*; Charles Lane, *A Poem on the Death of General Washington* (Alexandria, Va., 1800).

[103] "Elegy on Washington," *Historical Magazine*, I (August, 1857), 233–234.

[104] See John Lovett, *Washington's Birthday* . . . (Albany, N.Y., 1812); Cynthia Bullock, *Washington and Other Poems* (New York, 1847); William Whittlesey Badger, *Washington* . . . (New York, 1859).

in personifications and other figures. Of Washington's administration he wrote:

> And when recall'd from Vernon's peaceful shade,
> The matchless man his country's call obey'd!
> With ready zeal the sacrifice he made.
> Unmov'd by foreign menaces or smiles,
> Unaw'd by Faction's clamours, threats or wiles;
> With God-like port our Cincinnatus stood;
> Awful in virtue, firm in rectitude . . .[105]

Theodore Dwight, a younger brother of the better-known Timothy, wrote in similar vein of the plight of a "widow'd country."[106] Ministers and others who delivered funeral orations often included an ode or elegy of their own composition, and the black-bordered newspapers of December, 1799, and January, 1800, abound in verse which is for the most part similar to that of Low in style and treatment of Washington.[107]

During Jefferson's administration few versifiers seem to have sung the praises of the first President. Among poems of a Republican cast, two by a forgotten young man of Charleston, South Carolina, contain a few lines on Washington.[108] In a different political key,

[105] In Low, *op. cit.*, I, 9-15. Low treated Washington in several poems. Others than those already mentioned are "To Kotzebue," "Ode for the 4th of July, 1800," and "Lines Written at the Request of the Members of Holland Lodge . . ."

[106] Lines on the Death of Washington," in Kettell, *op. cit.*, II, 71-72. Cf. Thomas G. Fessenden, "Elegy on the Death of Washington," *ibid.*, II, 116-117; "An Elegy on the Death of General George Washington," *Publications of the Colonial Society of Massachusetts* (Boston, 1905), VII (Transactions, 1900-1902), 196-198; also the handbill of a funeral ceremony of the day, reprinted in the *Historical Magazine*, I (February, 1857), 38-39.

[107] See Henry Holcombe, "Introductory Hymn," in *A Sermon occasioned by the Death of . . . Washington . . .* ([Savannah, Ga., 1800]); Joseph Story, "Elegy to the Memory of General George Washington," in *An Eulogy on General George Washington* (Salem, Mass., 1800); "An Elegy on the Death of General Washington," *Virginia Argus* (Richmond, Va.), January 14, 1800; "Airs in the Monody," *J. Russell's Gazette* (Boston), January 9, 1800; "Lady Washington's Lament," in Jackson, *op. cit.*, pp. 95-97.

[108] George Heartwell Spierin, "Liberty, a Didactic Poem," and "A Poem on the Acquisition of Louisiana," in Spierin, *Poems* . . . (Charleston, S.C., 1805), pp. 69 ff., 115 ff. A note introducing the volume states that Spierin was a lad of humble circumstances but great promise who died at the age of seventeen.

Verse

William Cullen Bryant's bitter attack on Jefferson in "The Embargo," written when the poet was thirteen, includes a tribute to the veterans of the Revolution,

> Whom WASHINGTON our pride and glory led . . .[109]

The events leading to the War of 1812 reanimated the spirit of nationalism. Robert Treat Paine worked Washington into a lively war song.[110] A number of verse-writers accented commerce, shipping, and related phases of the national life. In Massachusetts a member of the Washington Benevolent Society, an organization designed to strengthen and popularize the Federalist Party, wrote of him:

> Defended by his powerful sway,
>   How high our Nation's honour rose!
> Our Commerce o'er the wat'ry way,
>   Rode fearless of contending foes.
>
> The veteran statesman, wise as brave,
>   With wealth and peace his country crown'd,
> With Trade, where Ocean roll'd a wave,
>   And Fame, the skies alone could bound.[111]

Many thus looked back to the times of Washington and Adams and found them good. Some treated Washington in long didactic poems favorable to Britain and antagonistic to France, as they contrasted the terrible situation of their own day with the good old days of the

---

[109] In William Cullen Bryant, *Representative Selections* . . . , ed. Tremaine McDowell (New York, 1935), p. 343.

[110] "Ode Written for . . . July 4, 1811," in Paine, *op. cit.*, p. 279. Cf. William Dunlap, *Yankee Chronology . . . to Which Are Added the Patriotic Songs of the Freedom of the Seas and the Yankee Tars* (New York, 1812).

[111] John Lathrop, Jr., "Ode, Composed for the First Celebration of the 'Washington Benevolent Society' . . . ," in William Sullivan, *An Oration Delivered before the Washington Benevolent Society of Massachusetts* . . . (2d ed.; Boston, 1812). Cf. Lucius M. Sargent, "Ode III," and E. Tisdale, "Ode II," both included in the Sullivan volume.

seventeen-nineties.[112] But Ralph Waldo Emerson, aged eleven, saw him against a background of eternity:

> In former years when Britain ruled these States
> And like a tyrant doom'd our hapless fates
> The God of Israel heard our groans and cries
> And bade to life a WASHINGTON arise.[113]

Robert S. Coffin, who styled himself "the Boston Bard," produced a large amount of newspaper verse which he published in book form in 1826.[114] Coffin found inspiration in all manner of subjects, and his volume includes several items touching upon Washington. Four of his themes are representative of Washingtonian verse of the period: he celebrated Washington in connection with Lafayette's last visit to America,[115] he spoke of him as "Columbia's . . . Saviour,"[116] he sounded a mournful, romantic strain on the subject of his death, and he urged the construction of a suitable monument or memorial.

Coffin was affected by a pleasant melancholy at times, as were many writers of the early nineteenth century. "Washington's Dirge," which was set to music, opens:

> Why moans the white surge on Potomac's proud tide,
> Why droop the green willows that grow by its side?

[112] John Pierpont, *The Portrait* . . . (Boston, 1812); Charles Prentiss, *A Poem Delivered at Brookfield, July 5th, 1813, before the Washington Benevolent Societies* . . . (Brookfield, Mass., 1813).

[113] "Lines on Washington Written at Concord Dec. 24th, 1814," in Ralph Waldo Emerson, *The Letters* . . . , ed. Ralph L. Rusk, 6 vols. (New York, 1939), VI, 329; cf. his "Poetical Essay," of the same period, *op. cit.*, VI, 330–332.

[114] [Robert S. Coffin], *Oriental Harp; Poems of the Boston Bard* (Providence, R.I., 1826). Duyckinck (*op. cit.*, II, 255–256) treats Coffin briefly.

[115] "Arrival of General La Fayette" and "La Fayette at the Tomb of Washington" in Coffin, *op. cit.* See also James Gates Percival, "Ode, for the Celebration at Bunker Hill, June 17, 1825," in Percival, *The Poetical Works* . . . , 2 vols. (Boston, 1826), I, 251–252; "Virginia," in *The Potomac Muse* . . . (Richmond, Va., 1825), p. 32, "by a Lady, a Native of Virginia" (Mrs. Alfred W. Elwes?). The author of the last-mentioned poem stated that Washington was too great a subject for her muse.

[116] "Light and Washington" and "Washington's Dirge" in Coffin, *op. cit.* See also Lydia H. Sigourney, "Mother of Washington," *Richmond Enquirer*, July 18, 1826. Another poem entitled "Mother of Washington," also by Mrs. Sigourney, is in Griswold, *Poets and Poetry of America*, pp. 192–193.

Verse

> Why chant Nature's minstrels their numbers so slow,
> Imparting their songs in the whispers of wo?[117]

Poets joined with Congressional and other speakers in agitation which led eventually to the erection of the Washington Monument. In "Impromptu: Written at Mount Vernon, 1816," Coffin used as epigraph a couplet from another versifier who regretted the nation's failure to provide an appropriate memorial for the first President. Coffin's own poem is brief and pointed:

> Thy country, spirit of the mighty dead,
>   To thee a lasting monument imparts;
> She rears, great Washington, above thy head,
>   A monument of most ungrateful hearts.[118]

When in 1832 the centennial of Washington's birth was celebrated, few versifiers rose to the occasion. Francis C. Gray included a "Hymn" with the published form of the oration that he delivered before the Massachusetts Legislature.[119] Gray's motif was religious: a trust that the Lord would always in time of need send America heroes like Washington. The fourth of his five stanzas runs:

> There, like an angel form,
> Sent down to still a storm,
>   Stood WASHINGTON—
> Clouds broke and rolled away;
> Foes fled in pale dismay;
> Wreathed were his brows with bay,
>   When war was done.

Verse writers continued to compare and contrast Washington with other great figures, particularly Napoleon. An anonymous

---

[117]In Coffin, *op. cit.* See also John G. C. Brainard, "On the Birthday of Washington . . . 1822," in Brainard, *The Literary Remains* . . . , ed. J. G. Whittier (Hartford, Conn., [1832]); Lucretia Davidson [aged twelve], "Lines after a Celebration of the Birth-Night of Washington," in Griswold, *The Poets and Poetry of America*, p. 432.

[118]Cf. Coffin's "Vision II," *op. cit.* The epigraph mentioned was taken from Pierpont, *op. cit.* See also Ebenezer Bailey, "The Triumphs of Liberty," in Kettell, *op. cit.*, III, 309-310. Bailey hailed Bolivar as a successor of Washington; Coffin treated the same theme in "The Sword of Washington." In "Patriotic Song" Coffin envisioned Washington waving the flag of freedom over the whole world.

[119]*Supra*, Chapter III, Section 3.

writer of "Lines on the Statue of Washington in the Capitol" pronounced the American leader:

> A perfect hero, free from all excess,
> Above Napoleon, though he dazzled less.[120]

St. Leger Landon Carter ingeniously combined a similar contrast with a plea that Washington's grave be suitably marked and tended. Carter pointed out that the despot's grave was a marble shrine, guarded day and night, while that of the real hero was "deserted and drear."[121]

7

By 1842 sectional differences had become definitely apparent in America. In that year a writer of magazine verse expressed the hope that the statue of Washington at the Capitol would exert such a unifying influence as the man himself had exerted against "party strife or private broils." The hero was apostrophized in grandiloquent terms:

> If Vandal hands should e'er assail again
> The sacred walls that Freedom loves so well,
> Be thou a Presence shall their rage restrain,
> As when upon a lashed sea's angry swell
> A gentle Saviour trod![122]

William Cullen Bryant's "Washington," in a volume of verse published in 1844, concludes with the idea that the "elastic chain"

---

[120]*Southern Literary Messenger*, II (March, 1836), 253. Cf. "Ode: Written at the Grave of Washington at Mt. Vernon," *Knickerbocker*, VIII (September, 1836), 329-330.

[121]"Washington and Napoleon," *Southern Literary Messenger*, I (November, 1834), 90.

Among other poems of the thirties which treat Washington are "Williamsburg Birth Night Ball," *Southern Literary Messenger*, I (April, 1835), 403-404; "Sung by the Ladies of the Ursuline Community after the Oration on February 22, 1838 . . . ," in John England, *The Works* . . . , ed. Ignatius Aloysius Reynolds, 5 vols. (Baltimore and New York, 1849), IV, 503; and the verse of Robert Francis Astrop.

[122]S. D. Dakin, "Lines on the Statue of Washington at the Capitol," *Knickerbocker*, XX (September, 1842), 281.

binding the states together should bind new states and old in a strong, peaceful company.[123] In John Greenleaf Whittier's "Yorktown," first published in 1847, Washington appears in glorious Revolutionary scenes; these are placed in strong contrast with scenes showing the continued existence of slavery in a region that should have been sacred to the cause of freedom.[124]

A great number of verse writers used Washington as a theme in the forties and fifties, and in much of their work there is little or no political significance. Few of these productions are as memorable as a single line of James Russell Lowell's, who said that he found in a cemetery,

> Sixty-two second Washingtons; two or three Jacksons . . .[125]

And few of them are so prophetic as a couplet written by St. George Tucker:

> And future ages, when thy fame they scan,
> Will deem thee Freedom's myth—thou more than man.[126]

---

[123] In William Cullen Bryant, *The White-Footed Deer, and Other Poems* (New York, 1844), p. 8. "Washington" is not included in most of the later editions of Bryant. It is a revision of an ode which Bryant wrote in 1839 to be sung at the New York celebration of the Jubilee of the Constitution, which was the semi-centennial of Washington's first inauguration. The earlier form, untitled, appears in John Quincy Adams, *The Jubilee of the Constitution* . . . (New York, 1839), p. 124. In both forms the poem consists of four quatrains, and the theme is the greatness of the Union and its founders.

Dixon Wecter mentions the poem which Bryant wrote for the 1839 celebration, but he erroneously quotes as of that date a stanza which actually is from "The Twenty-second of February," one of Bryant's last compositions. See Wecter, *The Hero in America, a Chronicle of Hero-Worship* (New York, 1941), p. 139. "The Twenty-second of February," first published in the *Sunday School Times* in 1878, is a graceful tribute wherein Washington's life and fame are likened to the calm and majestic course of the Hudson. It appears in Bryant, *The Poetical Works . . . with a Memoir of His Life by Richard Henry Stoddard* . . . (New York, 1910), pp. 399–400.

[124] In John Greenleaf Whittier, *The Writings* . . . , 7 vols. (large paper ed.; Cambridge, Mass., 1888), III, 128–130. Whittier's "The Vow of Washington" was written some thirty years later.

[125] James Russell Lowell, "A Fable for Critics" (1848), in Lowell, *The Complete Poetical Works* . . . (Cambridge ed.; Boston and New York, [1897]), p. 147.

[126] St. George Tucker, "A Poetical Address, Delivered before the Literary Societies of Washington College, Lexington . . . ," *Southern Literary Messenger*, XXV

162   *Verse*

Ann Pamela Cunningham, of South Carolina, in 1853 began the movement that resulted in the Mount Vernon Ladies' Association of the Union. The Association was composed largely of Southern women, and their appeals and those that others made for them, occasionally in verse, implied the hope that in some small way they might strenghten national ties.[127] But some writers cited Washington more pointedly. A Masonic "Hymn, to Be Sung at the Tomb of Washington, June 24, 1851," contains the couplet:

> Let the Union he founded forever remain!
> Strike powerless the arm which would sever its chain . . .[128]

And in 1856, when national attention was fixed on the violence in Kansas, Oliver Wendell Holmes wrote his "Ode for Washington's

---

(August, 1857), 113–121. This Tucker was the grandson of the St. George Tucker of Revolutionary days.

Among the poems of the forties and fifties are the following: John Pierpont, "Ode for the Fourth of July," in Griswold, *Poets and Poetry of America*, p. 59; H. T. Tuckerman, "Greenough's Statue of Washington," *Southern Literary Messenger*, VII (October, 1841), 742; "Lines, Written after Reading the Life of Gen'l Washington," *Magnolia*, III (February, 1841), 95; "George Washington," by "Horace," *Knickerbocker*, XXII (November, 1843), 445; George Rogers, *George Washington, Crowned by "Equality, Fraternity, and Liberty"* . . . (New York, 1849); Mary E. Hewitt, "Songs of Our Land," in Griswold, *Female Poets of America*, pp. 187–188; "Washington," by "Herbert," *Knickerbocker*, XXXVIII (January, 1851), 40; Thomas Holley Chivers, "Washington," in *The Lost Pleiad* (New York, 1845), p. 18; "The Mighty Dead," in *Eonchs of Ruby* . . . (New York, 1851), p. 31; "Ganymede" and "Liberty" in *Virginalia; or, Songs of My Summer Nights* . . . (Philadelphia, 1853), pp. 15–19, 100–109; "America," by "an Adopted Citizen," *Knickerbocker*, XLIII (April, 1854), 399; "Fable for Rechabites," quoted in "Editor's Table," *Knickerbocker*, XLIV (December, 1854), 651–652; G. W. P. Custis, "To Him Who Was First in War . . . ," in Hincks and Smyth, *op. cit.*, pp. 21–22; William Gilmore Simms, "The Battle Feast," in *The Forayers*, Chapter XLVI; Henry Pickering, "The House in Which I Was Born: Once the Headquarters of Washington," in Duyckinck, *op. cit.*, II, 26; John Weik, *Washington as a Child* . . . (Philadelphia, [1856]); R. R. Belshaw, "Ode to Washington," *United States Democratic Review*, New Series, XL (August, 1857), 170–171; James Gates Percival, "Washington's Name," in Percival, *op. cit.*, I, 370; "The Sword and the Staff," quoted in Benson J. Lossing, *Mount Vernon and Its Associations* . . . (New York, 1859), p. 121.

[127]"To the Daughters of Washington," *Southern Literary Messenger*, XXI (May, 1855), 318–321; "Mount Vernon," *ibid.*, XXI (December, 1855), 762; Isaac Maclellan, "A Vision of Mount Vernon," *Knickerbocker*, XLVIII (August, 1856), 118; George W. Young, "The Birth-day of Washington," in *Washington's Birth-day Celebration at Irving College* . . . (Baltimore, 1859), pp. 26–28.

[128]In Benjamin B. French, *An Address on the Masonic Character and Standing of Washington* . . . (Washington, D.C., 1851).

Verse 163

Birthday." He asked Americans to heed "the Father's dying voice," which admonished:

> Love your country first of all!
> Listen not to idle questions
> If its bands may be untied;
> Doubt the patriot whose suggestions
> Strive a nation to divide![129]

In the South, particularly in Virginia, enthusiasm for Washington did not wane. A patriotic celebration was held at Jamestown in 1857, the 250th anniversary of the English settlement there. The principal address, delivered by former President Tyler, was followed by the recitation of a long historical poem. James Barron Hope, the poet and reciter, concluded with a rather ominous figure. He proclaimed that the luster of Washington's name should be shed upon the form of Virginia:

> Its fittest place is on Virginia's brow,
> As, kneeling down, to God she sends her vow—
> That, as her great son left her, she will be;
> And live on proudly—free amid the free;
> Or, finding that she may not thus remain,
> Like Samson, grasp the pillars of the fane,
> And leave all wreck, where erst in pride it rose,
> Tomb for herself in common with her foes.[130]

The unveiling of Crawford's statue of Washington at Richmond on February 22, 1858, was celebrated in verse written by Hope and by John R. Thompson.[131] Thompson, editor of the *Southern Literary Messenger*, contributed the opening ode for the ceremony, a pseudo-Pindaric of over two hundred lines. He touched upon the importance of the occasion, the merit of the sculptor and the statue, and the past and future fame of Virginia and the nation. In the last

---

[129] In Oliver Wendell Holmes, *The Works* . . . , 13 vols. (New York, 1892), XII, 242. The ode consists of six stanzas; a portion of the fifth is quoted above. Cf. W. H. C. Hosmer, "Independence Ode," *Knickerbocker*, XLVI (August, 1855), 150.

[130] James Barron Hope, "Poem," *Southern Literary Messenger*, XXIV (June, 1857), 455–462.

[131] For speeches at the Richmond ceremonies, see *supra*, Chapter III, Section 4. Alfred Mitchell's *The Coloniad* was also written for this occasion.

of his four sections he made a plea for national unity. Asking what was the duty of those there assembled, the poet answered:

> 'T is that we here in gratitude renew
> The patriot-vows to country ever due,
> And on this holy altar firmly swear
> The blessed compact never to impair . . .[132]

Hope's terminal ode, on the other hand, is not entirely free of the gloomy note he sounded at Jamestown the year before. The first part is notable for eulogy of Virginia and for a Washington-Savior motif; visitors were welcomed to "our Bethlehem," where "the Messiah of the land was born." But after reminding Virginians that they could best applaud Washington by "standing by the Laws," Hope immediately added that if their rights should ever be denied they must unfurl their banner in the mountains and prepare to protect the freedom that Washington had left them. He even paraphrased some words attributed to the General during the Revolution, and so it was implied that Virginia might have to fight a similar war for freedom.[133]

After hostilities began, those who rallied to the Southern cause could look upon Washington as a son of the South who had led a struggle for freedom. A Confederate song entitled "The Gathering of the Southern Volunteers," sung to the tune of the "Marseillaise," has a stanza that begins:

> When Freedom plumed her radiant pinion,
> And soared to meet the western sun,
> She chose our shore for her dominion,
> And sought the home of Washington.
> And sought the home of Washington![134]

[132] John R. Thompson, "Inauguration of the Equestrian Statue of Washington . . . Opening Ode," *Southern Literary Messenger*, XXVI (March, 1858), 161-166.

[133] "The Washington Memorial Ode," in James Barron Hope, *A Wreath of Virginia Bay Leaves* . . . , ed. Janey Hope Marr (Richmond, Va., 1895), pp. 45-56. This poem is briefly and favorably reviewed, probably by John R. Thompson, in the *Southern Literary Messenger*, XXVI (March, 1858), 229-230.

Hope became a captain in the Confederate army. One of his later compositions, "Memoriae Sacrum" (1887), contains a prolonged comparison of Washington and Robert E. Lee, here called "twin rebels."

[134] *Southern Literary Messenger*, XXXII (June, 1861), 449.

Verse 165

More specific is a stanza of George H. Miles's "God Save the South," written in the early days of the war and intended as a national hymn:

> *Rebels* before,
> Our fathers of yore,
> *Rebel's* the righteous name
> *Washington* bore.
> Why, then be ours the same,
> The name that he snatched from shame,
> Making it first in fame,
> Foremost in war.[135]

That Washington was theirs is a recurrent theme in the work of Confederate poets. An anonymous piece of newspaper verse entitled "Rebels" presents the Southern attitude particularly well:

> Rebels! 'tis our family name—
> Our father, Washington,
> Was the arch-rebel in the fight
> And gave the name to us—a right
> Of father unto son.[136]

Northern bards, needless to say, saw the situation in a different light. Oliver Wendell Holmes wrote "Under the Washington Elm, Cambridge, April 27, 1861." Less than a century after the "brave old tree" had witnessed a glorious scene of the Revolution, mused Holmes, it appeared that only half of the work was done. He looked upon the current conflict as liberty's second battle.[137] To the same period belongs Walt Whitman's "Virginia—the West." In the first of three quatrains the poet envisioned Virginia, "noble sire fallen on evil days," advancing madly, knife in hand, "toward the

---

[135] In [Lizzie Cary Daniel, ed.], *Confederate Scrap-Book* . . . (Richmond, Va., 1893), pp. 214–216.
[136] In Nora Fontaine M. Davidson, ed., *Cullings from the Confederacy* . . . (Washington, D.C., 1903), p. 24. The stanza quoted is the second of eight. Cf. "The South's Appeal to Washington," *ibid.*, p. 30; "Men of the South!" by "G. B. J.," *Southern Literary Messenger*, XXXII (May, 1861), 369; William Gilmore Simms, "The Soul of the South, an Ode," *ibid.*, XXXIV (February and March, 1862), 101–102.
[137] In Holmes, *op. cit.*, XIII, 72–73.

Mother of All," evidently the Union. But in the second stanza "the noble son" from the prairie, followed by a blue-clad multitude, rushes to the Mother's defense. In the final lines she speaks:

> As to you Rebellious, (I seemed to hear her say,)
>   Why strive against me, and why seek my life?
> When you yourself forever provide to defend me?
> For you provided me Washington—and now these also.[138]

A few lines of "Lee in the Capital," written by Herman Melville some time after the cessation of hostilities, present an interesting new motif, a comparison of Washington and Robert E. Lee. The scene is the United States Congress:

> Awhile with curious eyes they scan
> The Chief, who led invasion's van—
> Allied by family to one,
> Founder of the Arch the Invader warred upon:
> Who looks at Lee must think of Washington;
> In pain must think, and hide the thought,
> So deep with grievous meaning is it fraught.[139]

Highly significant of the trend of American hero worship is Richard Henry Stoddard's "Abraham Lincoln, a Horatian Ode" (1865). Stoddard was one of the first to express an essential contrast in popular conceptions of Washington and Lincoln, a contrast which accelerated the acceptance of Lincoln as Washington's peer. Referring to Lincoln as his "country's father," a title which had been Washington's alone, the poet spoke of:

> The People, of whom he was one:
> No gentleman, like Washington,
>   (Whose bones, methinks, make room,
>   To have him in their tomb!)[140]

---

[138]In Walt Whitman, *Leaves of Grass*, 3 vols. in one (Garden City, N.Y., 1920), II, 56–57. "By Blue Ontario's Shore" (*ibid.*, II, 107–126) contains a mention of Washington.

[139]In Herman Melville, *The Works* . . . , 16 vols. (London, 1922–1924), XVI, 164. This poem was included in *Battle Pieces and Aspects of the War* (1866).

[140]In Richard Henry Stoddard, *The Poems* . . . (New York, 1880), p. 280. The stanza quoted echoes lines twenty and twenty-one of Ben Jonson's famous elegy

Verse

In tone, poetical representation of Washington varied little for about a century beginning with 1775. Bards who were his contemporaries hailed him in glowing terms from their classical idiom. "Godlike" was one of their favorite adjectives for him, and they likened him most often to Fabius and Cincinnatus, although sundry Roman, Greek, and Hebrew worthies likewise received their consideration. Their forms were epic, ode, and occasionally ballad. Discordant notes were few. Unpublished at the time it was written, Tom Paine's instruction to a sculptor was found among his posthumous papers:

> Take from the mine the coldest, hardest stone,
> It needs no fashion, it is Washington;
> But if you chisel, let your strokes be rude,
> And on his breast engrave *Ingratitude*.[141]

Several American verse writers were attracted to Washington during the period of the Virginia dynasty, but in quality their entire output is easily surpassed by the concluding lines of Byron's "Ode to Napoleon Buonaparte" (1814), frequently quoted:

> Where may the wearied eye repose
>   When gazing on the Great;
> Where neither guilty glory glows,
>   Nor despicable state?
> Yes—One—the first—the last—the best—
> The Cincinnatus of the West,
>   Whom Envy dared not hate,

"To the Memory of My Beloved, the Author Mr. William Shakespeare . . ." See also "The Ballad of Valley Forge," *ibid.*, pp. 246-260.

Among other verses touching upon Washington and written in the sixties are the following: Thomas Dunn English, "The Two Voices," *Southern Literary Messenger*, XXXI (November, 1860), 322-323; "The Eagle and the Harp," by "Billy Shields," *Knickerbocker*, LVIII (October, 1861), 371-373; "The President at the Washington Monument," *ibid.*, LVIII (November, 1861), 397-398; Sidney Hayden, untitled verses in Hayden, *Washington and His Masonic Compeers* . . . (New York, 1866), pp. 36-37.

[141] In Duyckinck, *op. cit.*, I, 200. Cf. Hesketh Pearson, *Tom Paine, Friend of Mankind* (New York, 1937), p. 218.

Bequeathed the name of Washington,
To make man blush there was but one.[142]

The two decades preceding the Civil War saw a renaissance of national interest in Washington and a corresponding increase in the bulk of verse touching upon him. Much of it treats the hero only incidentally in connection with the writers' views on slavery, secession, and related issues. In verse as in prose, Washington's name became an aegis for various groups: the Federalists in 1800 and 1812, and both the Union men and, to a lesser extent, the secessionists of the prewar period.

It is somewhat disappointing to find so little true poetry inspired by Washington during a time when he held undisputed reign as America's national hero. Apparently he made only occasional appeals to the better New England poets of the nineteenth century. Perhaps they felt that, as Emerson himself said, "Every hero becomes a bore at last." Certainly praise of Washington was a hackneyed subject in America long before poets of both genius and maturity made their appearance. But the situation was redeemed when James Russell Lowell wrote the best poem that has yet been written about Washington: "Under the Old Elm," a memorial poem read at Cambridge on July 3, 1875, the hundredth anniversary of Washington's taking command of the army on that spot.[143] The date lies not too far beyond the limits of this study to preclude quotation. Despite the vagueness and distortion of the accounts and descriptions at his disposal, the poet's intuition allowed him to see Washington,

No more a pallid image and a dream . . .

---

[142]In George Gordon, Lord Byron, *Poetry* . . . , ed. Ernest Hartley Coleridge, 7 vols. (London and New York, 1895-1905), III, 316. The statement about "Envy" is, of course, untrue.

Byron has in several of his poetical works stanzas or passages treating Washington which, though not so famous as the one quoted, are in some instances about as good: *Childe Harold*, Canto IV, Stanza 96, *ibid.*, II, 400; "The Vision of Judgment," Stanza LXXXIV, *ibid.*, IV, 516; *Don Juan*, Canto VIII, Stanza 5, and Canto IX, Stanza 8, *ibid.*, VI, 331 and 376; "The Age of Bronze," *ibid.*, V, 554.

[143]In Lowell, *op. cit.*, pp. 364-370.

Verse

Lowell's analysis is particularly keen in the last two stanzas of Section V:

> Minds strong by fits, irregularly great,
> That flash and darken like revolving lights,
> Catch more the vulgar eye unschooled to wait
> On the long curve of patient days and nights
> Rounding a whole life to the circle fair
> Of orbed fulfilment; and this balanced soul
> So simple in its grandeur, coldly bare
> Of draperies theatric, standing there
> In perfect symmetry of self-control,
> Seems not so great at first, but greater grows
> Still as we look, and by experience learn
> How grand this quiet is, how nobly stern
> The discipline that wrought through lifelong throes
> That energetic passion of repose.
>
> A nature too decorous and severe,
> Too self-respectful in its griefs and joys,
> For ardent girls and boys
> Who find no genius in a mind so clear
> That its grave depths seem obvious and near,
> Nor a soul great that made so little noise.
> They feel no force in that calm-cadenced phrase,
> The habitual full-dress of his well-bred mind,
> That seems to pace the minuet's courtly maze
> And tell of ampler leisures, roomier length of days.
>
> . . . . . .
>
> It was a world of statelier movement then
> Than this we fret in, he a denizen
> Of that ideal Rome that made a man for men.

Unlike most Northern writers, Lowell took full cognizance of the fact that Washington was a Virginian. The last section of his poem is a graceful plea for reconciliation between Virginia and the Union; it opens:

> Virginia gave us this imperial man
> Cast in the massive mould

Of those high-statured ages old
Which into grander forms our mortal metal ran;
She gave us this unblemished gentleman:
What shall we give her back but love and praise
As in the dear old unestrangëd days
Before the inevitable wrong began?
Mother of States and undiminished men,
Thou gavest us a country, giving him . . .

CHAPTER VI

DRAMA

AMERICAN ACHIEVEMENT in the field of drama was, throughout the period here studied, less considerable than that in the other major literary genres. Few towns were large enough to become theatrical centers. In New England a strong religious prejudice against the theater was overcome slowly. In no section was the writing of plays a profitable business; British, French, and German plays could be adapted to the American stage easily and without payment of royalty. Yet American playwrights made their appearance, and many of them dealt with native themes.[1]

From Revolutionary days onward, Washington was occasionally characterized in plays, some intended for the stage and some closet dramas. In nearly all he appears as General Washington, or, if the treatment is allegorical, his connection with the Revolution is pointed up. In addition, he is a topic of discussion in a number of plays in which he is not among the *dramatis personae*. Several significant examples of this indirect type of treatment are included in the present chapter.

The long shadow of Shakespeare lies on several of the plays here considered. Fully half of them are in verse. American playwrights felt that the dignity of dramatic verse was peculiarly fitted to so exalted a theme as Washington.[2]

[1] Later plays dealing with Washington have been treated in an excellent study: Samuel Blaine Shirk, *The Characterization of George Washington in American Plays since 1875* . . . (Easton, Pa., 1949). Shirk wrote this work as a doctoral dissertation at the University of Pennsylvania.

[2] Plays treated in the present chapter are in prose unless verse is mentioned or quoted.

I

In 1774 the Continental Congress passed an economy resolution discouraging the performance of plays and shows of all types. A number of dramatic satires soon made their appearance, however, some reflecting Patriot sympathies, others of Tory persuasion; only a few of them are known to have been produced. In one of the most important and interesting of the Patriot plays, *The Fall of British Tyranny*, published in Philadelphia in 1776, it seems that Washington made his first appearance in drama.[3] An American chronicle play, *The Fall of British Tyranny* opens with a clever and vigorous scene in the British Parliament, and then the scene shifts to Boston, to Virginia, and elsewhere in the New World. Lord Bute and one or two other English lords are made responsible for the war. Washington appears only in the last act, with the American army at Cambridge. In rather turgid prose he expresses his grief over news of General Montgomery's death, but there is some power in the scene in which he and Generals Charles Lee and Israel Putnam pledge themselves to continue the fight till death if need be.[4]

Another Patriot play, a little farce entitled *The Motley Assembly* and attributed to Mrs. Mercy Otis Warren, scores Tories and fainthearted Whigs of Boston society in 1779.[5] Washington is not in the cast, but in one particularly interesting scene a toast to "godlike glorious Washington" is proposed by Captain Aid, of the American army. The hostess on this occasion, Mrs. Flourish, is one of a group here satirized: ladies who, at a time when the Americans are not

---

[3]*The Fall of British Tyranny; or, American Liberty Triumphant* . . . ([Philadelphia, 1776]), reprinted in Montrose J. Moses, ed., *Representative Plays by American Dramatists*, 3 vols. (New York, 1918-1925), I, 277-350. The play is ascribed to John, or Joseph, Leacock. A full discussion is given by Moses Coit Tyler, *The Literary History of the American Revolution, 1763-1783*, 2 vols. (New York, [1941]), II, 198-207.

[4]Washington appears in Scenes 3 and 4 of Act V. In Act I, Scene 5, the British discuss his poltroonery at Braddock's fight.

[5][Mercy Otis Warren], *The Motley Assembly: a Farce* . . . (Boston, 1779).

faring well, sneer at the Revolutionary effort and speak patronizingly even of Washington. When the toast is proposed, she bridles a bit. The following dialogue ensues:

> Mrs. Flourish: Why, he is no more than man, Captain Aid.
> Aid: Then all mankind beside are less, madam.
> Mrs. Flourish: You have not seen all mankind, sir. I believe Mr. Washington, or General Washington, if you please, is a very honest, good kind of a man, and has taken infinite pains to keep your army together, and I wish he may find his account in it. But doubtless there are his equals—so say no more.
> Aid: If you meant that as a compliment, madam, it is really so cold a one, that it has made me shiver. I will, therefore, with your leave, drop the subject, and take another glass of wine.

Such intense partisanship is paralleled in Tory plays. An especially devastating Loyalist satire is an anonymous farce called *The Battle of Brooklyn*, published in New York by James Rivington.[6] This is a reply in kind to *The Fall of British Tyranny*, and the American cause and its leaders are ridiculed unmercifully. The military incompetence of the Americans is played up; Washington is presented as a usurper who fears a complete disaffection of his troops at any moment, and the other "Rebel Chiefs" make an even worse showing. But *The Battle of Brooklyn* is also a coarse and scurrilous attack on the private lives of the Patriots, including their Commander-in-Chief. A chambermaid, Betty, mentions that Washington has given her thirty dollars; and at one point he himself, in the midst of a soliloquy that shows his overweening ambition, stops short because, as he says, he must keep an appointment with Betty.

Entirely different from the dramatic satires of Revolutionary days are three verse productions of the next decade. The earliest of these is John Parke's "Virginia: a Pastoral Drama," written for Washington's Birthday in 1784. Nymphs, shepherds, and other pastoral characters rejoice at the return of peace and the homecoming of Daphnis (Washington). Daphnis himself does not appear. The

---

[6] *The Battle of Brooklyn, a Farce* . . . (New York, 1776), reprinted in *Long Island Publications*, No. 1 (Brooklyn, N.Y., 1873). The scenes mentioned occur in the first of the two acts.

piece has no plot but consists of songs, dialogues, monologues, and choruses. The following lines of Hylas are typical:

> Daphnis the great the good is come,
> To bless again his native home.
> He comes, he comes, the hero comes,
> From martial camps and noisy drums:
> To greet his own Virginia's shore,
> Where Daemon war shall rage no more . . .[7]

Whether "Virginia" was ever performed is uncertain, but in the fall of the same year General Washington's deeds were celebrated by the presentation of "A Masque Written at the Warm-Springs in Virginia," by Hugh Henry Brackenridge.[8] Brackenridge, a circuit judge at the time, was among the guests at the popular resort when it was learned that the nation's hero, on a tour of his western lands, would stop there for a day. Characters of the masque that he wrote for the occasion include the Potomac, the Delaware, the Ohio, and the Genius of the Springs, as well as Naiads. The Potomac is eloquent in praise of Washington, whom he calls his son:

> Go tell the naiads and the jocund deities,
> To cull their choicest flowers; a noble name,
> Has come this day to do them honour.
> That chief whose fame has oft been heard by them,
> In contest with Britannia's arms; that chief
> Whom I myself have seen quitting the farm,
> By no ambition, but by virtue led,
> Arising at his country's call, and swift
> The challenge of the vet'ran foe receiving.[9]

[7] [John Parke], "Virginia: a Pastoral Drama on the Birth-Day of an Illustrious Personage . . . ," in [Parke], *Translations from the Greek and Latin, with Original Poems* (Philadelphia, 1786), pp. 321-334. A number of the so-called translations of Horace in this volume are really adaptations, some of which bring in Washington, e.g., "Elegy 2," p. 211; "Ode 3 on Masonry," p. 259; "Ode IX," p. 141; "Ode XIV, on the Return of Augustus from Spain. Paraphrased on General Washington's Return to Virginia," p. 102; and "Ode 6, for the New Year, 1784," p. 266. The pieces are curious and clever.

[8] In Hugh Henry Brackenridge, *Gazette Publications* (Carlisle, Pa., 1806).

[9] *Ibid.*, p. 37. Brackenridge's biographer gives an interesting account of this production and Washington's visit. See Claude Milton Newlin, *The Life and Writings of Hugh Henry Brackenridge* (Princeton, N.J., 1932), pp. 65-68.

Drama

In a third dramatic effort of the period, the anonymous *Columbia and Britannia* (1787), Washington appears several times under the name of Fabius.[10] Designed for the use of elocution classes, the work consists of several discrete Revolutionary scenes in blank verse and couplets.

Colonel John Parke, whose "Virginia" is discussed above, published in the same volume with it a verse epistle to his friend Peter Markoe "On his Excellent Tragedy called *The Patriot Chief*."[11] Markoe was advised to turn his talents to American subjects. Over a century later, Paul Leicester Ford said of *The Patriot Chief* (1784) that it "was based on his [Washington's] Revolutionary services."[12] Arthur Hobson Quinn declares *The Patriot Chief* an early example of the drama used in America to promulgate political ideas, for Markoe states in his Preface that the schemes of the villain Otanes to overthrow King Dorus of Lydia show the evils of a strong aristocracy.[13] Sister Mary C. Diebels, in a scholarly study of Markoe and his works, finds parallels between the character of Dorus and that of Washington and states that the character of the ancient king is a deliberate tribute to the contemporary hero.[14] Markoe wrote strong tributes to Washington in some of his satirical and shorter verses, but resemblances between the protagonist of *The Patriot Chief* and Washington are not equally clear to all readers.[15]

Similar to the masquelike productions of Parke and Brackenridge is an elaborate masque in five acts, *Americana; or, A New Tale of*

---

[10]*Columbia and Britannia; a Dramatic Piece*, by a Citizen of the United States (New London, Conn., 1787). Oscar Wegelin (*Early American Plays*, New York, 1900, p. 2) dates this 1786.

[11]Parke, *op. cit.*, pp. 295-296.

[12]Paul Leicester Ford, *Washington and the Theatre* (New York, 1899), p. 25.

[13]Arthur Hobson Quinn, *A History of the American Drama from the Beginning to the Civil War* (2d ed.; New York, 1943), p. 88.

[14]Sister Mary Chrysostom Diebels, S.S.N.D., *Peter Markoe ... a Philadelphia Writer ...* (Washington, D.C., 1944), p. 13.

[15][Peter Markoe], *The Patriot Chief: a Tragedy* (Philadelphia, 1784). In "An Epistle to Mr. O-w-ld," (*Pennsylvania Journal*, February 21, 1787), Markoe refers to Washington as "The CHIEF." He also praises him, as "Tully," in the *Times* (Philadelphia, 1788) and in "Harmony; an Ode in Music, in Commemoration of the Birthday of His Excellency General Washington," in *Miscellaneous Poems* (Philadelphia, 1787), and in the *American Museum*, I (February, 1787), 161-162.

the *Genii*, supposedly written during the Revolution but not performed until 1798, when it was presented in Charleston, South Carolina. The motifs of the Revolution are dramatized for the edification of an old hermit who has lived in the Appalachians through the early years of the war and so knows nothing of it. Elutheria, the genius of liberty, is transplanted from England to America and so becomes the companion of Americana, the genius of America. Among those who assist Elutheria are Fulmenifer (Franklin) and Etherius, the American Commander-in-Chief. The unknown author showed considerable skill and originality in inventing and handling a great diversity of characters. In the climactic scene Etherius rescues and revives Elutheria, who has been abducted and mistreated by Typhon (tyranny) and Fastidio (pride). Among the lines which Etherius addresses to her are the following:

> Spotless innocence condemned to die,
> Sweet life repriev'd, or what's still valued more,
> Honour retriev'd is not so very dear
> As thou, fair Elutheria, art to us.
> As dear as virtue struggling with distress
> Is to the Heavenly Powers, so dear art thou,
> O Liberty, to our adoring souls![16]

Washington seems to have been portrayed infrequently in stage productions during his presidency,[17] but a few writers took opportunity to discuss his policies through the medium of stage dialogue. *The Traveller Returned*, by Mrs. Judith Sargent Murray, was produced in Boston early in 1796. The scene is Revolutionary, but the plot concerns a divided family and has no connection with the war.

[16] *Americana; or, A New Tale of the Genii* . . . (Baltimore, 1802), p. 63.
[17] An interesting French item is a classical tragedy by Edmé Louis Billardon de Sauvigny entitled *Vashington; ou, La Liberté du nouveau monde* (ed. Gilbert Chinard, Princeton, N.J., 1941), which was produced with some success in Paris in 1791. French Revolutionary situations are here presented under the guise of American Revolutionary incidents. The central character is the embodiment of all virtues. How remote is the rambling series of incidents from American historical fact may be judged by an example: in the third act Washington tells one Lincol, another Patriot, that his son, young Lincol, has been killed while rescuing Washington's wife and son.

Characters at one point discuss Washington's genius and only disagree as to whether, in view of his treatment of André, he is a man of sensibility.[18] More pointed and timely discussion occurs in John Murdock's *The Politicians*, published in Philadelphia in 1798 and evidently intended as a political commentary rather than for production. Bitter dissension over the Jay Treaty and ensuing developments enters into the conversation of various members of the cast. The author was apparently in sympathy with those who defended Washington's action. The dialogue on both sides is realistic and pungent. A Mrs. Turbulent declares that Washington "never was equal to the situation he was placed in; vastly has his talents been over-rated; he possesses none beyond that of being overseer to a Virginia plantation, or the superintendance of a horse-stable: he is an excellent judge of horses."[19]

The most important name in American drama during Washington's lifetime was that of William Dunlap. In 1789 Dunlap wrote an interlude in verse, "Darby's Return," wherein an Irish soldier goes back to Ireland and describes his adventures in America and elsewhere. Darby's allusion to the newly elected President is slight but has interest because Washington himself witnessed the first performance and was amused by the lines:

> Soon after that I saw another show,
> A man who'd fought to free the land from woe,
> Like *me* had left his *farm a sold'ring* for to go;
> But having gained the point, he had, *like me*,
> Return'd his own *potatoe ground to see;*

---

[18][Judith Sargent Murray], *The Traveller Returned*, in *The Gleaner* . . . by Constantia [pseud.], 3 vols. (Boston, 1798), III, 116-163. The portion treating Washington is pp. 122-123.

[19][John Murdock], *The Politicians; or, A State of Things* . . . (Philadelphia, 1798), Act I, Scene 1.

William Munford's "The Political Contest; a Dialogue" (in *Poems* . . . [Richmond, Va., 1798], pp. 163-175) is a verse treatment of the same theme. Both the Federalists and the Republicans are criticized, and the author seems opposed to extreme action in the direction of alliance with either France or Britain. "A," the moderate party to the dialogue, speaks of the Jay Treaty as:

> The signal of my country's shame,
> Which proves that Godlike Washington,
> For once a foolish thing has done . . .

But there he couldn't rest; with one accord
He's called to be a kind of—, not a lord—
I don't know what—he's not a great man, sure,
For poor men love him just as he was poor!
They love him like a father or a brother.

. . . . . .

KATHLEEN. How look'd he Darby? Was he short or tall?
DARBY. Why sure I didn't see him; to be sure,
As I was looking hard from out the door,
I saw a man in regimentals fine,
All lace and glitter, bother'um and shine;
And so I look'd at him till all was gone,
And then, I found that he was not the one.[20]

Dunlap relates that the President looked grave until the last of these lines was pronounced, then burst into hearty laughter.[21]

A far more important play is *André*, performed in New York in 1798, the first of Dunlap's attempts at tragedy on a native theme. Washington here has an important role. A young hero named Bland, an American friend of André, pleads in vain with the General in behalf of the condemned man.[22] A highly dramatic scene is that in which Washington learns that Sir Henry Clinton threatens to execute Bland's father, now a British prisoner, if André is executed. Washington's words to the British messenger at this point have dignity and vigor:

'Tis well, sir; bear this message in return.
Sir Henry Clinton knows the laws of arms:

[20]William Dunlap, "Darby's Return,—a Comic Sketch. As Performed at the Theatre in This City, with Universal Applause. Written in 1789 . . . ," *New York Magazine*, I (January, 1790), 47–51.
[21]William Dunlap, *A History of the American Theatre* (New York, 1832), pp. 84–85.
For interesting information on Washington's attendance at the theater, see Ford, *op. cit.*; "Darby's Return" is reprinted as an appendix of this.
[22]Major John André, painter, writer, and gallant, was captured out of uniform in 1780 while attempting to return to the British lines after an interview with Benedict Arnold regarding the betrayal of West Point. He was tried and sentenced to be hanged as a spy. André wrote General Washington asking that he be shot rather than hanged; the request was not granted.

Drama

He is a soldier, and I think, a brave one.
The prisoners he retains he must account for.
Perhaps the reckoning's near. I likewise am
A soldier; entrusted by my country.
What I shall judge most for that country's good
That shall I do. When doubtful, I consult
My country's friends; never her enemies.
In André's case there are no doubts; 'tis clear:
Sir Henry Clinton knows it.[23]

Moved by the power of Washington's speech, young Bland realizes that justice should proceed regardless of the persons involved. Dunlap's portrayal of General Washington is more convincing than that of many writers of Revolutionary romances in the following century.

André is now considered one of the best surviving American dramas of the eighteenth century. Yet its production on the stage met with little success. The incidents treated were near enough to the audience to arouse a great deal of prejudice; moreover, Dunlap here presented a Federalist point of view when political feeling ran high.[24]

2

During the Revolution and later, actors sometimes spoke from the stage a tribute to Washington in the form of prologue or epilogue, usually in verse. Of such nature is the epilogue written by Jonathan Mitchell Sewall for a production of Addison's *Cato* in 1778.[25] After

---

[23]William Dunlap, *André: a Tragedy in Five Acts* . . . (New York, 1798), reprinted in Moses, *op. cit.*, I, 499-564. The quotation is from Act III, Scene 3. The final act seems to show the influence of Otway's *Venice Preserved*, to which allusion is made in the dialogue.

[24]Cf. Quinn, *op. cit.*, p. 88.
In *The Glory of Columbia—Her Yeomanry* . . . (New York, 1803), a revision of *André*, Dunlap's treatment of Washington remains essentially the same.

[25]*Supra*, Chapter V, Section 5. Cf. "Occasional EPILOGUE to the CONTRAST: a COMEDY, Written by Royall Tyler, Esq.," *Massachusetts Magazine*, V (March, 1794), 179-180.
When Washington himself was a visitor, the students of Washington College, in Maryland, added a similar occasional epilogue to their presentation of a tragedy concerning Gustavus Vasa, the Swedish deliverer. See Nathaniel Wright Stephen-

news of his death was received, monodies and odes in Washington's honor were likewise pronounced in theaters. One delivered in the New-York Theatre on December 30, 1799, consists of a hundred lines in heroic couplets. In theme and sentiment it is similar to scores of other poems which marked the occasion.[26]

A curious work of 1800, probably not intended for production of any kind, is *Washingtons Ankunft in Elisium*, a Pennsylvania German sketch. Herein the hero is shown in heaven, conversing on sundry topics with Brutus, Columbus, Franklin, and William Penn. When Franklin and Penn inquire about conditions in America at the time of his departure, Washington deplores the violence of party feeling in Pennsylvania.[27]

The interest in Revolutionary themes which followed the publication of Cooper's *The Spy* extended in a limited degree to drama as well as fiction.[28] In March, 1822, Charles Powell Clinch's dramatization of *The Spy* itself began a long run in New York. Clinch, however, did not put Mr. Harper (Washington) on the stage; his part in the plot is presented indirectly in the conversation of various persons.[29] The reason for this omission can be only a matter for conjecture. Perhaps Clinch found the characterization of Washington difficult, or perhaps he felt that he was too sacred a figure for the stage.[30]

Throughout the period here considered, playwrights who used Revolutionary material put praise of Washington in the mouths of their characters in plays wherein he himself does not appear. The

---

son and Waldo Hilary Dunn, *George Washington*, 2 vols. (New York and London, 1940), II, 527-528.

[26]"Monody on the Death of George Washington . . . ," *Monthly Magazine and American Review*, I (December, 1799), 478-479. Cf. the ode by Samuel Low, also recited in the New-York Theatre: *supra*, Chapter V, Section 6.

[27]*Washingtons Ankunft in Elisium, eine Dialogiste Skizze* . . . (Lancaster, Pa., 1800).

[28]Cf. Quinn, *op. cit.*, pp. 269, 277, 291.

[29]Charles Powell Clinch, *The Spy* . . . , in *Metamora and Other Plays* . . . , ed. Eugene R. Page (Princeton, N.J., 1941), Vol. XIV of "America's Lost Plays," ed. Barrett H. Clark, 20 vols.

[30]Samuel Blaine Shirk, dealing with plays written after 1875, has found four stage adaptations of *The Spy*; in all, the role of Mr. Harper is retained. See Shirk, *op. cit.*, pp. 54-57.

hero of *King's Bridge Cottage* (1826) declares: "I have fought and bled by the side of that god-like hero—followed him through fields of carnage—gazed upon his calm collected features amid the din and rage of battle, and thought him more than mortal . . ."[31]

A new departure in dramatic treatment of Washington was made by George Washington Parke Custis in *The Indian Prophecy*, first produced in Philadelphia on July 4, 1827. This brief play concerns an incident prior to Revolutionary days, and the scene is the Kanawha region of Virginia, now West Virginia. Dr. James Craik, who accompanied Washington at the time, told Custis of an old Indian chief who recognized Washington in 1770 because he and his braves had shot at him in Braddock's fight in 1755. The chief declared that Washington was under the special protection of the Great Spirit; this conclusion he drew from the fact that the Indians had tried in vain to shoot him on the earlier occasion.[32] Custis added a few fictitious characters and situations, but the speech of Menawa, the Indian chief, is the climax of the play. Because he reveres a specially chosen person, Menawa refuses to smoke, drink, or eat with Colonel Washington. He drops dead at the conclusion of his speech, which runs in part:

Menawa is old, and soon will be gathered to the Great Council . . . but ere he goes, there is something here, which bids him speak in the voice of Prophecy. Listen! *The Great Spirit protects that man, and*

[31]*King's Bridge Cottage* . . . (New York, 1826), p. 26. The play is sometimes attributed to Samuel Woodworth.
Cf. William Dunlap, *The Father; or, American Shandyism* (New York, 1789), p. 20; Robert Munford, *The Patriots*, in *A Collection of Plays and Poems* (Petersburg, Va., 1798), pp. 78, 84, 93; and also in *William and Mary Quarterly*, Series 3, VI (July, 1949), 448–503; M. M. Noah, *She Would Be A Soldier* . . . (1819), in Moses, *op. cit.*, I, 644; Walter Lee, *Lafayette; or, The Fortress of Olmutz* (New York, 1824), pp. 20–21; Samuel Woodworth, *Lafayette; or, The Castle of Olmutz* (New York, 1824), pp. 21–22; George L. Stephens, *The Patriots; or, Union and Freedom* (Boston, 1834), pp. 15, 18, 26, 36, 65, 84; Oliver Bell Bunce, *Love in '76* (1857), in Moses, *op. cit.*, III, 207, 209; C. E. B. Howe, *Signing the Declaration of Independence* . . . (New York, [1866]), p. 10.

[32]George Washington Parke Custis, *The Indian Prophecy, a National Drama in Two Acts* . . . (Georgetown, D.C., 1828), Preface. The incident is also related in Custis's *Recollections and Private Memoirs of Washington*. See also Murray H. Nelligan, "American Nationalism on the Stage: the Plays of George Washington Parke Custis (1781–1857)," *The Virginia Magazine of History and Biography*, LVIII (July, 1950), 299–325.

guides his destiny. He will become the Chief of Nations, and a people yet unborn shall hail him as the Founder of a mighty Empire!

The Indian Prophecy is interesting because it brought to the stage a phase of Washington's career other than the Revolutionary. But it contributed little in the way of characterization. Colonel Washington here is much talked about and glorified but is himself a colorless figure.

Although Revolutionary themes attracted a number of American dramatists throughout the period 1825–1860, only about one fifth of their plays have been preserved. Among the lost plays are found many titles which indicate that Washington may possibly have been in the cast, and in the following, all of which were produced, he almost certainly had an important part: *Washington; or, The Savior of His Country* (1831); John Dumont, *Washington; or, The Retaliation* (1832); James Rees, *Washington; or, The Hero of Valley Forge* (1832); James Rees, *Washington Preserved* (1836); S. S. Steele, *Washington and Napoleon; or, The Conqueror's Dream* (1841); *Three Eras of Washington's Life* (1849); *General George Washington; or, The Traitor Foiled* (1850); *Washington; or, The Path to Fame and Glory* (1851).[33] But he appears in few surviving plays of the period.

Washington is a background figure, vaguely characterized by dignity and military competence, in Nathaniel H. Bannister's *Putnam, the Iron Son of '76*, which was first produced in 1844. This popular play features General Putnam's amazing adventures and narrow escapes. Washington too has a narrow escape when a villain plots to capture him in order to secure a reward from General Clinton. He is rescued by an Indian chief who—like the one in *The Indian Prophecy* of Custis—states that he was present at the Battle of the Monongahela, where he and his warriors fired their rifles many times at the Great White Chief without touching him.[34]

[33] The information in this paragraph is supplied by Quinn, *op. cit.*, pp. 277–278. In contrast, Quinn finds that of plays on Revolutionary themes produced before 1825 fully half are extant.

[34] Nathaniel H. Bannister, *Putnam, the Iron Son of '76* . . . (Boston, [1859]), Act III, Scene 3. Arthur Hobson Quinn states in the *DAB* that Bannister's *Richmond*

Drama

In *The Death of Capt. Nathan Hale* (1845), by David Trumbull, the Commander-in-Chief has a somewhat more important part. Although he sorely needs information, he is most reluctant to allow Hale to risk his life. Washington is more verbose here than in most of his roles in extant plays of the time. He soliloquizes in grandiloquent style, saying at one point:

How awfully important, yet welcome is my position! Immense responsibility! Interests beyond all computation hang on every passing day and hour. Future ages—uncounted millions yet to live depend on *me* for happiness or misery: upon me are cast all eyes—my fellow patriots, my country, wives, mothers, sinewy youths, gray-haired men and children, eager with interest watch my every motion. If by my faithlessness the cause of freedom fail, reproach, and an unresting conscience with sharper stings will never cease to goad my soul.[35]

The Miller of New Jersey, by John Brougham, concerns the valuable assistance rendered the American cause in 1776 through information supplied by a miller and his brother, semicomic figures.[36] Washington appears in each of the three acts. He thanks the brothers and makes one of them a captain. He is also shown in conference with officers of his staff. The first act ends with a "Tableau of Washington Crossing the Delaware," and in Act II is depicted the Battle of Princeton, wherein the Commander shouts orders and stops a retreat. In the final act the Americans, under orders from Washington, attack a British prison ship upon which atrocities have been committed. The author's lower class characters are interesting and well characterized, but the historical figures, who include General Conway and a number of other officers as well as Washington, are indistinct and lifeless.

The Miller of New Jersey was produced in New York in 1856, as was *Blanche of Brandywine*, a stage adaptation of George Lip-

---

Hill (1846), which was produced but apparently never published, introduced Washington and André.

[35]David Trumbull, *The Death of Capt. Nathan Hale* . . . (Hartford, Conn., 1845), Act III, Scene 3. The play was produced at Yale College.

[36]John Brougham, *The Miller of New Jersey; or, The Prison-Hulk* . . . (New York, [1858]).

pard's romance of the same name.[37] In the latter play Washington speaks more naturally, but some of the situations are extremely melodramatic. Costume directions for the large cast begin with "Washington—made up after Stuart's celebrated picture." The plot concerns the many captures and escapes of one Colonel Frazier, an American officer, and Blanche, his adopted daughter, but a variety of historical and legendary incidents of the Revolution are introduced. At one point in the third act Washington, alone in the woods, soliloquizes on the gravity of the American situation and then falls on his knees to pray. General Howe, who has lost his way, now appears and offers Washington a title of nobility on condition that he cease fighting. The American's indignant reply begins:

And your king wishes me to barter the blood of my countrymen for the bauble of a coronet—the empty jingle of a title! Go, and tell your king that were George Washington to betray the trust reposed in him there is not a soldier in the continental army who would hesitate to shoot the traitor like a dog!

Howe is permitted to depart unmolested.

An interesting bit of dialogue occurs near the end of the play, after Randulph, a brave young American, has rescued Blanche from the hands of the villain:

RANDULPH. Ask the soldier the name he shouts in the vanguard of battle. Ask the dying warrior the name he murmurs when his voice is husky with the flow of suffocating blood! Ask the mother the name she whispers when she presses her babe to her bosom! Ask prophecy the name which shall live in future ages, second only in sanctity to—
BLANCHE. God bless the name of Washington!

A number of plays, most of them closet dramas, deal with Arnold and André. In Horatio Hubbell's *Arnold; or, The Treason of West Point* (1847) Washington is not in the cast, but the actors frequently speak of him. A tragedy in the classical tradition, this closet play contains more exposition and narration than action. The senti-

[37] J. G. Burnett, *Blanche of Brandywine; an American Patriotic Spectacle* . . . (New York and London, 1858).

Drama

mentalizing which was frequently provoked by the fate of André is apparent in lines on Washington spoken by a Colonel Tallmadge near the end of the play:

> Stern policy alone compels him; throughout
> He has each gentler usage tried to soothe
> The suff'rer's lot, even to the furnishing
> His meals, with delicate attention, from
> His own table.[38]

Similar treatment is accorded to Washington in Joseph Breck's *West Point* (1840)[39] and W. W. Lord's *André* (1856),[40] the former in prose and the latter in verse. Both seem to have been intended for production. In Breck's play Major André from the scaffold absolves "that great man, George Washington," of all malice. Washington makes several brief appearances in *The Highland Treason* (1852), by Elihu G. Holland, a closet drama.[41] The language is bombastic and the verse halting.

The most interesting portrayal of Washington to be found in this group of plays occurs in the *Arnold* (1854) by J. R. Orton. Here the Commander not only appears as an Olympian figure but is also endowed with a certain amount of psychological insight. When Arnold asks to take command of West Point rather than engage in an attack on New York, Washington remarks:

> I am quite unable
> To comprehend his motives. Action is
> The breath of his existence; and the field
> Of battle is his home, where none excel him.
> The strife he loves is gathering around us,
> And he applies for rest.[42]

[38] Horatio Hubbell, *Arnold; or, The Treason of West Point* . . . (Philadelphia, 1847).
[39] Joseph Breck, *West Point; or, A Tale of Treason* . . . (Baltimore, 1840). The play was based on a novel by Joseph Holt Ingraham, evidently *The Treason of Arnold*.
[40] In W. W. Lord, *The Complete Poetical Works* . . . , ed. Thomas Ollive Mabbott (New York, 1938), pp. 191–265.
[41] Elihu G. Holland, *Essays and a Drama in Five Acts* (Boston, 1852).
[42] J. R. Orton, *Arnold, and Other Poems* (New York, 1854), Act III, Scene 2.

After the discovery of Arnold's treachery, Washington's comment is:

> In turning against his country, Arnold has
> Lost that acuteness which has hitherto
> Distinguished him. Affection for his wife
> Would seem the only noble quality
> Left to him now. His formal resignation
> Of his commission is gratuitous.
> His threats of vengeance on his countrymen,
> By murderous reprisals, if André
> Be brought to punishment, show to what a depth
> A brave and haughty spirit may descend.[43]

In his characterization of the protagonist, Orton is more successful than most dramatists who used the Arnold-André story. Emotional conflict is apparent as Arnold, once a gallant soldier, gradually loses his pride and ideals and finally becomes a traitor.

Washington appears in the first and last scenes of George Henry Calvert's *Arnold and André* but does not speak, and in his Preface the author remarks that Washington seems to "enfold the whole action in his vast paternal arms." As the play begins, he and other officers are shown on their way to West Point, where one of the officers finds opportunity shortly thereafter to describe the Commander-in-Chief to a friend; the characters refer to him frequently. The legend that an Indian chief declared he was under the protection of the Great Spirit is skillfully brought into conversation at one point, and at another an old officer becomes eloquent in his praise:

> No smiling time
> Is this for hypocritical ambition
> To cheat men's minds with virtue's counterfeit.
> What made him Washington makes him the chief
> Of this vast league,—and that's integrity,
> The which his noble qualities enlinks
> In one great arch, to bear the sudden weight

[43]*Ibid.*, Act V, Scene 6.

Drama

Of a new cause, and, strength'ning ever, hold
Compact 'gainst time's all-whelming step.⁴⁴

In the second act Arnold soliloquizes to the effect that Washington is himself a traitor—to England; Arnold hates his chilly stateliness and reserve, and it angers him to feel that his nature is rebuked by Washington's. In the final scene Washington is seen silently signing André's death warrant. After he retires, the situation is discussed by Greene, Knox, Lafayette, and other generals. The playwright seems to have followed the injunction that John R. Thompson gave to Thackeray: to let Washington do no more than cross the stage.⁴⁵

Ida G. Everson, who wrote a scholarly study of Calvert, found his *Arnold and André* better suited for reading than for stage presentation. It was written many years before its publication in the full form, and Calvert stated that he brought it out in 1864 because Arnold's treason was "a suitable theme in a time of greater treason."⁴⁶

More definitely linked with sectional conflict is an anonymous work entitled *America: a Dramatic Poem*, published a year earlier.⁴⁷ Among the characters of this curious piece are America, the South Wind, the North Wind, and several ghosts, including that of George Washington. America speaks in grief:

O chief of heroes, and of patriots first!
Great father of thy country! proved thy tomb

⁴⁴George Henry Calvert, *Arnold and André* . . . (Boston, 1864), Act I, Scene 2. This scene was published in the *Southern Literary Messenger*, I (June, 1835), 555–557. The play is listed as of 1876 by Shirk, *op. cit.*, p. 54, note 31. A new edition appeared in that year.
Still another drama with the same theme is Joseph Addison Turner's *West Point: a Tragedy*, published in a Georgia magazine, *The Countryman*, Vol. IV, Nos. 1–9 (December 22, 1862–February 24, 1863), not seen by the present writer. B. H. Flanders reports that this play presents "a very sympathetic portrayal of Washington's magnanimity toward his military rival." See Flanders, *Early Georgia Magazines, Literary Periodicals to 1865* (Athens, Ga., 1944), p. 173.
The Arnold-André incident has inspired more dramas than any other single episode of the Revolution. Cf. Shirk, *op. cit.*, p. 44.
⁴⁵*Infra*, Chapter VII, Section 4.
⁴⁶Calvert, *op. cit.*, Preface. See also Ida G. Everson, *George Henry Calvert* . . . (New York, 1944).
⁴⁷New York, 1863.

Drama

> Too narrow also, when its walls received
> The tumult of our strife?

The poem has little merit but is an example of literary treatment of Washington in a time of national confusion and conflict.[48]

Except in the Tory plays of Revolutionary days, there is little variety in the treatment of Washington in drama before 1865. Extant plays, together with a few titles of others, show that his standard role was that of the great, yet kindly Commander-in-Chief. Unfortunately, few pertinent dramas from the latter part of the period survive. We know that Washington was a favorite figure in historical plays and that producers were hard pressed to find actors to represent him adequately.[49] No doubt it was his appearance and bearing which were hard to approximate, for, if extant plays are at all representative, actual characterization of Washington was slight indeed. Playwrights evidently felt that putting him on the stage, suitably made up and provided with a few patriotic and rhetorical lines, was characterization enough. They relied upon the preconception of the audience to do the rest. In all probability they even feared to go further in the direction of definite portrayal, lest they offend that same preconception. To make him the central figure in anything other than a pageant or pantomime would have been especially difficult. In one extant play, Custis's *The Indian Prophecy* (also unique in presenting a non-Revolutionary scene, although the Revolution is prophesied), Washington is the center of interest, but even here he has a minor role on the stage. An American audience wished to see Washington either as the perfect leader or as an abstract national symbol; his appearance in drama usually filled both specifications.

[48]C. E. B. Howe's *Signing the Declaration of Independence* . . . (New York, [1866]), which is described as "a National Sketch in One Act, Dedicated to the Union Men of America," attempts to show that freeing the slaves was in line with the Declaration. Washington is not in the cast and is mentioned only casually, as a brave and great leader in the Revolution.

[49]See Quinn, *op. cit.*, p. 278.

In considering the inconsequence of most of the plays here treated, it must be remembered that the best playwrights of the period 1825–1860 did not deal with historical themes. As regards the American scene, they doubtless realized that Revolutionary events and personalities were not yet far enough in the past to allow the dramatist much freedom of interpretation. In particular was this true of the Father of His Country.

CHAPTER VII

FICTION

THE AWE AND VENERATION which Americans felt for Washington made it difficult for novelists and romancers to portray him in the early part of the nineteenth century. Their problem was almost the same as that of a good Moslem endeavoring to put Mohammed into a work of fiction. Even in 1858 a reviewer attacking Thackeray's presentation of Washington in *The Virginians* said: "Mr. Thackeray should never have ventured upon bringing Washington into his story farther than to permit him to cross the stage and be seen no more."[1]

Examination of a hundred and fifty romances and other works of fiction dealing with Washington's day and locale and written before 1865 revealed sixty which contain no reference to him and so are not a present concern. Over fifty others mention his name or contain discussion of him, but in them he does not make a personal appearance. In the remaining group of more than thirty, which require closer analysis, Washington appears in person. Many of these romances and tales were beneath the attention of critics, and some were twenty-five-cent paper-backed thrillers.[2]

A clear distinction must be made between fiction in which Washington is presented as a character and that in which he is spoken of by the characters or the author but does not appear. Writers could

[1][John R. Thompson], "Editor's Table," *Southern Literary Messenger*, XXVI (February, 1858), 153.
[2]Lyle H. Wright, analyzing the matter of American romances written before 1850, found a total of one hundred and thirteen dealing with the Revolution. See "A Statistical Survey of American Fiction, 1774–1850," *Huntington Library Quarterly*, II (April, 1939), 309–318.

Fiction 191

discuss the glory of Washington or allow their personages to do so without doing violence to the public veneration, which was almost religious, of the national hero. Those who had occasion to deal with the military situation at any point of the American Revolution mentioned Washington quite naturally, and frequently they added a few words of admiration or eulogy. The usual tone of such passages may be seen in the following excerpt: "When the names of Caesar and Alexander shall have been forgotten, those of Washington and his brave compatriots shall flourish in the freshness of youth and the splendour of an undying immortality."[3]

One author, James Kirke Paulding, expressly stated his objection to the presentation of Washington in a work of fiction. In *The Old Continental* (1846) a proud old Colonel tells the young hero, who aspires to the hand of his daughter, that he may marry the girl provided he conducts himself so gallantly in the Patriot army as to win the attention and approbation of Washington.[4] When the young man finally sees the General, he contemplates him "with affectionate reverence, unlimited confidence, and profound gratitude."[5] Eventually he performs such exploits as the old Colonel demanded and is, with the Colonel, scheduled to interview General Washington. Here was a perfect opportunity to present Washington as a character in the romance, but Paulding did not make use of it. Instead, he gave his reasons for the omission:

Far be from us the presumption of attempting to portray or caricature the face, person, and deportment of the illustrious man, to whose presence the colonel was now, at his earnest request conducted. The severe simplicity of his character—the natural, unaffected dignity of his deportment—the beautiful symmetry which blended all his great qualities and virtues in one harmonious whole—while it constitutes the perfection of our nature, will forever defy the presumption of those who attempt to portray either his person or his character. Washington was no hero

[3] [T. S. Fay], *Herbert Wendall: a Tale of the Revolution* . . . , 2 vols. (New York, 1835), I, 113-114.
[4] [James Kirke Paulding], *The Old Continental; or, The Price of Liberty*, 2 vols. in one (New York, 1846), I, 30-31.
[5] *Ibid.*, I, 85.

of romance, and his name associates but illy with fiction. It is too sacred for such profanation . . .[6]

Yet many romancers were bold—or profane—enough to use Washington as a character. Most of them presented him as Commander-in-Chief. A few chose the obscure period of Braddock's defeat, which offered material much less encumbered with historical detail. Fictional treatment of Washington's childhood, as of all the other periods of his life, is almost negligible, and so the young George and the venerable President are dwarfed by General Washington.

Fictional portraits of General Washington, taken as a group, make him something of a paradox. On the one hand, he is the perfect military leader, poised and wise in council, energetic and efficient at his desk, magnificent on horseback, formal, impersonal, Jovian. On the other hand, he has a heart of gold, and apparently spends a large portion of his time comforting the widow and the orphan, the female in distress, and the dying soldier. The first aspect predominates in most stories, but often the second accompanies it, and in a few cases the sentimental view is the only one. The background for these sentimental portrayals of Washington was laid in the eighteenth-century novel of sentiment.

Another influence upon the fiction in which Washington appears was the Gothic, seen to some extent in James Fenimore Cooper's *The Spy* and much more in the works of George Lippard, a third-rate writer whose portrayals of Washington are nevertheless among the best of the period. But by far the greatest influence operating upon most of the writers here to be considered, beginning with Cooper, was that of Walter Scott. A few writers treated Washington in tales and short stories, but his standard appearance in American fiction after 1820 is in the historical romance, for which the "Author of Waverley" set the pattern.

[6] *Ibid.*, I, 189. Cf. Catharine Maria Sedgwick's Introduction to *The Linwoods: infra*, Section 2.

Fiction

I

One of the earliest mentions of Washington in fiction was made by Hugh Henry Brackenridge in 1779. From January to July of that year Brackenridge published in the *United States Magazine* a story the very title of which shows Gothic influence: "The Cave of Vanhest." This is a rambling tale of a young man and his tutor and of their visiting a cultured family—father, mother, two beautiful daughters, and dwarf servant—who live in a cave near the field of the Battle of Monmouth. Having recently visited the scene of the battle, the tutor tells the story for the benefit of the company. The account of the battle seems fairly accurate, but details of individual deaths and other episodes are inserted so profusely that it is difficult for the reader who does not have the general picture in mind to understand it. Washington's language upon meeting with General Charles Lee is not so warm here as it is sometimes given, but it is warm enough. No description of Washington is included, and the entire treatment of him, wholly in the words of a fictional character, is brief.[7]

In Brackenridge's best-known work, *Modern Chivalry*, written for the most part in the seventeen-nineties, Washington appears as President. The protagonists of *Modern Chivalry*, Captain Farrago and his rough Irish servant, Teague, manage to enter one of Washington's levees to beg preferment for the latter. Upon seeing Teague, Washington stares in astonishment for a moment; as the two are being ushered to the door, he remarks that doubtless the gentleman's merits will receive the consideration they deserve.[8] A slightly more consequential treatment of Washington written about the same time occurs in Jeremy Belknap's *The Foresters*, a clever allegory of American history. The titular characters, "the foresters," represent the colonies, and Walter Pipeweed represents Vir-

---

[7]*United States Magazine*, I (April, 1779), 149-150.
[8]Hugh Henry Brackenridge, *Modern Chivalry*, ed. Claude M. Newlin (New York, 1937), p. 15. Washington is mentioned several times, usually with a word of praise, and he appears again on a similar occasion, pp. 253-254.

ginia; George Washington, Walter Pipeweed's grandson, is chief counsel for the foresters in a lawsuit brought to a hearing at Trenton and York.[9] George's exploits both before and after he became President are discussed at some length by the other characters.[10]

The sentimental strain got an early start in novels and tales of the Revolution. In *The Female Review* (1797), a poorly written story of a woman dressed as a man who served in the American army, General Washington appears briefly. He is greatly affected by the surrender of Cornwallis: "Tears trickled from his eyes during the most of the scene. And a view of him in these moments must have forced the tear of reverential gratitude from the most obdurate."[11] Sentimental treatment of Washington continues in fiction throughout the period under consideration, often in the exaggerated form just cited. It is, of course, a notable example of distortion of the man's actual personality.

Five years before the appearance of *The Spy*, Samuel Woodworth wrote *The Champions of Freedom; or, The Mysterious Chief*, an amorphous romance about the War of 1812. The young hero, George Washington Willoughby, who has inherited a sword once belonging to Washington, is visited at crises of love and war by a kind of Gothic daemon in the form of an Indian chief, who appears out of thin air to tender advice and assistance. For instance, at a fashionable masquerade party in Boston the Indian tells George that war has begun and that he must now become a soldier and fight for his country. At almost the same hour, as George learns

[9]Jeremy Belknap, *The Foresters, an American Tale: Being a Sequel to the History of John Bull the Clothier* . . . (2d ed.; Boston, 1796), pp. 142, 163. *The Foresters* was first published as a book in 1792 but had appeared serially, in slightly different form, in the *Columbian Magazine*, beginning in June, 1787.

[10]*Ibid.*, pp. 105, 136, 145, 189, 229, 235.

[11][Herman Mann], *The Female Review; or, Memoirs of an American Young Lady . . . a Continental Soldier* . . . (Dedham, Mass., 1797), p. 155. Mrs. E. F. Ellet discussed this work and its heroine, Deborah Sampson, an actual person, in "Heroic Women of the Revolution," *Godey's Lady's Book*, XXXVII (July 1, 1848), 6–9; another view is in the *Historical Magazine*, X, Supplement II (1866), 86–87.

Sentimental treatment of Washington began still earlier in British fiction. The American General weeps freely in Samuel Jackson Pratt, *Emma Corbett* . . . , 3 vols. (London and Bath, [1780]), III, 69–70, as quoted in Robert B. Heilman, *America in English Fiction, 1760–1800* (Baton Rouge, La., 1937), p. 375.

Fiction

from a letter a few days later, the Indian appears to George's father at their home some distance from Boston to say almost the same things.[12] Although the chief tells George at one point during the war that eventually he will explain himself, his discovery in the final scene is not very convincing to the reader. There the chief makes the declaration that he is "the spirit of Washington": "Think of me as an ALLEGORY . . . whenever Americans would succeed, either in peace or war, their counsels must be actuated and their heroes inspired by the *Spirit of Washington*."[13] Despite the subtitle, the Indian's part is not integral to the plot, and probably the book would have been better without him.

Since *The Spy* (1821) was the first noteworthy historical romance using an American scene, its success paved the way for scores of others. In writing it, Cooper made an abrupt shift from the eighteenth-century novel of sentiment to the romance of history. Cooper's first work, *Precaution*, modeled upon a novel by Mrs. Amelia Opie or more probably upon Jane Austen's *Persuasion*, deals with an English scene. Influenced by the suggestions of friends, he chose a native setting and theme for *The Spy*, his second novel.[14] He had once heard from John Jay the story of a man who served Washington as a spy while ostensibly serving the British.[15] From this slight suggestion Cooper developed the noble character of Harvey Birch, who, like Locksley and Rob Roy, is of humble background. Other components of the Scott formula are here also: a beautiful young heroine, often in distress; a rather colorless young hero, who finally marries the heroine after sundry misadventures have long prevented the union; and, of especial interest in the pres-

---

[12]Samuel Woodworth, *The Champions of Freedom; or, The Mysterious Chief* . . . (New York, 1816), pp. 34–40. This version is slightly different from a two-volume edition of the same year.

[13]*Ibid.*, pp. 55 and 126.

About thirty years later Woodworth wrote a brief tale about an old fortune-teller who served the British as a spy for money, and Washington for love of the Patriot cause: "The Female Spy," printed at the back of Robert F. Greeley, *Arthur Woodleigh; a Romance of the Battle Field in Mexico* (New York, 1847), pp. 77–94.

[14]James Fenimore Cooper, *The Spy, a Tale of the Neutral Ground*, with an Introduction by Tremaine McDowell (New York, [1931]).

[15]*Ibid.*, Introduction, pp. xii ff.

ent connection, an important historical personage, who is not a main character but comes into the story occasionally and is at times a *deus ex machina* who solves problems for the fictitious characters.[16]

The scene of *The Spy* is Westchester County, New York, toward the end of 1780, when this region lay between the British in the city and the Americans up the Hudson and was consequently known as "the Neutral Ground." The action centers around the adventures of the Wharton family: the head of the family, a country squire; his beautiful daughters, Sarah and Frances, the elder a Tory, the younger a Patriot; and young Henry, or Harry, Wharton, who is a lieutenant in Clinton's army. There are in the household or connected with it an elderly spinster aunt, Miss Jeanette Peyton; Colonel Dunwoodie, Captain Lawton, Lieutenant Singleton, and a comic doctor named Sitgreaves, all American officers; a villainous Britisher named Colonel Wellmere; and several others. Contrasting with these gentlefolk are a colored servant, Caesar, and his wife, Dinah; groups of cowboys and skinners, partisans with Tory and Patriot leanings respectively; Betty Flanagan, a comic sutler for the American forces; and Katy Haynes, a comic housekeeper for the peddler spy, Harvey Birch.

Henry (or Harry) Wharton has a role more integral to the action of the story than that of Birch, though the latter appears on the scene more often. Harry is captured by the Americans when, in disguise, he visits his father and sisters behind the American lines, and much of the action centers around efforts to prevent his being hanged as Major André had been a few months previously. The complications and episodes relevant to this situation are too numerous for summary. Frances Wharton loves Colonel Dunwoodie, a Virginian, who has captured her brother, and throughout she attempts to save Henry without Dunwoodie's being dishonored. She succeeds with the help of Harvey Birch and the mysterious Mr. Harper, and she finally marries Dunwoodie. While his father's

---

[16]See G. Harrison Orians, "The Romance Ferment after Waverley," *American Literature*, III (January, 1932), 408–431.

funeral is in progress, Harvey is captured by the Americans and is sentenced to be hanged, but he escapes by disguising himself as Betty Flanagan, who is enjoying a somewhat drunken slumber in the same cell. It is Harvey who prevents the marriage of Sarah Wharton and Colonel Wellmere of the British army, who, as it develops, has a wife in England already. Dressed as a minister, Harvey admirably performs a rather comic part in order to direct the proceedings of Harry's final escape from the Americans who intend to hang him; Harry is disguised on this occasion as a black servant, Caesar, who replaces him in his cell. The pages are filled with sword fights, brushes with the enemy, house burnings, unexpected captures, hangings, and dangerous escapes; and Harvey Birch is ubiquitous, appearing whenever and wherever there is need for his services.

Harvey is somewhat Byronic in his great loneliness of soul and his feeling of inadequacy under the burden of the double-dealing role he is forced by circumstances to play. Only Washington knows his loyalty to the American cause, and his life is constantly in danger from the Patriot forces he really loves. Yet, in contrast with his selfless patriotism, he exhibits a Yankee practicality and shrewdness amounting almost to avarice.

Washington, who wears until near the end of the book the disguise of Mr. Harper, appears in person on only three occasions, but he is ever in the background, sending timely notes and oral directions in various crises. His first appearance occurs early in the story; a benevolent, highly dignified stranger, he arrives unexpected at the home of the Whartons, where he resides for several days, ostensibly because of bad weather. There he becomes friendly with the family, who are enormously curious as to what business could draw the handsome gentleman to so dangerous a region. They never suspect, though the reader does, that he is there to see Harvey Birch, with whom he has some casual conversation. One circumstance which leads them to trust the mysterious stranger is that Caesar, the servant, reports having seen him in prayer. They realize that he is a keen observer when he penetrates Harry's disguise, but they learn to love and trust him when he does nothing about it.[17] Throughout the remainder of the book, in which neither Harper nor Washington appears in person till near the end, all the characters mention him frequently, in one form or the other,[18] and usually they say or imply that he is very impressive and kindly, just as he is represented in the first four chapters. Here is Cooper's description of Mr. Harper:

> On taking an extra handkerchief from his neck and removing a cloak of blue cloth, with a surtout of the same material, he exhibited to the scrutiny of the observant family party, a tall and extremely graceful person, of apparently fifty years of age. His countenance evinced a settled composure and dignity; his nose was straight, and approaching to Grecian; his eye, of a gray color, was quiet, thoughtful, and rather melancholy; the mouth and lower part of his face being expressive of decision and much character. His dress, being suited to the road, was simple and plain, but such as was worn by the higher class of his countrymen; he wore his own hair, dressed in a manner that gave a military air to his appearance, and which was rather heightened by his erect and conspicuously graceful carriage. His whole appearance was so impressive and decidedly that of a gentleman, that as he finished laying aside the garments, the ladies arose from their seats, and, together with the master of the house, they received anew, and returned the complimentary greetings which were again offered.[19]

Harper's second personal appearance occurs after four fifths of the book is completed. Harry has just eluded the Patriots detailed to guard him until time for his hanging in the morning, and his sister Frances, doubting that his attempt at escape will be successful, has made her way up a steep, rocky incline to a secluded cabin, where she by chance has caught a glimpse of Harvey Birch in the distance. There she discovers not Harvey but Mr. Harper, whose aid several have been seeking in behalf of Harry. Harper with sympathetic kindness promises to do what he can to save the life of the

[17]Cooper, *op. cit.*, pp. 47 ff.
[18]*Ibid.*, pp. 84–87, 123, 146–148, 240, 253, 274, 294, 307, 321, 344, 357, 363, 380, 385, 387, 389–390, 393–395, 398–400, 417, 456–458, 460, 472, 492–500.
[19]*Ibid.*, p. 8.

British officer. Birch and Harry arrive, and Harper hides while they interview Frances and concert a plan for her to marry Dunwoodie in the next two hours and so prevent his following the fugitive. After they depart, Harper assures Frances that if she can detain Dunwoodie and his men for two hours, her brother will be safe. He swears her to secrecy about having seen him; then he takes her hand and gives her his parting benediction, saying in part:

"God has denied to me children, young lady; but if it had been his blessed will that my marriage should not have been childless, such a treasure as yourself would I have asked from his mercy. But you are my child: all who dwell in this broad land are my children, and my care; and take the blessing of one who hopes yet to meet you in happier days."[20]

In the penultimate chapter, which is an interview between Harper and Harvey Birch just before the departure of the American armies for Yorktown, Harper is discovered to be Washington, and Harvey is revealed as actually his spy while in the service of General Clinton. Harvey heroically refuses the gold proffered as a reward for his services. He says that if any doubt his loyalty, Washington can tell them he refused the money. Washington gives him a signed note, avouching his patriotism, and this Harvey bears with him until his death in 1814 at the Battle of Lundy's Lane. Typical of the interview and of Washington-Harper's part in the romance is the speech that he makes when Harvey refuses the bag of gold:

"Now, indeed, I know you; and although the same reasons which have hitherto compelled me to expose your valuable life will still exist, and prevent my openly asserting your character, in private I can always be your friend; fail not to apply to me when in want or suffering, and so long as God giveth to me, so long will I freely share with a man who feels so nobly and acts so well. If sickness or want should ever assail you, and peace once more smile upon our efforts, seek the gate of him you have so often met as Harper, and he will not blush to acknowledge you in his true character."[21]

[20]*Ibid.*, pp. 449–450.
[21]*Ibid.*, p. 497.

The Spy was favorably received by American readers, and William Howard Gardiner reviewed it at great length, hailing the appearance of a new genre in fiction.[22] But the Harper-Washington role did not meet with universal favor. Sentimental readers doubtless liked the bombastic speech and overformal manners that Cooper attributed to the Father of His Country, but more exacting critics did not. In the words of Gardiner, "the author has got more dignity upon his hands than he knows how to manage; and accordingly it is starched up with stiff bows, awkward courtesies, and glum looks."[23] A second objection, raised by reviewers and general readers alike, was that it was unnatural and disrespectful to show the Commander-in-Chief, unattended and far from his forces, hiding in a hut to interview a peddler-spy. Tremaine McDowell, who has made an intensive study of *The Spy*, including the part of Mr. Harper therein, reports that Cooper himself later regretted this attempt to portray Washington in fiction.[24]

Although the scene of *The Spy* never shifts from New York, the roles of Colonel Dunwoodie and several other Southern officers and soldiers, as well as that of Washington, make it in a sense America's first intersectional novel. Yet Cooper, except possibly in Captain Jack Lawton, made no attempt at distinctive characterization of his Southerners. As for Mr. Harper himself, he is stiff and colorless in comparison with Harvey Birch and some of the other characters. It has often been pointed out that he even crosses his legs "with steady composure."

John Neal, in his day a rival of Cooper in the field of American fiction, included in his epistolary novel *Randolph* (1823) several rather significant remarks about the contemporary attitude toward Washington. Early in the book one of the characters declares: "I

[22] *North American Review*, XV (July, 1822), 250-282.
[23] *Ibid.*, p. 262.
[24] Cooper, *op. cit.*, Introduction, p. xxi. McDowell lists several reviews. See also Alexander Cowie, *The Rise of the American Novel* (New York, [1948]), pp. 122-125.
Cooper made incidental references to Washington in later novels laid in Revolutionary times, notably *The Pilot* (1823), *Lionel Lincoln* (1825), and *Wyandotte* (1843).

Fiction

cannot write or speak the name of GEORGE WASHINGTON, without a contraction, and dilation of the heart, if I do it irreverently."[25]

But another character, Molton, displays a different attitude.[26] Writing to an English friend, he states that his father knew Washington well and that from him he learned that the well-known Stuart portraits are "less what Washington was than what he ought to have been." Molton's point is that Stuart infused into his paintings a grandeur that he saw in the character and sensed in the personality of Washington but which did not actually appear in his face. In other words, the writer considers the portraits impressionistic, and he indicates that they are in a sense better likenesses than are the more realistic portraits of Washington. From these observations Molton, probably the mouthpiece of the author, proceeds to a character sketch of the American hero. He assures his friend that, contrary to the popular belief, Washington was no exception to the rule that a man's faults are in proportion to his virtues. Molton mentions three or four serious errors in military strategy; he notes also Washington's "terrible passions" and says that he was sometimes violent in his treatment of associates, particularly Charles Lee and Alexander Hamilton. The conclusion of his remarkable discussion is worthy of quotation:

George Washington had his infirmities, in the same measure as his virtues. And thanks be to God that he *had!* Now we have an example to encourage us. Were he perfect, we should be repelled, intimidated and discouraged. You will be astonished, Stafford, to hear that his character is not understood by his own countrymen; but it is not. They have so long listened to hyperbolical eulogy, intemperate, and unmeaning praise, that he has lost to their eyes, the chief attributes of humanity—and become a God. For shame—Gods are manufactured by the feeble of mind, who, having no discrimination, no power of analysis; find it easier to take all their clay from one bank, than to compound it judiciously, of many, when they would exhibit the workmanship of their hands.

---

[25] [John Neal], *Randolph*, 2 vols. (Philadelphia, 1823), I, 65.
[26] *Ibid.*, II, 62–66. Arthur Hobson Quinn points out that Neal was a pioneer in several ways. See Quinn, *American Fiction, an Historical and Critical Survey* (New York and London, [1936]), p. 49.

Thus in 1823 John Neal was completely aware of "the Washington Legend," which more than one student discovered a century or more later. With an inconsistency typical of Neal's hasty workmanship, it is this same Molton who later writes, apropos of Cooper's *The Spy*, for which he had no good words: "Washington—George Washington is profanely introduced and always profanely employed, in situations totally unworthy of him—perilous—foolish—and ridiculously mysterious . . ."[27]

Neal himself had already introduced Washington into a novel. Shortly before turning off *Randolph* in thirty-six days—according to his own statement—he had written *Seventy-Six* in twenty-nine. The latter, probably Neal's best work, is a Revolutionary romance in which Washington appears several times, although his part in the action is negligible and he never speaks at any length. At one point General Washington interviews the young hero of the story after the latter has killed a man while fencing; he has the case investigated and gives the young man a commission upon finding him innocent and worthy.[28] Neal described the General's appearance on horseback, a favorite subject with writers of Revolutionary romance:

Washington passed us now, at a slow, warlike movement, his tall martial person habited in a uniform which I will try to describe:—the waistcoat was buff, plain buff, without an atom of gold upon it, very long and opening at the bottom, with flaps; the coat, what we call a French blue, rather worn and dusty, exceedingly tight in the arms and open always;—breeches buff, and boots in the clumsy fashion of the day, reaching to the knees—but without any expression [sic]: the whole costume wearing the look of what is meant for service, rather than parade. As he passed us, he uncovered to our general salutation, with a dignity and plainness that I never saw equalled. But do what he would—he was always George Washington—full of beautiful simplicity and power.[29]

[27]Neal, *op. cit.*, II, 213. The book also contains some discussion of Trumbull's picture "The Surrender of Cornwallis" (II, 126) and of Judge Marshall's biography (II, 226-227).

[28][John Neal], *Seventy-Six*, 2 vols. (Baltimore, 1823), II, 13-15. Although Neal followed Cooper in the use of Revolutionary material, *Seventy-Six*, like Neal's earlier novels, is primarily a romance of passion, not in the Scott tradition. See Quinn, *op. cit.*, pp. 48-49.

[29]Neal, *Seventy-Six*, II, 60.

Fiction

The Commander's appearances in *Seventy-Six* are always stately and inspiring—in one case he speaks briefly to a young recruit, who then declares himself no longer weak and no longer a boy—[30] and there is here no departure from the conventional conception of Washington.

Probably the most prolonged and ambitious of early attempts to treat Washington in fiction was made by James McHenry in *The Wilderness*, also published in 1823. McHenry, Irish-born physician, novelist, and versifier, chose to deal with the frontier region in the vicinity of Fort Duquesne, with which he was familiar, and Braddock's fight provides the climax of his story. *The Wilderness* contains a multitude of characters, including Gilbert Frazier, an old settler from Ulster; his wife, Nelly; their sons, Paddy and Archy, woodsman and farmer respectively; and their daughter, Nancy, and adopted daughter, Maria. Nancy is a buxom, blooming girl, but Maria is fragile and refined, unsuited for rough work, though skilled with her needle and fond of poetry. Maria's fiancé is Charles Adderly, a young man from Philadelphia. Dr. Killbreath, who is not so humorous as his name, is a suitable match for Nancy. There are also historical characters: Christopher Gist and Van Braam, De Villiers and Captain Joncaire; and Indians—some historical, others not—Aliquippa, Halmanna, Shingiss, Carrawissa, and Carrawoona.[31]

The main plot is the love affair of Adderly and Maria; a subplot is the matter of Dr. Killbreath and Nancy; but the historic events of the time and place often push these stories into the background. Throughout, incidents and events are piled together in unrestrained profusion, as may be seen in the high points of those portions of the narrative which concern Washington.

Sent to Fort Le Boeuf by Governor Dinwiddie, Washington steps into the Frazier family circle as a correct young officer. Traveling with Paddy Frazier on his return journey, he goes into the icy

[30] *Ibid.*, I, 134.
[31] [James McHenry], *The Wilderness; or, Braddock's Times. A Tale of the West* . . . 2 vols. (New York, 1823). The book appeared under the pseudonym of Solomon Secondsight. A slightly earlier edition was published in London under the same pseudonym: *The Wilderness; or, The Youthful Days of Washington. A Tale of the West* (London, 1823). Cooper's *The Pioneers*, first of his romances of frontier life, appeared in 1823 also.

river first through accident and again to rescue Paddy; previously they have been ambushed by Indians and have captured one and then set him free.[32] Washington has fallen in love with Maria on the way out, and now, before returning to the settlements, he gives her a volume of William Shenstone, containing passages so marked as to form a declaration.[33] Maria is embarrassed by Washington's attentions because she has given her heart to Charles Adderly, but the young officer is blindly in love, and eventually he attempts to speak. Maria says that she is unworthy and that he should seek another, and in reply Washington grows eloquent:

> "Maria!" he exclaimed—"Oh, tantalizing girl! Another choice, did you say! No; let heaven hear me! I swear that, unless thou dost peremptorily and finally refuse to be mine, I shall never form another choice; and even then, should that ever be, which heaven forbid, my choice may be the dictate of duty, but I shall never be impelled to it by that warm, that irresistible feeling of the heart and soul, which urges me to sue thee to become the partner of my love, the mistress of my fortune, the fondly-cherished wife of my bosom, the dear, the sweet source of all my earthly happiness. O Maria! wilt thou not yield to it? wilt thou not become mine?"[34]

Refused and dejected, the prim young man continues on his way to the fateful encounter with Jumonville, where Paddy Frazier does the actual shooting, and to Fort Necessity, where Washington's successful bluff enables a small band of soldiers to escape the clutches of untold numbers of villainous Frenchmen and Indians.[35] In due course he fights valiantly with Braddock at the Monongahela,[36] and after that he discovers that Maria is a captive of the cruel De Villiers. Disguised as an Indian chieftain, Washington manages to rescue her.[37]

[32]McHenry, *op. cit.*, Vol. I, Chapter XIX. McHenry made still more sensational two exciting incidents related by Washington and by Christopher Gist, Washington's real guide on this trip.
[33]*Ibid.*, Vol. I, Chapter XXI.
[34]*Ibid.*, II, 77.
[35]*Ibid.*, Vol. II, Chapters VII and VIII.
[36]*Ibid.*, Vol. II, Chapter XI.
[37]*Ibid.*, Vol. II, Chapter XVI.

Fiction

A little later he has occasion also to rescue Charles Adderly as Indians are about to burn the favored lover at the stake.[38] Throughout these and all the other events which follow Maria's rejection of his suit, Washington bears a heavy heart, guided by thought not of earthly happiness but of duty and patriotism. Chastened and purified by the flames of unrequited love, he ever after is to be swayed only by the highest motives. He realizes that never again will he devote his affections to a woman "so rapturously," and hence he can dedicate himself to "the graver interests of mankind" and especially to those of his country.[39]

The Wilderness, McHenry's first novel, was taken to pieces in a long review, the ironic tone of which may be seen in a few sentences that bear upon Washington's role:

We have indeed, before this, seen Washington placed in extraordinary situations, but who beside our author ever imagined him,

> "Sighing like furnace, with a woful ballad
> Made to his mistress' eyebrow?"

Who ever before thought of General Washington thridding the mazes of a cotillon upon "light fantastic toe," or marching with the true aboriginal parrot toed gait in an elegant costume of party colored feathers and porcupine's quills![40]

The Wilderness has little to recommend it, but in regard to some points the last laugh is probably on the reviewer. Today it is common knowledge that the youthful Washington wrote verses to

---

[38] *Ibid.*, Vol. II, Chapter XVIII.

[39] *Ibid.*, II, 290–292.

Dr. Ernest E. Leisy in a brief discussion of *The Wilderness* identifies Maria with Mary Phillipse, who lived in New York City (*The American Historical Novel*, Norman, Okla., [1950], pp. 62–63).

Josiah Priest's *A History of the Early Adventures of Washington among the Indians of the West* . . . (Albany, N.Y., 1841) is a plagiarism, a sixty-page condensation of McHenry's two volumes. Though much of the historical background has been omitted, the work has all the faults of the original except its length.

McHenry made incidental mentions of Washington in *The Betrothed of Wyoming* (Philadelphia, 1830), a Revolutionary romance. Washington appears briefly, interviewing the hero, in *Meredith; or, The Mystery of the Meschianza* (Philadelphia, 1831), p. 147.

[40] *North American Review*, XIX (July, 1824), 209–223; quotation, p. 222. Cf. *Knickerbocker*, IV (July, 1834), 19.

young ladies and that he enjoyed dancing as he did also in maturity. Yet less than twenty-five years after his death such activities were considered inconsonant with his character.

The influence of Cooper can be seen in McHenry's work and is still more evident in three other forgotten novels of the twenties. Gilbert, the hero of *The Refugee* (1825), belongs to a Tory family, and he himself serves in the British army until he becomes convinced he is on the wrong side and changes to the Patriot forces. Washington's attempt to ride into British fire at Kip's Bay is used here;[41] Gilbert, who is in command of the British troops involved, is so much moved by Washington's appearance that he at first orders them not to shoot; but he rescinds his order as Washington is withdrawing, and the company (sixty men) all shoot—and miss! The General appears towering, noble, and stately as he vainly tries to stop the retreat of the Patriot militia. Later he twice interviews Gilbert: first he hears the young man's reasons for changing sides; on the second occasion he asks Gilbert whether he would be willing to kill his father, a belligerent Tory, and commends the negative answer. In both interviews the General is genial. "The Godlike Washington" is often a topic of conversation in the book, notably in a barber-shop conversation between Farmer Stallfeeder and Schoolmaster Flagel, who weigh the Commander's merits against those of General Gates.[42]

Morton, an anonymous romance of 1828, presents General Washington in one scene. Late at night the protagonist interviews the General alone in his headquarters, and Washington, the tired executive, tries to dissuade him from the perilous work of a spy; he strongly impresses the young hero by his dignity and benevolence.[43] General Washington sends the hero of *Donald Adair*, another forgotten romance of 1828, on a mission from Valley Forge to Vir-

[41] For an account of the incident see Nathaniel Wright Stephenson and Waldo Hilary Dunn, *George Washington*, 2 vols. (New York and London, 1940), I, 365.
[42] [James Athearn Jones], *The Refugee. A Romance*, by Captain Matthew Murgatroyd [pseud.], 2 vols. (New York, 1825). Washington's appearances: I, 176-180; II, 21 ff., 60 ff.; the barbershop scene: II, 11-15. The book is unfavorably reviewed in the *North American Review*, XXI (July, 1825), 83-86.
[43] *Morton, a Tale of the Revolution* . . . (Cincinnati, Ohio, 1828), pp. 262-268.

Fiction

ginia, but Washington is not on this occasion presented to the reader.[44] Later the author discusses the Battle of Monmouth, including the famous interview between Washington and Charles Lee, but again there is no portrayal of Washington.[45] Eventually he does appear at the bedside of a dying major, where he talks most sentimentally of the consolations of religion: "Can any of you, my brave associates, doubt the validity of the Christian religion? Only see what a veil of light it casts upon the dying."[46]

2

Catharine Maria Sedgwick, a Massachusetts schoolteacher and a prolific writer, was more successful with the genre of Scott and Cooper than the prim tone of much of her work would lead one to expect. Her portrayal of Washington in *The Linwoods* (1835) is at least as good as Cooper's presentation of him in *The Spy*. She may have felt more than the usual interest in the national hero, for her father had been well acquainted with Washington,[47] but she wished it known that she presented him with fear and trembling. In her Introduction she wrote:

A very few of our "immortal names" have been introduced, with what propriety the reader must determine. It may be permitted to say, in extenuation of what may seem presumption, that whenever the writer has mentioned Washington, she has felt a sentiment resembling the awe of the pious Israelite when he approached the ark of the Lord.[48]

Despite this feeling, Miss Sedgwick introduced Washington into eleven scenes of her novel, and both he and Mrs. Washington figure to some extent in the action. A high light is the scene in which

---

[44][A. M. Lorraine], *Donald Adair: a Novel by a Young Lady of Virginia . . .*, 2 vols. (Richmond, Va., 1828), II, 136-138.

[45]*Ibid.*, II, 32-36.

[46]*Ibid.*, II, 40. Cf. II, 44.

[47]*Life and Letters of Catharine M. Sedgwick*, ed. Mary E. Dewey (New York, 1871), pp. 30 ff.

[48][Catharine Maria Sedgwick], *The Linwoods; or, "Sixty-Years Since" in America*, 2 vols. (New York, 1835), xii.

Eliot Lee, a young American officer who is the hero of the story, shrewdly thwarts a British plot to capture Washington.[49] Eventually the General sends young Lee into New York under a flag of truce with papers for General Clinton. Upon his return, Eliot has to report to his Commander that without his knowledge a friend, the hotheaded Herbert Linwood, accompanied him, disguised as his servant, and that Linwood was captured and is held as a spy by the British. Though visibly enraged, Washington controls himself well.[50]

In an earlier scene Herbert Linwood presents to Washington a young lady's petition that she be allowed to visit her brother, an officer on a British sloop anchored nearby. Miss Sedgwick may have put into the General's words her own reaction to fulsome eulogy of Washington:

He passed his eye again over the note and there was an expression of displeasure and contempt in his curling lip as he read such expressions as the following: "I cannot be disappointed, for I am addressing one who unites all virtues, whose mercy even surpasses his justice."—"I write on my knees to him who is the minister of Providence, dispensing good and evil, light and blessing with a word." "Miss Ruthven should remember that flattery corrupts the giver as well as the receiver. I have no choice in this matter. We have an inflexible rule preventing all discourse with the enemy."[51]

A scene in which Washington dines with Mr. Ruthven, an old friend, is almost unique; in fiction the General has almost no social life. The author thus envisioned his appearance:

That expression of repelling and immoveable gravity, that look of tension (with him the bow was always strained) that characterized Washington's face, had vanished like a cloud; and it now serenely reflected the social affections (bright and gentle spirits!) that, for a time, mastered his perplexing cares. He was retracing the period of his boyhood; a period, however cloudy in its passage, always bright when surveyed

[49]*Ibid.*, I, 151–159.
[50]*Ibid.*, I, 169–170: II, 34–37.
[51]*Ibid.*, I, 145.

Fiction

over the shoulder. He recalled his first field-sports, in which Ruthven had been his companion and teacher; and they laughingly reviewed many an incident by flood and field.[52]

The plot of *The Linwoods* follows a common pattern: the hero and heroine meet, are separated by the manifold exigencies of war, but are united at the end. Miss Sedgwick handles several subplots efficiently.

Among now forgotten American writers of the thirties and forties were a number who tried their hand at Revolutionary tales and romances, and a few saw fit to introduce Washington in person. In many of their works he merely adds historical interest to the narrative and has no part in the plot.

A "young gentleman of Nashville," believed to be Wilkins Tannehill, depicted the crossing of the Delaware in one of his *Tales of the Revolution.* Washington contemplates "the maddening Delaware," and then, "raising his head as if in benediction to heaven," he dashes into the water on horseback. Upon reaching the opposite bank he kneels to pray before advancing on Trenton.[53] Tannehill seems not to have known that most of Washington's men were infantry and that the crossing was made in boats. Another brief treatment of the General occurs in a *nouvelle* called "The Deserter," included in *The Romantic Historian,* an anonymous work. Here Washington, benignant and sympathetic, has an essential role though he appears only at the end of the story. The wife of a soldier who is falsely accused of desertion from the Patriot forces gains access to the General, and the latter investigates the case, punishes the villain, and exonerates the innocent.[54]

The hero of John R. Willis's *Carleton,* another romance of war and love, was the son of a Tory. On joining the Patriot army, Henry Carleton had high hopes of distinguishing himself and looked

---

[52]*Ibid.,* I, 156.
[53]"The Hermit of the White Cliff," in *Tales of the Revolution, by a Young Gentleman of Nashville . . .* (Nashville, Tenn., 1833), pp. 174-176.
[54]"The Deserter," in *The Romantic Historian; a Series of Lights and Shadows . . .* (Philadelphia, 1834), pp. 85-120. Washington is mentioned incidentally in other tales in the volume: pp. 2, 14, and 57.

forward rapturously to the thanks of General Washington.[55] The author found occasion to remark on the high motives of several of the Patriot leaders, including "the immortal Washington."[56] On the other hand, Henry discussed his prospects with his enraged parent, who prophesied that Washington would be a prisoner or a fugitive within six months.[57] The young soldier's first interview with the General gave opportunity for a detailed pen portrait of the great man at his desk in headquarters.[58] At this time Henry was deeply awed, and later he felt that Washington had treated him as he would have treated his own son.[59]

A full-length romance entitled *The Deserter, a Legend of Mount Washington* was written by John H. Mancur, who used Revolutionary material a number of times.[60] The plot is commonplace, another story of misunderstanding, with the "deserter" finally exonerated. Washington's role is not integral to the plot, but he appears in a description of the retreat from Long Island, and the events of the next few days, related with some vividness, lead up to the Kip's Bay episode. Here Washington is in tears, and dashing his sword to the ground, he attempts to ride into the enemy because his men refuse to fight.[61] He is shown in tears again at the slaughter of his troops at Fort Washington.[62] On the other hand, he laughs heartily at an amusing tale told him by a French woman.[63]

One of Washington's rare appearances in a novel dealing with the frontier rather than the Revolution occurs in *Old Fort Duquesne*,

[55] John R. Willis, *Carleton; or Patriotism, Love, and Duty. A Tale of Seventeen Hundred and Seventy-Six* (London, 1842), p. 13.
[56] *Ibid.*, p. 20.
[57] *Ibid.*, pp. 23–24.
[58] *Ibid.*, pp. 26–28.
[59] *Ibid.*, pp. 27 and 63. Cf. pp. 133–134.
[60] John H. Mansur, *The Deserter* . . . (New York, 1843) is No. 2 of the author's series, "Tales of the Revolution."
[61] *Ibid.*, pp. 97–106.
[62] *Ibid.*, pp. 127–132.
[63] *Ibid.*, p. 131. Washington is mentioned in Mancur's *Christine. A Tale of the Revolution* (New York, 1843) and in *Paul Jones: a Tale of the Sea* (Philadelphia, 1843) and *Ernest Harcourt; or, The Loyalist's Son* (Philadelphia, 1843). The last two were published anonymously but are attributed to Mancur by Theodore Hunt, *Le Roman américain, 1830–1850* . . . (Paris, 1937).

Fiction

a stilted anonymous romance which has as background the events leading to the shooting of Jumonville, the climax of the story. Apparently the author was seeking to disseminate his idea of this event because he felt that some misunderstanding was current. Washington, a youthful Colonel, does not appear until near the conclusion. He is rather heavily jocose in rallying a fellow officer who is in love: "Now preserve us from the rattling tongue of a self-conceited lover. Sit down calmly, Carroll, and compose yourself."[64] The author makes the point that the atmosphere of Washington's camp was highly informal and that he accepted the advice of older subordinates quite readily.[65]

More in the tradition of Cooper is a chapter appended to Maturin Ballou's *Fanny Campbell, the Female Pirate Captain*. Here, muffled in a greatcoat which hides his uniform, Washington is shown obtaining information about the British from a female spy named Moll Pitcher and called "the Fortune Teller of Lynn."[66] The story as a whole takes place mainly on shipboard and in the East Indies.

Joseph Holt Ingraham introduced Washington five times into *Burton; or, The Sieges* (1838). First, the General penetrates the disguise of a young female transvestite, Eugenie de Lisle, who is pursuing in headquarters the libertine Richard Burton (Aaron Burr). Washington reproves the handsome villain for his immorality. With his wife, whom he calls "Mary," he takes Eugenie into their quarters to recover from the ill effects of her adventurous journey from Canada, and they undertake to reveal the true character of Burton, who has seduced one girl and is leading on another in addition to the heroine. Ingraham shows Washington briefly in the middle of the Battle of Brooklyn, calm amid disaster. His fourth

---

[64] *Old Fort Duquesne, a Tale of the Early Toils, Struggles and Adventures of the First Settlers at the Forks of the Ohio, 1754* . . . (Pittsburgh, Pa., 1844), p. 72. Cf. p. 70. Dr. Ernest E. Leisy (*op. cit.*, p. 220) says this book concerns "Braddock's Defeat," which occurred in 1755.

[65] *Old Fort Duquesne*, pp. 68–69.

[66] [Maturin Murray Ballou], *Fanny Campbell, the Female Pirate Captain; a Tale of the Revolution*, by Lieutenant Murray [pseud.] (Boston, 1845), pp. 95–97.
The tale of Moll Pitcher of Monmouth, who continued the firing of a cannon after the cannoneer, her husband, was killed, took many forms and is a minor legend.

appearance is at his headquarters again, where Eugenie, again in male clothes, arrives just in the nick of time to warn him of a plot to capture him there; he captures the plotters instead. Finally, he gives away the bride in the concluding chapter when Eugenie marries an honest Patriot officer. The triviality of the book is evident from the fact that the action takes place in New York in the summer of 1776, a season when the Commander-in-Chief had little time to interest himself in the amours of seventeen-year-old girls.[67]

Washington is mentioned frequently by the other characters of Ingraham's *The Treason of Arnold* (1847), and he appears on the scene briefly when, arriving at Beverly House, he expects to meet Arnold but finds him departed. He engages in dialogue, his longest speech being as follows:

"Well, gentlemen, it is fortunate for us that General Arnold has gone over to the garrison in advance of us, for we shall now have a salute, and the roaring of the cannon will have a fine effect among these mountains."[68]

When the defection of Arnold is discovered, Washington sends Hamilton to intercept him. Ingraham says that although he refused to see André in captivity, Washington read a letter penned by him and was deeply moved by it.[69]

Ingraham's *Neal Nelson* (1847) contains also a highly conventional portrait of Washington although the author passes up a splendid opportunity to introduce the Commander-in-Chief to the reader when the hero visits a wounded comrade in the General's headquarters.[70] Eventually Neal, a seaman, does interview the great

[67][Joseph Holt Ingraham], *Burton; or, The Sieges. A Romance* . . . , 2 vols. (New York. 1838), Vol. II, Chapters II, IV, X, XVI, and XVII. Washington is frequently mentioned by the author or by the other characters: pp. 51, 71, 74, 77, 79, 83, 89, 101, 107, 134, 145, 178, 196, 210, 219 ff., 249 ff., 262 ff.

[68][Joseph Holt Ingraham], *The Treason of Arnold: a Tale of West Point during the American Revolution* (Jonesville [Templeton], Mass., 1847), p. 36. Lyle H. Wright attributes this romance to Ingraham. See Wright, *American Fiction, 1774–1850* . . . (San Marino, Calif., 1939).

[69]*The Treason of Arnold*, p. 41.

[70][Joseph Holt Ingraham], *Neal Nelson; or, The Siege of Boston. A Tale of the Revolution* (New York, 1847), pp. 28 ff.

Fiction

man and from him obtains command of a cruiser. Washington speaks once.⁷¹ In the conclusion, Washington gives away the bride at a wedding performed on July 4, 1776.

The Buckskin, published anonymously in 1847, is one of the best of the several romances that show Washington in his relations with secret agents. A mysterious stranger caught in a rainstorm at the cabin of Uncle Sy Rumsey, near Yorktown in 1781, is a reincarnation or literary descendant of Cooper's Mr. Harper. This stranger has come to obtain information from Uncle Sy, a recluse and a connoisseur of snakes. At the cabin, the stranger converses with a droll rustic servant and gives him a letter asking his master to release him for military service; the rustic is delighted somewhat later to find that his letter is signed by General Washington. Throughout the romance Washington often has business with the young hero, Mark Moorland, a leader of guerrillas. He sends Mark into besieged Yorktown to obtain information and incidentally to rescue the heroine of the story from British captivity. On one occasion, Uncle Sy Rumsey saves Washington's life by knocking upward the rifle of a villainous Tory who has drawn a bead on him.⁷² The role of Washington in *The Buckskin* is notably similar to that of Mr. Harper in *The Spy*.

Newton Mallory Curtis, a prolific writer of his day, introduced Washington somewhat unexpectedly in the last chapter of *The Marksmen of Monmouth*. He is shown on horseback in battle, viewing from a slight eminence a desperate charge led by Anthony Wayne, which turns the tide against the British after all hope of a complete victory is lost. There is nothing of Washington's famous

---

⁷¹*Ibid.*, p. 39. In later life, after Ingraham became an Episcopal clergyman, he regretted the romanticism and sensationalism of his early writing and endeavored to suppress its further publication. A large number of romances are attributed to him. See David H. Bishop, "Joseph Holt Ingraham," in *Library of Southern Literature*, ed. Edwin Anderson Alderman, Joel Chandler Harris, and Charles William Kent, 16 vols. (New Orleans, 1908-1913), VI, 2591-2596. On the other hand, Arthur Hobson Quinn (*op. cit.*, p. 125, note) doubts that Ingraham wrote all the romances attributed to him. See also Don C. Seitz, "A Prince of Best Sellers," *Publishers' Weekly*, CXIX (February 21, 1931), 940.

⁷²*The Buckskin; or, The Camp of the Besiegers. A Tale of the Revolution* . . . (New York, 1847), Chapters VI, X, XIV, XXII, XXVII, XXIX, XXX.

meeting with Charles Lee, which is the most dramatic incident of the Battle of Monmouth.[73]

3

George Lippard, who died at the age of thirty-two, devoted more pages to the treatment of Washington than any other writer of fiction up to the present day. Lippard was an eccentric Philadelphia lawyer, journalist, social reformer, and lecturer, as well as a writer of tales and romances which had a wide circulation in the eighteen-forties and -fifties.[74] To write of Washington did not paralyze his vivid imagination, and some of his presentations of the national hero are remarkably convincing. Lippard's admiration for Washington was so great that he called himself "Supreme Washington" of the Brotherhood of the Union, a pre-Marxian socialistic organization of which he was founder. He steeped himself in Revolutionary and Washingtonian lore, which became his principal stock in trade for lectures as well as romances. He showed easy familiarity with his material, but he wrote in haste, for unlearned rather than critical readers, and his stories are marred by sensationalism, voluptuousness, and preposterous Gothic elements, which make the best of them uneven and some of them unintelligible.[75]

Lippard's longer Revolutionary romances are *Herbert Tracy*, *Blanche of Brandywine*, and *The Rose of Wissahikon*. Using largely materials already contained in these three earlier works,

---

[73]Newton Mallory Curtis, *The Marksmen of Monmouth: a Tale of the Revolution* . . . (Troy, N.Y., [1848]), pp. 143-147. *The Scout of the Silver Pond* (New York, 1847), by the same author, contains inconsequential mentions of Washington.

[74]There is an informative chapter on Lippard in Ellis Paxson Oberholtzer, *The Literary History of Philadelphia* (Philadelphia, 1906). Cowie, *op. cit.*, pp. 319-326, has a good discussion of Lippard's studies of city life. Edgar Allan Poe befriended Lippard on one or two occasions; see Arthur Hobson Quinn, *Edgar Allan Poe* (New York, 1941), pp. 385, 403 note, 618 ff.

[75]One book, *The Nazarene; or, The Last of the Washingtons. A Revelation of Philadelphia, New York, and Washington in the year 1844* (Philadelphia, [1854]), which came out originally in 1846, is largely incomprehensible, perhaps because of symbolism involving current events. Despite the title, the volume contains nothing about Washington except a few inconsequential mentions: pp. 4, 41, 43. Apparently only the first volume was published; the story is incomplete.

Fiction

Lippard brought out in 1847 a group of "legends" entitled *Washington and His Generals*. *Washington and His Men*, which appeared in 1850, contains much new material and includes some of Lippard's most original portrayals of Washington, showing him not only as Commander-in-Chief but also as a young man.

In *Herbert Tracy*, a scout of that name rides up to General Washington's headquarters, where a council of war is in progress. The time is October, 1777. After hearing Tracy's report, Washington speaks:

"Your information, Captain Tracy," said the Commander-in-Chief, "agrees in every essential point with the data already in my possession. So, gentlemen, our original plan of battle holds good. While the divisions of Generals Wayne and Sullivan enter the village by way of Chestnut Hill, the divisions of Greene and Stephens, flanked by McDougall's brigade, will take a circuit along the Limekiln Road, some two miles eastward from Chew's House, and attack the enemy's right wing. The militia of Maryland and New Jersey, under command of Generals Smallwood and Forman, will march down the Old York Road, which lies three miles to the east of the Limekiln Road, and engage with the rear of the right. General Armstrong's Pennsylvania brigade will attack the enemy's left at Vanduring's Mill, at the junction of the Wissahikon with the Schuylkill. Think you, Captain Tracy, that we shall be able to surprise the enemy?"

"I think the movement might be effected with care and celerity, your Excellency."

A shade of thought came over the noble brow of the Commander-in-Chief, and he leaned his head musingly upon his hand for an instant.

"Gentlemen," he exclaimed, after the pause of a moment, "I need not tell you that every thing depends upon the suddenness and secrecy of our movements. If we surprise the enemy, we shall terminate this disastrous war, and win the best of all boons, our country's independence; if the enemy are on the alert, and ready to receive us, it is more than probable that the superior discipline of his troops will triumph over the irregular bravery and undisciplined courage of a great portion of the army which I have the honor to command. What think ye, Gentlemen?"[76]

[76] George Lippard, *Herbert Tracy; or, The Legend of the Black Rangers. A Romance of the Battlefield of Germantown* (Philadelphia, 1844), pp. 83–84.

Lippard's reference to "the noble brow of the Commander-in-Chief" is elevated, but the words attributed to Washington are for the most part such as a man might speak when planning a battle. Twice in the same romance Lippard describes Washington leading cavalry charges,[77] and in the second the General narrowly escapes capture. The situation at Chew's house, where the pursuit of the fleeing British pauses, and where the American leaders disagree among themselves, is shown succinctly but graphically.[78] In his final appearance Washington chooses volunteers to fire the house held by the British and gives them directions, concluding: "Now, Captain Tracy, I leave the matter to your discretion. God be with you."[79]

Herbert Tracy, which Lippard dedicated to James Fenimore Cooper, is almost wholly the story, historical and legendary, of the Battle of Germantown. *Blanche of Brandywine* is much longer and has a more complicated plot. There are some fairly good humorous touches, as well as many ill-advised Gothic scenes and numerous sensational incidents. At a midnight meeting, when the two men are alone in a wood, General Howe offers Washington the title of duke, which Washington indignantly refuses; Howe admiringly gives him the title anyway.[80] The final scene of the novel is sensational and Gothic; the hero, Randulph Waldemar, kills his villainous brother, Percy, in the presence of Washington, who on the spot has a horrible vision of Blood and Death.[81] Only less sensational is an earlier scene in which, while a Quaker is delivering to Washington a mysterious packet, of untold importance, the two are surrounded by the British; the Quaker stabs the leader, and Washing-

[77]*Ibid.*, pp. 110 and 124.
[78]*Ibid.*, pp. 118–119.
[79]*Ibid.*, p. 131.
[80]George Lippard, *Blanche of Brandywine; or, September the Eleventh, 1777* . . . (Philadelphia, [1846]), pp. 150–158. Howe proclaims him "His Grace, George, Duke Washington, Viceroy of America." Some such offer was actually considered at one time. See Carl Van Doren, *Secret History of the American Revolution* . . . (New York, 1941), pp. 80 ff.
[81]*Blanche of Brandywine*, pp. 343–345.

ton leaps his horse over the heads of the astonished redcoats to flight and safety.[82]

Many of the better scenes of *Blanche of Brandywine* parallel those of *Herbert Tracy:* the General is twice in council with his officers; he appears with his staff in the midst of the battle; he rides madly down a hill with Pulaski at his side, to join the forces of Lafayette in combat; and he has another narrow escape from capture, being saved this time by Randulph Waldemar and Pulaski.[83]

The action of *The Rose of Wissahikon* is more rapid than clear. Except for the love interest, which is considerable, the story is concerned with the efforts of a young lady named Rose and an Indian named Mayaniko to deliver to Washington at his headquarters an advance copy of the Declaration of Independence; also involved are the plots of two factions, one seeking to make Washington king, the other seeking to replace him as General.[84] The treatment of Washington is essentially the same as that in Lippard's earlier romances.

One of the most remarkable incidents contained in *Washington and His Generals* is entitled "The Consecration of the Deliverer." Here an old prophet or man of religion in 1775 waits in the forest three hours after midnight because of a revelation from God that he should consecrate a deliverer. A handsome stranger (Washington) appears, riding on horseback, and he is duly anointed. The prophet proclaims:

"The voice of God has spoken to me, in my thoughts by day, in my dreams by night—*I will send a* DELIVERER *to this land of the New World, who shall save my people from physical bondage*, even as my Son saved them from the bondage of spiritual death."[85]

Washington and His Generals is loosely constructed and apparently even more hastily written than the three romances.

[82]*Ibid.*, pp. 130–131.
[83]*Ibid.*, pp. 128 and 138; 234, 255–259.
[84]*The Rose of Wissahikon; or, The Fourth of July, 1776; a Romance Embracing the Secret History of the Declaration of Independence* (Philadelphia, 1847).
[85]*Washington and His Generals; or, Legends of the Revolution* . . . (Philadelphia, 1847), p. 92.

218   Fiction

Washington and His Men is comparatively well organized. It is divided into fourteen "legends," most of which are short stories, but some of which may more properly be called *nouvelles*. Such are Legend 13 and Legend 14, condensations of *The Rose of Wissahikon* and *Herbert Tracy*, respectively. In Legend 12, "Washington's Christmas, a Legend of Valley Forge," Washington arrives at the farmhouse of Israel Kuch just in time to prevent the old man's killing a young Tory who is in love with his daughter. The Tory has fired at Washington, missed, and apparently killed old Kuch's son, Washington's bodyguard. When at length it is found that the bodyguard was merely scratched, the kindhearted Washington forgives the Tory, with advice to shoot straighter thereafter.[86] In Legend 11, King George III appears to Washington in a vision on one of the battlefields of the Revolution, a fantastic tale which appears in slightly different form in *Washington and His Generals*.[87]

Lippard did not confine himself to Revolutionary tales but in the first ten legends of *Washington and His Men* dealt with events dating from about 1450 until 1755. In writing these he could allow his imagination to range more freely than he could when treating the Washington of 1775–1783. The first legend is the story of a baron's daughter, Washington's supposed ancestress, who eloped with a man of humble origins. In Legend 2 Lippard followed Parson Weems[88] in telling of two sets of visions experienced by Mary Washington, one a vision of his actual career, the other of his career as it might have been if he had not been guided aright. "The Youth of Washington," Legend 3, is a retelling of the tradition that he climbed up the rocky wall beside the Natural Bridge to write his initials higher than those of any other.[89] In Legend 4, "The Boy and the Book," he pores over the old family Bible, especially the stories of Moses, David, and Jesus. Legends 5 and 6, "The Challenge," and

[86] *Washington and His Men: a New Series of Legends of the Revolution* . . . (New York, 1850), pp. 71–80.
[87] *Washington and His Generals*, pp. 119 ff.
[88] Mason Locke Weems, *A History of the Life and Death, Virtues & Exploits of General George Washington* (New York, 1927), pp. 93–96.
[89] For an earlier mention of this tradition, see William A. Caruthers, "Climbing the Natural Bridge," *Knickerbocker*, XII (July, 1838), 32–35.

Fiction

"The Duel; or, Courage That Is Not Afraid of the Name of Coward," enlarge upon Parson Weems's story of a little man named Payne who knocked Washington down with a stick after the latter had called him a liar on election day.[90] In Lippard's story Washington's friends arrange for a duel, but Washington's conscience shows him that he is in the wrong, and so he apologizes and asks for a reconciliation, which Payne willingly grants. Legends 7, 8, and 10 deal with Braddock's campaign and conform in general to the usual account, except that Braddock as he lies dying admits that he erred in neglecting Washington's advice.

Legend 9, "Washington in Love," the most original piece in the book, also deals with the time of Braddock's defeat. A beautiful girl named Marion lives in the wilderness near the Monongahela with her guardian, supposedly her grandfather. Washington arrives at their cabin just in time to save Marion from Michael Burke, the "Red Wolfe," who is forcing his attentions upon her. The young Colonel remains for the night and hears from Old Abraham, the guardian, strange tales of Marion's birth and parentage. That same night Washington falls into a fever and delirium, during which Marion nurses him. To the sick man she seems to be an angel, and on the next day both are deeply in love; but Washington must leave to rejoin Braddock's forces and fight in the Battle of Monongahela. His return is delayed for several days. As he approaches the region of the cabin at last, his mind is filled with visions of Marion's chestnut hair, bright eyes, full bosom, and graceful figure, and he happily imagines their meeting; but when he arrives, he finds that the victorious Indian allies of the French have scalped both Marion and her grandfather. Securing a lock of Marion's hair, he places it in a locket bearing the inscription "Marion, July 11th, 1754," and this he still has with him many years later when he is President.[91]

Lippard's presentation of young Washington in the grip of the tender passion is one of very few such fictional efforts to be found

[90]Weems, *op. cit.*, pp. 311–316.
[91]*Washington and His Men*, pp. 47–59. Lippard got his dates a year too early throughout this story: Braddock's defeat occurred in July, 1755.

in the period under consideration. Despite its gruesome ending, the story is definitely superior to McHenry's *The Wilderness,* and, perhaps because of its brevity, it also seems more graphic than does Washington's part in a somewhat similar story written by John Esten Cooke several years later.

Sentimental portrayal of Washington as General reaches a high point in *The Lone Dove* (1850), by Diana Treat Kilbourn. The story concerns the fate of an orphan who has become separated from her foster father and now lives with some friendly Indians who call her the "Lone Dove." An Indian princess takes her to see General Washington in the hope that he will intervene to free the foster father—who in the end is discovered to be the orphan's real grandfather—from captivity in the hands of the British. The plight of the Lone Dove immediately fascinates Washington, and, in a scene which is visited by an angel from heaven, he promises to intercede for the captive and offers to let the girl remain with him in Boston as his daughter. Talking with the Indian princess and the Lone Dove, Washington falls into a sort of Indian lingo, which has no first or second person: "The General pressed his lips to the pure brow of the sweet child, and murmured as he raised his eyes above: —'The prayers of such innocence must bring a blessing! But where will the Lone Dove stay, till the white-chief has spoken to his brother?'"[92] Washington's intervention is unavailing, but in the course of the next several years the Lone Dove meets the General several times. Her career includes life in an Indian village, education by an English officer and his wife, presentation to New York society, abduction, rescue, and finally departure for England with her English benefactors. Each time the Lone Dove crosses Washington's path, he treats her as his own, the daughter whom he would have adopted if it had been practicable. On the night before she leaves for England, he takes leave of her thus:

"My good, my gentle child," he said, with much emotion: "Had heaven willed that you should have remained under my care, my protection, I

---

[92][Diana Treat Kilbourn], *The Lone Dove: a Legend of Revolutionary Times* . . . (Philadelphia, 1850), p. 52.

Fiction

should have viewed it as one of its choicest blessings. But he, who knows what is for the best, has ordered it otherwise, and I must not complain; though it is with feelings of the deepest regret that we part with you, my sweet child!"[93]

More in the tradition of Cooper are two romances by Emerson Bennett, a prolific writer whose works were very popular in the fifties: *The Female Spy* and its sequel, *Rosalie Du Pont*.[94] Rosalie, the heroine of both stories, pretends to be a Tory spy but actually is spying for the Americans. Like Lafayette, who is seen here in a very kindly light because of Washington's esteem for him, she is of French origin. The plot of *The Female Spy* involves the story of Arnold and André, and portions of the narrative are reminiscent of Ingraham's *The Treason of Arnold*. Washington is here characterized by a mixture of dignity and kindliness. In the final chapter of *Rosalie Du Pont* he makes a long bombastic speech thanking Rosalie and her fiancé for their aid.

In Henry A. Buckingham's *Harry Burnham, the Young Continental*, Washington is frequently on the scene. He interviews Harry, his friend Frank Fairfax—just out of Yale—and their factotum, Ki, an older man whom Washington chooses for a spy because of his huge bulk, physical strength, and knowledge of the countryside.[95] A little later he chooses Harry for an aide and entrusts him with important dispatches.[96]

An unusual scene is that in which Washington plays quoits with Ki, the big semicomic servant and spy, and allows Ki to

---

[93]*Ibid.*, p. 246. For further appearances of Washington, see Chapters XII, XVIII ("Scenes at Valley Forge"), XL, XLI, LIII, and LIX.

[94]Emerson Bennett, *The Female Spy; or, Treason in the Camp* . . . (Cincinnati, Ohio, [1851]); *Rosalie Du Pont; or, Treason in the Camp* . . . (Cincinnati, Ohio, [1851]).

The Seven Brothers of Wyoming . . . (New York, [1850]) is an anonymous romance in which General Washington appears very briefly when one of the characters applies to him for a furlough for his son, a soldier.

[95]Henry A. Buckingham, *Harry Burnham, the Young Continental; or, Memoirs of an American Officer during the Campaigns of the Revolution, and Sometime a Member of Washington's Staff* (New York, [1852]), p. 37.

[96]*Ibid.*, p. 117.

win by one point. The author makes a comment upon this incident:

It is a wrong idea in the minds of many, that Washington had no pleasantry about him. It is true that, among mere strangers, he seldom permitted himself to be gay. But, in his own family, and when surrounded by his favorites, he could now and then be as amusing as the best. But vulgar wit he never uttered, nor dared any one to utter it in his presence.[97]

On one occasion Washington interviews Nathan Hale and tells him of the great danger of his mission.[98] The scene at Kip's Bay, where Washington is infuriated by the cowardly retreat of his green troops, is given in some detail and rather graphically. When Ki seizes his bridle to prevent his riding in singlehanded attack upon the British, Washington composes himself and says: "You have done right."[99] On another occasion, when he sends Ki into New York after it is feared that Hale has been captured, he is moved to tears by Ki's devotion to his country and willingness to take any risk. The author says that although Washington is remembered for "his inflexible sternness, which cast over him throughout his whole life, civil and military, an almost godlike sublimity," he nevertheless could weep at such pure patriotism.[100] Washington draws the coverlet over the dead Ki, who has been mortally wounded in the fall of Yorktown, and declares that there was never a more faithful or patriotic soldier.[101]

John Richter Jones, author of *Slavery Sanctioned by the Bible*, produced in 1858 a Revolutionary romance which contains three unusual touches in its characterization of Washington. Several times he is called "rebel";[102] he is compared with Cromwell, whom the author admires;[103] and the critical attitude of those who wanted

[97] *Ibid.*, p. 172.
[98] *Ibid.*, pp. 190–191.
[99] *Ibid.*, pp. 212–213.
[100] *Ibid.*, p. 232.
[101] *Ibid.*, p. 255.
[102] [John Richter Jones], *The Quaker Soldier; or, The British in Philadelphia* . . . (Philadelphia, [1858]), pp. 181, 290, 392, 429.
[103] *Ibid.*, pp. 326 ff.

to replace him in 1777–1778 is here shown quite clearly.[104] Still, in half a dozen appearances, the General does not differ greatly from the portrayal in other romances. He interviews the hero Lynnford in headquarters and appoints him a special aide; he entertains Lynnford at a most solemn dinner with his other aides; on horseback, from a little hill, he reviews passing troops and then sends the hero with dispatches. At Chew's house, in the midst of battle, he decides to take the impoverished fortress instead of pursuing the fleeing redcoats with all speed. Under fire in the battle of Germantown he coolly gives orders. Later he speaks inspiringly to troops drawn up ready for an attack which never comes. He visits the wounded Lynnford and tells him of the woeful straits of his troops. Finally, he sends Lynnford, armed with a letter, to Congress for a promotion. There Lynnford, in conversation with Charles Thomson, Secretary of Congress, says Washington is not "one of us—the men of everyday life," to defend him from the Secretary's judgment that he is "cold and reserved."[105]

There is less embroidery upon history in the part Washington plays in *The Rivals*, by Jeremiah Clemens, one-time United States Senator from Alabama.[106] Clemens traced the relations of Aaron Burr and Alexander Hamilton, taking the unusual position that Hamilton was a subtle rascal and Burr an upright gentleman. Washington appears frequently, although he is not integral to the plot. Since the General is deceived in his good opinion of Hamilton throughout the book, the reader is likely to conclude that he was a poor judge of men. But Clemens probably did not consider this angle; at any rate, characterization of Washington was not a primary object with him. The General's various military moves come in for praise, and he seems the embodiment of almost all qualities desirable in a Commander-in-Chief.

[104] *Ibid.*, pp. 478 ff.
[105] *Ibid.*, p. 480. Washington's appearances are in Chapters XX, XXII, XXIII, XXIV, XXXI, and XXXIV.
[106] Jeremiah Clemens, *The Rivals: a Tale of the Times of Aaron Burr and Alexander Hamilton* (Philadelphia, 1860). The book was reissued in 1900 as *An American Colonel*.

Fiction

A somewhat better romance than most of those considered in the present section is John Esten Cooke's *Lord Fairfax*.[107] Cooke presented Washington as Cupid's victim at the age of sixteen. The setting of the story is the Shenandoah Valley in the neighborhood of Winchester, Virginia, where the young man is surveying lands for Lord Fairfax. While he is working alone in the woods one day, he hears a call for assistance. Hastening to the source of the cry, George (no other name is given until the end of the book) rescues a beautiful girl from drowning.[108] He takes her to the cabin where she resides with her grandfather, and in the course of time he becomes a frequent visitor. Soon he and the girl, whose name is Cannie Powell, fall in love. Indian marauders carry off Cannie and other captives, so that the frontiersmen are constrained to unite for battle. Despite his extreme youth, George performs valiantly in the fight which ensues, and Cannie is rescued.[109] But her health, never very good, has been undermined by the exposure and hardship of her captivity, and she dies with George at her side, smiling through his tears.[110] Years later, when returning from the Battle of Yorktown, General George Washington goes far from his direct route to visit the grave of Cannie, to whose epitaph he adds a note that his heart has died with her.[111] Such is the subplot of Cooke's *Lord Fairfax*.

Fortunately, the main plot is more interesting, and some of the other characters—including Falconbridge, the hero; Lightfoot, a noble Indian; Yellow Serpent, a villainous half-breed; and an eccentric young woman named Bertha Argal—are much more vividly portrayed than is young George. The reader repeatedly has evidence that the boy is brave, warmhearted, and good, but he is not

---

[107] John Esten Cooke, *Lord Fairfax; or, The Master of Greenway Court* (New York, 1896). Also published as *Fairfax; or, The Master of Greenway Court* (1868), the story first appeared serially in the *Southern Literary Messenger* in 1858 under the title *Greenway Court*.
[108] *Ibid.*, pp. 55 ff.
[109] *Ibid.*, pp. 377 ff.
[110] *Ibid.*, pp. 394 ff.
[111] *Ibid.*, pp. 402 ff.

further characterized and so seems less real than most of the other persons in the story.[112]

Far more realistic treatment is accorded the national hero in Theodore Winthrop's *Edwin Brothertoft* (1862), but here Washington's role is a very small one. Early in the story, one of Winthrop's characters speaks rather irreverently of the young Washington: "Our strapping young friend from Virginia, Master George Washington, has caracoled off, with a tear in his eye and a flea in his ear."[113] The reference is to his courtship of Mrs. Custis after his (supposed) rejection by Mary Phillipse. Later a few scraps of conversation are attributed to Washington, now Commander-in-Chief.[114] The words are informal, almost flippant, and Winthrop takes occasion to remark that the Commander "was not the stilted prig that modern muffs have made him."[115] But a critic pronounced the portrayal of both Washington and Putnam in *Edwin Brothertoft* unfaithful and found it a great blemish.[116] Just a few years earlier, critics had been seriously disturbed by a more extended characterization of Washington in a British novel.

4

William Makepeace Thackeray's *The Virginians, a Tale of the Last Century* appeared serially in *Harper's Monthly Magazine*, contemporaneously with its publication in Britain, over a two-year

---

[112]Washington is mentioned in Cooke's *The Virginia Comedians* (1854) and in *Henry St. John, Gentleman* . . . (1857), where he is called "the sword of the Revolution."
"Excalibur: a Story for Anglo American Boys" appeared in a Cincinnati magazine called *The Dial* early in 1860. The mystic sword of King Arthur was here traced to Frederick the Great, George Washington, and John Brown. Moncure Daniel Conway, the author, discusses it in his *Autobiography, Memories and Experiences* . . . , 2 vols. (Boston and New York, 1904), I, 310–311.
Three dime novels issued before 1865 and said to present Washington as a character are listed in Albert Johannsen, *The House of Beadle and Adams and Its Dime and Nickel Novels*, 2 vols. (Norman, Okla., [1950]), I, 83 and 86; II, 429.
[113]Theodore Winthrop, *Edwin Brothertoft* (8th ed.; Boston, 1865), p. 26.
[114]*Ibid.*, pp. 96–98, 123–124.
[115]*Ibid.*, p. 98.
[116]"Critical Notices," *North American Review*, XCV (October, 1862), 561–562.

period that began in November, 1857. The American reaction to the treatment of Washington therein gives reason for inclusion of *The Virginians* in the present chapter. Incidentally, English realism had by 1859 gone much further than American, and Thackeray could hardly have aroused there in any way such an angry critical response as he drew forth in America.

Thackeray twice traveled in America on lecture tours, and it seems to have been during the latter of these visits (1855–1856) that the plan for a novel laid in Revolutionary Virginia crystallized in his mind. He spoke of the idea to John Pendleton Kennedy and to John Esten Cooke, and at one point he added that he would wait at least two years in order to collect material and get his project well in mind before the actual writing.[117] In the primary matter of getting "material" Thackeray ran into difficulty. Kennedy was helpful in showing him something of plantation life and introducing him to several Virginians, but Thackeray did not feel that from conversation with Kennedy and others he got anything concrete on Washington's personality.[118]

Several years earlier, Thackeray had run afoul of the popular veneration for Washington. American readers found fault with a casual reference to "Mr. Washington" in the opening pages of *The Newcomes*, and the novelist published a graceful letter of explanation. His closing words were: ". . . let me say, in perfect faith and gravity, that I think the cause for which Washington fought entirely just and right, and the champion the very noblest, purest, bravest, best of God's men."[119] Today it is difficult to understand the objection raised to the passage in *The Newcomes*, and it is still

---

[117] Thackeray's story did not evolve exactly as he at first envisioned it. For the genesis of *The Virginians*, see Jay B. Hubbell, "Thackeray and Virginia," *Virginia Quarterly Review*, III (January, 1927), 76–86.

[118] *Ibid.*, p. 83. From Kennedy's diary comes the information that Thackeray borrowed from him Alexander Graydon's *Memoirs*, William Heath's *Memoirs*, and Alexander Garden's *Anecdotes of the Revolutionary War;* see Henry T. Tuckerman, *The Life of John Pendleton Kennedy* (New York, 1871), p. 364. For these reminiscences of Revolutionary soldiers: *supra*, Chapter II, Section 1.

[119] To the editor of the *Times*, November 22, 1853, in *The Letters and Private Papers of William Makepeace Thackeray*, ed. Gordon N. Ray, 4 vols. (Cambridge, Mass., 1945–1946), III, 321. Cf. III, 327–328, 331–332.

more difficult to understand the strictures of American critics on *The Virginians*.

Washington, as a Colonel aged twenty-three, is not one of the central figures in *The Virginians* but enters the story as financial adviser and friend to Madam Esmond Warrington. Madam Warrington is a charming widow whose twin sons are just four years younger than Washington himself. When he visits at the Warrington plantation, Mrs. Mountain, the housekeeper, who is jealous of her influence in the establishment, leaps to the conclusion that he has come to woo. She conveys this idea to the boys, Harry and George, the former of whom is rather hotheaded, and the latter of whom has already suspected Washington's attentions to his mother. Mrs. Mountain's suspicions are apparently confirmed when she reads, in a personal letter which Washington has written to his brother, that he intends to marry a rich young widow with two children. Aroused by Harry and Mrs. Mountain, and assisted by several arrogant drunken officers of General Braddock, George Warrington insults Washington at a tavern and contrives to challenge him to a duel, as do a couple of the brawling officers also. With the intention of fighting, Washington writes several letters which Mrs. Mountain also reads, and these make it evident that his marital intentions are directed not toward Madam Warrington but toward a Mrs. Curtis [sic]. So Mrs. Mountain herself rushes to the scene and averts the duel in the nick of time. After reconciliations Washington's visit ends, and in the thirteenth chapter of the first volume he leaves the story, to return no more until the final chapter of Volume II. All told, he is involved in the action of less than one eighth of the entire book.

More than twenty years elapse between the tavern episode and the glimpse of General Washington which is presented through the eyes of Harry Warrington at the close of the story. In the interim Harry has fought in the Revolution as an American officer, and his brother, now Sir George, has served with the British forces. Most of the Warrington family is united at the end, and Harry reminisces at some length. He recalls that once he quarreled with the General and wished to resign his commission because the young Marquis de Lafayette was given a high rating over the heads of himself and other Patriot officers. Washington on this occasion kept his temper and justified Lafayette's commission, deeply impressing and mollifying Warrington. Harry also describes the familiar and moving scene of Washington's farewell to his officers at Fraunces' Tavern, near Whitehall Ferry, in 1781.[120]

Thackeray's treatment of Washington was unusual in two important respects. In the first place, he showed him against the background of Virginian society in pre-Revolutionary days. The few Americans who treated Washington's youth in works of fiction did so against a wilderness background. The Britisher was remarkably successful in depicting eighteenth-century Virginia although only a comparatively small portion of the action of *The Virginians* takes place there.[121] Secondly, Thackeray was far more realistic in handling Washington than any American author had been. He everywhere speaks highly of the young Colonel; yet he contrives to make him human. After considerable needling on the part of the Warrington boys and Braddock's officers at the tavern, Washington yells with rage. He calls one of the tipsy officers a hog, and at one point he addresses the entire group:

"Is this some infernal conspiracy in which you are all leagued against me?" shouted the Colonel. "It would seem as if I was drunk, and not you, as you all are. I withdraw nothing. I apologize for nothing. By heavens! I will meet one or half-a-dozen of you in your turn, young or old, drunk or sober."[122]

It has been said that Thackeray's portrayal of young Washington is too unconventional to please his contemporary American readers

---

[120] *The Virginians, a Tale of the Last Century*, 2 vols., VII–VIII in Thackeray, *The Complete Works* . . . with Introductions by William P. Trent and John Bell Henneman; 30 vols. in 15 (New York, [1904]), II, 498–508.

[121] Cf. Hubbell, *op. cit.*, pp. 84–86.

[122] *The Virginians*, I, 111. It was this passage and a few similar ones that caused Frederick S. Cozzens to comment, in a letter otherwise favorable to Thackeray's novel: "I must except to your making George Washington use language unbecoming an officer and a gentleman, as you do."—Cozzens to Thackeray, March 21, 1858, in Thackeray, *Letters and Private Papers*, IV, 74.

Fiction

and that it is too conventional to please present-day historians.[123] Unable to get any specific information of the kind he sought, the author realized only that Washington must be staid and proper on all occasions. To enliven the picture, he created the tavern scene wherein the young Colonel's display of anger is—as Thackeray probably thought—entirely justified. It is possible that Thackeray himself felt some annoyance with the perfect youth he had chosen to deal with, and that he conveyed his own attitude to some of his characters.[124] Mrs. Mountain finds the Colonel very old for his age and is scornful because he seems to have sowed no wild oats.[125] And George Warrington, in a journal addressed to his family, pronounces the Colonel "as perfectly stupid and correct as Prince Prettyman need be." He adds: "Hang him! He has no faults, and that's why I dislike him. When he marries that widow—ah me! what a dreary life she will have of it."[126] Harry, on the other hand, is Washington's devoted friend.

After only eight chapters of *The Virginians* had appeared, John R. Thompson wrote of it in the *Southern Literary Messenger*. Thompson, who had met Thackeray,[127] served warning that it was a dangerous business "to involve Washington in the machinery of a work of fiction," for he was in no way a fit subject for satire.[128] When four more chapters had appeared, including the tavern scene, Thompson expressed himself as "out of patience with Mr. Thackeray's 'Virginians.' " He mentioned inaccuracies, particularly that of having Washington acquainted with Mrs. Custis before Braddock's campaign. Then Thompson added:

But these faults are trivial compared with the liberty taken by Mr. Thackeray in hurrying Washington into a couple of duels with a pair of drunken youths, which, though arrested before an actual exchange of shots with either party, place our venerated hero in a somewhat

---

[123]Hubbell, *op. cit.*, pp. 82-83.
[124]Cf. *ibid.*, p. 83.
[125]*The Virginians*, I, 51.
[126]*Ibid.*, I, 124.
[127]Hubbell, *op. cit.*, pp. 76-77.
[128]"Editor's Table," *Southern Literary Messenger*, XXVI (January, 1858), 75-77.

Fiction

ridiculous position. Mr. Thackeray should never have ventured upon bringing Washington into his story farther than to permit him to cross the stage and be seen no more.[129]

Cornelius C. Felton, classical scholar and educator, found opportunity to attack Thackeray on much the same grounds. According to Felton, that novelist's characters are "compounds of many vices and few if any virtues"; if the virtues in any case predominate, the character is simply a fool. Particularly incensed because some Americans were pleased to see Washington made "like other men," Felton declared: "Why, this is the very essence of falsehood. Washington was not like other men; and to bring his lofty character down to the level of the vulgar passions of common life, is to give the lie to the grandest chapter in the uninspired annals of the human race."[130]

It has been shown that a great many American writers followed Cooper's lead in including General Washington as a character in Revolutionary romances and tales. Yet no other outstanding American writer did so before 1865 although a few wrote historical romances. Perhaps they were forewarned by Cooper's own failure; perhaps too they realized that the conception of Washington to which they fell heir was not material sufficiently real to handle. In most of the works of the minor writers General Washington is remarkably similar to Cooper's Mr. Harper, although in many instances he has a smaller—and less mysterious—role than that famous prototype. Catharine Maria Sedgwick's portrait is far more human and convincing than the average, and George Lippard's genuine

---

[129] *Ibid.*, XXVI (February, 1858), 152–153.
Criticism of Thackeray's treatment of Washington became so general that the editorial staff of Harper's came to the Britisher's defense. See "Editor's Easy Chair," *Harper's Monthly Magazine*, XVI (March, 1858), 558–559; also "Thackeray's Washington," *Harper's Weekly*, II (February 20, 1858), 114–115. George William Curtis, an influential littérateur, wrote both articles. To his friend Thackeray, Curtis wrote: "It has been the most tempestuous teapot you ever heard."—June 17, 1858, in Thackeray, *Letters and Private Papers*, IV, 92–93.

[130] *North American Review*, XCI (October, 1860), 580–582. Felton's words on Thackeray were incidental; he here reviewed Everett's biography of Washington.

Fiction

enthusiasm gives his work an ease and a vigor that are often lacking in stories of the Revolution.

Some increase of interest in Washington is evident in fiction of the eighteen-forties and -fifties, as compared with that of the preceding decades. But the formula remains the same: the august and all-capable, yet kindly General. Exceptions are the stories by Lippard and John Esten Cooke in which these authors portray the youthful Washington in love. Their stories, and also an earlier one by James McHenry, are quite dissimilar in point of detail but remarkably similar in pattern and philosophy: the object of the young man's affection in each case is an unspoiled daughter of the wilderness, each affair ends unhappily, and there is the statement or implication that the hero's character was strengthened by the experience.[131]

It must not be forgotten that Washington is mentioned, incidentally or—more often—with a few words of praise, in dozens of stories in which he does not actually appear.[132] Occasionally such

---

[131] A similar interpretation of Washington's life occurs in a modern novel by Mrs. Bernie Babcock, *The Heart of George Washington* (Philadelphia, 1932), and, more significantly, in the biography by Rupert Hughes, *George Washington . . .* 3 vols. (New York, 1926–1930). See also John Corbin, *The Unknown Washington . . .* (New York, 1930); Henry M. Edmonds, *Studies in Power* (Nashville, Tenn., 1931).

[132] Among those not otherwise treated in these pages are the following: [Peter Markoe], *The Algerine Spy in Pennsylvania . . .* (Philadelphia, 1787); Obadiah Benjamin Franklin Bloomfield [pseud.], *The Life and Adventures . . .* (Philadelphia, 1818); Eliza Lanesford Foster Cushing, *Yorktown* (Boston, 1826); "The Battle of Monmouth," in *Tales of the Fireside, by a Lady of Boston* (Boston, 1827); James Ewell Heath, *Edge-Hill . . .* (Richmond, Va., 1828); John Pendleton Kennedy, *Swallow Barn . . .* (1832), ed. Jay B. Hubbell (New York, 1929); William Alexander Caruthers, *The Kentuckian in New York* (New York, 1834); William Gilmore Simms, *The Partisan: a Tale of the Revolution* (New York, 1835); A. B. Longstreet, "The Turn Out," in *Georgia Scenes* [1835] (2d ed.; New York, 1854); *Tales of the Revolution* (New York, 1836); Sarah J. Hale, "The Soldier of the Revolution," in *Sketches of American Character* (Boston, 1838); *The Deserter, a Romance of the American Revolution . . .*, *Southern Literary Messenger*, Vols. III–IV (September, 1837–January, 1838); Julia Putnam Henderson [?], *Lionel Granby*, Chapter XI, *Southern Literary Messenger*, IV (January, 1838), 22–24; *The Treason of Arnold and Other Tales* (Boston, 1840); Mary Stanley Bunce Dana, *Charles Morton . . .* (New York, 1843); Benjamin Barker, *Ellen Grafton . . .* (New York, 1845); Jephtha Root Simms, *The American Spy . . .* (Albany, N.Y., 1846); Benjamin Barker, *The Dwarf of the Channel* (Boston, 1846); A. J. Herr, *The Maid of the Valley . . .* (New York, 1847); Charles F. Sterling, *Buff and Blue . . .* (New York, 1847); J. H. Robinson, *The Boston Conspiracy . . .*

Fiction

references have some particular significance, like those in John Neal's *Randolph*.[133]

By 1860 the transition to realism in the American novel was beginning, and one young writer, Theodore Winthrop, dared to treat the Revolutionary heroes, even including Washington, as mere human beings. Winthrop's casual words presaged later developments. Although interest in Washington ran particularly high for a score of years just before the Civil War, realistic treatment of him was for that very reason out of the question. Americans were hoping that veneration for Washington would help prevent disunion, and

(Boston, 1847); A. H. Brisbane, *Ralphton; or, The Young Carolinian of 1776* . . . (Charleston, S.C., 1848); Charles F. Sterling, *The Red Coats* . . . (New York, 1848); Charles Douglas Paterson, *Grace Dudley; or, Arnold at Saratoga* (Philadelphia, [1849]); Edgar Allan Poe, "Mellonta Tauta" (1849), in *Complete Works* . . . , ed. James A. Harrison, 17 vols. in 11 (New York, 1902), VI, 197–215; Robert F. Greeley, *The Partisan's Oath* . . . (New York, 185–); *Anna Archdale . . . and Other Tales* (Boston, [185–]); Sylvanus Cobb, Jr., *The Golden Eagle* . . . (Boston, 1850); Lawrence Labree, *Rebels and Tories* . . . (New York, [1851]); William Gilmore Simms, *Katharine Walton* . . . [1851] (New York, 1882); "The Two Sisters," *Knickerbocker*, XLVI (July, 1855), 65–73; William Gilmore Simms, *Eutaw* . . . [1856] (New York, 1882); Oliver Wendell Holmes, *The Professor at the Breakfast Table* [1860] (New York, 1892); N. C. Iron, *The Maid of Esopus; or, The Trials and Triumphs of the Revolution* (New York, [1861]); Oliver Wendell Holmes, *Elsie Venner* [1861] (New York, 1892).

[133]An interesting tangent to the treatment of Washington in fiction is the occasional use of his name in humorous sketches. In the latter part of the period here considered, humorists sometimes burlesqued the heroic tradition by bestowing upon their characters such appellations as Martha Washington Greene Swink and George Washington Snubbins; see "Some Scenes in the Life of a Fastidious Man," by "J. F. K.," *Southern Literary Messenger*, XIII (March, 1847), 147–151. In a magazine sketch ("Editor's Table," *Knickerbocker*, XLVI (November, 1855), 535, someone known as K. N. Pepper writes to P. Pepper Podd about his "reverens & aw" for his friend's character, which he says is "similar to WASHINGTON'S." Several such passages occur in *Artemus Ward: His Book* (1862). Among the objects displayed by Ward, the traveling showman, were wax figures of "G. Washington, Gen. Tayler, John Bunyan, Capt. Kidd," and others. When Mr. Ward is seen intoxicated, he explains that he has been drowning his sorrow, for vandals had painted Washington's nose red, set his wig awry and his tricorn at an angle, put his pants in his boots, and stuck a clay pipe in his mouth. See Charles Farrar Browne, *The Complete Works of Artemus Ward* . . . (London, 1899), pp. 37, 71; cf. pp. 86, 110, 122, 152, 217, 221, 261, 297–298, 305, 410. Artemus Ward's Fourth of July speech is quoted *supra*, Chapter III, Section 4.

For further humorous references to Washington see "Editor's Table," *Southern Literary Messenger*, XXVIII (May, 1859), 395–398; "Bunkum's Flagstaff," *Knickerbocker*, XXXIV (August, 1849), 155; "The Prince of Pickpockets," *Knickerbocker*, LV (March, 1860), 16; [Robert Henry Newell], *The Orpheus C. Kerr Papers*, 3 vols. (New York, 1862–1865), I, 90, 103; Ivan Benson, *Mark Twain's Western Years* . . . (Stanford University, Calif., 1938), p. 186.

they had no desire to read anything that would seem to indicate that he was "like other men." Particularly offensive was something of that nature from the pen of an Englishman, as Thackeray discovered.

On the whole, the story of Washington in fiction before 1865 is a story of failure. American writers displayed little need of the warning that a critic gave Thackeray:

Washington's character has come to us spotless, and if you impute to him the little follies that have belonged to other great men, the majestic apparition you have called up may visit you, pure and white as you see him in Houdon's statue, and freeze you into silence with his calm, reproachful gaze.[134]

[134] [John R. Thompson], "Editor's Table," *Southern Literary Messenger,* XXVI (January, 1858), 75–77.

CHAPTER VIII

*C*ONCLUSION

*I*N THE WRITINGS of his contemporaries, particularly their letters, memoirs, and journals, it is possible to find the traits that his own generation valued in Washington: moral integrity, devotion to duty, steady perseverance, sound judgment, unlimited courage, and great military competence. Later generations did not lose sight of these characteristics, but speakers and writers shifted the emphasis and applied their own interpretations freely. In addition, many contributed details and anecdotes in accord with their respective ideas of what would constitute the perfect character. The way in which Washington thus became all things to all men has been skilfully traced by Dixon Wecter, who compares and contrasts the man's actual characteristics, as revealed by modern biographical research, with some of the traits popularly attributed to him.[1]

But in one very important respect Americans were remarkably consistent in their conception of Washington until the coming of sectional conflict confused their thinking. As was proclaimed by many a Fourth of July orator, Washington showed the world the type of man the new nation could produce. He was, in short, the ideal American and so represented the nation itself. In all likelihood every young nation has something of an "inferiority complex." Americans found it good at frequent intervals to assure and remind themselves of their dignity and importance, and this they could well do through contemplation of the character and career of Washing-

[1] "President Washington and Parson Weems," in Dixon Wecter, *The Hero in America, a Chronicle of Hero-Worship* (New York, 1941), pp. 99–147.

Conclusion

ton. They were extremely sensitive on many points touching their national status, and, as Thackeray learned, one such point was that sacrosanct figure.

It is, then, impossible to study the literary aspect of Washington's fame without likewise considering some of its historical and political aspects. The funeral eulogies seem to have crystallized in grandiose terms the conception of national virtue that prevailed at the close of the eighteenth century, and in a way they marked the formal acceptance of Washington as America's hero. Many of them, however, displayed a strong Federalist bias, and it was the memory of his Federalist leanings that somewhat impaired Washington's fame during the ensuing period of the Virginia dynasty. Yet at no time were the Federalists able to secure a firm, exclusive hold on him. The whole nation had need of his beneficent influence, to use a common nineteenth-century expression.

The Washington of the Stuart portraits is not greatly different from the hero of the funeral sermons of 1800. Encountering one of these portraits while abroad, Nathaniel Hawthorne said he "was proud to see that noblest face and figure here in England; the picture of a man beside whom (considered merely as a physical man) any English nobleman would look like common beef or clay."[2] This was a typical American reaction, but a more critical one was that of Thackeray, who, according to tradition, showed off his Stuart portraits of General and Mrs. Washington with the remark: "Look at him. Does he not look as if he had just said a good, stupid thing?"[3] There is much to be said for Thackeray's opinion as well as for Hawthorne's, and certainly the Stuart portraits, though apart from the subject of the present study, tended to reinforce the impersonal impression given by the orators.[4]

[2]Nathaniel Hawthorne, *The English Notebooks* . . . , ed. Randall Stewart (New York and London, 1941), p. 225. Cf. pp. 47, 217, 612.
[3]William Makepeace Thackeray, *The Letters and Private Papers*, ed. Gordon N. Ray, 4 vols. (Cambridge, Mass., 1945-1946), III, 180 note.
[4]For discussion of Washington in art see: John Hill Morgan and Mantle Fielding, *The Life Portraits of Washington and Their Replicas* (Philadelphia, 1931); G. A. Eisen, *Portraits of Washington*, 3 vols. (New York, 1932); Francis D. Whittemore, *George Washington in Sculpture* (Boston, 1933); Elizabeth Bryant Johnston, *Original Portraits of Washington* (Boston, 1882).

Conclusion

In 1823, when many persons who had seen and known Washington were still alive, an American novelist wrote apropos of the Stuart portraits that his countrymen had stripped their hero of "the chief attributes of humanity" and made him a god. From the literary evidence it is clear that this dehumanizing process was in operation in Washington's own lifetime. It began in Revolutionary days and, despite bitter political attacks, was well under way before 1800. Historians point out that Washington himself became the rallying point of the Revolution and, later, the chief unifying force that enabled the thirteen colonies to establish one government rather than several. He was, therefore, a living personification of the idea of unity and, in a very real sense, the Father of His Country.

America's need of unifying forces grew greater when sectional differences and disputes became acute. As Edward Everett proclaimed, Washington in the flesh was no longer with them, but Americans could still cling to his memory. Beginning nearly a quarter of a century before the Civil War, a gradual increase of interest in Washington is discernible in American literature. To just what extent it was due to the political situation cannot, of course, be determined. American literature itself was maturing rapidly and increasing in bulk, and Washington was a theme certain of some appeal in any case. Another important fact was the appearance in the thirties of Sparks's edition of Washington's own writings, making available for the first time a valuable body of source material. But the tone of much of the literature of the forties and fifties shows that the ever-growing tension had a share in turning men's thoughts to the hero who symbolized the nation itself and personified national unity.[5]

One of the most striking aspects of the literary treatment of Washington is the way in which various Americans fitted him into their dialectic at the time of national confusion and crisis. It is a truism that the Bible can be used to prove almost any proposition.

[5] For Washington's place in "Pre-Sumter Symbolism," see Ralph Henry Gabriel, *The Course of American Democratic Thought* . . . (New York, [1940]), pp. 91–94.

Conclusion 237

Almost the same could be said of Washington in mid-nineteenth-century America. When serious controversy arose, both sides agreed in using his name as a charm against sectional strife and disunion; yet each found in various phases of his career support for its own position in that very strife. Both hoped that his unifying influence would heal the breach, but at the same time representatives of either camp undertook to show that their side was that of Washington.

Several factors made literary treatment of Washington extremely difficult in the entire period here considered. In the thinking of nineteenth-century Americans he was, as we have seen, less a personality than a collection of abstractions, a catalogue of virtues. Even the writers of his own day tended so to regard him. Almost any treatment more concrete than an oratorical or metrical eulogy was likely to meet with disfavor. Moreover, the writer who wished to characterize Washington realistically was at a loss for material, unless he was willing to engage in considerable research on both the man and his milieu. Finally, American literature was itself in the formative stage when Washington took his conspicuous place in the national consciousness.

Patriotic orators could and did grow eloquent on the subject of his greatness. Versifiers, too, celebrated his fame in measures which pleased their contemporaries and which in some instances still have charm—as graceful, sincere eulogy rather than as characterization of Washington.

The figure whom orators and poets constantly called to the attention of their fellow citizens was, of course, the mature man of later Revolutionary days or of the presidency. One got the impression that Washington was never young. Eulogists frequently mentioned the young soldier's exploits in the colonial wars, but the man they described even for that period was prudent, dignified, and staid. The anecdotes of Weems, the first of a long succession of writers who have set out to humanize Washington, were not seriously at variance with this impression, for they presented the type of childhood that adults would foist upon their offspring if they could. This ever-dignified portrayal of the hero met two needs: it presented the young of Victorian days with an excellent model, and it held up before the world an American who exemplified a quality in which Americans were sometimes thought to be deficient.

Fiction and drama require more concrete character portrayal than do oratory and verse. After the publication of *The Spy* led the way, Revolutionary romances and plays were popular in America for several decades. They soon became stereotyped in many ways, and their treatment of General Washington was especially formalized. Even Cooper's reverent portrayal was looked upon as lese majesty, for he showed Washington in lowly, undignified situations. The public could accept anecdotes that merely illustrated their hero's peerless qualities, but to go further—as writers of fiction were likely to do—was to tread on dangerous ground. Following Cooper, novelists and playwrights frequently included the General in their stories, but almost invariably they made him a conventional figure, having little or no part in the plot, and characterized only by dignity, competence, and in some cases benevolence.

Very few writers before 1865 were brash enough to exercise their imaginations on the subject of Washington's love life, but the early efforts should be remembered; later novelists, playwrights, and biographers were to favor this theme. James McHenry, the earliest of all, visualized the young colonel as a rejected suitor, and George Lippard and John Esten Cooke as a disappointed one.

For biographers Washington early became a challenging figure. The grandiose concept presented by Marshall and the priggish portrayal of Weems—the former the stanchest of old Federalists, the latter a pure Republican—in addition to the work of the orators and versifiers, produced a total effect with which some Americans were vaguely dissatisfied and which a few endeavored to alter long before 1865. Washington Irving was undoubtedly the most successful of the biographers of the period. His work is readable and scholarly, and his characterization of the hero shows improvement upon that of Marshall and that of Jared Sparks. Yet Weems's book was far more popular than any other written before 1865, and it has, in-

Conclusion 239

deed, had the greatest influence of all works on Washington to the present day.

From the standpoint of literary merit Irving's *Life of George Washington* is again preeminent among works of any length considered in the present study, but it appeared too late in the period to have much influence on the fiction, poetry, and drama treated here. In judging the fiction and drama of the latter portion of the period, it must be remembered that none of the better American writers produced drama, and of the better novelists and romancers only Cooper found the Revolution an attractive subject. As we have seen, the concept of Washington to which they fell heir did not constitute good material even for writers of Revolutionary romance. Yet the numerous appearances of the Commander-in-Chief in the works of minor novelists and playwrights are significant of the popularity of that stereotyped figure. In such appearances were combined the patriotic motif and the romantic appeal of warfare. The year 1847, when America was at war with Mexico, was a high point in the publication of cheap Revolutionary thrillers and of paper-backed lives of Washington and his generals.

A play and a novel on the matter of Arnold's attempt to betray West Point to the British were published in 1847, and this became the most popular of Revolutionary subjects with dramatists and romancers. Eight plays and two romances dealing with it are treated in the present study. A people need a villain as well as a hero, and Arnold was obviously the people's choice to contrast with Washington.

The difficulty of obtaining concrete material on Washington's personality, as distinct from his character and achievements, has been mentioned. The process known at the present day as the "build up," which is as old as Rome, has operated to obscure for future ages the personalities of many historic Americans.[6] When the Patriots of the Revolutionary period and the Federalists of the time of his presidency sang Washington's praises to the skies, they

[6] Cf. Gerald W. Johnson, *America's Silver Age* . . . (New York and London, 1939), pp. 19–20.

were making more difficult the task of any who might wish to understand his personality in the future.

Sparks's edition of his writings in the thirties gave an impetus to biographical and other study of Washington. But it included considerably less than half of the extant Washington manuscripts. Worthington Chauncey Ford's edition (1889–1893) made some additional materials available, but only with the publication of the bicentennial edition (1931–1944) has the great bulk of Washington's letters and papers become public property. And until the publication of his diaries under the auspices of the Mount Vernon Ladies' Association in 1925, only a small fraction of this important record had appeared in print.

Equally great was—and still is—the difficulty of understanding Washington's background. He was the product and representative of a society that was as remote from many Americans in 1850 as it is today. The eighteenth-century squirearchy of the South persisted there in attenuated form until the Civil War and then expired. Lincoln's semifrontier world has now passed away also, but in 1865 and for many years thereafter it was the everyday world of millions of Americans. As Amy Lowell remarked: "Washington and Lincoln are the two great symbols of American life. But to deal adequately with Washington needs a historical sense, a knowledge of the eighteenth-century, which few of our poets yet possess."[7] Washington's most recent biographer, Douglas Southall Freeman, has seen fit to include in his first volume an excellent chapter on "Virginia during the Youth of Washington," over a hundred pages in length.

The mature nation that emerged from the fires of the Civil War had less need to point to a venerable Father as its symbol of nationality or national unity. Interest in Washington declined somewhat after Appomattox. When it revived, as it did, a great change was evident. Americans were able to study and write of their first President with comparative objectivity. They tended to regard him as a

[7] Amy Lowell, *Tendencies in Modern American Poetry* (Boston and New York, [1926]), p. 185.

Conclusion 241

man, a personality, rather than a symbol or a tradition. Moreover, America now had a second great national hero in Abraham Lincoln, and the South for many years paid at least as much tribute to Robert E. Lee as to Washington.

Comparisons of Washington and Lincoln, in accord with modern interpretations of their respective milieus, characters, personalities, and achievements, are too numerous to warrant the inclusion of yet another in the present study, but two points connected with their renown and the treatment accorded them in literature are worthy of mention. Washington was a hero to the majority of his countrymen during his lifetime. Until the day he died a martyr's death, Lincoln was not looked upon as a hero even by a majority of persons in the North.[8] In the second place, American literature had come of age by 1865, and Lincoln—or rather his memory—benefited accordingly. The abstraction, symbolism, and vagueness that clung to Washington so early and so long have proved exceedingly difficult to dispel.

A mere glance at later years may be in order. Particularly since the publication of larger portions of his own writings, scholars and writers have complained that early writers and speakers obscured Washington's real personality. He has, in fact, become an almost tantalizing figure, especially for biographers. Many of the titles of biographies written in the last sixty years indicate the attitude of the authors: *The True George Washington* (1896), *George Washington: the Image and the Man* (1926), *George Washington, the Human Being and the Hero* (1926–1930), *The Unknown Washington* (1930), and *George Washington the Man* (1932).[9]

Washington's fame survived the debunking of the nineteen-twenties, and it seems safe to predict that it will endure for some time to come. He is the subject of a biographical study now in progress, that of Douglas Southall Freeman, involving research on an enormous scale. Novelists, playwrights, and poets continue to

---

[8] Cf. Edward H. O'Neill, *A History of American Biography, 1800–1935* (Philadelphia, 1935), p. 155.

[9] Authors of the biographies mentioned are Paul Leicester Ford, W. E. Woodward, Rupert Hughes, John Corbin, and Carl Russell Fish.

find him an interesting and a challenging subject. The limits of the present study preclude details, but it is notable that the more recent literary treatments exhibit greater variety than those of the period 1775–1865. For various reasons, as has been seen, the earlier writers left many phases of his career and several aspects of his personality largely untouched. His youth and love life have aroused considerable interest in recent years, as have his social life and family relationships, his business interests, and his farming activities.

How well modern writers have succeeded in portraying the "real" George Washington is a matter of opinion. But such complaints as the following, in a newspaper editorial of 1944, are not uncommon even today:

Everybody feels as if he knows Lincoln and merely knows of Washington . . . We have had studies of the "real" Washington, of Washington as a young blade, surveyor, general, President, host and gentleman farmer, but to most of us he still remains austere, unapproachable, a sort of plaster saint, a figure who matured long before his time and never ripened or mellowed.[10]

Books that treat Washington have become almost as numerous as the leaves on the trees, but, partly because of dissatisfaction with those now existing, it appears that there is always demand for still another.

[10] *Boston Herald*, February 22, 1944.

APPENDIX

CHRONOLOGICAL TABLE OF EVENTS IN WASHINGTON'S LIFE[1]

1732 February 22	George Washington born.
1743	Augustine Washington, his father, dies.
1748–1749	Accompanies expedition surveying lands of Lord Fairfax.
1749	Appointed surveyor of Culpeper County.
1751	Accompanies half-brother Lawrence to Barbados.
1752	Comes into possession of Mount Vernon.
November 4	Admitted to Fredericksburg Lodge of Masons.
November 6	Appointed district adjutant general of Virginia militia.
1753–1754	Delivers Governor Dinwiddie's message to Fort Le Boeuf.
1754 May 24	Skirmish with a French force, and death of its commander, Jumonville.
July 3	Surrenders to French at Fort Necessity.
October	Colonel Washington resigns commission.
1755 July 9	Braddock's last fight.
August 14	Appointed commandant of Virginia militia in charge of border defense.

[1] Based upon W. S. Baker, *Itinerary of General Washington* . . . (Philadelphia, 1892); W. S. Baker, *Washington after the Revolution* (Philadelphia, 1898); Albert Bushnell Hart, ed., *George Washington Year by Year* (Washington, 1931).

Appendix

1756 February–March	Visits Governor Shirley of Massachusetts, commander of British forces in America.
1757	Attends conference of colonial governors at Philadelphia.
1758	Takes part in General Forbes's expedition against Fort Duquesne.
	Colonel Washington resigns commission.
1759 January 6	Marries Martha Dandridge Custis.
February 22	For the first time occupies a seat in the Virginia House of Burgesses, a position which he held for fifteen years.
May	Takes up residence at Mount Vernon.
1762 May	Becomes vestryman of Truro Parish in Fairfax County.
1769 May 17	With other Burgesses, signs nonimportation agreement at Raleigh Tavern.
1770	Accompanied by Dr. Craik, makes trip of 265 miles down the Ohio River.
1772	Secures charter for the Potomac Company, to develop navigation.
1773 May–June	Trip to New York to put John Parke Custis in King's College.
1774 May 24	Meeting of Burgesses at Raleigh Tavern to renew nonimportation agreement and call for colonial congress.
September–October	Attends first Continental Congress in Philadelphia.
1775 June 15	Appointed Commander-in-Chief of Patriot armies.
July 3	At Cambridge assumes command of armies around Boston.
1776 March 4	Places cannon and fortifications on Dorchester Heights.
March 17	Occupies Boston as British leave.
April–June	Prepares for defense of New York.
July 9	Has Declaration of Independence read to army assembled in New York.
August 27	Battle of Long Island.
August 29	Retreat from Long Island.

Appendix

	October 28	Battle of White Plains.
	November–December	Retreat through New Jersey.
	December 26	Battle of Trenton.
1777	January 3	Battle of Princeton.
	September 11	Battle of Brandywine.
	October 4	Battle of Germantown.
1777–1778		Winter quarters at Valley Forge.
1780	September 21	First conference with Rochambeau.
1781	October 19	Surrender of Cornwallis at Yorktown.
1782	May 22	Refuses to become king.
1783	March 15	Address to officers at Newburgh.
	December 4	Farewell to officers at Fraunces' Tavern.
	December 23	General Washington resigns his commission at Annapolis.
1784	September	Trip to lands beyond the Alleghenies.
1785	May 17	Made president of Potomac Navigation Company.
1787	May–September	Presides over Constitutional Convention.
1789	February 4	Unanimously elected President.
	April 30	Inauguration at New York.
1790	August 3	Removal to Philadelphia, temporary capital.
1791	April–June	Tour through Southern states.
1792	April 5	Uses veto power on first of two occasions.
	December 5	Unanimously re-elected.
1793	April 2	Proclamation of neutrality.
	August 1	Asks cabinet to take measures leading to recall of Genêt by France.
1794	April 16	Appoints John Jay envoy to England.
	September–October	Visits troops collected in Pennsylvania to suppress Whiskey Rebellion.
1795	March 30	Refuses to submit to House of Representatives papers relative to Jay Treaty.
1796	September 17	Publishes Farewell Address.
1797	March 4	Attends inauguration of John Adams.
1798		Accepts appointment as Lieutenant-General.
1799	December 14	Death, following a throat infection.

SELECTIVE BIBLIOGRAPHY

I. Primary Sources

A. VERSE

Alsop, Richard. A Poem: Sacred to the Memory of George Washington . . . Adapted to the 22nd of February, 1800. Hartford, Conn.: Hudson and Goodwin, 1800.

"The American Farmer," *American Museum*, VII (January, 1790), 38–39.

Astrop, Robert Francis. Original Poems, on a Variety of Subjects, Interspersed with Tales . . . Philadelphia: E. L. Carey and A. Hart, 1835.

Barlow, Joel. The Vision of Columbus: a Poem, in Nine Books, with Explanatory Notes (from a Revised Edition of the Author) . . . Hagerstown, Md.: W. D. Bell, 1820.

Bryant, William Cullen. Representative Selections . . . , ed. Tremaine McDowell. New York: American Book Company, 1935.

—— The White-footed Deer, and Other Poems. New York: I. S. Platt, 1844.

Byron, George Gordon. Poetry . . . , ed. Ernest Hartley Coleridge. London: John Murray; New York: Scribner, 1895–1905. 7 vols.

Calvert, George Henry. A Nation's Birth and Other National Poems. Boston: Lee & Shepard, 1876.

Carter, St. Leger Landon. "Washington and Napoleon," *Southern Literary Messenger*, I (November, 1834), 90.

Case, Wheeler. Revolutionary Memorials . . . , ed. Stephen Dodd. New York: M. W. Dodd, 1852.

[Coffin, Robert S.] Oriental Harp; Poems of the Boston Bard. Providence, R.I.: Smith & Parmenter, 1826.

Dakin, S. D. "Lines on the Statue of Washington at the Capitol," *Knickerbocker*, XX (September, 1842), 281.

[Daniel, Lizzie Cary, ed.] Confederate Scrap-Book . . . Richmond, Va.: J. H. Hill, 1893.

248 *Selective Bibliography*

Davidson, Nora Fontaine M., ed. Cullings from the Confederacy . . . Washington, D.C.: Rufus H. Darby, 1903.

Dwight, Timothy. The Conquest of Canaan, a Poem in Eleven Books . . . Hartford, Conn., 1785; London: Reprinted for J. Johnson, 1788.

Eggleston, George Cary, ed. American War Ballads and Lyrics . . . New York and London: Putnam, [1889]. 2 vols. in one.

"Elegy on Washington," *Historical Magazine*, I (August, 1857), 233–234.

Emerson, Ralph Waldo. "Lines on Washington Written at Concord Dec. 24th, 1814," in The Letters . . . , ed. Ralph L. Rusk. New York: Columbia University Press, 1939. 6 vols. VI, 329.

French, Benjamin B. "Hymn, to Be Sung at the Tomb of Washington, June 24, 1851," in French, An Address on the Masonic Character and Standing of Washington . . . Washington, D. C.: Gideon & Co., 1851.

Freneau, Philip. The Last Poems of Philip Freneau, ed. Lewis Leary. New Brunswick, N.J.: Rutgers University Press, 1945.

—— The Poems of Philip Freneau, Poet of the American Revolution, ed. Fred Lewis Pattee. Princeton, N.J.: University Library, 1902–1907. 3 vols.

"The Gathering of the Southern Volunteers," *Southern Literary Messenger*, XXXII, 449 (June, 1861).

Gibson, Henry Richard. The Washingtoniad . . . Geneva, N.Y.: W. Johnson, 1861.

Griswold, Rufus W. The Female Poets of America. 2d ed.; Philadelphia: Parry & McMillan, 1859.

—— The Poets and Poetry of America . . . Philadelphia: Carey and Hart, 1842.

Haines, Hiram. Mountain Buds and Blossoms . . . Petersburg, Va.: Yancey & Burton, 1825.

Holmes, Oliver Wendell. The Works . . . New York: Houghton Mifflin, 1892. 13 vols.

Honeywood, St. John. Poems, with Some Pieces in Prose. New York: T. and J. Swords, 1801.

Hope, James Barron. "Poem," *Southern Literary Messenger*, XXIV (June, 1857), 455–462.

—— A Wreath of Virginia Bay Leaves, ed. Janey Hope Marr. Richmond, Va.: West, Johnston & Co., 1895.

Hopkinson, Francis. "Poems on Several Subjects," separately paged at back of third volume of The Miscellaneous Essays . . . Philadelphia: T. Dobson, 1792. 3 vols.

Humphreys, David. The Miscellaneous Works . . . New York: Hodge, Allen, and Campbell, 1790.
—— The Miscellaneous Works . . . New York: T. and J. Swords, 1804.
—— A Poem on Industry . . . Philadelphia: Mathew Carey, 1794.
Jackson, George Stuyvesant, ed. Early Songs of Uncle Sam, with an Introduction by Kenneth B. Murdock. Boston: Bruce Humphries, Inc., 1933.
Kettell, Samuel, ed. Specimens of American Poetry . . . Boston: S. G. Goodrich & Co., 1829. 3 vols.
Lathrop, John, Jr. "Ode, Composed for the First Celebration of the 'Washington Benevolent Society' . . . ," in William Sullivan, An Oration Delivered before the Washington Benevolent Society of Massachusetts . . . 2d ed.; Boston: John Eliot, Jr., 1812.
Lewis, Eldad. An Eulogy, on the Life and Character of His Excellency George Washington . . . Published at the Request of the Audience. Pittsfield, Mass.: Chester Smith, 1800.
"Lines on the Statue of Washington in the Capitol," *Southern Literary Messenger*, II (March, 1836), 253.
Linn, John Blair. The Death of Washington, a Poem, in Imitation of the Manner of Ossian. Philadelphia: John Ormrod, 1800.
Low, Samuel. Poems. New York: T. & J. Swords, 1800. 2 vols.
Lowell, James Russell. The Complete Poetical Works . . . Cambridge ed.; Boston and New York: Houghton Mifflin, [1897].
McGill, Walter Marshall. The Western World; a Poem, Founded on the Facts Recorded of the Revolutionary War; Consisting of Several Books, in One Volume. Together with a Description of American Scenery, &c. Maryville, Tenn.: F. A. Parham, 1837.
Maclellan, Isaac. "A Vision of Mount Vernon," *Knickerbocker*, XLVIII (August, 1856), 118.
Mayo, William Starbuck. Romance Dust from the Historic Placer. New York: Putnam, 1851.
Melville, Herman. "Lee in the Capital," in The Works . . . London: Constable, 1922–1924. 16 vols. XVI, 164.
Miner, Louie M. Our Rude Forefathers; American Political Verse, 1783–1788. Cedar Rapids, Iowa: Torch Press, 1937.
Mitchell, Alfred. The Coloniad, a Narrative in Verse on Washington's War . . . Richmond, Va., 1858.
"Monody on the Death of George Washington . . . ," *Monthly Magazine and American Review*, I (December, 1799), 478–479.

Moore, Frank, ed. Songs and Ballads of the American Revolution. New York: Appleton, 1856.

Morton, Sarah Wentworth. My Mind and Its Thoughts . . . Boston: Wells and Lilly, 1823.

"Mount Vernon," *Southern Literary Messenger*, XXI (December, 1855), 762.

"Ode," in C. W. Bowen, "The Inauguration of Washington," *Century Magazine*, XXXVII (April, 1889), 817.

"An Ode; for the Birth Day of the President of the United States," by "The Volunteer Laureate," *Massachusetts Magazine*, IV (February, 1792), 118.

"An Ode upon the Arrival of THE PRESIDENT OF THE UNITED STATES," *Massachusetts Magazine*, I (October, 1789), 653.

Paine, Robert Treat. The Works, in Verse and Prose . . . Boston: J. Belcher, 1812.

Pierpont, John. The Portrait; a Poem Delivered before the Washington Benevolent Society of Newburyport, October 27, 1812. Boston: Bradford & Read, 1812.

Prentiss, Charles. A Poem Delivered at Brookfield, July 5th, 1813, before the Washington Benevolent Societies . . . Brookfield, Mass., 1813.

"The Retreat of Seventy-six," *Knickerbocker*, XVI (October, 1840), 335–338.

[Richards, George]. "Zenith of Glory," *Massachusetts Magazine*, I (June, August, September, October, December, 1789), 384–385, 519, 586, 655, 789–790; II (March, May, 1790), 184, 311–312; III (January, May, August, December, 1791), 53–54, 309, 510, 765; IV (March, June, August, September, December, 1792), 192–193, 390–391, 518–519, 637–638, 747.

Sargent, Winthrop, ed. The Loyalist Poetry of the Revolution. Philadelphia: Privately printed, 1857.

Sewall, Jonathan Mitchell. Miscellaneous Poems . . . Portsmouth, N.H.: William Treadwell, 1801.

Smyth, Mary W. "Contemporary Songs and Verses about Washington," *New England Quarterly*, V (April, 1932), 281–292.

Snowden, Richard. The Columbiad; or, A Poem on the American War, in Thirteen Cantoes . . . Baltimore: W. Pechin, [*circa* 1796].

Spierin, George Heartwell. Poems by the Late George Heartwell Spierin. Charleston, S.C.: W. P. Young, 1805.

Stansbury, Joseph, and Jonathan Odell. The Loyal Verses of Joseph Stansbury and Doctor Jonathan Odell; Relating to the American Revolution, ed. Winthrop Sargent. Albany, N.Y.: J. Munsell, 1860.

Selective Bibliography

Stevenson, Burton Egbert, ed. Poems of American History. Boston and New York: Houghton Mifflin, [1922].

Stoddard, Richard Henry. The Poems . . . New York: Scribner, 1880.

Thompson, John R. "Inauguration of the Equestrian Statue of Washington . . . Opening Ode," *Southern Literary Messenger*, XXVI (March, 1858), 161–166.

"To the Daughters of Washington," *Southern Literary Messenger*, XXI (May, 1855), 318–321.

Trumbull, John. The Poetical Works . . . Hartford, Conn.: Samuel G. Goodrich, 1820. 2 vols.

Tucker, St. George (1828–1863). "A Poetical Address, Delivered before the Literary Societies of Washington College, Lexington . . . ," *Southern Literary Messenger*, XXV (August, 1857), 113–121.

[——] (1752–1823). The Probationary Odes of Jonathan Pindar . . . Philadelphia: B. F. Bache, 1796.

Wallace, William Ross. Meditations in America . . . New York: Scribner, 1851.

Wharton, Charles Henry. A Poetical Epistle to George Washington . . . from an Inhabitant of the State of Maryland . . . London: C. Dilly, 1780; [New York: Privately reprinted by J. Munsell, 1865].

Wheatley, Phillis. Poems and Letters . . . , ed. Charles Fred. Heartman. New York: C. F. Heartman, [1915].

Whitman, Walt. Leaves of Grass. Garden City, N.Y.: Doubleday, 1920. 3 vols. in one.

Whittier, John Greenleaf. The Writings . . . Large paper ed.; Cambridge, Mass.: Riverside Press, 1888. 7 vols.

B. DRAMA

America; a Dramatic Poem. New York: A. D. F. Randolph, 1863.

Americana; or, A New Tale of the Genii: Being an Allegorical Mask in Five Acts. Baltimore: W. Pechin, 1802.

Bannister, Nathaniel H. Putnam, the Iron Son of '76. A National Military Drama in Three Acts. Boston: W. V. Spencer, [1859].

The Battle of Brooklyn, a Farce . . . (New York: 1776) Reprinted in "Long Island Publications," No. 1, Brooklyn, N.Y., 1873.

Brackenridge, Hugh Henry. "A Masque Written at the Warm-Springs in Virginia," in *Gazette Publications*. Carlisle, Pa.: Alexander & Phillips, 1806.

Breck, Joseph. West Point; or, A Tale of Treason. An Historical Drama,

in Three Acts, Dramatised from Ingraham's Romance of American History . . . Baltimore: Bull & Tuttle, 1840.
Brougham, John. The Miller of New Jersey; or, The Prison-Hulk. An Historic Drama-Spectacle in Three Acts, as Performed at the Bowery Theatre . . . New York: Samuel French, [1858].
Burnett, J. G. Blanche of Brandywine; an American Patriotic Spectacle . . . New York and London: Samuel French, 1858.
Calvert, George Henry. Arnold and André . . . Boston: Little, Brown, 1864.
Clinch, Charles Powell. The Spy . . . , in Metamora and Other Plays . . . , ed. Eugene R. Page. Princeton, N.J.: Princeton University Press, 1941. Vol. XIV of "America's Lost Plays," ed. Barrett H. Clark, 20 vols.
Columbia and Britannia; a Dramatic Piece, by a Citizen of the United States. New London, Conn.: T. Greene, 1787.
Custis, George Washington Parke. The Indian Prophecy, a National Drama in Two Acts, Founded on a Most Interesting and Romantic Occurrence in the Life of General Washington . . . Georgetown, D.C.: James Thomas, 1828.
Dunlap, William. André: a Tragedy in Five Acts . . . (New York: 1798). Reprinted in Moses, Representative Plays by American Dramatists, I, 499–564.
—— "Darby's Return,—a Comic Sketch. As Performed at the Theatre in This City, with Universal Applause. Written in 1789 . . . ," *New York Magazine*, I (January, 1790), 47–51.
—— The Glory of Columbia—Her Yeomanry . . . a Play in Five Acts . . . New York: D. Longworth, 1803.
The Fall of British Tyranny; or, American Liberty Triumphant . . . [Philadelphia: 1776], reprinted in Moses, Representative Plays by American Dramatists, I, 277–350.
Holland, Elihu G. Essays and a Drama in Five Acts. Boston: Phillips, Sampson and Company, 1852.
Hubbell, Horatio. Arnold; or, The Treason of West Point. A Tragedy in Five Acts. Philadelphia: [Copyrighted by Horatio Hubbell], 1847.
King's Bridge Cottage. A Revolutionary Tale Founded on an Incident Which Occurred a Few Days Previous to the Evacuation of New York by the British. A Drama in Two Acts, Written by a Gentleman of New York and Performed at the Amateur Theatre. New York: E. Dunigin, 1826.
Lord, W. W. "André," in The Complete Poetical Works . . . , ed. Thomas Ollive Mabbott. New York: Random House, 1938.

[Markoe, Peter]. The Patriot Chief: a Tragedy. Philadelphia: Printed for the Author . . . , 1784.
Moses, Montrose J., ed. Representative Plays by American Dramatists . . . New York: Dutton, 1918–1925. 3 vols.
[Murdock, John]. The Politicians; or, A State of Things. A Dramatic Piece, Written by an American and a Citizen of Philadelphia. Philadelphia: Printed for the author, 1798.
[Murray, Judith Sargent]. "The Traveller Returned," in The Gleaner; a Miscellaneous Production . . . by Constantia [pseud.]. Boston: J. Thomas and E. T. Andrews, 1798. 3 vols. III, 116–163.
Orton, J. R. Arnold and Other Poems. New York: Partridge and Brittan, 1854.
[Parke, John]. "Virginia: a Pastoral Drama on the Birth-Day of an Illustrious Personage . . . ," in [Parke], Translations from the Greek and Latin, with Original Poems. Philadelphia: Eleazer Oswald, 1786.
Trumbull, David. The Death of Capt. Nathan Hale . . . Hartford, Conn.: E. Geer, 1845.
[Warren, Mercy Otis]. The Motley Assembly: a Farce, Published for the Entertainment of the Curious. Boston: Nathaniel Coverley, 1779.
Washingtons Ankunft in Elisium, eine Dialogiste Skizze . . . Lancaster, Pa.: Christian Jacob Hütter, 1800.

C. FICTION

[Ballou, Maturin Murray]. Fanny Campbell, the Female Pirate Captain; a Tale of the Revolution, by Lieutenant Murray [pseud.]. Boston: F. Gleason, 1845.
Belknap, Jeremy. The Foresters, an American Tale: Being a Sequel to the History of John Bull the Clothier . . . 2d ed.; Boston: I. Thomas and E. T. Andrews, 1796.
Bennett, Emerson. The Female Spy; or, Treason in the Camp . . . Cincinnati, Ohio: Lorenzo Stratton, [1851].
—— Rosalie Du Pont; or, Treason in the Camp. Cincinnati, Ohio: Lorenzo Stratton, [1851].
Brackenridge, Hugh Henry. "The Cave of Vanhest," United States Magazine, I (January–July, 1779), 14–15, 61–63, 106–110, 149–150, 213–116 [sic], 253–255, 311–313.
—— Modern Chivalry, ed. Claude M. Newlin. New York: American Book Company, 1937.
Buckingham, Henry A. Harry Burnham, the Young Continental; or, Memoirs of an American Officer during the Campaigns of the Revo-

lution, and Sometime a Member of Washington's Staff. New York: Burgess and Garrett, [1852].

The Buckskin; or, The Camp of the Besiegers. A Tale of the Revolution . . . New York: William H. Graham, 1847.

Clemens, Jeremiah. The Rivals: a Tale of the Times of Aaron Burr and Alexander Hamilton. Philadelphia: Lippincott, 1860.

Cooke, John Esten. Lord Fairfax; or, The Master of Greenway Court. New York: G. W. Dillingham, 1896.

Cooper, James Fenimore. The Spy, a Tale of the Neutral Ground, with an Introduction by Tremaine McDowell. New York: Scribner, [1931].

Curtis, Newton Mallory. The Marksmen of Monmouth: a Tale of the Revolution . . . Troy, N.Y.: L. Willard, [1848].

"The Deserter," in The Romantic Historian; a Series of Lights and Shadows, Elucidating American Annals . . . Philadelphia: Hogan & Thompson, 1834.

[Fay, T. S.] Herbert Wendall: a Tale of the Revolution . . . New York: Harper, 1835. 2 vols.

[Ingraham, Joseph Holt]. Burton; or, The Sieges. A Romance. By the author of "The Southwest" and "Lafitte." New York: Harper, 1838. 2 vols.

–– Neal Nelson; or, The Siege of Boston. A Tale of the Revolution. New York: Williams Bros., 1847.

–– The Treason of Arnold: a Tale of West Point during the American Revolution. Jonesville (Templeton), Mass.: James M. Barnes, 1847.

[Jones, James Athearn]. The Refugee. A Romance, by Captain Matthew Murgatroyd [pseud.]. New York: Wilder & Campbell, 1825. 2 vols.

[Jones, John Richter]. The Quaker Soldier; or, The British in Philadelphia. An Historical Novel. Philadelphia: T. B. Peterson and Brothers, [1858].

[Kilbourn, Diana Treat]. The Lone Dove: a Legend of Revolutionary Times . . . Philadelphia: Appleton, 1850.

Lippard, George. Blanche of Brandywine; or, September the Eleventh, 1777 . . . Philadelphia: G. B. Zieber & Co., [1846].

–– Herbert Tracy; or, The Legend of the Black Rangers. A Romance of the Battlefield of Germantown. Philadelphia: R. G. Berford, 1844.

–– The Rose of Wissahikon; or, The Fourth of July, 1776. A Romance Embracing the Secret History of the Declaration of Independence. Philadelphia: G. B. Zieber & Co., 1847.

Selective Bibliography 255

— Washington and His Generals; or, Legends of the Revolution . . . Philadelphia: G. B. Zieber & Co., 1847.
— Washington and His Men: a New Series of Legends of the Revolution . . . New York: Stringer & Townsend, 1850.
[Lorraine, A. M.] Donald Adair: a Novel by a Young Lady of Virginia . . . Richmond, Va.: Peter Cottom, 1828. 2 vols.
[McHenry, James]. The Wilderness; or, Braddock's Times. A Tale of the West . . . New York: E. Bliss and E. White, 1823. 2 vols.
Mancur, John H. The Deserter, a Legend of Mount Washington . . . New York: William H. Colyer, 1843.
[Mann, Herman]. The Female Review; or, Memoirs of an American Young Lady . . . a Continental Soldier . . . Dedham, Mass.: Nathaniel and Benjamin Heaton, 1797.
Morton, a Tale of the Revolution . . . Cincinnati, Ohio: Hatch, Nichols & Buxton, 1828.
[Neal, John]. Randolph. Philadelphia: Charles I. Jack, 1823. 2 vols.
— Seventy-Six. Baltimore: J. Robinson, 1823. 2 vols.
Old Fort Duquesne, a Tale of the Early Toils, Struggles and Adventures of the First Settlers at the Forks of the Ohio, 1754 . . . Pittsburgh, Pa.: Cook's Literary Depot, 1844.
[Paulding, James Kirke]. The Old Continental; or, The Price of Liberty. New York: Paine and Burgess, 1846. 2 vols. in one.
Priest, Josiah. A History of the Early Adventures of Washington among the Indians of the West . . . Albany, N.Y.: J. Munsell, 1841.
[Sedgwick, Catharine Maria]. The Linwoods; or, "Sixty-Years Since" in America. New York: Harper, 1835. 2 vols.
The Seven Brothers of Wyoming . . . New York: H. Long & Brother, [1850].
[Tannehill, Wilkins]. "The Hermit of the White Cliff," in Tales of the Revolution, by a Young Gentleman of Nashville . . . Nashville, Tenn.: Hunt, Tardiff and Co., 1833.
Thackeray, William Makepeace. The Virginians, a Tale of the Last Century. 2 vols., VII–VIII in The Complete Works . . . with Introductions by William P. Trent and John Bell Henneman. New York: T. Y. Crowell, [1904]. 30 vols. in 15.
Willis, John R. Carleton; or Patriotism, Love, and Duty. A Tale of Seventeen Hundred and Seventy-six. London: J. Cunningham, 1842.
Winthrop, Theodore. Edwin Brothertoft. 8th ed.; Boston: Ticknor and Fields, 1865.
Woodworth, Samuel. The Champions of Freedom; or, The Mysterious Chief . . . New York: Charles N. Baldwin, 1816.

—— "The Female Spy," printed at the back of Robert F. Greeley, Arthur Woodleigh; a Romance of the Battle Field in Mexico. New York: W. B. Smith & Co., 1847.

D. ORATORY, BIOGRAPHY, AND MISCELLANEOUS

Abbott, John S. C. Lives of the Presidents . . . Boston: B. B. Russell, 1867.

"An Account of the Battle of Bunker Hill. By H. Dearborn . . . A Letter to Major General Dearborn . . . by Daniel Putnam, Esq.," *North American Review*, VII (July, 1818), 225–258.

Adams, Abigail. Letters of Mrs. Adams, the Wife of John Adams . . . , ed. Charles Francis Adams. Boston: Little, Brown, 1840. 2 vols.

Adams, John. Correspondence of John Adams and Thomas Jefferson (1812–1826), ed. Paul Wilstach. Indianapolis: Bobbs-Merrill, 1925.

—— "Correspondence between John Adams and Mercy Warren . . ." in Collections of the Massachusetts Historical Society, Fifth Series, Vol. IV. Boston: The Society, 1878.

—— The Works of John Adams, with a Life of the Author, Notes and Illustrations, by His Grandson, Charles Francis Adams. Boston: Little, Brown, 1850–1856. 10 vols.

Adams, John Quincy. The Jubilee of the Constitution; a Discourse Delivered at the Request of the New York Historical Society . . . New York: S. Colman, 1839.

Alexander, Caleb. A Sermon; Occasioned by the Death of His Excellency George Washington . . . Boston: Samuel Hall, 1800.

Allen, William. An American Biographical and Historical Dictionary . . . Cambridge, Mass.: W. Hilliard, 1809.

Baker, W. S. Itinerary of General Washington . . . Philadelphia: Lippincott, 1892.

—— ed. Character Portraits of Washington . . . Philadelphia: Robert M. Lindsay, 1889.

—— ed. Early Sketches of George Washington . . . Philadelphia: Lippincott, 1894.

Bancroft, Aaron. An Eulogy on the Character of the Late Gen. George Washington . . . Worcester, Mass.: Isaiah Thomas, 1800.

—— The Life of George Washington . . . Philadelphia: Porter & Coates, 1808. 2 vols. in one.

Barbé-Marbois, François, Marquis de. Our Revolutionary Forefathers, the Letters of François, Marquis de Barbé-Marbois . . . 1779–1785, ed. Eugene Parker Chase. New York: Duffield & Co., 1929.

Selective Bibliography

Barlow, Joel. "An Oration, Delivered at the North Church in Hartford . . . July the Fourth, 1787 . . . ," *American Museum*, II (August, 1787), 135–142.

Bayard, Ferdinand M. Voyage dans l'interieur des États-Unis . . . Augm. de Descriptions et d'Anecdotes sur la vie militaire et politique de Georges VVashington. 2d ed.; Paris: Batilliot frères, [1798].

[Bentley, William]. "Washington's Birth-Day Oration at Salem, Mass., February 22, 1793," *Historical Magazine*, Series 2, VII (January, 1870), 3–8.

Berrien, John Macpherson. An Oration, Commemorative of the Anniversary of American Independence . . . Savannah, Ga.: Seymour & Woolhopter, 1808.

Bigelow, Henry. A Sermon, Delivered at Castleton, on the 22 of February 1814, before the Washington Benevolent Society, of the County of Rutland, in Commemoration of the Birth of Washington. Middlebury, Vt.: Timothy C. Strong, 1814.

Boucher, Jonathan. Reminiscences of an American Loyalist, 1738–1789 . . . , ed. Jonathan Bouchier. Boston and New York: Houghton Mifflin, 1925.

—— A View of the Causes and Consequences of the American Revolution, in Thirteen Discourses, Preached in North America between the Years 1763 and 1775. London: G. G. and J. Robinson, 1797.

Brown, Charles Brockden. "Hints for a Funeral Oration," *Monthly Magazine and American Review*, II (February, 1800), 102–105.

Browne, Charles Farrar. The Complete Works of Artemus Ward . . . London: Chatto & Windus, 1899.

Burnett, Edmund C., ed. Letters of Members of the Continental Congress. Washington, D.C.: The Carnegie Institution of Washington, 1921–1936. 8 vols.

Caldwell, Charles. An Oration Commemorative of the Character and Administration of Washington, Delivered before the American Republican Society of Philadelphia . . . Philadelphia: Bradford and Inskeep, 1810.

Calhoun, John C. The Works . . . , ed. Richard K. Crallé. New York: Appleton, 1854–1860. 6 vols.

[Carpenter, Stephen Cullen]. Memoirs of the Honorable Thomas Jefferson . . . [New York]: Printed for the purchasers, 1809.

Carrington, Mrs. Edward. "A Visit to Mount Vernon—a Letter of Mrs. Edward Carrington to Her Sister, Mrs. George Fisher," *William and Mary College Quarterly*, Series 2, XVIII (April, 1938), 198.

Chinard, Gilbert, ed. George Washington as the French Knew Him, a

Selective Bibliography

Collection of Texts. Princeton, N.J.: Princeton University Press, 1940.

Clark, Willis Gaylord. The Literary Remains . . . , ed. Lewis Gaylord Clark. New York: Burgess, Stringer, & Co., 1844.

Coleman, William. A Collection of the Facts and Documents, Relative to the Death of Major-General Alexander Hamilton . . . by the Editor of the *Evening Post*, [1804]. Reprinted, Boston and New York: Houghton Mifflin, 1904.

Colton, Calvin, ed. The Life, Correspondence, and Speeches of Henry Clay. New York: A. S. Barnes & Co., 1857. 6 vols.

Condie, Thomas. Biographical Memoirs of the Illustrious Gen. Geo. Washington . . . Philadelphia: Charless & Ralston, 1800.

—— "Memoirs of George Washington, Esq., Late President of the United States . . . ," *Philadelphia Monthly Magazine; or, Universal Repository of Knowledge and Entertainment*, I (January, February, March, May, June, 1798), 15–20, 65–71, 121–127, 241–249, 297–308.

Crafts, William, Jr. An Oration . . . on the Fourth of July . . . Charleston, S.C.: W. P. Young, 1812.

Custis, George Washington Parke. An Address Occasioned by the Death of General Lingan, Who Was Murdered by the Mob at Baltimore. Delivered at Georgetown, September 1, 1812. Boston: Bradford & Read, 1812.

—— Recollections and Private Memoirs of Washington . . . with . . . Illustrative and Explanatory Notes by Benson J. Lossing . . . New York: Derby & Jackson, 1860.

Danforth, J. N. "Thoughts on the Fourth of July, 1847," *Southern Literary Messenger*, XIII (August, 1847), 502–505.

Davies, Samuel. Sermons on Important Subjects . . . New York: Dayton and Saxton, 1842. 3 vols.

Davis, John. Travels of Four Years and a Half in the United States of America; during 1798, 1799, 1800, 1801, and 1802, ed. A. J. Morrison. New York: H. Holt, 1909.

Davis, M. Darnell. "British Newspaper Accounts of Braddock's Defeat," *Pennsylvania Magazine of History and Biography*, XXIII (January, 1899), 310–328.

Dunlap, William. A History of the American Theatre. New York: Harper, 1832.

Dutcher, Salem, Jr. An Oration Commemorative of the Birth of Washington; Delivered at the Baptist Church, on the 23d of February, 1824. Albany, N.Y.: J. B. Van Steenbergh, 1824.

Duyckinck, Evert A. National Portrait Gallery of Eminent Americans

Selective Bibliography 259

. . . with Biographical and Historical Narratives. New York: Johnson, Fry & Company, [1862]. 2 vols.

Duyckinck, Evert A., and George L. Duyckinck. Cyclopaedia of American Literature . . . New York: Scribner, 1856. 2 vols.

Emerson, Ralph Waldo. The Complete Works . . . with a Biographical Introduction and Notes by Edward Waldo Emerson. Centenary ed.; Boston and New York: Houghton Mifflin, 1903. 12 vols.

—— Journals . . . , ed. Edward Waldo Emerson and Waldo Emerson Forbes. Boston and New York: Houghton Mifflin, 1909–1914. 10 vols.

—— The Letters . . . , ed. Ralph L. Rusk. New York: Columbia University Press, 1939. 6 vols.

England, John. The Works . . . , ed. Ignatius Aloysius Reynolds. Baltimore and New York: John Murray, 1849. 5 vols.

Eulogies and Orations on the Life and Death of General George Washington . . . Boston: Manning and Loring, 1800.

Everett, Edward. Orations and Speeches on Various Occasions. 2d ed.; Boston: Little, Brown, 1850–1868. 4 vols.

—— The Life of George Washington. New York: Sheldon & Co., 1860.

[Felton, Cornelius C.] "The Life of George Washington. By Edward Everett . . . ," *North American Review*, XCI (October, 1860), 580–582.

Franklin, Benjamin. The Writings . . . , ed. Albert H. Smyth. New York and London: Macmillan, 1905–1907. 10 vols.

Frost, John. Lives of the Heroes of the American Revolution . . . Boston: Phillips & Sampson, 1848.

—— The Presidents of the United States from Washington to Pierce . . . Boston: Phillips, Sampson and Company, 1855.

Garden, Alexander. Anecdotes of the Revolutionary War in America . . . Charleston, S.C.: Printed for the author by A. E. Miller, 1822.

Gilmer, Thomas W. "An Address . . . ," *Southern Literary Messenger*, III (February, 1837), 97–102.

[Goodrich, Samuel G.] The Life of George Washington, Illustrated by Tales, Sketches and Anecdotes . . . New York: Collins and Hannay, [1832].

Gray, Francis C. Oration Delivered before the Legislature of Massachusetts at Their Request, on the Hundredth Anniversary of the Birth of George Washington. Boston: Dutton and Wentworth, 1832.

Graydon, Alexander. Memoirs of a Life, Chiefly Passed in Pennsylvania . . . Harrisburg, Pa.: John Wyeth, 1811.

Griswold, Rufus W. The Republican Court; or, American Society in the Days of Washington . . . New York: Appleton, 1854.

Selective Bibliography

[——] Washington and the Generals of the American Revolution . . . Philadelphia: Carey and Hart, 1847. 2 vols.
Hamilton, Alexander. The Works . . . , ed. Henry Cabot Lodge. New York: Putnam, 1886. 9 vols.
Hamilton, James A. Reminiscences . . . New York: Scribner, 1869.
Hamilton, John C. The Life of Alexander Hamilton . . . New York: Halsted & Voorhies, 1834.
Harrington, H. F. "Anecdotes of George Washington . . . ," *Godey's Lady's Book*, XXXVIII (December, 1849), 427.
Hawks, Francis L., ed. Appleton's Cyclopedia of Biography. New York: Appleton, 1856.
Hawthorne, Nathaniel. The English Notebooks. Based upon the Original Manuscripts in the Pierpont Morgan Library, ed. Randall Stewart. New York: Modern Language Association of America; London: Oxford University Press, 1941.
—— Notes of Travel, Vols. XIX–XXII in Complete Writings . . . Old Manse ed.; Boston and New York: Houghton Mifflin, 1903. 22 vols.
Hayden, Sidney. Washington and His Masonic Compeers. New York: Masonic Publishing and Manufacturing Co., 1866.
Headley, J. T. The Illustrated Life of Washington . . . Social Circle, Ga.: Nebhut, 1859.
—— Washington and His Generals. New York, Baker and Scribner, 1847. 2 vols.
[Heady, Morrison]. The Farmer Boy, and How He Became Commander-in-Chief, by Uncle Juvinell . . . Boston: Walker, Wise, and Company, 1864.
Hincks, William, and F. H. Smyth. Washington's Birthday; Congressional Banquet in Honor of George Washington, and the Principles of Washington. Washington, D.C.: Buell & Blanchard, 1852.
Holmes, Abiel. The Counsel of Washington, Recommended in a Discourse Delivered at Cambridge, February 22, 1800. Boston: Samuel Hall, 1800.
Hopkinson, Francis. The Miscellaneous Essays . . . Philadelphia: T. Dobson, 1792. 3 vols.
Humphreys, David. "An Essay on the Life of . . . Major-General Israel Putnam," in The Miscellaneous Works . . . New York: Hodge, Allen, and Campbell, 1790. Pp. 185–330.
Irving, Washington. Life of George Washington. New York: Putnam, 1855–1859. 5 vols.
Jay, John. The Correspondence and Public Papers . . . , ed. Henry P. Johnston. New York and London: Putnam, 1890–1893. 4 vols.

Selective Bibliography

Jefferson, Thomas. The Writings . . . , ed. Albert Ellery Bergh. Washington, D.C.: Thomas Jefferson Memorial Association, 1904–1905. 20 vols.

—— The Writings . . . , ed. Paul Leicester Ford. New York: Putnam, 1892–1899. 10 vols.

Judson, L. Carroll. The Sages and Heroes of the American Revolution. Philadelphia: The author, 1852.

King, Rufus. The Life and Correspondence . . . , ed. Charles R. King. New York: Putnam, 1894–1900. 6 vols.

Kirkland, Caroline Matilda. Memoirs of Washington. New York: Appleton, 1857.

Lee, Henry. A Funeral Oration on the Death of George Washington Delivered at the Request of Congress . . . London: Button, 1800.

The Lee Papers, 4 vols., in Collections of the New York Historical Society, Vols. IV–VII. New York: 1871–1874.

Leland, John. An Oration . . . Cheshire, Massachusetts, July 5, 1802. 2d ed.; Hudson, Mass., 1802.

Lempriere, John. Universal Biography. New York: E. Sargeant, 1810.

Lincoln, Abraham. Complete Works, Comprising His Speeches, Letters, State Papers, and Miscellaneous Writings, ed. John G. Nicolay and John Hay. New York: Century Co., 1902. 2 vols.

Lindsley, Philip. An Address Delivered at Nashville, February 22, 1832 . . . Nashville, Tenn.: Tardiff, 1832.

Lossing, Benson J. Life of Washington; a Biography, Personal, Military, and Political. New York: Virtue & Company, [1860]. 3 vols.

—— The Lives of the Presidents of the United States . . . New York: H. Phelps & Co., 1847.

—— Our Countrymen . . . New York: Ensign, Bridgman, & Fanning, 1855.

—— The Pictorial Field-Book of the Revolution . . . New York: Harper, 1851–1852. 2 vols.

Maclay, William. The Journal of William Maclay, United States Senator from Pennsylvania, 1789–1791, with Introduction by Charles A. Beard. New York: Boni, 1927.

M'Guire, E. C. The Religious Opinions and Character of Washington. New York: Harper, 1836.

Marshall, John. The Life of George Washington . . . Compiled under the Inspection of the Honourable Bushrod Washington, from Original Papers . . . to Which Is Prefixed, an Introduction Containing a Compendious View of the Colonies Planted by the English on the

Continent of North America . . . Philadelphia: C. P. Wayne, 1804–1807. 5 vols.

Maxcy, Jonathan. The Literary Remains of the Reverend Jonathan Maxcy, with a Memoir of His Life . . . New York: Blake, 1844.

Meade, William. Old Churches, Ministers, and Families of Virginia. Philadelphia: Lippincott, 1857. 2 vols.

Minot, George Richards. An Eulogy on George Washington, Late Commander in Chief of the Armies of the United States . . . 2d ed.; Boston: Manning & Loring, 1800.

Morse, Jedidiah. The American Geography . . . Elizabeth Town, N.J.: Shepard Kollock, 1789, pp. 127–132.

—— A Prayer and Sermon . . . Charlestown, Mass.: Samuel Etheridge, 1800.

Munford, William. Poems and Compositions in Prose on Several Occasions. Richmond, Va.: Samuel Pleasants, 1798.

Murray, John. Jerubbaal; or, Tyranny's Grove Destroyed, and the Altar of Liberty Finished . . . a Discourse on America's Duty and Danger, Delivered at the Presbyterian Church in Newbury-Port, December 11, 1783 . . . Newburyport, Mass.: John Mycall, 1784.

Norton, John N. Life of General Washington . . . New York: General Protestant Episcopal Sunday School Union and Church Book Society, 1860.

Paine, Thomas. The Life and Works . . . , ed. William M. Van der Weyde. New Rochelle, N.Y.: Thomas Paine National Historical Association, 1925. 10 vols.

Parker, Theodore. Historic Americans, ed. Samuel A. Eliot. Boston: American Unitarian Society, [1908].

Paulding, James K. A Life of Washington . . . New York: Harper, 1835. 2 vols.

Payson, Phillips. A Sermon Delivered at Chelsea, January 14, 1800 . . . on the Sorrowful Event of the Death of General Washington. Charlestown, Mass.: Samuel Etheridge, 1800.

Poyas, Mrs. Elizabeth Anne. Our Forefathers . . . Charleston, S.C.: Walker, Evans & Co., 1860.

Quincy, Eliza. Memoir of the Life of Eliza Susan Morton Quincy. Boston: [Printed by J. Wilson and Son], 1861.

Ramsay, David. The Life of George Washington . . . New York: Hopkins & Seymour, 1807.

Randall, Henry Stephens. The Life of Thomas Jefferson. New York: Derby & Jackson, 1858. 3 vols.

Selective Bibliography 263

Rayner, B. L. Life of Thomas Jefferson . . . Boston: Lilly, Wait, Colman, & Holden, 1834.

[Reed, Anna C.] The Life of George Washington . . . Philadelphia: American Sunday School Union, [1832].

[Renwick, Henry B. and James]. Lives of John Jay and Alexander Hamilton. New York: Harper, 1845.

"Review of an Inquiry into the Formation of Washington's Farewell Address," *Quarterly Review*, CVII (April, 1860), 382–383.

"Review of M'Guire's Religious Opinions of Washington," *New York Review*, I (March, 1837), 225–237.

Rush, Benjamin. The Autobiography of Benjamin Rush; His "Travels through Life" together with His Commonplace Book for 1789–1813, ed. with Introduction and notes by George W. Corner. [Princeton, N.J.]: Published as Vol. XXV of the "Memoirs of the American Philosophical Society" by Princeton University Press, 1948.

Rush, Richard. Washington in Domestic Life. From Original Letters and Manuscripts. Philadelphia: Lippincott, 1857.

Schmucker, Samuel Mosheim. The Life and Times of Thomas Jefferson. Philadelphia: J. W. Bradley, 1857.

Shaw, Samuel. The Journals of Major Samuel Shaw, the First American Consul at Canton; with a Life of the Author by Josiah Quincy. Boston: W. Crosby and H. P. Nichols, 1847.

Skeel, Emily Ellsworth Ford, ed. Mason Locke Weems, His Works and Ways. Norwood, Mass.: Privately printed, 1929. 3 vols.

Sparks, Jared. The Life of George Washington . . . Boston: Tappan & Dennett, 1839.

—— The Life of Gouverneur Morris . . . Boston: Gray & Bowen, 1832. 3 vols.

—— "Pulaski Vindicated from an Unsupported Charge . . . ," *North American Review*, XX (April, 1825), 357–392.

Stephens, Alexander H. Address . . . before the Maryland Institute in Baltimore, 23rd February, 1852 . . . Washington, D.C.: J. T. Towers, 1852.

"Stray Leaves from an Autograph Collection," *Historical Magazine*, IV (July, 1860), 193–203.

Sullivan, William. The Public Men of the Revolution . . . Philadelphia: Carey and Hart, 1847.

Thackeray, William Makepeace. The Letters and Private Papers . . . , ed. Gordon N. Ray. Cambridge, Mass.: Harvard University Press, 1945–1946. 4 vols.

Tucker, George. The Life of Thomas Jefferson . . . London: Charles Knight & Co., 1839. 2 vols.

Tuckerman, Henry T. Biographical Essays . . . Boston: Phillips, Sampson and Company, 1857.

Tyler, John. "An Oration Delivered by John Tyler . . . ," *Southern Literary Messenger*, III (December, 1837), 747–752.

U.S. Congress. Annals of Congress, 1789–1824. Washington, D.C.: U.S. Government Printing Office, 1834–1856. 42 vols.

—— Register of Debates . . . Washington, D.C.: U.S. Government Printing Office, 1825–1837. 14 vols. in 29.

Upham, Charles W. The Life of Washington, in the Form of an Autobiography . . . Boston: Marsh, Capen, Lyon, and Webb, 1820. 2 vols.

Varnum, James M. "An Oration, Delivered July 4, 1788, at Marietta, in the Territory of the United States, North-west of the River Ohio, by . . . One of the Judges of Said Territory," *American Museum*, V (May, 1789), 452–456.

Walpole, Horace. The Letters . . . , ed. Mrs. Paget Toynbee. New York: Oxford University Press, 1903–1905. 16 vols.

Washington, George. The Diary of George Washington, from 1789 to 1791 . . . , ed. Benson J. Lossing. New York: C. B. Richardson & Co., 1860.

—— The Writings . . . , ed. Worthington Chauncey Ford. New York and London: Putnam, 1889–[1893]. 14 vols.

—— The Writings . . . Prepared under the Direction of the United States George Washington Bicentennial Commission . . . , ed. John C. Fitzpatrick. Washington, D.C.: U.S. Government Printing Office, [1931–1944]. 39 vols.

—— The Writings . . . with a Life of the Author . . . , ed. Jared Sparks. Boston: American Stationers' Company; J. B. Russell, 1834–1837. 12 vols.

"Washington's Birth-Day Oration at Salem, Mass., February 22, 1793," *Historical Magazine*, Series 2, VII (January, 1870), 3–8.

Watson, John F. Annals of Philadelphia and Pennsylvania, in the Olden Time . . . Philadelphia: Whiting & Thomas, 1865. 2 vols.

Webster, Daniel. The Writings and Speeches . . . Boston: Little, Brown, 1903. 18 vols.

Weems, Mason Locke. A History of the Life and Death, Virtues & Exploits of General George Washington. New York: Macy-Masius, 1927.

[Weld, Horatio Hastings]. Pictorial Life of George Washington . . . Philadelphia: Lindsay and Blakiston, 1845.

Whipple, Edwin P. Character and Characteristic Men. Boston: Ticknor and Fields, 1866.
Whitney, Peter. Weeping and Mourning at the Death of Eminent Persons a National Duty. A Sermon . . . Brookfield, Mass.: E. Merriam, 1800.
Willard, Joseph, and David Tappan. An Address in Latin, by Joseph Willard . . . and a Discourse in English, by David Tappan . . . Delivered before the University in Cambridge, February 21, 1800, in Solemn Commemoration of General George Washington. [Charlestown, Mass.]: Samuel Etheridge, 1800.
Williams, J. M. "Biographical Outline of General George Washington," in Washington's Political Legacies, to Which Is Annexed . . . a Biographical Outline of His Life and Character . . . Boston: John Russell and John West, 1800.
Williston, Seth. The Agency of God, in Raising up Important Characters, and Rendering Them Useful . . . Geneva, N.Y.: Eaton, Walker, & Co., [1800].
Wilmer, James Jones. The American Nepos . . . 2d Baltimore ed.; Baltimore: A. Miltenberger and John Vance & Co., 1811.
Winthrop, Robert C. Addresses and Speeches on Various Occasions. Boston: Little, Brown, 1852–1886. 4 vols.
[Wise, Henry A.] "The Celebration of the Twenty-second . . . ," *Southern Literary Messenger*, XXVI (April, 1858), 241–244.
—— "Governor Wise's Oration, at Lexington, Virginia, 4th July, 1856," *Southern Literary Messenger*, XXIII (July, 1856), 1–19.
Yancey, William Lowndes. "Washington's True Legacies," in Library of Southern Literature, ed. Edwin Anderson Alderman, Joel Chandler Harris, and Charles William Kent. New Orleans: Martin & Hoyt Company, 1908–1913. 16 vols. XIII, 6027–6033.

II. Secondary Sources

Adair, Douglass. "The Authorship of the Disputed Federalist Papers" (Part I), *William and Mary College Quarterly*, Series 3, I (April, 1944), 97–122.
Baker, W. S. Bibliotheca Washingtoniana; a Descriptive List of the Biographies and Biographical Sketches of George Washington. Philadelphia: R. M. Lindsay, 1889.
—— Washington after the Revolution. Philadelphia: Lippincott, 1898.
Basler, Roy P. The Lincoln Legend. Boston and New York: Houghton Mifflin, 1935.

Bassett, John Spencer. The Middle Group of American Historians. New York: Macmillan, 1917.
Beveridge, Albert J. The Life of John Marshall. Boston: Houghton Mifflin, 1916–1919. 4 vols.
Boynton, Percy H. "Patriotic Songs and Hymns," in The Cambridge History of American Literature. New York: Putnam, 1917–1921. 4 vols. IV, 493.
Brigance, William Norwood, ed. A History and Criticism of American Public Address. New York: McGraw-Hill, 1943. 2 vols.
Bryan, W. A. "The Genesis of Weems' 'Life of Washington,'" *Americana*, XXXVI (April, 1942), 147–165.
—— "George Washington: Symbolic Guardian of the Republic, 1850–1861," *William and Mary Quarterly*, Series 3, VII (January, 1950), 53–63.
Conway, Moncure Daniel. The Life of Thomas Paine . . . New York: Putnam, 1892. 2 vols.
Cowie, Alexander. The Rise of the American Novel. New York: American Book Company, [1948].
Cuningham, Charles E. Timothy Dwight . . . New York: Macmillan, 1942.
Diebels, Sister Mary Chrysostom, S.S.N.D. Peter Markoe (1752?–1792); a Philadelphia Writer. A Dissertation . . . of the Catholic University of America . . . Washington, D.C.: The Catholic University of America Press, 1944.
Everson, Ida G. George Henry Calvert, American Literary Pioneer. Number 160 of the "Columbia University Studies in English and Comparative Literature." New York: Columbia University Press, 1944.
Faÿ, Bernard. The Two Franklins: Fathers of American Democracy. Boston: Little, Brown, 1933.
Fisher, Sydney George. The Struggle for American Independence. Philadelphia and London: Lippincott, 1908. 2 vols.
—— The True History of the American Revolution. Philadelphia and London: Lippincott, 1902.
Fitzpatrick, John C. George Washington Himself; a Common-Sense Biography Written from His Manuscripts . . . Indianapolis: Bobbs-Merrill, [1933].
—— The George Washington Scandals. Alexandria, Va.: Washington Society of Alexandria, 1929.
Ford, Paul Leicester. Washington and the Theatre. New York: Dunlap Society, 1899.

Freeman, Douglas Southall. George Washington, a Biography. New York: Scribner, 1948– 6 vols. projected; 4 published, 1948–1951.
—— R. E. Lee, a Biography. New York: Scribner, 1934–1935. 4 vols.
Gabriel, Ralph Henry. The Course of American Democratic Thought . . . New York: Ronald Press, [1940].
Goodman, Nathan G. Benjamin Rush, Physician and Citizen, 1746–1813 . . . Philadelphia: University of Pennsylvania Press, 1934.
Griffin, Appleton P.C. A Catalogue of the Washington Collection in the Boston Athenaeum . . . Cambridge, Mass.: University Press, J. Wilson and Son, 1897.
Hart, Albert Bushnell, ed. George Washington Year by Year. Washington, D.C.: U. S. Government Printing Office, 1931.
—— "A Study of Washington Biography," *Publishers' Weekly*, CXIX (February 19, 1931), 820–822.
Hellman, George S. "Irving's Washington; and an Episode in Courtesy," *Colophon*, Vol. I, Pt. 1 (March, 1930).
Hough, Franklin B. Bibliographical List of Books and Pamphlets Containing Eulogies, Orations, Poems, or Other Papers, relating to the Death of General Washington, or to the Honors Paid to His Memory . . . Albany, N.Y.: Privately printed, 1865.
Howard, Leon. The Connecticut Wits. Chicago: University of Chicago Press, [1943].
Hubbell, Jay B. "Thackeray and Virginia," *Virginia Quarterly Review*, III (January, 1927), 76–86.
Hughes, Rupert. George Washington, the Human Being and the Hero. New York: W. Morrow & Company, 1926–1930. 3 vols.
Johnson, Gerald W. American Heroes and Hero-Worship. New York and London: Harper, 1941.
—— America's Silver Age . . . New York and London: Harper, 1939.
Kellock, Harold. Parson Weems of the Cherry Tree . . . New York and London: Century Co., [1928].
Kraus, Michael. A History of American History. New York: Farrar & Rinehart, [1937].
Krout, John A. "The Washington Legend," New York *Times Book Review*, July 1, 1945, p. 3.
Leary, Lewis. That Rascal Freneau, a Study in Literary Failure. [New Brunswick, N.J.]: Rutgers University Press, [1941].
Leisy, Ernest E. The American Historical Novel. Norman, Okla.: University of Oklahoma Press, [1950].
Literary History of the United States, ed. Robert E. Spiller, Willard

Thorp, Thomas H. Johnson, Henry Seidel Canby. New York: Macmillan, 1948. 3 vols.
Lowell, Amy. Tendencies in Modern American Poetry. Boston and New York: Houghton Mifflin, [1926].
Mott, Frank Luther. American Journalism . . . New York: Macmillan, 1941.
Newlin, Claude Milton. The Life and Writings of Hugh Henry Brackenridge. Princeton, N.J.: Princeton University Press, 1932.
Oberholtzer, Ellis Paxson. The Literary History of Philadelphia. Philadelphia: Jacobs, 1906.
O'Neill, Edward H. A History of American Biography, 1800–1935. Philadelphia: University of Pennsylvania Press, 1935.
Orians, G. Harrison. "The Romance Ferment after Waverley," *American Literature*, III (January, 1932), 408–431.
Otis, William Bradley. American Verse, 1625–1807; a History. New York: Moffat, Yard and Company, 1909.
Parrington, Vernon L., ed. The Connecticut Wits. New York: Harcourt, Brace, [1926].
Pearson, Edmund. Queer Books. Garden City, N.Y.: Doubleday, 1928.
Quinn, Arthur Hobson. American Fiction, an Historical and Critical Survey. New York and London: Appleton-Century, [1936].
—— A History of the American Drama from the Beginning to the Civil War. 2d ed.; New York: Crofts, 1943.
Rowe, Margaret. George Washington: the Legend. Unpublished master's thesis of Columbia University, 1920.
Sedgwick, Catharine Maria. Life and Letters . . . , ed. Mary E. Dewey. New York, Harper, 1871.
Shirk, Samuel Blaine. The Characterization of George Washington in American Plays since 1875. Easton, Pa.: John S. Correll Co., 1949.
Stephenson, Nathaniel Wright, and Waldo Hilary Dunn. George Washington. New York and London: Oxford University Press, 1940. 2 vols.
Stillwell, Margaret Bingham. Washington Eulogies; a Checklist of Eulogies and Funeral Orations on the Death of George Washington . . . New York: New York Public Library, 1916.
Tuckerman, Henry T. The Life of John Pendleton Kennedy. New York: Putnam, 1871.
Tyler, Moses Coit. The Literary History of the American Revolution, 1763–1783. New York: Barnes & Noble, [1941]. 2 vols.
Umbreit, Kenneth. Founding Fathers; Men Who Shaped Our Tradition. New York and London: Harper, 1941.

Selective Bibliography

U. S. Library of Congress, Legislative Reference Service. The United States Congress on George Washington . . . Compiled by Myrtis Jarrell under the Direction of H. H. B. Meyer. Washington, D.C.: George Washington Bicentennial Commission, 1932.

Wecter, Dixon. The Hero in America, a Chronicle of Hero-Worship. New York: Scribner, 1941.

Wegelin, Oscar. Early American Plays, 1714–1830. New York: Dunlap Society, 1900.

—— Early American Poetry . . . 2d ed.; New York: P. Smith, 1930.

Williams, Stanley T. The Life of Washington Irving. New York: Oxford University Press; London: Humphrey Milford, 1935. 2 vols.

Wright, Lyle H. American Fiction, 1774–1850; a Contribution toward a Bibliography. San Marino, Calif.: Huntington Library Publications, 1939.

—— "A Statistical Survey of American Fiction, 1774–1850," *Huntington Library Quarterly*, II (April, 1939), 309–318.

Wroth, Lawrence C. Parson Weems; a Biographical and Critical Study. Baltimore: Eichelberger Book Company, 1911.

INDEX

"Abraham Lincoln . . ." (Stoddard), 166
Adams, Abigail, 28, 43
Adams, John, 17, 137, 145, 157; on Marshall's *Life of W.*, 14; on character of W., 29; inauguration, 41; envious of W.: eulogy of him at death, 42; on funeral eulogies, 60
Adams, John Quincy, 71
"Adams and Liberty" (Paine), 153
Addison, Joseph, 179
"Address to the Armies of America" (Humphreys), 128
"Address to the Commander-in-Chief . . . An" (Freneau), 122
Agency of God, The . . . (Williston), 63
Agriculture, W.'s scientific study of, 5, 7
Aikin, Dr., 129*n*
Alexander, Caleb, 61
Alsop, Richard, 154
America: a Dramatic Poem, 187
Americana; or, A New Tale of the Genii, 175
American Geography, The (Morse), 57, 87
"American Liberty, a Poem" (Freneau), 122
American Revolution, 6 ff.
American Sunday School Union, 97
"American Taxation" (St. John), 133
Ames, Fisher, 61
Anas (Jefferson), 47
André (Dunlap), 178
André (Lord), 185
André, John, story of, as theme in drama, 177, 184–87
Anecdotes of the Revolutionary War (Garden), 27
Anglican Church, 6
Anglo-American relations, 11
Armstrong, John, 38
Arnold (Orton), 185

Arnold, Benedict, 32, the villain to contrast with W., 239
Arnold; or, The Treason of West Point (Hubbell), 184
Arnold and André (Calvert), 186
Arnold-André story as theme in dramas, 184–87
Artemus Ward: His Book (Browne), 82, 232*n*
Astrop, Robert Francis, 141
Aurora, 10*n*, 12
Austen, Jane, 195

Bache, Benjamin Franklin, 10*n*, 12, 152
Bache, Mrs. Richard, 28
Ballou, Maturin, 211
Bancroft, Aaron, 62, 96
Bangs, Edward, 131
Bannister, Nathaniel H., 182
Barbados, 4
Barbé-Marbois, François, marquis de, on W.'s physical characteristics, 30
Barlow, Joel, 53, 138
Battle of Brooklyn, The 173
Battle of Concord, 95
Battle of Germantown, 116
Battle of Lexington, 95
Battle of Monmouth, Lee's conduct at, 26, 36
"Battle of Trenton, The," 133*n*
Bayard, Ferdinand, 46
Belknap, Jeremy, 193
Bell, John, 18, 87
Bennett, Emerson, 221
Bentley, William, 54*n*
Beveridge, Albert J., 89
Bigelow, Timothy, 20*n*, 61
"Biographical Outline of . . . Washington" (Williams), 89
Biography, 86–120
Birthday odes, 150
Blanche of Brandywine (Burnett), 183
Blanche of Brandywine (Lippard), 214, 216

Index

Boston, eulogies delivered in, 61
Boswell, James, 86
Boucher, Jonathan, estimate of W., 33 ff.; emphasis upon his slowness, 37, 48
Boudinot, Elias, interview with W., 26
Bowen, C. W., 149
Brackenridge, Hugh Henry, 174, 193
Braddock's campaign, 8
Breck, Joseph, 185
Brotherhood of the Union, 214
Brougham, John, 183
Brown, Charles Brockden, 56, 62, 155
Browne, Charles Farrar, 82, 232n
Bryant, William Cullen, 160; attack on Jefferson, 157
Buckingham, Henry A., 221
Buckskin, The, 213
Bunker Hill Monument, 73
Burlesques of Washingtonian orations, 82
Burton; or, The Sieges (Ingraham), 211
Byron, George Gordon, lord, 167

Cabal, Conway, 37
Calhoun, John C., 20, 75, 80, 81; eloquence, 51; literary merit, 83
Callender, James, Thompson, 12
Calvert, George Henry, 136, 186
Carey, Mathew, 92
Carleton (Willis), 209
Carrington, Mrs. Edward, 43
Carter, St. Leger Landon, 160
Case, Wheeler, 143
Cato (Addison), 179
"Cave of Vanhest, The" (Brackenridge), 193
Champions of Freedom . . . The (Woodworth), 194
"Character of Washington, The" (Everett), 78
Charleston, Catholic bishop of, 71
Cherry-tree story, 94, 95
Civil War, role of W. in prewar controversy, 18 ff., 74 ff.; verse of prewar period, 160-68
Clark, Willis Gaylord, 72
Clay, Henry, eloquence, 51; motion for purchase of manuscript of Farewell Address, 75
Clayton, Augustin, 69, 72
Clemens, Jeremiah, 223
Clinch, Charles Powell, 180
Cobbett, William ("Peter Porcupine"), 12

Coffin, Robert S., 158, 159
Coloniad, The (Mitchell), 142
Columbia and Britannia, 175
Columbiad, The (Snowden), 139
Condie, Thomas, 57, 88
"Congress, The, A Song . . . ," 132
Conquest of Canaan, The (Dwight), 137
"'Constellation' and the 'Insurgente', The," 135
Constitutional Convention, 7, 11, 38; verse inspired by, 148
Continental Congress, resolution re performance of plays and shows, 172
"Convivial Song" (Tyler), 153
Conway, Thomas, 37
Cooke, John Esten, 220, 224, 226, 231, 238
Cooper, James Fenimore, 15, 195-200; regretted attempt to portray W., 200; influence, 230; portrayal of W. looked upon as lese majesty 238; found Revolution an attractive subject, 239
Cooper Institute, Lincoln's speech in, 81
"Cornwallis's Surrender," or "Cornwallis Burgoyned," 134
Cozzens, Frederick S., 228n
Craik, James, 181
Crawford, Thomas, equestrian statue in Richmond, 79, 163
Cunningham, Ann Pamela, 162
Curtis, George William, 230n
Curtis, Newton Mallory, 213
Custis, George Washington Parke, *Recollections and Private Memoirs of Washington*, 17, 108; on Martha and Mary Ball Washington, 117; dramatic treatment of W., 181, 188
Custis, Martha, see Washington, Martha

"Dance, The," 134
"Darby's Return" (Dunlap), 177
Davies, Samuel, 52, 128
Davis, John, 61
Dean, Silas, 25
Death of Capt. Nathan Hale, The (Trumbull), 183
Death of Washington, The (Linn), 140
"Deserter, The," 209
Deserter, The, a Legend of Mount Washington (Mancur), 210
Diary, W.'s, 4, 240
Diebels, Sister Mary C., 175
Disunion, see Union
Donald Adair (Lorraine), 206

Index

Douglas, Stephen A., 81
Drama, 171–89; indirect treatment of W., 171; satires of Revolutionary days, 172–73; tribute to W. in form of prologue or epilogue, 179; titles of lost plays, 182
Duane, William, 12
Dumas, Mathieu, count, 31
Dumont, John, 182
Dunlap, William, 177–79
Dwight, Theodore, 156
Dwight, Timothy, 137

Edwin Brothertoft (Winthrop), 225
Eliot, Samuel Atkins, 99
"Embargo, The" (Bryant), 157
Emerson, Ralph Waldo, 22, 168; attitude toward W., 71; on Stuart portrait of W., 72
Ervin, James, 67
Everett, Edward, 19, 83, 110, 236; Birthday oration, 78 f., 80
Everson, Ida G., 187

Fairfax, Lord, 4
Fall of British Tyranny, The (Leacock), 172, 173
Fanny Campbell . . . (Ballou), 211
Farewell Address, clear statement of foreign policy of W.'s administration, 13; counsel against sectionalism and disunion, 18; motion for purchase of manuscript, 19, 75; Hamilton's share in drafting, 41, 115; W.'s views on national union and foreign relations, 76; Madison's share in drafting, 115n
Farmer Boy . . . , The (Heady), 110
"Father of His Country," 22, 87n
Federalists, disagreements over national finance, 11; confirm W. as hero, 13; monopoly of W.'s glory, 14; opposition to War of 1812, 65
Felton, Cornelius C., on Thackeray, 230
Female Review, The, 194
Female Spy, The (Bennett), 221
Fenno, John, 12
Fiction, 190–233; Cooper's *The Spy,* 192, 195–200, 230; Neal, 200–203; McHenry, 203–6; Sedgwick, 207–9, 230; Ingraham, 211 ff.; Lippard, 214–20, 230, 231; Thackeray's *The Virginians,* 225–30
"First in war, first in peace . . . ," 64
Ford, Paul Leicester, 175
Ford, Worthington Chauncey, 105, 240

Foreign policy of W.'s administration, 13
Foresters, The (Belknap), 193
"Fort Duquesne" (Plimpton), 136
Fort Le Boeuf, journal of mission to, 4, 8
Fort Necessity, 5, 8
Fort Washington, 27
Fourth of July oratory, 64, 65, 72, 77
France, W.'s reputation in, 29 ff.
Franco-American relations, 11
Franklin, Benjamin, 17, 20n; on W.'s reputation in France, 29
Freeman, Douglas Southall, 4n, 5n, 240, 241
French view of W., 10, 29
Freneau, Philip, 12, 47, 48, 151, 154; poems, 121–27
Funding and banking system, 60
Funeral oratory, *see* Oratory, funeral

Gage, Thomas, 8
Garden, Alexander, 27
Gardiner, William Howard, 200
"Gathering of the Southern Volunteers, The," 164
"General Howe's Letter," 133
"Genius of America . . . , The" (Trumbull), 143
George Washington (Lodge), 118
Gibson, Henry Richard, 142
Gist, Christopher, 102, 141
Glass, Francis, 97n
Goddard, William, 9
Godey's Lady's Book, 112
"God Save the Rights of Man" (Freneau), 124
"God Save the South" (Miles), 165
Goodrich, Samuel G., (Peter Parley), 97
Graham's Magazine, 102
Grasse, Compte de, 134
Gray, Francis C., 159
Graydon, Alexander, 27
Griswold, Rufus W., 102, 109, 118

"Hail Columbia" (Hopkinson), 153
Haines, Hiram, 140
Hamilton, Alexander, and the Federalists, 11, 12; friendship with W., 40; share in drafting Farewell Address, 115; influence, 127; W.'s treatment of, 201
Harper's Monthly Magazine, 225

Harrington, H. F., 112
Harry Burnham . . . (Buckingham), 221
Hawthorne, Nathaniel, 84, 101; on Stuart portrait, 235
Headley, J. T., 102, 120
Heady, Morrison, 110
Herbert Tracy (Lippard), 214, 215, 218
Higginson, Stephen, 38
Highland Treason, The (Holland), 185
"Hints for a Funeral Oration" (Brown), 56
"His Excellency General Washington" (Wheatley), 144
Historical Magazine, 113
History of the American Revolution (Ramsay), 96
History of the Life . . . of . . . Washington, A (Weems), 14, 70, 86, 89, 92–96, 118, 119
Hodgkinson, John, 155
Holland, Elihu G., 185
Holmes, Abiel, 62
Holmes, Oliver Wendell, 62, 162, 165
Honeywood, St. John, 152
Hope, James Barron, 163, 164
Hopkinson, Francis, 133, 145
Hopkinson, Joseph, 153
Houdon, statue of W., 77
House of Burgesses, 6
Howe, C. E. B., 188*n*
Hubbell, Horatio, 184
Humphreys, David, 47, 114, 147; biography of Putnam, 115; poems, 121, 127–30, 154
"Hymn" (Gray), 159
"Hymn, to Be Sung at the Tomb of Washington, June 24, 1851," 162

"I go to Washington and glory" (Humphreys), 127
Illustrated Life of Washington, The (Headley), 102
"Impromptu: Written at Mount Vernon, 1816" (Coffin), 159
Independence Day orations, 53, 54
Indian Prophecy, The (Custis), 181, 188
Ingraham, E. D., 102
Ingraham, Joseph Holt, 211 ff.
"Invention of Letters, The" (Paine), 152
Irving, Washington, *Life of . . . Washington*, 16, 86, 103–5, 118, 119*n*, 120, 238, 239

Jay, John, 41*n*, 195
Jay Treaty, 12, 152, 177
Jefferson, Thomas, 62, 65, 81; and The Republicans, 11; effort to prevent Federalist monopoly of W.'s glory, 14; estimate of W., 46 ff., 64; biographies, 114; Bryant's attack on, 157
Jeffersonians depreciated policy and character of W., 18; *see also* Republicans
Johnson, Andrew, 12*n*
Johnson, Samuel, 14
"Jonathan Pindar, a cousin of Peter's" (Tucker), 151
Jones, James Athearn, 206*n*
Jones, John Richter, 222
Jones, Walter, 114
Journal of mission to Fort Le Boeuf, 4, 8
Jubilee of the Constitution, 71
Judson, L. Carroll, 112
Jumonville (Thomas), 137*n*
Jumonville, Coulon de, 5, 8, 10

Kennedy, John Pendleton, 226
Kilbourn, Diana Treat, 220
King, Rufus, 41*n*
King's Bridge Cottage, 181
Kirkland, Caroline Matilda, 119; *Memoirs of Washington*, 86, 106–7
Knox, Mrs., 47

Lafayette, marquis de, 32, 72, 136, 158
"Lament of Washington, The," 136
"Last Words of Washington" (Wallace), 142
Lathrop, John, Jr., 157
Lear, Tobias, 39
Lee, Charles, 9, 201; W.'s altercation with, 18, 26, 35 ff.; criticism of W.'s slowness, 37, 48
Lee, Henry, resolutions presented to Congress on death of W., 55, 63 f.
Lee, Robert E., 21, 166, 241
"Lee in the Capital" (Melville), 166
Lewis, Eldad, 155
Lewis, Nellie Custis, 43
Life and Times of Thomas Jefferson, The (Schmucker), 114
Life of George Washington . . . , The (Bancroft), 96
Life of George Washington (Irving), 16, 86, 103–5, 118 119*n*, 120, 238, 239
Life of George Washington, The (Sparks), 98–101, 118, 120

Index

Life of George Washington . . . The (Weems), see *History of the Life . . . of . . . Washington, A*
Life of George Washington in Latin Prose, A (Glass), 97n
Life of Washington, The (Marshall), 89–93, 95
Life of Washington . . . A (Paulding), 100
"Light Horse Harry," see Lee, Henry
Lincoln, Abraham, 22, 83, 121; Cooper Institute speech, 20; on W., 70, 72, 81, 82; rebuttals to arguments of secessionists, 81; contrast in popular conceptions of W. and, 166; second great national hero, 241
"Lines Intended for Mr. Peale's Exhibition" (Freneau), 123
"Lines on the Statue of Washington in the Capitol," 160
Linn, John Blair, 140
Linwoods, The (Sedgwick), 207 ff.
Lippard, George, romances and legends portraying W., 183 f., 192, 214–20, 230, 231, 238
Livingston, William, 26
Lodge, Henry Cabot, 118
Lone Dove, The (Kilbourn), 220
Lord, W. W., 185
Lord Fairfax (Cooke), 224
Lorraine, A. M., 207n
Lossing, Benson J., 108, 109, 120
Low, Samuel, 148, 155
Lowell, Amy, 240
Lowell, James Russell, 161; best poem about W., 168
Loyalists, see Tories
Luzerne, Countess du la, 28

M'Caula, Dr., 28
McDowell, Tremaine, 200
M'Fingal (Trumbull), 137, 138
McGill, Walter Marshall, 141
M'Guire, E. C., 16, 101
McHenry, James, 203 ff., 231, 238
Maclay, William, *Journal*, 44
Madison, James, 7, 12, 65, 81; share in drafting Farewell Address, 115n
Magazine articles featuring W., 112
Mahon, Lord, 99
Mancur, John H., 210
Markoe, Peter, 175
Marksmen of Monmouth, The (Curtis), 213
Marlborough, Duke of, 79

Marshall, John, Lee's resolutions offered in Congress by, 55, 63 f.; *Life of Washington*, 13, 86, 89–93, 95; conception of W., 118, 238
"Mary the Mother of Washington," 73, 118
Mason, James, 75
Masonry, 6
"Masque Written at the Warm-Springs . . . , A" (Brackenridge), 174
Massachusetts Magazine, 139
Maurois, André, 107
Maxcy, Jonathan, 54
Mayo, William Starbuck, 136
Meade, William, 17, 108
Melville, Herman, 166
"Memoirs of George Washington" (Condie), 57, 88
Memoirs of . . . Jefferson (Carpenter), 114
Memoirs of Washington (Kirkland), 106–7
Mercer, George, physical description of young W., 24
Miles, George H., 165
Mill, Robert, 19n
Miller of New Jersey, The (Brougham), 183
Milns, William, 148
Minot, George Richards, 61
Mitchell, Alfred, 142
Modern Chivalry (Brackenridge), 193
Morris, Gouverneur, 39
Morse, Jedidiah, 57, 63, 87
Morton, 206
Motley Assembly, The (Warren?), 172
Mount Vernon, 4, 7, 8, 79; routine at, 39; daily life at, 88
Mount Vernon Ladies' Association of the Union, 19, 78, 80, 162, 240
Munford, William, 54, 177n
Murdock, John, 177
Murgatroyd, Matthew, 206n
Murray, Judith Sargent, 176

Napoleon, 159
National Gazette, 122, 124, 151
National Intelligencer, 108
National unity, pleas for, in name of W., 18 ff., 74 ff.
Neal, John, 200–203
Neal Nelson (Ingraham), 212
Negroes, proposal of a colony for, in Central America, 82

Newburgh, W.'s treatment of dissatisfied officers and men at, 29, 38
Newcomes, The (Thackeray), 226
New England, tradition of elegiac oratory, 52; funeral orations, 60
New York, W.'s inauguration, 40
New York Historical Society, 71
North, use of name of W. in appeals for national unity, 18; bards of the, 165 f.
North American Review, 98
Northwest Territory, W.'s stand against spread of slavery into, 20, 81
Norton, John N., 108
Novels, *see* Fiction
Nullification movement, 68

"Occasioned by the Debate of this Day" (Freneau), 124
"Ode V, to a Truly Great Man" (Tucker), 151
"Ode for Washington's Birthday" (Holmes), 162
Odell, Jonathan, 147
"Ode on the Death of . . . Washington" (Low), 155
"Ode to Napoleon Buonaparte" (Byron), 167
"Ode upon the Arrival of the President of the United States, An," 149
Old Churches, Ministers, and Families of Virginia (Meade), 17
Old Continental, The (Paulding), 191
Old Fort Duquesne, 210
"On a Proposed Negotiation with the French Republic . . ." (Freneau), 124
"On the Demolition of Fort George" (Freneau), 124
"On the War Projected with . . . France" (Freneau), 124
Opie, Amelia, 195
Oratory involving W., 51–85; funeral, 14, 16, 52, 54–64, 155; Fourth of July, 64, 65, 72, 77; W.'s birthday, 65–68 *passim*, 71, 72, 76–80 *passim*; protests against sentimental panegyric of W., 69, 72, 74
Orton, J. R., 185

Paine, Robert Treat, 152, 157
Paine, Thomas, attitude toward W., 45; instruction to a sculptor, 167
Parke, John, 173, 175

Parker, Theodore, 17, 20*n*
Parley, Peter, 97
"Passaic . . . ," 135
Patriot Chief, The (Markoe), 175
Patriots, rhetorical fashion in speaking of W., 25; *see also* Whigs
Paulding, James Kirke, 86, 100, 191
Payson, Phillips, funeral eulogy, 58 ff.
Persuasion (Austen), 195
"Peter Porcupine," 12
Philadelphia Monthly Magazine, 57
Pickell, John, 106*n*
Pictorial Field-Book of the Revolution, The (Lossing), 109, 120
Pictorial Life of . . . Washington (Weld), 101
Pitcher, Moll, 211
Plays, *see* Drama
Plimpton, Florus B., 136
Pocahontas, 69
Poe, Edgar Allan, 97*n*, 100, 102, 106
Poem, A: Sacred to the Memory of . . . Washington . . . (Alsop), 154
"Poem Containing Some Remarks on the Present War, A," 131
Poem on Industry, A (Humphreys), 129
"Poem on the Death of . . . Washington, A" (Humphreys), 154
"Poem on the Happiness of America . . . A" (Humphreys), 128
"Poetical Epistle to . . . Washington . . . A" (Wharton), 145
"Political Ballad . . ." (Hopkinson), 133
"Political Catechism, A" (Hopkinson), 145
Political parties, rise of, 7; division between disciples of W. and of Jefferson, 18
Politicians, The (Murdock), 177
Potomac Company, 7
Potts, Quaker, 16, 94
Powers, Hiram, 19*n*
Poyas, Elizabeth Anne, 21*n*
Precaution (Cooper), 195
"Probationary Odes," 151
Propaganda of the American Revolution, 9
Public opinion determined and expressed by oratory, 51
Pulaski, General, 116
Putnam, Israel, 115
Putnam, the Iron Son of '76 (Bannister), 182

Index

Quaker Soldier, The (Jones), 222
Quinn, Arthur Hobson, 175, 182n

Ramsay, David, 96
Randall, Henry Stephens, 114
Randolph (Neal), 200 ff.
Rayner, B. L., 114
"Rebels," 165
Recollections and Private Memoirs of Washington (Custis), 17, 108
Reed, Anna C., 97
Rees, James, 182
Refugee, The (Jones), 206
Religious Opinions and Character of Washington, The (M'Guire), 16, 101
Republican Court . . . The (Griswold), 102
Republicans, attacks upon W., 10n, 11 ff.; confirmed W. as hero, 13
Revolutionary War ballads, 130–36
Richards, George, 139
"Rising Empire, The" (Freneau), 124
Rivals, The (Clemens), 223
Rivington, James, 9, 173
Romances, see Fiction
Romantic Historian, The, 209
Rosalie Du Pont (Bennett), 221
Rose of Wissahikon, The (Lippard), 214, 217, 218
Royal Gazette, 147
"Rules of Civility," 4
Rush, Benjamin, 20n, 30; on first toast to "The Commander-in-Chief," 25; on Charles Lee, 37
Rush, Richard, 105

Sages and Heroes of the American Revolution, The (Judson), 111 f.
St. John, Samuel, 133
Salem, Mass., celebration of W.'s birthday, 54
"Saratoga Song," 133
Sauvigny, Edmé Louis Billardon de, 176n
Schmucker, Samuel Mosheim, 114
Scott, Walter, 192
Scott, Winfield, 133n
Secessionists, Lincoln's rebuttals to arguments of, 81
Sectional division, W.'s warning to beware of, 75
Sedgwick, Catharine Maria, 207 ff., 230
Seventy-Six (Neal), 202
Sewall, Jonathan Mitchell, 132, 144, 152, 179

Shaw, Samuel, 25
Signing the Declaration of Independence (Howe), 188n
Simms, William Gilmore, 102
Slavery, W.'s attitude toward, 6, 8, 18, 107; prohibited in Northwest Territory, 20, 81; Whittier on, 161
Smith, John, 69
Snowden, Richard, 139
"Song for a Venison Dinner at Mr. Bunyan's . . ." (Stansbury), 147
South, use of name of W. in appeals for national unity, 18 ff.; enthusiasm for W., 163 ff.
South Carolina, nullification movement, 68
Southern Literary Messenger, 163, 229
Sparks, Jared, W.'s own writings edited by, 16, 71, 236, 238, 240; The Life of . . . Washington, 86, 98–101, 118, 120; Irving's indebtedness to, 104; criticism of Irving, 105; defense of Pulaski, 116; on Martha Washington, 117
Sparks-Mahon controversy, 99
Speechmaking, see Oratory
Spirit of Washington, 195
Springfield Washingtonian Temperance Society, 72
Spy, The (Cooper), 15, 192, 195–200; Clinch's dramatization, 180
Stansbury, Joseph, 147
"Stanzas to the Memory of General Washington . . ." (Freneau), 125
"Stanzas upon the Same Subject" (Freneau), 125
"Stanzas Written on a Visit to . . . 'The Military Ground' . . ." (Freneau), 126
States' rights doctrine, 80
Steele, S. S., 182
Stoddard, Richard Henry, 166
Stuart, Gilbert, portraits of W., 16, 201, 235; Emerson's comment on portrait, 72
Sullivan, William, on funeral eulogies, 56

Tales of the Revolution (Tannehill), 209
Tannehill, Wilkins, 209
Tappan, David, 62
Taxation, 5 per cent impost, 38
"Taxation of America" (St. John), 133

Thackeray, William Makepeace, liberties he took with character of W., 16; presentation of W. in *The Virginians*, 187, 190, 225–30; on Stuart portraits of General and Mrs. Washington, 235
Thompson, John R., 163, 187, 229; warning to Thackeray, 233
Tories, English and American, 9; defamation of W., 33; verse, 146 f.
"To the President of the United States" (Freneau), 124
Traveller Returned, The (Murray), 176
Treason of Arnold, The (Ingraham), 212
Trenton, as theme for poetry, 143
"Trip to Cambridge, The," 131
Trumbull, David, 183
Trumbull, John, 137, 163, 143
Tucker, George, 114
Tucker, Nathaniel Beverley, 19n
Tucker, St. George (1752–1823), 151
Tucker, St. George (1828–1863), 161
Tuckerman, Henry T., 104, 113
Turner, Joseph Addison, 187n
Tyler, John, 70, 163
Tyler, Royall, 153

"Under the Old Elm" (Lowell), 168
"Under the Washington Elm . . ." (Holmes), 165
Union, name of W. invoked in rift between North and South, 18 ff., 74 ff.
United States Gazette, 108
United States Magazine, 193
Upham, Charles W., 101

Valley Forge, W. praying in woods near, 16, 94
Vashington; ou, La Liberté du nouveau monde (Sauvigny), 176n
Verse, 121–70; Freneau and Humphreys, 121–30; Revolutionary War ballads, 130–36; epic, 136–42; inspired by events of the Revolution, 142–54; Tory, 146; Birthday odes, 150; period of presidency, 151; on W.'s death, 154–56; pre-Civil War, 160–68; best poem about W., 168; tribute to W. in prologue or epilogue to drama, 179
"Verses Occasioned by . . . Washington's Arrival in Philadelphia . . ." (Freneau), 123
View of the Causes and Consequences of the American Revolution . . . , A (Boucher), 35

Virginia, W. as officer of militia, 4, 5, 8; House of Burgesses, 6; enthusiasm for W., 163; plea for reconciliation between the Union and, 169
"Virginia: a Pastoral Drama" (Parke), 173
"Virginiad, The," (Haines), 141
Virginia Historical and Philosophical Society, 69
Virginia House of Burgesses, W. a member, 68
Virginia Military Institute, unveiling of replica of Houdon's statue of W., 20, 77
Virginians, The (Thackeray), 16, 28, 187, 190, 225–30
"Virginia—the West" (Whitman), 165
Vision of Columbus, The (Barlow), 53, 138
"Volunteer's March, The" (Freneau), 126

Wallace, William Ross, 141
Walpole, Horace, 8
"War and Washington" (Sewall), 132, 144
Ward, Artemus, 82, 85, 232n
War of 1812, opposition to, 65; Webster's sectional criticism of, 65
Warren, Mercy Otis, 172
Washington, Bushrod, 89
Washington, George, chronological table of events in life of, 3, 243–45; in House of Burgesses, 6; as delegate to Constitutional Convention, 7, 11, 38, 148; elevated to Valhalla of national heroes, 13; a national symbol, 15 f.; name used as a charm against disunion in pre-Civil War controversy, 18 ff., 236 f.; Father of His Country, 22, 87n; as seen by his contemporaries, 23–50, 234; reputation in France, 29 ff.; became all things to all men, 234; less a personality than a collection of abstractions: efforts to humanize, 237; comparisons of Lincoln and, 241, 242
——biography, 86–120; sketches written before death, 87 f.; Biographies of 1800–1865, 89–120; Marshall (q.v.), 89–93; Weems (q.v.), 92–96; short sketches, 111 ff.; works about W.'s associates, 113–18; Sparks (q.v.) 98–101; Irving (q.v.), 103–5; minor writers, 96 f., 100–103, 105–11; paper-

Index

backed lives of, during war with Mexico, 239
——Commander-in-Chief, 25–38; quality of his military genius, 7; altercation with Charles Lee, 18, 26, 35 ff., 100, 193, 201; first toast to, as, 25; resignation of authority, 29
——death: funeral oratory, 54–64; project of removing remains to Richmond, 67; to Washington, 69
——in drama, 171–89; resolution passed by Continental Congress, 172; Patriot plays, 172; Tory plays: satires, 173; Dunlap, 177–79; Revolutionary themes, 179–89; Arnold-André story as theme, 184–87
——in fiction, 190–233; W. as character in, and as spoken of by characters, 190 ff.; Gothic influence, 192, 193; sentimental strain, 194; Cooper's *The Spy*, 195–200, 230; Neal, 200–203; McHenry, 203–6; Sedgwick, 207–9, 230; Ingraham, 211 ff.; Lippard, 214–20, 230, 231; Thackeray's *The Virginians*, 225–30
——in verse, 121–70; Freneau and Humphreys, 121–30; Revolutionary War ballads, 130–36; epic, 136–42; inspired by events of Revolution, 142–54; on W.'s death, 154–56; pre-Civil War, 160–68
——oratory involving, 51–85; funeral oratory, 54–64; Birthday oratory, 65–80 *passim*
——personality: character: appearance, 24, 30 ff., 43, 78; Jefferson's word portrait, 49–50
——portraiture: Stuart portraits, 16, 201, 235; unveiling statue in New York, 77; Crawford's equestrian statue, Richmond, 79, 163; statue at the Capitol, 160
——presidency: rise of political parties, 7; praise and criticism, 11 ff.; foreign policy, 13; Farewell Address (*q.v.*), 13, 18, 20, 76, 152; installation, 40; relations with Senate, 44
——private life, 3–7, 39, 88; scientific farmer, 5, 7; ill health, 7; religion, 16, 17, 18, 108; rode colt to death, 117; few attempts to write of love life, 238
——writings: diary, 4, 240; Sparks's edition of W.'s own, 16, 71, 236, 238, 240; other editions, 240

Washington, Lawrence, 4
Washington, Martha, 109, 116
Washington, Mary Ball, 4*n*, 117
"Washington" (Bryant), 160
"Washington" (Calvert), 136
"Washington, My Son, a Lamentation," 154
Washington and His Generals (Headley), 102, 120
Washington and His Generals (Lippard), 215, 217, 218
Washington and His Masonic Compeers (Hayden), 111
Washington and His Men (Lippard), 215, 218
Washington and the Generals of the American Revolution (Griswold), 102
Washington Benevolent Society, 15
Washington Benevolent Society of Massachusetts, 157
Washington Benevolent Society of Portsmouth, N.H., 65
Washington Benevolent Society of Rutland County, Vt., 66
Washingtoniad, The (Gibson), 142
"Washingtonian, an Epic Poem, The" (Astrop), 141
Washington in Domestic Life (Rush), 106
Washington-Jesus parallel, 73, 118, 164, 217
Washington Monument, 19, 56, 73, 159
Washingtons Ankunft in Elisium, 180
"Washington's Birth-Day Oration at Salem . . . 1793" (Bentley), 54
"Washington's Dirge" (Coffin), 158
"Washington's First Battle . . ." (Mayo), 135
Wayne, C. P., 89
Webster, Daniel, eloquence, 51, 83; sectionalism of 1812, 65; nationalism of 1832, 65, 68; allusions to W., 69, 73; veneration for W., 76
Wecter, Dixon, 234
Weems, Mason Locke, 218, 219; *A History of the Life . . . of . . . Washington*, 14, 70, 86, 89, 92–96, 118, 119; knew reading taste of public, 14, 94; portrayal of W., 15, 16, 85, 238; set out to humanize W., 237
Weld, Horatio Hastings, 101
West, W.'s awareness of, 6, 7
Western World, The (McGill), 141

West Point (Breck), 185
West Point: a Tragedy (Turner), 187n
Wharton, Charles Henry, 145
Wheatley, Phillis, 144
Whigs, British, 10
Whipple, Edwin P., on panegyric of W., 74
Whitman, Walt, 121, 165
Whitney, Peter, 63
Whittier, John Greenleaf, 161
Wilderness, The (McHenry), 203 ff.
Willard, Joseph, 62
Williams, J. M., 89
Willis, John R., 209
Williston, Seth, 63
Winthrop, Robert C., 74
Winthrop, Theodore, 225, 232

Wise, Henry A., 20; fight-within-the-Union policy, 77; plea for national unity, 79
Woodworth, Samuel, 194
Writings of George Washington ... The (Sparks), 98

Yancey, William Lowndes, 80 f.
"Yankee Doodle," 130
"Yankee's Return from Camp, The," 130
Yorktown, fall of, 27
"Yorktown" (Whittier), 161
Young Men's Lyceum of Springfield, 70

"Zenith of Glory" (Richards), 139